FOURTH EDITION

LIVES ACROSS CULTURES

CROSS-CULTURAL
HUMAN DEVELOPMENT

Harry W. Gardiner
University of Wisconsin–La Crosse

Corinne Kosmitzki
University of California, Berkeley

PEARSON

Boston   New York   San Francisco
Mexico City   Montreal   Toronto   London   Madrid   Munich   Paris
Hong Kong   Singapore   Tokyo   Cape Town   Sydney

Series Editor: Stephen Frail
Series Editorial Assistant: Allison Rowland
Marketing Manager: Pamela Laskey
Production Editor: Beth Houston
Editorial Production Service: Nesbitt Graphics, Inc.
Composition Buyer: Linda Cox
Manufacturing Buyer: JoAnne Sweeney
Electronic Composition: Nesbitt Graphics, Inc.
Photo Researcher: Poyee Oster
Cover Administrator: Linda Knowles

For related titles and support materials, visit our online catalog at *www.ablongman.com*.

Between the time website information is gathered and then published, it is not unusual for some sites to have closed. Also, the transcription of URLs can result in typographical errors. The publisher would appreciate notification where these errors occur so that they may be corrected in subsequent editions.

Library of Congress Cataloging-in-Publication Data

Gardiner, Harry W.
    Lives across cultures : cross-cultural human development / Harry W. Gardiner, Corinne Kosmitzki. — 4th ed.
        p. cm.
    ISBN-13: 978-0-205-49475-0
    ISBN-10: 0-205-49475-7
    1. Ethnopsychology—Cross-cultural studies. 2. Socialization—Cross-cultural studies. 3. Cognition and culture—Cross-cultural studies. 4. Personality and culture—Cross-cultural studies. 5. Developmental psychology—Cross-cultural studies. I. Kosmitzki, Corinne. II. Title.
    GN502.G37 2008
    155.8'2—dc22

                                                                    2007002097

Printed in the United States of America
10   9   8   7   6   5   4   11   10   09

CONTENTS

◇ CHAPTER THREE
CULTURE AND SOCIALIZATION   53

◇ CHAPTER FOUR
CULTURAL ASPECTS OF PHYSICAL
GROWTH AND DEVELOPMENT   83

◇ CHAPTER ELEVEN
LOOKING TO THE FUTURE   298

REFERENCES   322

AUTHOR INDEX   347

SUBJECT INDEX   353

FOREWORD

I enjoy looking at human hands. Regardless of culture, hands can help to indicate one's general livelihood, hardships, usually one's gender, and certainly one's approximate age. I have especially marveled at the delicate hands of newborn babies, blemish-free and soft as the finest silk with tiny fingers. I find it relaxing to touch them.

In mid-April 2006, my wife and I flew to Denver, Colorado, to see our fourth grandchild, who was born about three weeks earlier. Alena has joined her three-year-old sister, Sophia, as members of the current youngest generation. We are proud grandparents, just as we were and are proud parents. Their lives will develop in different ways—some predictable, some unpredictable, but always unfolding in a complex cultural context—one of the central themes of this book.

Accompanying me during our visit was a small portfolio of manuscripts, all focused on different aspects of culture and its influence on human behavior. Among these were several final drafts of chapters for this book. I especially looked forward to reviewing the many ways Harry Gardiner and Corinne Kosmitzki had improved the already successful third edition of their now-classic *Lives Across Cultures*. It is truly impressive how the authors have integrated new material from large numbers of culturally-oriented developmental psychologists throughout the world into this volume. Many of these significant changes are described in the Preface under the "Features New to the Fourth Edition" section.

While thinking about the Foreword to this fourth edition, my thoughts were a hodgepodge of interrelated ideas and topics, many of them fueled by my fascination with the hands of infants. I wondered what Alena's hands, with their dimpled knuckles, would eventually touch and feel, who they would touch, and why they would touch certain objects or people during the course of a long, happy and productive life in what we all hope will be a more peaceful and rational world. Would the little index fingers push buttons or flip switches to turn on technical equipment not yet even imagined? Would one of the thumbs be sucked for as long as she wanted, either to the dismay or to the resigned acceptance of her parents? Would the ring finger of her left hand eventually be adorned with a diamond or some other piece of jewelry to signify that she has joined hands in matrimony? Indeed, when she reaches an appropriate marrying age, will the vows and expectations she may take be the same as they are now, or will marriage have a completely different meaning? Will her little fingers learn to play the piano, or eventually calculate complex formulas, or get dirty while digging for hidden treasures in some other land? Will they help change diapers of her own babies, or as a physician help bring other babies into the world? What will these fingers be doing when Alena takes her last breath in, we hope, well into the twenty second century? With respect to this text, how will all of the above be played out or understood in other cultures or ethnic groups?

This book is about thousands of topics and issues that developmental psychologists, and others, take into consideration when they study human lives as they unfold across the globe. It is fascinating to think about all of the questions inherent in this field of inquiry. As you turn the pages of this book, look at your own hands and think about what they have already told about you and your culture.

One of the more exciting developments in psychology in the last generation has been the attention given to the cultural context of human behavior. *Lives Across Cultures*, in its three previous editions, has made significant contributions to these efforts and continues to do so with this new edition. An increasing number of psychologists are paying careful attention to important issues when considering key questions in the field: To what extent can psychologists generalize various theories and laws governing human developmental processes across cultural or ethnic groups? What is the nature of psychology's data base? What is it about the context, texture, and structure of human societies that produces differences in thought and behavior? And not simply to emphasize differences (as interesting and intriguing as they can be), what is it about human societies—with all their complexities in language, beliefs, values, attitudes, and so on—that produce a wealth of universals? Is there a "best" way for humans to behave, or to raise children? If so, can we learn from other cultures what these best ways may be? I suggest that trying to answer these questions, and many others asked by developmental psychologists, is essential in a rapidly globalizing world. Harry and Corinne ask many of these questions and provide some of the answers in a thoughtfully organized and readable book that has become a favorite of students and professionals alike.

Today, there is a substantial and growing group of developmental psychologists who consider a broad range of topics and perspectives in their research that encompasses other cultures or ethnic groups. Specifically, such individuals often identify with the title "cross-cultural developmental psychologist." Harry Gardiner, the senior author of this book, is one of them and has been in that particular camp for about forty years. He knows its history, its strengths, its weaknesses, and he identifies what is important for him and others to learn. With the kind of background he brings to a book like this, the reader can be assured that the voice of authority is speaking directly to you through the medium of the printed page. And in this case there are two authoritative voices, because Corinne Kosmitzki brings her own strong credentials and background to the table. Both of them, and an ever-increasing number of colleagues, see the great value in looking beyond not only one's cultural and national borders for insightful information and data about the entire human lifespan, but also the theoretical and practical advantages of reaching beyond the often narrow constraints of one's disciplinary borders.

Harry Gardiner and Corinne Kosmitzki, and their own very capable hands, skillfully and in an engaging and personal style, have energetically and generously updated and extended the coverage provided in the third edition of *Lives Across Cultures*. Covering all of the major developmental topics from cradle to grave, they take the reader through the labyrinth of lives that work and play and, unfortunately, fight through occasional major crises and the vexing problems of growing up. The style and tone of the book is genuinely comfortable. Reading it is like having a friendly dialogue with gentle and caring friends.

I encourage you to read this book carefully. As an introduction to the ways in which psychologists and others cover the unfolding of human development as it is played out on the global stage, this book is a treat to read.

This Foreword opened with a photograph of the hands of three-week-old Alena, representing the "Alpha," or beginning, of life. It closes with a photograph of the hands of 102-year old Khun Mae Kasorn, the mother of Harry's Thai wife, Ormsin, representing the "Omega," or end, of a long and productive life (she passed away on April 23, 2005). She was respected by everyone who knew her for her genuine kindness, helpfulness, and modesty throughout her life. She remained healthy and strong into her later years and was an inspiration to all who knew her. Separated by more than a century in age and by very different cultures thousands of miles apart, Alena and Khun Mae Kasorn symbolize two unique examples of the ongoing development of millions of "lives across cultures."

Walter J. Lonner
Professor Emeritus
Western Washington University
Bellingham, Washington

Walter J. Lonner has been involved in cross-cultural psychological research for nearly 40 years. He is Founding and Special Issues Editor of the *Journal of Cross-Cultural Psychology*, the flagship publication in this area of international scholarship. A charter member, past president, and Honorary Fellow of the International Association for Cross-Cultural Psychology, Lonner has been involved in various capacities with about forty books on cross-cultural psychological research and applications. Retired since 2001, he remains active in cross-cultural psychology. For example, he is coeditor of the forthcoming sixth edition of *Counseling across Cultures*. Another of his current projects is coauthoring a book-length biography of Swiss psychologist Ernest E. Boesch, a significant figure in cultural psychology.

PREFACE

It gives us great pleasure to place in the hands of readers this fourth edition of *Lives Across Cultures*. When we began work on the first edition more than a decade ago, we never dreamed we would one day still be happily involved in this project. Over the years we have been extremely gratified by the acceptance of the first three editions and the many kind and helpful comments made by students, faculty, and others who have told us how much they have enjoyed the book and the benefits they have derived from it. Our goal, as always, is to continue our journey of exploration into the exciting and ever expanding world of cross-cultural human development begun in the groundbreaking first edition. As we have done in each of the previous editions, basic principles are linked to practical everyday events to help readers cultivate a global and multicultural perspective on behavior and gain an improved understanding of, and appreciation for, development as it takes place in diverse cultural settings throughout the world.

Each of us is a teacher and cross-cultural researcher, with extensive experience in small college and large university settings in this country and abroad. In common with previous editions, we focus on connections between these personal experiences and the more formal theories and research that make up this discipline and present it all in a manner that is easy to understand, engaging, and informative to readers.

◇ ORGANIZATION OF THE BOOK

In this latest edition, our presentation of cross-cultural material continues to differ in a number of significant ways from other books. Most notable, we believe, is our effort to integrate and synthesize viewpoints and perspectives from a variety of disciplines, including psychology, anthropology, sociology, and the health sciences.

We look at development from a **cross-cultural perspective**, designed to provide opportunities to expand awareness and sensitivity to global similarities and differences in behavior, while helping to reduce any ethnocentric thinking on the part of readers, whether conscious or not. We allow readers to experience variations in behavior not normally found in their own societies, thereby helping to contribute to an understanding of human adaptation. Most importantly, this approach encourages readers to look more closely at the interconnections among culture, development, and behavior in their *own* lives as well as in others.

Another major focus is on understanding development within a wide range of cultural contexts, using Bronfenbrenner's **ecological model** and Super and Harkness's concept of the **developmental niche**—both of which recognize the bidirectional or reciprocal influence of individuals and their environments.

We also take a **chronological-within-topics approach.** As the table of contents indicates, selected topics, for which a substantial amount of cross-cultural research exists, are discussed chronologically. This approach demonstrates how behavioral processes unfold and change, as individuals in a variety of cultures pass from infancy and childhood through adolescence and into adulthood and old age.

In the introductory chapter, we define cross-cultural human development, discuss its connections to other social sciences, provide a historical context for the increasing interest in cross-cultural research and its findings, and present and illustrate the major themes of the book.

Chapter 2 focuses on theories and methodology. Each of the major theories discussed throughout the book is first presented here, followed by a presentation of the methodologies used in conducting cross-cultural studies in human development.

The focus in Chapter 3, "Culture and Socialization," is on ecological systems, the developmental niche, and cultural variations in such important socialized behaviors as sleep, feeding, and crying during infancy; formal versus informal learning during childhood; adolescent rites of passage; and adult interpersonal relationships.

Cultural aspects of physical growth and development are examined in Chapter 4, with attention given to the role of genetic factors; nutrition and its effects on physical growth and motor development during infancy and early childhood; cross-cultural studies of physical change in adolescence; and cultural reactions to physical changes associated with the transition to adulthood, including menopause and senescence.

In Chapter 5, "Culture, Language, and Cognition," attention is given to the link among these three topics along with language socialization, second language acquisition and bilingualism, development of analytical thinking and problem-solving, and communication in the years of later adulthood as well as variations in cognitive and language development across cultures.

Chapter 6, "Culture, Self, and Personality," looks at the development of self and personality, beginning with temperament in infancy and progressing to the emergence of the self-concept in childhood, identity in adolescence, and personality changes during adulthood and aging.

"Culture and Issues of Gender and Sexuality" are examined in Chapter 7, including a discussion of some universal gender differences and cultural influences on the socialization of women and men. Attention is given to gender relationships in childhood, sexual activity and cultural taboos during adolescence, division of labor in early and middle adulthood, and changes in gender roles and status in old age.

Chapter 8, "Culture and Social Behavior," opens with a focus on ecological contexts and early child–caretaker relationships; moves to influences of family and peer culture during the years of childhood and adolescence; development of aggression, work, and leisure activities in middle adulthood; and concludes with a discussion of social support and well-being in the years of later adulthood.

Chapter 9, "The Family in Cultural Context," looks at the birth process and variations in the family life cycle across cultures, including differences in parental belief systems and cultural views of mate selection, parenthood, and grandparenthood.

Issues related to culture and health are examined in Chapter 10. Topics include difficulties in medical diagnosis across cultures, cultural differences in children's health, adolescent eating disorders and depression, mental health issues during early and middle adulthood, and cultural views on caring for the elderly, many of them suffering from dementia and Alzheimer's disease.

Finally, in Chapter 11, "Looking to the Future," the major themes are briefly reviewed and suggestions are made for applying more theoretically and culturally useful approaches to the study of human development. The chapter concludes with some thoughts and suggestions related to directions the study of cross-cultural human development might take in the future.

◇ FEATURES NEW TO THE FOURTH EDITION

The fourth edition retains the basic structure and emphases of previous editions. However, a number of significant changes are reflected in this revision. For example, the text has been completely updated with the addition of several new topics and the inclusion of the latest in research findings and references. New photographs and boxed material have been added. Each chapter contains new suggestions for further readings and a section on Study Questions has been added. Chapter 1 includes an expanded discussion of culture and its definitions. Coverage of major approaches, such as the ecological model and the developmental niche, has been significantly expanded and includes discussions of the latest research findings. Chapter 3 on socialization contains new sections on cultural influences on academic achievement and childhood obesity, along with new material on handedness. In Chapter 4, there is an introduction to the Human Genome Project and an extensive discussion of the influences and effects of genes on human development and behavior. Chapter 5 on culture and cognition has been expanded to include new material on second-language acquisition and bilingualism as well as the latest findings on physical and mental abilities among the elderly. Chapter 6, "Culture, Self, and Personality," includes new material on conceptions of the self, self-efficacy, and contextual and cultural influences on identity development. A new section has been added on the Big Five personality traits. The focus of Chapter 7 is now on cultural issues of gender and sexuality with new material on gender role socialization. In Chapter 8, "Culture and Social Behavior," the latest research on family and peer influences on adolescent social behavior has been added. Chapter 9 includes new material on mate selection, nurse-midwife success in delivering babies, "shared mothering," advances in fathering research, expansion of material on cross-cultural differences in adolescent peer relationships, and the latest issues related to grandparenthood. Expanded health care coverage is reflected in Chapter 10, along with new sections on illness, stress and coping, ecological influences on early coping behavior, acculturation and adaptation, and coping with chronic illness in old age. The final chapter, "Looking to the Future," has been revised and updated to reflect some of the newest suggestions and speculations on thoughts and challenges for the design of future research. The reference section has been significantly revised to include the latest citations of work published between 2005 and 2007.

◇ SPECIAL FEATURES

Most of the special features appearing in the third edition have been retained, although some have been revised, in this fourth edition. These include a number of interesting and readable pedagogical aids to assist readers in learning, remembering, and making practical use of the material covered.

Opening Vignettes. Most chapters open with vignettes of two individuals from different geographical areas of the world who illustrate one or more of the behaviors described in the chapter. Since one of our major goals is to familiarize the reader with as many cultures as possible, we decided to open each chapter with stories of different individuals living in more than fifteen different cultures around the globe. The development of these individuals is integrated into each chapter in which they appear.

Recurring Themes. Throughout each chapter, the principal themes (e.g., ecological and contextual approaches, developmental niche, and developmental and cross-cultural perspectives) are regularly interwoven into the narrative to provide a comprehensive and cohesive understanding of development.

Key Ideas. Efforts have been taken to make concepts easy to understand by placing them in bold type the first time they appear, immediately defining them, and providing numerous examples to illustrate their cultural relevance. For a quick review or preview, each chapter ends with a concise summary of important points.

Cultural Diversity. Unlike some books that claim to focus on culture but only sprinkle a few selected boxes or features in several chapters, this book contains scores of examples of cross-cultural research and findings in every chapter.

Further Readings. Each chapter closes with an annotated listing of recommendations for further reading. The books and articles suggested have been selected for their ability to expand on topics covered in each chapter as well as for their interesting and often amusing writing style.

Developmental Analysis. New to this edition is a series of nine Developmental Analysis boxes appearing in Chapters 3–10. Written in the first person, they tell the life story of Matilda "Maddi" Skelton, who engagingly applies important concepts to her own development over the lifespan. This pedagogical feature helps to clarify the material and provide continuity across chapters. It also encourages students to write their own developmental analysis for a better understanding of how they became the people they are today.

◇ NOTE TO INSTRUCTORS

Lives Across Cultures can be used as a core text in a course focusing on cultural similarities and differences in human development, whether it is in psychology, anthropology, or sociology. It can also be effectively used as a supplement to basic courses such as General Psychology, Child and Adolescent Development, Lifespan Development, Cross-Cultural Psychology, Social Psychology, Cultural Anthropology, Sociology of the Family, and similar courses in which the instructor might want to provide a cultural focus not represented in standard textbooks. In its three previous editions, this book has been successfully used in international business classes to familiarize students with a wide range of cultural behaviors they may encounter in the global market and some of the reasons for individual differences.

◇ NOTE TO READERS

You, the reader, will live in the world of tomorrow, where understanding and interacting with people of diverse cultural backgrounds will be a prerequisite for success in the family, school, workplace, and society. It is for you that this book has been written. We hope it will help you develop an appreciation for and sensitivity to the cultural similarities and differences that characterize those of us who live on this planet Earth today, including your parents and grandparents, and those who will call it home in future generations, including your children and grandchildren. We hope you will find this book enjoyable and informative reading.

◇ SUPPLEMENTS

An *Instructor's Manual,* containing suggestions for teaching, ideas for student projects, guide to films and videos, and test items, is available for download. Allyn & Bacon's World Wide Web site is: *http://www.ablongman.com.* For more information about *Lives Across Cultures,* visit *http://www.ablongman.com* and search the catalog By Author, typing *Gardiner* into the search box.

◇ A FINAL COMMENT

We spent many exciting and busy years working on the first three editions of this book. Now, after about ten months, we have completed work on the current edition. It has now passed from our hands to yours. We began the original project because we felt there was a need for a book like this. Wide acceptance of the first three editions has (happily) proved us right, and now you are able to read about some of the new developments in this latest edition. We are proud to have been able to make a contribution to better understanding of development across cultures. Only you, the readers, can tell us if we have succeeded or how we might do better in the future, as many of you did following the appearance of each new edition. Let us know your thoughts by writing or e-mailing us at the addresses that follow. We'd really enjoy hearing from you.

◇ ACKNOWLEDGMENTS

Urie Bronfenbrenner, upon whose ideas much of our work is based, died at his home in Ithaca, New York, on September 25, 2005, at the age of 88. Widely regarded as one of the world's leading scholars in developmental psychology and childrearing, he is credited with creating the interdisciplinary field of human ecology that receives such prominent attention throughout this book. We wish to acknowledge his contributions that, in large measure, stimulated us to write this volume.

The completion of a book like this can not be accomplished without the generous assistance of a great many people. To those who reviewed the plans for this fourth edition and offered suggestions and revisions for its improvement, we owe a genuine debt of gratitude: Julie Johnson-Pynn, Berry College; Carolyn Cass Lorente, The George Washington University; David W. Shwalb, Southeastern Louisiana University, and M. L. Corbin Sicoli, Cabrini College.

To the editorial, production, and marketing staff at Allyn & Bacon who contributed their time and talent to making this fourth edition possible, we thank you.

Finally, we thank our families, who didn't see a great deal of us while we stared at our computer screens late into the night or early in the morning. Special thanks from Harry to Ormsin Gardiner and to our children—Alisa Jarin, Alan Verason, Alexina Tippa, and Aldric Harin, whose bicultural lives have provided many of the examples for this book, and to Maciness Charoen, Malinee Kathyrn, and Sirina Francis, our grandchildren who represent the next generation of biculturalism. Corinne extends her appreciation to Gloria Solomon for her continued support and the many valuable suggestions on topics represented in this book.

Harry W. Gardiner
Professor Emeritus
Psychology Department
University of Wisconsin–La Crosse
La Crosse, WI 54601
harry@gardiner.net

Corinne Kosmitzki
Graduate Division
University of California
Berkeley, CA 94720
ckosmitzki@berkeley.edu

ABOUT THE AUTHORS

Harry Gardiner. I am Professor Emeritus at the University of Wisconsin–La Crosse, where I designed and taught courses in cross-cultural human development for more than 25 years. It was the inability to find a textbook for a course in cross-cultural human development that led to the writing of this book. I also offered courses in child development, cross-cultural psychology, the hurried child, and humor in education for teachers. My interest in culture also led me to teach a course entitled "Orientation to Study Abroad" for students planning extended study and research at foreign universities. I continue to volunteer to orient international students to the university campus and help with their adjustment to life in the American culture. My undergraduate degree is from American International College, in Springfield, Massachusetts where I began my "international" quest so many years ago. My M.A. is from the University of Hawaii, where the real seeds of my interest in cross-cultural psychology were first planted. I completed my Ph.D. at Manchester University in England, where my personal journey into culture was forever changed when I met a young lady from Thailand,

Ormsin Sornmoonpin, who was studying to be an electrical engineer. I followed her to Asia, where we were married in Buddhist and Christian wedding ceremonies. I taught in the graduate program at Chulalongkorn University in Bangkok for two years before we moved to the United States. I live in an Asian American family, consisting of our two sons (Alan and Aldric) and two daughters (Alisa and Alexina), in which I am a minority—"the one with the blond hair and the blue eyes!" I was a charter member of the International Association for Cross-Cultural Psychology and served as president of the Society for Cross-Cultural Research. In addition, I serve as consulting editor for the *Journal of Cross-Cultural Psychology* and assistant editor for teaching for the *Cross-Cultural Psychology Bulletin*. In addition to publishing articles in a wide variety of journals and participating in national and international meetings, I have coauthored a chapter with my wife on "Women in Thailand," revised a chapter on "Child and Adolescent Development" for a book on cross-cultural topics in psychology, and prepared a chapter on cross-cultural development for a handbook on culture and psychology. I have engaged in training, teaching, and research in Europe, Asia, and the United States for more years than I will admit. As my children frequently remind me, I have been celebrating my thirty-ninth birthday annually for as long as they can remember. In my "spare time" I enjoy writing for *Cobblestone*, a history magazine for young children, and have contributed interviews with Supreme Court Justice Sandra Day O'Connor and Muppet creator Jim Henson, among others. Another great joy is watching the development of our grandchildren, Macinnes Charoen Lamont, born on March 6, 2000; Malinee Kathryn Lamont, born on January 4, 2002, and Sirina Francis Lamont, born on November 2, 2004.

Corinne Kosmitzki. I was born and raised in Germany, where I grew up in a fairly traditional household (although Sauerkraut is not one of my favorite foods!). My interest in the lives of people led me to study clinical and counseling psychology at the Universität Münster. I earned my Ph.D. in psychology at the University of California at Berkeley. As an international student I experienced many of the challenges discussed in this book. I have been able to share these experiences with other international students in workshops and seminars I held at various universities. After being an active teacher and researcher at universities in Virginia, New Jersey, and Texas I have now returned to California. At the University of California at Berkeley, I continue to work with students and faculty from many different cultural and national backgrounds. I have enjoyed traveling in most of Western and Eastern Europe and North America. I also try to visit my family in Germany as often as I can. Like Harry Gardiner, who enjoys spending time with his grandchildren, I too enjoy watching my niece and nephew (Alexa and Hendrik Abraham) grow up in a multicultural world. I live with my two dogs and a cat, and, in my spare time, I like to read, write, and explore the beautiful California waterways by motorboat and kayak.

CHAPTER ONE

INTRODUCTION

Many books begin by introducing their readers to the history of the field. This is certainly essential (though sometimes boring), but will come later in this book (you can always skip it if you don't find it very interesting). As one of the authors (Gardiner), I would like to begin this book as I begin most of my classes—by relating a few of my humorous cross-cultural experiences.

In About the Authors, I mentioned that my wife, Ormsin, is from Thailand and we have raised our four children in an Asian American family, where I am the minority—the one with the blond hair and blue eyes. I don't like to admit it, but I'm also the shortest, making me a double minority! As you might imagine, raising children in a cross-cultural and bilingual home has resulted in many interesting developmental experiences, some of which may help you to understand the processes involved in cross-cultural human development.

One experience concerns our eldest daughter, Alisa, and the way in which she became bilingual. Our cross-cultural family setting provided a unique opportunity for this to occur. We had been advised that the best approach to helping her become bilingual was to let her hear and speak both languages without emphasizing that they *were* two languages. So, when she was an infant and young child, her mother spent much of the day speaking to her in Thai, while I spoke to her in English. Then, one evening, when she was about three years old, one of my Chinese students came to babysit. Alisa opened the door, saw an Asian face, and began speaking to the student in Thai. The young lady patiently listened to her and then said, "I'm Chinese and I understand English, but I bet you were speaking to me in Thai, weren't you?" I watched as she thought about this and then turned to me and said, "I speak two languages, don't I? Daddy, I speak two languages!" I told her that indeed she did and asked, "What did you think was happening?" Her reply, based on the experience of her unique developmental niche in a bilingual home, was, "I thought it was all one big language and Mommy understood some words and you understood others and I understood them all!"

Throughout the chapters that follow, we make reference to how important it is to understand another culture and realize that not everyone everywhere has the same understanding of topics and events. Sometimes, when traveling, studying, or working in another culture, our experiences are frustrating, scary, or humorous. I had an opportunity to live in England for three years while completing my doctoral studies at the University of Manchester. During that time, there was one food craving I found nearly impossible to fulfill—*popcorn!* My roommate and I searched everywhere for it. The only place anything resembling it was available was at the cinema. The only problem: it was sticky, caramel-covered goop, not the white, fluffy kernels sprinkled with salt and hot butter with which we were familiar. Eventually, using the skills of Sherlock Holmes and Doctor Watson, we discovered small (tiny, actually) thirty-kernel bags of popping corn at the airport and bought the entire stock! A few days later, we visited a British family that had befriended these two "Yanks from across the pond" and took some with us. When we asked the husband if we could make some popcorn, he replied (much to our surprise), "No, that's impossible." When we asked why, he said, "Popcorn grows on bushes. You pick it and put caramel on it." We told him he might be confusing this with cotton, which grows on bushes but is not eaten. Nevertheless, he supplied us with a pot, and we put in some oil and threw in some kernels. When it began to make noise, we tried to explain that this was the corn popping. When it was done, we showed him. He took one look and disappeared out the back door! A few minutes later, he returned with his neighbors, looked at us, and said, "Do it again!" One day I think I'll open a popcorn stand on a street corner in London and surprise and amaze the public with the wonders of popcorn! Now, if I could only get it to grow on bushes! The moral of this story: we all grow up in cultures where we understand what happens around us because the experiences are a familiar part of our developmental niche. These experiences are not always easily understood by those living in different ecological settings.

More than two decades ago the anthropologist Theodore Schwartz, writing about the acquisition of culture, declared that "anthropologists had ignored children in culture while developmental psychologists had ignored culture in children" (1981, p. 4). Just two years later, John Berry, a Canadian psychologist and pioneering researcher in cross-cultural psychology, noted that the discipline was "so culture-bound and culture-blind . . . [that] . . . it should not be employed as it is" (1983, p. 449). Shortly thereafter, Gustav Jahoda, a well-known European psychologist and early contributor to the developing discipline, was able to express a more optimistic view and point out that cross-cultural studies of human development had been steadily increasing (1986). Yet, at the same time, he also criticized the field for being "too parochial in its orientation" (p. 418).

These were once serious criticisms of the newly emerging field of cross-cultural psychology. Fortunately, in recent years, great strides have been made in our approaches to, and understanding of, cross-cultural human

Harry Gardiner and his British friends making popcorn 30 years later.
(Courtesy of authors)

development. Throughout this book, we hope to show the progress, excitement, and promise of this increasingly important area of study.

In this first chapter we set the stage for the rest of the book by introducing some historical perspectives and expanding on some of the major concepts, themes, and issues briefly presented in the Preface. Let us begin by exploring the origins of cross-cultural human development.

◇ WHAT IS CROSS-CULTURAL HUMAN DEVELOPMENT?

The field of cross-cultural psychology is remarkably diverse, and those who contribute to it bring with them a variety of viewpoints, including different definitions of the field itself. In Volume 1 of the revised *Handbook of Cross-Cultural Psychology*, Berry, Poortinga, and Pandey (1997) define **cross-cultural psychology** as *"the systematic study of relationships between the cultural context of human development and the behaviors that become established in the repertoire of individuals growing up in a particular culture"* (p. x). This definition clearly states that this is a scientific endeavor that shares with more familiar disciplines the use of theories, scientific methodologies, statistical procedures, and data analysis.

The term *human development* has also been defined in a variety of ways. For the purpose of this book, we view **human development** as *changes in* *physical, psychological, and social behavior as experienced by individuals across the lifespan from conception to death.* Although this definition encompasses a wide range of experiences, the intention of this book is not to provide exhaustive and comprehensive coverage of all aspects of human development (aren't you glad to hear that!). Instead, our goal is more limited, focusing on a number of selected topics that provide insight and understanding into how individuals develop and live their lives in different cultural settings. In doing this, we provide examples from literally scores of societies throughout the world. Considering the important dimensions just discussed, and not finding the term **cross-cultural human development** defined elsewhere, we have chosen to view it as *cultural similarities and differences in developmental processes and their outcomes as expressed by behavior in individuals and groups* (Gardiner, 2001b).

Since we just mentioned the term *culture,* it should be pointed out that most researchers agree that this is one of the most difficult terms in the social sciences to define. Almost everyone who studies culture has a different way of looking at it, reflecting in part, different theories for understanding the concept as well as for describing various forms of human behavior. According to Berry, Poortinga, Segall, and Dasen (2002), E. B. Tylor was the first anthropologist to use the term in his two-volume work titled *Primitive Culture* (1871). He defined *culture* as *"that complex whole which includes knowledge, belief, art, morals, laws, customs and any other capabilities and habits acquired by man as a member of society"* (p. 42). More than fifty years ago, two other anthropologists, Kroeber and Kluckhohn (1952), compiled a list of 164 definitions of the term.

As recently as the year 2002, UNESCO, an agency of the United Nations, stated that culture is the *"set of distinctive spiritual, material, intellectual and emotional features of society or a social group, and that it encompasses, in addition to art and literature, lifestyles, ways of living together, value systems, traditions and beliefs"* (UNESCO, 2002, p. 1). We have no intention of listing all possible definitions here but provide the following as examples: *"the man-made part of the environment"* (Herskovits, 1948, p. 17), *"an abstraction based on the commonalities displayed in the behavior of a given community of people"* (Barnlund & Araki, 1985, p. 9), *"a field of action, whose contents range from objects made and used by human beings to institutions, ideas, and myths"* (Boesch, 1991, p. 29), and *"a socially interactive process with two main component processes: the creation of shared activity (cultural practices) and the creation of shared meaning (cultural interpretation)"* (Greenfield, 1997, p. 303).

Azuma (2005) has even proposed a new conceptualization of culture "beyond nationality, geography, class, and even ethnicity" which he tentatively calls "functional culture" (p. xii). It is his contention that "traditional culture" of past generations, uncontaminated, and with distinct and static systems "envisioned by cultural anthropologists in the early 1900s no longer exists" (p. xii). Rather, in the contemporary world, individuals come into contact with a variety of cultures as a result of the media, travel, reading, migration, and other activities. As a result, "cultures interact with and influence each other"; and traditions, which are part of functional culture, are "more fluid or fragmented" than they once were. In fact, cultures today import many of their features from other cultures and societies—features which Azuma points out "were quite foreign to people even a half century ago, and change and substitution of elements are constant" (p. xii). However, he goes on to emphasize that global culture does not become homogeneous, because the way in which these features are distributed within cultures will differ as a result of "traditional emphasis, condition of industry and labor, natural resources, climate, or just by chance" (p. xii); and this will determine cultural specificity. He stresses that "such culture forms a developmental niche not as a loose collection of fragments but as a configuration that is structured yet inevitably fluid . . . [and] . . . Human development must be studied as embedded in a dynamically functioning group culture . . . [in which] . . . More lively understanding results from carefully analyzing how specific behaviors interact with cultural conditions that are always bound by time and place" (p. xii). As you will see, later in this chapter and throughout the rest of this book, Azuma's view of culture fits very well with our definition and theoretical approach to understanding cross-cultural human development.

In the absence of an as yet commonly agreed-upon definition of **culture,** when we use the term in this book we shall be referring to *the cluster of learned and shared beliefs, values (achievement, individualism, collectivism, etc.), practices (rituals and ceremonies), behaviors (roles, customs, traditions, etc.), symbols (institutions, language, ideas, objects, and artifacts, etc.), and attitudes (moral, political, religious, etc.) that are characteristic of a particular group of people and that are communicated from one generation to another.*

A caveat regarding this definition may be in order before we proceed. Since there is no consensus regarding "the" definition of culture (and it is likely there never will be), our definition is a thoughtful compilation of aspects of several previously published definitions combined with some thoughts of our own as to what constitutes this concept. As Shwalb has accurately pointed out, in most comparative studies culture is "unfortunately equated with nationality, which is convenient for readers to understand . . . but not satisfying . . ." (personal communication, 2005). He goes on to say that he would like to see culture "better distinguished conceptually from nationality, ethnicity, race, and religion." (personal communication, 2005). We, and other social scientists, would surely agree, but, as the reader might imagine, this effort, like defining culture, is a most difficult task and better left for another time. If we were to attempt to provide definitions for these terms at this point, they would likely be as "unsatisfying" to many as some definitions of culture are to others and would distract us from our major focus—describing and explaining cross-cultural human development.

As the field of cross-cultural psychology has evolved, concerns in the area of development have undergone a number of significant shifts. Parke, Ornstein, Rieser, and Zahn-Waxler (1994) have succinctly summarized and discussed the changes in developmental focus over the past hundred years by looking at three periods. One hundred years ago, five major areas were of interest: emotional development, the biological basis of behavior, cognitive development, conscious and unconscious processes, and the role of self in development. During the 1950s and 1960s, the focus shifted to learning theory, the rise of experimental child psychology, interest in operant analysis of children's behavior, the emergence of investigations of infant sensory and perceptual development, and the objective measurement of cognitive understanding among preverbal infants. Today, there is a revitalized interest in emotional development and cognitive abilities of children, the biological bases of behavior, and social relationships. According to the authors, the "most unanticipated theme is the continuing discovery of the precocity of infants and young children—not only cognitively but also socially and emotionally" (p. 8). We shall see this point illustrated numerous times throughout this book.

◇ CROSS-CULTURAL HUMAN DEVELOPMENT AND THE OTHER SOCIAL SCIENCES

In commenting on the central role that culture plays in our efforts to better understand behavior, Segall, Lonner, and Berry (1998) posed an interesting and critical question: "Can it still be necessary, as we approach the millennium (as measured on the Western, Christian calendar), to advocate that all social scientists, psychologists especially, take culture seriously into account when attempting to understand human behavior?" (p. 1101). Unfortunately, while the situation has dramatically improved and only continues to get better, even now as we are nearing the end of the first decade of the twenty-first century, the answer remains (a qualified)—yes!

When discussing cross-cultural psychology and its sub-discipline of cross-cultural human development, it is obvious they share a long historical connection with general psychology. Although, as the well-known psychologist–anthropologist Otto Klineberg has pointed out, "There is no specific date that can be identified with the onset of interest in cross-cultural comparisions" (1980, p. 34). Jahoda and Krewer have suggested it may be as early as the seventeeth century, since the "dominant perspective of enlightenment philosophy was highly compatible with cross-cultural psychology's model of man" (1997, p. 11). Since the 1960s, much of our psychological research, particularly that which has emphasized the cross-cultural approach, has focused on the areas of abnormal, cognitive, social, and developmental psychology.

In terms of the other social sciences, the closest links are to anthropolgy and sociology with shared interests in specific approaches, methodological procedures, and research interests, including the socialization process and family influences on development. At the same time, this relationship has not always been a smooth one. Some of the difficulties, especially those centering on comparative studies of infant development, were pointed out by Super (1981), when he stated that, for several decades, psychology and anthropology "seem to have withdrawn from the interface . . . to tend to their own theories. Very few studies . . . achieve, or even attempt, an integration of infant care and development, on the one hand, with functional and value characteristics of the larger culture, on the other" (pp. 246–247). At the same time, he noted that success in these areas would require researchers to improve their ethnographic knowledge of cultures as well as to develop quantitative baselines of information for use in future studies. As you will discover in reading this book, this is precisely the path that much of present-day, cross-cultural, human development research has taken (Gardiner, 2001b).

In a lively and entertaining book titled *Psychology and Anthropology: A Psychological Perspective*, Gustav Jahoda, a psychologist with a true appreciation and understanding of both psychology and anthropology, noted that "Anthropologists have always been concerned with psychology, even if unwittingly. . . . However, this interest has, in many respects, remained narrowly culture-bound, largely ignoring the wider perspectives provided by anthropology" (1982, back cover).

In bringing this section to a close, it is our sincere hope that cross-cultural psychologists, in particular those interested in human development, will be able to forge a bond with other social scientists, notably anthropologists, and work together as partners in laying a firm foundation for an empirically based understanding of human behavior that places a greater focus on developmental processes within cultural contexts. A welcome step in this direction has been made with recent volumes that focus on emerging concepts and methods for measuring environment (or context) across the lifespan (Friedman & Wachs, 1999; Sternberg & Grigorenko, 2004) and childhood and family life (Weisner, 2002). Another important contribution is the recent book, *Developmental Psychology and Social Change*, by Pillemer & White (2005) discussing the historical evolution of developmental psychology, its goals, and its current challenges. The chapter by Super on the globalization of developmental psychology is of particular interest. Efforts such as these and others will greatly enrich our understanding of development and the vital role that culture plays in it.

◇ SOME IMPORTANT THEMES

This book differs in significant ways from most other volumes that focus on cross-cultural aspects of human behavior, most notably in its efforts to integrate a variety of important themes. Let us look at these in some detail and discover how they will weave through subsequent chapters.

A Cross-Cultural Perspective

Over the past two decades, and especially in the last five years, social scientists have become increasingly aware of the contributions that cross-cultural research findings can make to our understanding of human development. Reviews of recently published developmental books, compared with those of just a few years ago, reveal that references to cross-cultural topics and findings have grown tremendously (Gardiner, 1996; Woolf, Hulsizer, & McCarthy, 2002).

Any attempt to include all or even most of these findings in a book of this length would be difficult, if not impossible. Therefore, we have decided to be selective and discuss representative areas of interest using a chronological-within-topics approach. For readers desiring a more comprehensive view of cross-cultural human development, or for those wishing to explore particular topics in greater depth, we refer you to the "Further Readings" section at the close of each chapter as well as the references listed at the end of this book. If you are eager to get started, you might consider looking at such classics as *Two Worlds of Childhood: U.S. and U.S.S.R.* (1970) by Urie Bronfenbrenner and a series of volumes on *Six Cultures* by Whiting (1963), Whiting and Whiting (1975), and Whiting and Edwards (1988). There is the revised three-volume *Handbook of Cross-Cultural Psychology* (1997), edited by John Berry and others, which contains several chapters relevant to the study of cross-cultural development as well as the role of cross-cultural theory and methodology. In addition, there is the *Encyclopedia of Psychology*, eight volumes providing a definitive guide to the major areas of psychological theory, research, and practice (Kazdin, 2000). Finally, there is the *Handbook of Culture and Psychology* presenting the state of the art of major areas and issues in cross-cultural psychology, including development (Matsumoto, 2001).

Goals for the Field

As to the nature and purpose of the cross-cultural method, Berry, Poortinga, Segall, and Dasen (2002), in a comprehensive overview of cross-cultural psychology, set forth three goals for the field. The first goal involves *testing or extending the generalizability of existing theories and findings.* In earlier writings, Berry and Dasen (1974) referred to this as the "transport and test goal" in which hypotheses and findings from one culture are transported to another so that their validity can be tested in other cultural settings. For example, are parental speech patterns in English-speaking families similar or dissimilar to those in Spanish-speaking families? Are the stages of cognitive development proposed by Jean Piaget specific to certain types of cultures, or are they universal?

The second goal focuses on *exploring other cultures in order to discover variations in behavior that may not be part of one's own cultural experience.* In other words, if findings cannot be generalized, what are the reasons for this, and are these behaviors unique to these other cultures? A good example is a study by Jablensky and colleagues (1992) that successfully demonstrates that a number of symptoms characteristic of schizophrenia (a serious psychologi-cal disorder) exist in ten very different cultures, but that there is no single factor to explain differences in the formation or outcome of the disorder. At the same time, other psychological conditions appear to be "culture-bound" and occur only among certain groups of people. One example is *pibloktoq*, found only among specific groups of Eskimos, in which individuals, with lit-tle or no warning, perform irrational acts (e.g., ripping off clothes, shouting obscenities, throwing objects, and running wildly into snowdrifts, from which they are often rescued by others), lasting a few minutes or as long as an hour (Kirmayer & Minas, 2000).

The third goal, which follows from the first two, is aimed at *integrating findings in such a way as to generate a more universal psychology applicable to a wider range of cultural settings and societies.* Examples of this include efforts by many cross-cultural researchers to refine and expand the usefulness of sev-eral theories, including the various ecological approaches cited in this book.

At this point, you might be wondering, "How can a cross-cultural per-spective contribute to our understanding of human development?" In answer to this question, Gardiner (2001b) has pointed to a number of impor-tant benefits. First, looking at behavior from this perspective compels re-searchers to reflect seriously on the ways in which their cultural beliefs and values affect the development of their theories and research designs. In-creased awareness of cross-cultural findings provides an opportunity to extend or restrict the implications of research conducted in a single cultural group, most notably the United States and similar Western societies. Nothing helps to reduce ethnocentrism as quickly as looking at behavior as it occurs in other cultures. **Ethnocentrism** is defined as *the tendency to judge other peo-ple and cultures by the standards of one's own culture and to believe that the behavior, customs, norms, values, and other characteristics of one's own group are natural, valid, and correct while those of other's are unnatural, invalid, and incorrect.* Second, the number of independent and dependent variables to be investigated can be greatly increased in a cross-cultural design. Examples of studies in which this has been done include investigations of gender differences (Morinaga, Frieze, & Ferligoj, 1993), effects of parent–child relationships in diverse cultures (Gielen & Roopnarine, 2004), and individualism-collectivism and the atti-tudes toward school bullying of Japanese and Australian students (Nesdale & Naito, 2005). We generally think of an **independent variable (IV)** as *the condition introduced into or systematically manipulated in an experiment by the researcher,* and a **dependent variable (DV)** as *the subject's response or the behavior being measured in an experiment.* Without getting too complicated, it should be noted that in the context of cross-cultural research, these are really quasi-IVs and DVs, representing both a strength (more "real worldly") as well as a weakness (some loss of control and/or increased ambiguity). For an excellent discussion of culture as an antecedent, dependent, independent, or intervening variable, the reader is referred to several chapters in Volume 1 of the *Handbook of Cross-Cultural Psychology* (Berry, Poortinga, & Pandey, 1997).

Third, cross-cultural studies help us to separate **emics,** or *culture-specific concepts,* from **etics,** or *universal or culture-general concepts.* As Lonner (2005) points out, this poses an important question: "Can anyone outside any specific human group (culture) understand completely the workings of the group (culture) to the same degree as an insider does?" (p. 15). The **emic** (insider) **approach** focuses on a single culture, using criteria that are thought to be relative to it, and studies behavior from *within* the system itself. An example is an anthropological field study in which a researcher lives with a group of people and tries to understand the culture through their eyes and experiences, avoiding the ethnocentrism of his or her own cultural background. The **etic** (outsider) **approach,** on the other hand, looks at several cultures, comparing and contrasting them using criteria thought to be absolute or universal, and studies behavior from *outside* the system. An example, which (happily) we don't see as often as we once did in cross-cultural psychology, involves an investigator conducting what has been called "safari research." An illustration is a professor (not very familiar with the field) who goes on vacation to several countries, taking along a favorite questionnaire concerning _____ (you fill in the blank). He or she visits several universities, collects data from available students (who may or may not understand many of the colloquial English language terms), returns home, and publishes the findings as "universal" attitudes of those living in cultures X, Y, and Z.

Separating emics from etics is better accomplished by testing theories or principles developed in one cultural context in another. The work of Freud, Piaget, and Kohlberg are examples. In some cases, findings lend support to the universality of behaviors in vastly different cultural settings (e.g., stages in language development and the sequence and timing of such behaviors as smiling, walking, stranger and separation anxiety, and pubertal development). On the other hand, results have sometimes suggested a need for modification of certain culture-bound concepts (e.g., intelligence, medical diagnosis, and, sometimes, gender behavior). For a comprehensive review of some of the significant findings of indigenous psychologists, see Kim & Yang (2005).

By focusing throughout this book on cross-cultural material, we hope to provide readers with opportunities to expand their awareness and sensitivity to global similarities and differences in human development and to reduce any ethnocentric thinking. The cross-cultural perspective complements and extends the work of earlier researchers who successfully presented the more traditional, but often culture-specific, approach to understanding life-span development by offering a broader world view. By allowing readers to experience variations in behavior not normally found in their own societies (e.g., accelerated formal operational thought among some Asian populations, decreased susceptibility to visual illusions among certain African groups, and highly developed mathematical skills among Dutch children), this perspective contributes to our understanding of human adaptation. Perhaps most important, it encourages a closer look at the interconnections among culture, development, and behavior—a major theme in contemporary developmental psychology.

While we certainly are not the first to stress the importance of looking at cross-cultural data, we believe we give it greater emphasis because, as Segall so aptly stated nearly three decades ago, "It is to . . . theories of ecological, cultural, and socialization forces that we must turn for the most promising insights into why different peoples develop different . . . skills or develop the same skills at different rates" (1979, p. 129).

The mention of socialization practices, and the variety of ways in which we are influenced by ecological factors, leads us to another of our major themes.

An Ecological Model

The importance of viewing behavior within its social setting was first recognized not by psychologists but by sociologists, who stressed the importance of the individual's subjective view. Among the early proponents of this view were C. H. Cooley (1902), W. I. Thomas and F. Znaniecki (1927), and G. H. Mead (1934). When psychologists became interested in the topic, they tended to ignore the social context in favor of the cognitive processes (Koffka, 1935; Kohler, 1938; Piaget, 1954). Such analysis was extended beyond the individual to the study of the environment with the introduction of the concepts of "psychological field" and "life space" by Kurt Lewin (1935). Explicit recognition of the need to study an individual's subjective view of social reality came with the pioneering work of MacLeod (1947).

One of the most important contributions to these evolving ideas, and one of the ones on which much of our presentation is based, is the ecological model presented in the work of Urie Bronfenbrenner (1975, 1977, 1979, 1986, 1989, 1993, 2005). In its original form, this model divided a child's environment into four nested and interrelated systems or contexts (one more was added later) and allowed us to see and understand (within a broad framework) how patterns of interaction within the family and the wider society are influenced by and in turn influence the connection between development and culture. Each of these systems involves relationships and are defined by expected behaviors and roles. For example, a child behaves very differently at home, in school, or with playmates. When relationships between systems are in harmony, development proceeds smoothly. Consider the relationship between home and school as an example. If expectations are much the same in both settings (e.g., try to do your best work, be careful and neat, etc.), individuals are more likely to succeed and do well than if expectations differ significantly from one setting or environment to another. Bronfenbrenner's family-centered approach has allowed others to adapt and apply his model to a variety of contemporary issues and to develop applied programs involving parent education, counseling, disabilities, day care, and early childhood programs. This approach is presented and discussed in detail in Chapter 2.

Can you find the Western anthropologist in this picture? (© David R. Austen/Stock Boston)

Noted anthropologist Dr. Dawn Chatty, discussing local problems with Harsous tribal member in Sahmah, Oman, in the Arabian Peninsula. (© James L. Stanfield/National Geographic Society)

The Developmental Niche

If Bronfenbrenner is correct in his view that culture and environment make significant contributions to one's development (and we, as well as others, believe that they do), one might ask, "How does this happen and how can we better understand the processes taking place?"

One possible answer is provided by the cross-cultural developmental work of Harkness (2005), Parmar, Harkness, & Super (2004), and Super and Harkness (1986, 1994, 1999, 2002). Based on an extensive series of studies among Kipsigis-speaking communities in western Kenya, Super and Harkness, a psychologist–anthropologist research team, have presented a way of bringing together and integrating findings from the two disciplines. Called the **developmental niche,** it provides *a framework for understanding how various aspects of a culture guide the developmental process by focusing on the child as the unit of analysis within his or her sociocultural setting or context.* In this regard, it is compatible, in certain respects, with the ideas put forth by Bronfenbrenner and, in combination with it, comprises another major theme of this book. It, too, is presented and discussed in detail in Chapter 2.

A Developmental Orientation

It is well-recognized that most of our behavior does not take place at isolated periods in our lives but rather evolves and continually develops throughout the lifespan. Although the body of cross-cultural research literature is significant, it frequently resembles "a confused mosaic of contradictory findings" (Gardiner, 1994). This may explain, in part, why none of the books that currently examine cross-cultural topics systematically presents a developmental perspective as we do here. Not all of the behaviors covered in this book will always fit neatly into this orientation or be easily explained by some of the other themes or approaches. However, many do and, where appropriate, we attempt to demonstrate how these behaviors evolve and change as individuals develop across the lifespan and across cultures.

To illustrate the importance of looking at behavior from a developmental orientation, let us briefly consider the development of memory and attention, or the increased ability to organize information. As children we begin to think, attend, and store away memories. As adolescents and adults we develop the ability to make inferences, understand reversibility, and make use of abstract thought. Information that may have been remembered in childhood as a list can now be recalled in adulthood as a total pattern.

The implications of studying this topic from a lifespan developmental perspective have been nicely summarized by Forman and Sigel (1979), who write that "it is not clear whether the decline in memory and attention that occurs in old age is a function of reduced general cognitive competence or an inadequate problem-solving attitude due to social isolation, fear of failure, and other factors. But it is clear that the error rate of the elderly decreases when tests are not timed and social acceptance is reinforced. We can venture the tentative conclusion that poor performance in the 4-year-old is probably due to lack of a general cognitive competence, while poor performance in the 70-year-old is likely the result of an attitude toward solving problems (provided, of course, that the person shows no pathological signs of neurological deterioration)" (p. 89). A more recent effort to understand the lifespan development of human memory from an interdisciplinary perspective, employing a variety of research methods and theoretical approaches, is found in the work of Graf and Ohta (2000).

This brings us to another theme that will occur throughout this book—the chronological-within-topics approach.

A Chronological-Within-Topics Approach

In a book of this size, it is impossible to do all things—that is, provide a comprehensive view of development in all the necessary detail and also focus on all the important cross-cultural findings. Recognizing this, we have decided to look at selected topics for which a large literature of cross-cultural research exists and discuss these topics chronologically—from the early beginnings of development through the last years of life.

Using this *chronological-within-topics approach*, we hope to effectively demonstrate how behavioral processes evolve and change as individuals pass from infancy and childhood through adolescence and into adulthood. As a result, it should become clear that our behavior is dynamic and involves change, that it is at times orderly and predictable and at other times chaotic and unreliable, that both individual and cultural similarities and differences exist, and that specific cultural influences become important at different times and in different cultures. This approach includes basic concepts, principles, and theories that describe physical, psychological, cognitive, social, and personality changes that occur across the lifespan in a variety of cultural contexts.

◇ PRACTICAL APPLICATIONS

We believe that a book emphasizing process, content, and skill (at understanding and interpreting cross-cultural behavior), but avoiding unnecessary jargon and seeking a broad perspective, provides a number of benefits to readers. Therefore, part of our focus is on the *everyday experiences* encountered by individuals of differing ethnic backgrounds within their own society as well as between individuals of different cultural settings. We further believe that if readers come to understand the processes involved, they can begin to understand how to apply these principles for a deeper insight into the events and issues that touch their lives beyond the boundaries of their home, neighborhood, classroom, community, and nation. Throughout this book, material is continually related to issues and concerns that are important and relevant to all of us. Efforts are made to encourage critical thinking by using exercises that allow one to examine, question, explore, analyze, and evaluate a variety of everyday situations within diverse cultural contexts.

There is an adage that states "Tell me and I'll forget . . . show me and I'll probably remember . . . involve me and I'll never forget." Simply stated, this is another of our important themes—practical application. Many of today's texts are written for social science majors planning graduate study and frequently emphasize laboratory research—a shortcoming already recognized in our earlier comments on the need for an ecological point of view. While we feel a developmental text should be grounded in carefully researched theory, we also believe that if it is to be maximally useful, it should avoid jargon and focus on readers' "real-life" experiences, and ultimately assist them to relate more effectively with other individuals and in diverse environments. This is especially true today as our world, even at the local neighborhood level, becomes increasingly multicultural.

These goals are accomplished in several ways. In writing this book we have selected topics that have meaning for one's daily living: socialization (Chapter 3), physical development (Chapter 4), cognition and language (Chapter 5), personality (Chapter 6), issues of gender and sexuality (Chapter 7), social behavior (Chapter 8), the family (Chapter 9), and health issues (Chapter 10).

We don't expect you to accept what we say without question. We believe in the adage mentioned earlier, and we try to practice what we preach by providing opportunities for you to question, explore, and analyze the topics presented. In doing this, we hope you will arrive at a better understanding of your own behavior, modifying it where necessary and desirable and developing and improving your cross-cultural interactions with others, now and in the future.

◇ OVERVIEW OF THE BOOK

Since the transition from theory to practice cannot be accomplished simply by reading about applications, we make an effort to present the material in each chapter in such a way that it explicitly encourages your active involvement.

First, as you notice, each chapter opens with vignettes focusing on issues and behaviors to be addressed by the material presented in a particular chapter. This gives you an idea of what is covered in each chapter, and it allows you to formulate your own ideas as you read the material. For example, "What are the benefits of studying development cross-culturally?" "What are the effects of culture on socialization?" "How does children's play differ from one culture to another?" "In what ways are adolescents similar or different throughout the world?" "How do cultures treat their elders or older adults?"

Second, within the narrative, each new idea is defined, highlighted, and illustrated with cultural examples (many from the authors' own experiences) that, hopefully, you find both relevant and entertaining.

Third, real-life examples are described of cultural variations in childbirth, effects of culture on learning styles, growing old in different cultures, cultural variations in adolescent identity, and other important topics.

Finally, each chapter closes with a section on "Further Readings." Included are materials from a variety of sources that we think are interesting, informative, entertaining, and easy for you to locate. You will also find several "Study Questions" to help you focus on important points in each chapter.

◇ SOME CROSS-CULTURAL TEASERS

As we bring this chapter to a close, we'd like to leave you with a few "cross-cultural teasers," or questions for which we provide partial answers. Each of these receives further attention in future chapters.

- Is there a unifying concept that might explain reasons for cultural variations in development? The answer lies in the area of adaptation, or the various ways in which peoples of diverse cultures have adapted or adjusted to the events occurring in their lives.

- Are there any universals in human development? If so, what are they? One example of a universal is gender-role assignment. All societies appear to socialize boys and girls into gender roles (e.g., allowing more aggressive behavior among boys and encouraging more caring behavior among girls).

- How can we explain cross-cultural differences in such behaviors as dependence and independence? Part of the answer depends on where infants sleep after they are born. The United States is known as a culture that greatly emphasizes individual achievement; parents generally place babies in their own cribs in their own rooms. Japan, a collectivist culture, encourages dependence; children are allowed to sleep with parents, often for many years. How does this affect development?

- Adolescents in many of the world's cultures confront the problem of identity, or trying to answer the question "Who am I?" For some, living in Nigeria, it is a relatively easy task. For others, growing up bicultural in New York City, it is more difficult.

- Eating disorders, such as anorexia and bulimia, are common in many Western societies. Do young people throughout the world all strive to attain the ideal body image? You may be surprised by some of the answers found in Japan, Australia, and other countries.

- How do different cultures view their elderly? Is grandparenting the same everywhere? We'll give you some answers to these questions from China, Japan, and the United States.

- How does family life differ from one culture to another? In some societies, the roles of mothers and fathers may surprise you. Did you know children in some cultures become more closely attached to their fathers than to their mothers? Why would this be the case? We'll find out later in this book.

- An increasingly common disorder among older adults today is Alzheimer's disease. Did you know that people suffering from this disease are treated differently by their caregivers if the patient and caregiver are Hispanic, Native American, or Anglo?

- What's important in selecting a marriage partner—money, good looks, security, health? You'll be surprised at some of the views expressed by men and women from cultures around the world. How many chickens or cows do you think you're worth on the marriage market?

Have we gotten your attention? Do you want to know the answers to these and other interesting cross-cultural questions? Would you like to know some of the similarities and differences in human behavior and how people live their "lives across cultures?" Then turn the page and read on.

◇ SUMMARY

This chapter introduced the topic of cross-cultural human development and provided definitions of important terms and concepts. Discussion centered on several themes to be used in organizing developmental topics in a variety of cultural settings. These themes included a cross-cultural perspective, an ecological model, the developmental niche, a developmental orientation, a chronological-within-topics approach, and an emphasis on practical applications. Suggestions were given for using the material in ways to help readers develop a greater understanding of, and sensitivity to, those of a different cultural background than their own and develop and improve any cross-cultural interactions they might experience.

◇ STUDY QUESTIONS

Explain what is meant by the term *cross-cultural human development*.

Demonstrate a familiarity with the important themes presented in this chapter including the cross-cultural perspective, ecological model, developmental niche, developmental orientation, and chronological-within-topics approach.

Comment on the three goals set forth for the field of cross-cultural psychology.

◇ FURTHER READINGS

R. E. Axtell. (1993). *Do's and Taboos Around the World*, (3rd ed.). New York: Wiley & Sons.

Updated and expanded guide to international behaviors. Most useful for business travelers but also of value for tourists and travelers or anyone living or interacting with a culture other than their own.

Dave Barry. (1992). *Dave Barry Does Japan*. New York: Fawcett Columbine.

An irreverent view of Japanese culture by one of America's premiere humorists. Witty and sometimes insightful. Contains discussion of such topics as "Failing to Learn Japanese in Only Five Minutes (Very much good morning, Sir)," "Lost in Tokyo (Looking for plastic squid)," and "Humor in Japan (Take my tofu! Please!)."

Hubert J. M. Hermans and Harry J. G. Kempen. (1999). Moving Cultures: The Perilous Problems of Cultural Dichotomies in a Globalizing Society." *American Psychologist*, 54, 1111–1120.

The authors discuss the impact of globalization and compare Western cultural tradition with the rest of the world. They comment on the potential influence of cultural connections and some of the complexities associated with cultural change.

Joseph Lemasolai-Lekuton. (2003). *Facing the Lion: Growing Up Maasai on the African Savanna*. National Geographical Children's Books.

The author's memoir of childhood in one of Kenya's poorest tribes, his mischievous antics as a young Maasai cattle herder, coming-of-age initiation, boarding school experiences, and journey to America for a college education. While written for children, the author gives any reader a feeling for his unique culture, its traditions, and how he became the successful and inspirational person he is today. Well worth reading at any age.

CHAPTER TWO

THEORIES AND METHODOLOGY

Justin Tyme, an undergraduate major in psychology, has returned from a month in Thailand, where he attempted to collect data for his senior thesis. This was his first visit to a foreign country and it was a memorable, but unsatisfying, experience. Why? Because Justin was not well-prepared and made several serious (and avoidable) mistakes. First, he traveled to a culture he knew little about (because it sounded exotic). People spoke a language (Thai) he did not understand and which he found difficult to read, write, or speak in the brief time he was there because of its complexity (44 consonants, 28 vowel forms, 5 tones, and written in script). He found the weather too hot and humid, the food too spicy, and life in the village where he was doing his research "too slow." He had difficulty finding people to help translate his English-language, Western-designed, marital-role preference scale so that it would have comparable meaning in Thai. He was upset because the few subjects he was able to get often didn't arrive exactly on time (Asians, in general, are not as time conscious as Westerners, especially Americans), and when they did, they usually told him "Mai pen rai" (Don't worry). Finally, representative samples were difficult to obtain in a rural area that would match his samples back in Chicago, Illinois.

Dr. Kitty Litter, an anthropologist from Cornell University, recently spent six months doing an ethnographic field study among a group of Indians in the highlands of Peru. Not only was she fluent in Spanish, the most widely spoken language in the country, but she also had a working knowledge of two native languages—Quechua and Aymara—from two previous trips to the country. She had read extensively about the customs of the tribal groups in this area and was very fond of the food. She especially enjoyed the tropical climate along the coast and the cooler temperatures in the mountains. She had spent considerable time designing the questions she was going to ask and had even prepared a Quechuan-language version of a psychological instrument she hoped to validate while there.

Theories and methodology—sound exciting, don't they? Perhaps not, but these two topics are central to understanding what happens both in cross-cultural human development and in the chapters that follow. In this regard, we have two goals for this discussion of theories: first, to provide a foundation for those who do not have a background in human development (or could benefit from a review of major concepts) to appreciate their contributions to our efforts to better understand behavior; second, to provide a framework for identifying complex human behavior and experience as it occurs within different cultural contexts and to explore possible reasons for the similarities and differences that are found in societies around the world. If research (cross-cultural or otherwise) is not carefully designed, conducted, analyzed, and understood, any findings that result are of little value. So, we'll try to make the discussion of these topics as simple, relevant, and interesting as possible.

◇ THEORIES OF DEVELOPMENT

Why do we study human development? There are many reasons, but basically we do it to *understand, explain, predict,* and (in some instances) *control behavior.* To achieve these goals successfully, we need to be familiar and comfortable with theories and their important concepts. As a graduate student in England, I (Gardiner), while trying to select a topic for my doctoral dissertation, was asked by my major adviser if there was an area of psychology with which I felt particularly uncomfortable. Without hesitation, I immediately replied, "Theories." (I shouldn't say this but, as an undergraduate student, I frequently skipped over theories because I found them boring, confusing, and too abstract.) When it was suggested that I devote the next three years to the development of my own theory in order to decrease this discomfort (a form of theoretical desensitization, I guess), I thought this was a "daft idea." Of course, I didn't tell this to my adviser! However, develop my own theory I did (Gardiner, 1966). Not only did I really enjoy doing my original doctoral research (on "newspapers as personalities"), but, when it was over, I felt much less threatened by theoretical concepts and gained a greater appreciation for the central role theories play in the social sciences. We hope you feel the same way when you reach the conclusion of this chapter (don't skip over them; they *are* important!).

What Is a Theory?

Simply stated, a **theory** is *a set of hypotheses or assumptions about behavior.* A theory consists of guesses or speculations that allow us to answer such questions as "Why does a particular behavior occur?" For example, why are Chinese children generally calmer, less active, and easier to soothe when distressed than Western children? Why are ethnic customs and values of greater importance to some minority youths than others? What factors most influence the ways in which contemporary cultures treat their elderly?

When we study human development, we can't look at all aspects of an individual's, group's, or culture's behavior. Theories help us organize our ideas and limit what we look at, and serve as a guide (or blueprint) in the collection of data. Sometimes, it seems as if there are as many theories as there are people. In a sense, there are, because each of us has our own informal, unscientific, unverified, and highly idiosyncratic theories. Built up over years of personal observation and experience, these informal theories help us to understand the behavior of those with whom we come into contact. For example, when we meet someone for the first time, our informal theory of personality helps us decide whether we like or dislike this person, if we want to interact with this person again, and so on. However, we must go beyond these informal theories to truly understand and explain the complexity of human development. We need theories that are more formalized and rooted in scientific principles if we are to be able to compare and contrast behavior within and across cultures and draw conclusions about similarities and differences. In the pages that follow, we discuss six theories. While you may (or may not) be familiar with some or all of them, it might be helpful, in terms of our discussion, to think of the theories of Piaget, Kohlberg, and Erikson as traditional or mainstream psychological theories that focus on the individual, with primary attention to internal cognitive processes (e.g., knowing and thinking, moral reasoning, and psychosocial development). On the other hand, the theories of Bronfenbrenner, Super and Harkness, and Vygotsky can be viewed as interactionist theories, because they focus on the interactions between the individual and his or her environment in specific psychological domains (e.g., ecology and the interrelationship of the developing individual and his or her changing physical and social environment, links between children's behavior and the developmental niche in which they are raised, and cultural influences on development of language, thinking, and guided participation).

Bronfenbrenner's Ecological Model

In the previous chapter, we briefly noted that one of the most important contributions to the study of human development within cultural contexts, and one on which much of our presentation is based, is the ecological model presented in the pioneering work of Urie Bronfenbrenner (1975, 1977, 1979, 1986, 1989, 1993, 2005). At the center of Bronfenbrenner's thinking is his contention that human beings create the environments in which they live and that these, in turn, help shape their own development.

Simply stated, this model views behavior and development as a shared function of the characteristics of the individual (biological or genetic factors and personality) and the environment (social, physical, and cultural aspects of one's present surroundings, such as, family, school, and neighborhood), along with the larger contemporary and historical contexts of which these are an integral part, such as, society and period in which one is born and lives his or her life.

Bronfenbrenner's original model has been "undergoing successively more complex reformulations to attain its present, still-evolving form" (Bronfenbrenner, 1999, p. 4). The most recent version of this approach (Bronfenbrenner, 2005; Bronfenbrenner & Evans, 2000; Bronfenbrenner & Morris, 1998), has been renamed the *bioecological model*. By doing so, it identifies a child's own biology as a critical environmental factor affecting development, while incorporating earlier concepts, along with new ideas, into a series of propositions that focus more directly on the role of environment and the concept of time in the processes of human development. Those readers who want to know more about this evolving model, which remains more theoretical than practical at the moment, are directed to the references mentioned earlier.

In this book, we focus primary attention on Bronfenbrenner's earlier model (without the recent propositions), which we believe continues to offer advantages for viewing and understanding the connection between culture and human development. Where appropriate, we refer to some of his more recent ideas and formulations.

The **ecology of human development,** as defined by Bronfenbrenner, involves *"the scientific study of the progressive, mutual accommodation throughout the life course, between an active, growing human being and the changing properties of the immediate settings in which the developing person lives, as this process is affected by relations between these settings, and by the larger contexts in which the settings are embedded"* (2005, p. 107). In short, an individual is seen not as a passive, static, and isolated entity on which the environment exerts great influence (much like a *tabula rasa,* or blank slate), but as a dynamic and evolving being that interacts with, and thereby restructures, the many environments with which it comes into contact. These interactions between individual and environment are viewed as two-directional and characterized by reciprocity. For example, while a child's development is being influenced and molded by parents, family, school, and peers, she is, at the same time, influencing and molding the behavior of others.

Building on Bronfenbrenner's definition, the concept of environment is expanded to include increasingly complex interconnections among settings and is a considerably broader and more differentiated view than those previously presented in psychology in general and in developmental psychology in particular.

Bronfenbrenner has suggested that an individual's perception of the environment is often more important than "objective reality," and that this perception influences one's expectations and activities. A recognition and acceptance of the critical role played by the cultural or environmental context seem particularly suited to the study of human behavior and development.

In his critique of traditional research carried out on children, Bronfenbrenner has stated, "Much of contemporary developmental psychology is the science of the strange behaviors of children in strange situations with strange adults for the briefest possible periods of time" (1977, p. 513). In other words, while striving to achieve experimental rigor and control, we have often lost sight of the scientific and practical relevance of our findings by ignoring how the same phenomena might occur outside such artificial environments. One of the other major goals of this book is to stress the relevance and practicality of such findings.

The ecological model allows us to go beyond the setting being immediately experienced—whether in a laboratory, a classroom, or a backyard—and permits the incorporation of indirect, but nevertheless very real, effects from other settings, as well as from the culture as a whole. Bronfenbrenner originally divided the ecological environment into four **nested systems:** *microsystem, mesosystem, exosystem, and macrosystem* (see Figure 2.1 on page 24). This conceptualization of the ecological environment has been retained in his more recent bioecological model and is given attention in our discussions throughout this book. A fifth system, the *chronosystem*, with its focus on time and sociohistorical conditions, has been mentioned only occasionally in the literature, and seldom by Bronfenbrenner himself. However, as we soon see, the concept and importance of time has become a more significant part of the newly reformulated bioecological model and was so recognized in the last integrative book he wrote on his model before he died in 2005 (Bronfenbrenner, 2005).

The Microsystem. In Figure 2.1, the first level, the microsystem, is the layer closest to the child and contains those structures with which the child has direct contact. It represents the interactions or direct contacts between the child and her immediate surroundings (e.g., family or preschool) and resulting behaviors, such as dependence or independence and cooperation or competition. This is the most basic level, the one at which individuals engage in face-to-face interactions, and their behaviors frequently reflect social position. Bronfenbrenner (1994) expanded his original definition of the **microsystem** to include *"a pattern of activities, social roles, and interpersonal relations experienced by the developing person in a given face-to-face setting with particular physical, social, and symbolic features that invite, permit, or inhibit engagement in sustained, progressively more complex interaction with, and activity in the immediate environment"* (p. 1645). Examples include home, church, school, hospital, or day-care center. Other factors to consider include the effects of the physical environment on behavior, including background noise, crowding, and the number and types of toys available to a child.

The Mesosystem. The second level, the mesosystem, recognizes that the individual microsystems in which a child functions are not independent but

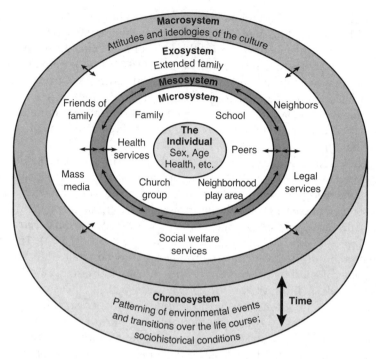

FIGURE 2.1   Bronfenbrenner's Ecological Model of Human Development

Source: From *The Ecology of Human Development* by U. Bronfenbrenner, 1979. Cambridge, MA: Harvard University Press. In *The Child: Development in a Social Context* by C. B. Kopp and J. B. Kaslow, 1982, p. 648. Reading, MA: Addison-Wesley. Reprinted by permission of Addison Wesley Longman, Inc.

are closely interrelated or connected and influence each other. This layer provides the connection between these structures. According to Bronfenbrenner's newly revised definition, the **mesosystem** *"comprises the linkages and processes taking place between two or more settings containing the developing person"* (1993, p. 22). This is a system made up of two or more microsystems (e.g., home and day care, day care and school, or family and peer group). It is the mesosystem that links or ties together information, knowledge, and attitudes from one setting that help to shape behavior or development in another setting. For example, while parents emphasize the importance of learning at home, preschool teachers provide stimulating activities at school that motivate a child to learn more. Steinberg and Brown (1989), in an effort to define and demonstrate the properties of the mesosystem, took this idea one step further by investigating the effect of parental and peer support of academic activities on performance of high school adolescents. At the conclusion of their investigation, they argued forcefully for the need to focus on multiple environmental influences as they affect development. They suggested that a failure to do so contributes to "the typically low proportion of explained variance in developmental research" (Bronfenbrenner, 1993). More recently, Steinberg, Darling, and Fletcher (1995) looked at authoritative parenting and adolescent adjustment within the ecological setting and reported a number of benefits, including lower levels of delinquency and substance abuse among both male and female adolescents.

The Exosystem.   Beyond the child's immediate environment are social settings of which he may not be a part but which, nevertheless interact with one or more structures in his microsystem and influence his development in significant ways. These settings or institutions make up the third level— the exosystem. As defined by Bronfenbrenner, the **exosystem** *"comprises the linkages and processes taking place between two or more settings, at least one of which does not contain the developing person, but in which events occur that indirectly influence processes within the immediate setting in which the developing person lives"* (1993, p. 22). Included here are formal settings, such as parents' place of work or community health and welfare institutions (e.g., hospitals). Bronfenbrenner (2005) provides an example of the link between the home and a parent's workplace for the developing child and of the link between the home and her children's peer group for the developing adult. Other less formal settings might include the extended family (aunts, uncles, cousins, friends, and neighbors.

The Macrosystem.   This is the most complex system and is found in the outermost circle and consists of the customs, values, and laws considered important in the child's culture. Bronfenbrenner (1993), in an expanded definition, states that the **macrosystem** *"consists of the overarching pattern of micro-, meso-, and exosystems characteristic of a given culture, subculture, or other extended social structure, with particular reference to the . . . belief systems, resources, hazards, lifestyles, opportunity structures, life course options and patterns of social interchange that are embedded in such overarching systems"* (p. 25). The focus is on the consistencies among a wide variety of settings within a given society or culture. For example, in many countries there are striking similarities in the form and function of such familiar settings as school playgrounds, post offices, shopping malls, and even fast food restaurants.

The Chronosystem.   In Bronfenbrenner's ecological model, the exact role of the **chronosystem** is somewhat difficult to describe because it has not received the same attention as have the other four systems. In fact, the term does not always appear in the reformulated bioecological model, although the elements that characterize it—time and sociohistorical conditions—constitute a major part of the new model (Bronfenbrenner, 2005). In his final writing, Bronfenbrenner makes the point that "The chronosystem is a methodological construct; the remaining four are theoretical but can also become substantive when put to empirical use" (p. 165). In general, this layer focuses on time as it relates to a child's various environments. For example, the physiological changes that occur as the child matures and his or her reactions to these changes as well as the changed environment in which he or she now functions. Another example is the timing of the death of an important person in the child's life, such as, a parent or sibling.

When studying individual behavior, a great deal of past and present developmental research has tended to view it either at a fixed point in time or, if over a long period of time (and if conducted longitudinally), has assumed little or no change in an individual's personal characteristics or in his or her environmental or ecological setting. As Muuss (1996) has pointed out, "time used to be perceived as synonymous with changes in chronological age. In the ecological model, the constancy or change over time (of both E and P) is essential to assessing the nature of the changes during the life course" (p. 320). Bronfenbrenner has used this chronosystem model to help explain how time simultaneously affects the environment (E) and the person (P). According to Muuss, Bronfenbrenner "emphasizes the interacting nature of these changes, and it is the interacting nature of (E) and (P) that Lewin, and more explicitly, Bronfenbrenner, have brought to our attention" (p. 320).

In his recent writings, Bronfenbrenner (2000), while not employing chronosystem terminology, placed increasing emphasis on "time and timing as they relate to features of the environment, as opposed to characteristics of the person" (p. 20)—what he has called "space through time: environment in the third dimension" (p. 20). Much of the progress in this area has emerged from researchers, primarily sociologists, using what Elder has called the "life course perspective" (1998a). For a discussion of the basic principles of this perspective, see Elder, 1998b.

In his final writings on the bioecological model, Bronfenbrenner (2005) discussed the defining properties of the chronosystem by stating that ". . . *its design permits one to identify the impact of prior life events and experiences, singly or sequentially, on subsequent development*" (p. 83). As examples, he explains these may occur either in the external environment (e.g., the birth of a sibling) or within the individual (e.g., one's first menstruation). He credits Baltes and his colleagues (1980) with further differentiating between *normative* experiences (e.g., entry into school or work, puberty, marriage, and retirement) and *nonnormative* events (e.g., a family illness or death, divorce, or even winning the sweepstakes). He emphasizes that both types of these experiences occur throughout the lifespan and frequently affect developmental change. Bronfenbrenner also suggests three types of research strategies that might be employed to study the chronosystem and its effects on development, including cross-sectional designs, short-term longitudinal designs, and the life course perspective proposed by Elder (1998 a,b).

Muuss (1996) provides an example of chronosystem research that might be conducted to investigate behavior among family members and the role time or timing might play in it. He points to the effect the arrival of a new baby might have on parents' interactions with each other and with other children. "By assessing the mother's interaction (with the older siblings) before, during, and after pregnancy, research suggests that the mother's inter-action patterns change rather noticeably as a function of these pregnancy/ child-bearing conditions" (Muuss, 1996, p. 320). Steinberg and his colleagues, in several studies (1987, 1988, 1995) examined the relationship between the timing of puberty and its effects on family relationships and parent–adolescent distance.

The ecological model, with its emphasis on the analysis of specific behaviors in increasingly complex settings, nicely complements our other themes and provides one of the central focal points around which these themes cluster. In fact, such a multilevel approach significantly expands the possibilities for explaining a variety of behaviors.

Super and Harkness's Developmental Niche

The concept of the developmental niche (at least the "niche" part) was orig-inally borrowed from the field of biological ecology, where *niche* describes the combined features of a particular animal's, or species of animal's, envi-ronment or habitat (Super & Harkness, 1994a). They use the example of a robin and a pigeon, both of which might live in the same section of a city park but differ in where they build their nests, the kinds of materials they use, and the kind of food they eat from the surrounding environment. The birds create a distinct niche for themselves based on each of these behaviors. The fact that this concept of a niche can be employed in biology and in psychology demonstrates, as we indicated earlier, that there is some unity to scientific efforts. In fact, much of the usefulness of the developmental niche concept lies in its ability to serve as an integrative framework provid-ing connections among culture, socialization, and ecology. In fact, the framework has been used by the authors and others in conducting research in a wide variety of areas, including cognitive, motor, and language devel-opment; temperament; sleep and arousal; emotional expression; literacy; and health. In recent years, it has been used extensively in the study of **ethnotheories,** or *parents' cultural belief systems about the nature of children, the processes of development, and the meaning of behavior* (Harkness & Super, 1996), as well as in intervention programs for inner-city children (Harkness et al, 2005).

As Sara Harkness and her colleagues (2005) have pointed out, the developmental niche concept owes much to the theoretical thinking and research of several earlier pioneers. For example, there are the "culture and personality" studies of the anthropologists Ruth Benedict and Margaret Mead, as well as Beatrice Whiting's idea of parents as "providers of settings" in which children were able to explore a variety of social behaviors. The authors refer specifically to the approach ". . . interwoven in early anthropological accounts of parenting in other cultures, . . . [which] . . . has emerged more recently as a distinctive focus in the developmental, as well as anthropological, literature, drawing from psychological research on parents' ideas as a force in children's development and on the anthropological construct of 'cultural model'" (p. 338). While each of these perspectives resulted in critical contributions, Harkness et al (2005) state that . . . " none of them accommodate sufficiently two core issues . . . the integration of various elements in the child's culturally structured environment and the endogenous aspects of individual development that alter the specifics of individual-environment interactions. The developmental niche is a theoretical framework that attempts to acknowledge and integrate this set of considerations" (p. 338).

In applying the term to psychology, Super and Harkness (1994a) state that "at the center of the developmental niche, therefore, is a particular child, of a certain age and sex, with certain temperamental and psychological dispositions. By virtue of these and other characteristics, this child will inhabit a different cultural 'world' than the worlds inhabited by other members of his family—and further, the child's world will also change as the child grows and changes" (pp. 96–97). In recent writing, Harkness and her colleagues (2005) state that "the primary view is to take the place of the child and look outward to the everyday world" (p. 338). Harkness (1999) has also pointed out that, while the approach has been used to analyze the niche of single individuals, it has more often been used to compare and contrast cultures or societies "widely separated in geographic place and historical background. However, flexibility in the degree of generalization is a useful feature of the framework, as it has proved useful in examining variation within a single physical community and in documenting changes in child care that are due to migration or seasonal change" (pp. 284–285). See, for example, Eldering (1995).

Every child's developmental niche consists of three interrelated components (see Table 2.1 on page 29). First, there are the physical and social settings of daily life in which a child lives (e.g., nuclear family living typically found in many Western cultures versus extended family arrangements found in many Asian or African countries). Aspects of this component include (1) the kind of company a child keeps (e.g., in rural Kenya families frequently consist of eight or more children, who serve as ready-made playmates and caretakers); (2) the size and shape of one's living space (e.g., in a large North American home children have their own rooms compared with families living in overcrowded apartments in Tokyo, where small rooms sometimes serve as living, dining, and sleeping areas); and (3) presence or absence of multiple generations living together (e.g., children, parents, grandparents,

TABLE 2.1   Components of the Developmental Niche

1. PHYSICAL AND SOCIAL SETTINGS OF DAILY LIFE

Size, shape, and location of living space

Objects, toys, reading materials

Ecological setting and climate

Nutritional status of children

Family structure (e.g., nuclear, extended, single parent, blended)

Presence of multiple generations (e.g., parents, grandparents, other relatives)

Presence or absence of mother or father

Presence of multiple caretakers

Role of siblings as caretakers

Presence and influence of peer group members

2. CUSTOMS OF CHILD CARE AND CHILD REARING

Sleeping patterns (e.g., co-sleeping vs. sleeping alone)

Dependence vs. independence training

Feeding and eating schedules

Handling and carrying practices

Play and work patterns

Initiation rites

Formal vs. informal learning

3. PSYCHOLOGY OF THE CARETAKERS

Parenting styles (e.g., authoritarian, authoritative, laissez-faire)

Value systems (e.g., dependence, independence, interdependence)

Parental cultural belief systems or ethnotheories

Developmental expectations

and other relatives). The differences in these components are clearly observable in the case of Kamuzu and Jeremy described in the opening vignette of Chapter 3.

The second component of the developmental niche focuses on culturally regulated customs of child care and childrearing practices. These include (1) informal versus formal learning (e.g., family teaching of important skills within most rural African tribal groups versus formal in-school learning characteristic of most Western societies); (2) independence versus dependence training (e.g., independence practiced by most Western parents versus dependence or even interdependence found among the majority of Asian parents); and (3) eating and sleeping schedules (e.g., in many North American and European homes, there are three meals a day at specified times, versus the five to six small meals at unscheduled times customary in many Asian cultures). Again, consider and contrast the educational experiences of Jeremy and Kamuzu mentioned above. Other examples include the customary use of playpens in Holland to keep infants happy and safe and the care of younger siblings by older ones in Kenya (Super & Harkness, 1994a).

Finally, the third component relates to the psychology of the caretakers or the psychological characteristics of a child's parents (e.g., developmental expectations, parental cultural belief systems, and types of parenting styles). According to Super and Harkness (1994a), this component "is an important channel for communicating general cultural belief systems to children, through very specific context-based customs and settings" (p. 98). These authors, like us, see a connection between the developmental niche and Bronfenbrenner's approach when they comment: "Drawing from ecological and systems theory, we suggest that the three components interact with each other as a system . . . to maintain consonance among them. The niche is an 'open system,' however, in that each component interacts independently with elements in the larger culture" (Harkness & Super, 1995, p. 227).

Super and Harkness propose that these components interact and function as a dynamic but not always completely coordinated system in which the individual and the developmental niche adapt and are mutually influential (see Figure 2.2). For example, although there is a conformity among certain elements of the niche (ecological settings consistent with parental beliefs), inconsistency can result from many factors, including external influences, limited resources, or historical change. Consistent with their recent ideas, Super and Harkness (1999) stress that these three subsystems of the niche "constitute elements of the environment as they are culturally structured in the child's experience" (p. 286). They point out that this framework can be equally well applied to adult development by expanding the third component—the psychology of the caretakers—to include the psychology of others (e.g., mates, coworkers) who might affect the adult. For an interesting example of the developmental niche in Somalia, see Box 2.1.

In an important extension of their pioneering approach to development, Super and Harkness (1999) look more closely at "the environment as culture in developmental research." They discuss, in depth, two anthropological concepts of culture they believe are of critical importance to understanding behavior within context—the immediacy of culture and its integrating nature.

For example, as to the immediacy of culture, it is their position (similar to our comments in Chapter 1) that psychologists (primarily in the past, but many even today) have either ignored culture when considering development

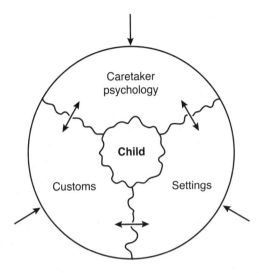

FIGURE 2.2 A Schematic Representation of the Developmental Niche

Source: From John W. Berry et. al., *Handbook of Cross-Cultural Psychology,* Volume 2, 2nd edition. Published by Allyn and Bacon, Boston, MA. Copyright © 1997 by Pearson Education. Reprinted by permission of the publisher.

or have tended to "keep it at great distance from the individual" (p. 281). In this regard, they are critical of Bronfenbrenner's original model, which represents culture as the macrosystem. It is their view that "the macrosystem's placement at the top of a nested hierarchy leaves it with no direct connection to the individual . . . culture exists as the outermost of several circles, while the developing child stands at the center, insulated from the cultural macrosystem by family, neighborhood, school, and other settings and institutions in the microsystem, mesosystem, and exosystem" (p. 281). Super and Harkness go on to suggest, "The anthropological insistence on the immediacy of culture not only better reflects the phenomenological experience of daily life but also brings the cultural environment into reach for the empirical scientist" (p. 282). We agree with this, as you will see in the many examples referred to throughout this book.

The integrating nature of culture is seen in the pioneering work of many anthropologists, including Margaret Mead, Ruth Benedict, and John and Beatrice Whiting, and in much of the research being done today. As Super and Harkness (1999) point out, these efforts suggest "a relatively new and promising agenda for interdisciplinary psychologists as they seek a more sophisticated understanding of behavior and development: Look for structures that integrate experience, and look for their immediacy in everyday life" (p. 283). For more on the ways in which culture serves as an integrating

BOX 2.1

 CHILDHOOD IN SOMALIA: AN EXAMPLE
OF THE DEVELOPMENTAL NICHE

In an extremely informative and detailed study, Norwegian psychologist Ragnhild Dybdahl explored childhood within the Somali sociocultural context, using the concept of the developmental niche. As part of her study, she conducted open-ended interviews in Mogadishu, Somalia, with twenty mothers, ranging in age from twenty-two to forty (mean age equals thirty), and twenty-three children (mean age equals ten). Most of the women lived with their husbands, and about one-fourth of them had been raised as nomads. The average number of family members was 7.5 and included various combinations of parents, children, grandparents, parents' siblings, and distant relatives staying as long-term guests. Topics of interest included reasons for having children, normative child care, and the roles played by parents and children in the Somali culture.

According to Dybdahl, the first component of the Somali developmental niche is characterized by the culture's economic and health problems; the nomadic way of life, with its emphasis on the extended family and clan; and the child's social and physical settings organized around school and Quaranic school, play, work, and household chores, especially care of younger siblings. The second component is characterized by socialization practices in which the infant, initially spending all its time with its mother, is gradually "distanced from the mother's back, breast and bed to be cared for by someone else." Although formal schooling plays a role, informal education is far more important and is the means by which children are taught such activities as household chores. Quaranic school serves as a mode of traditional education. The third component, based on interview comments from mothers, is characterized by mothers' focus on "physical health, obedience, resourcefulness, helpfulness and hard work," with expectations differing according to a child's age.

Dybdahl reported on the emergence of several themes associated with Somali childhood: (1) a clear responsibility for family and relatives; (2) the importance of such values as pride, hard work, loyalty, and obedience; (3) a constant struggle for survival and good physical health; and (4) the emotional importance attached to children as sources of short- and long-term security.

As a result of her interviews and observations, Dybdahl argues that Somali society represents a mix of "traditionalism and modernism, and collectivism and individualism." According to Dybdahl, her interviews with children provided a look at "the niche from the inside." She points out that "in spite of the difficult living conditions at the time . . . [just before "Operation Restore Hope" in 1989] . . . with war breaking out and relatively poor health

BOX 2.1 CONTINUED

conditions, beliefs in the future and in the possibility to change and improve one's life were recurring themes." She suggests that this may be due to a combination of factors, including the nomadic tradition of "moving on to another place," stoicism, and the belief that family and relatives will provide help if needed.

Dybdahl concludes that children must be studied in the "context and culture in which they live, and of which they are a part." Since developmental outcomes in Western societies have often come to be the norm for many of the world's children, "to avoid ethnocentrism and develop a global psychology, it is necessary to do cross-cultural research." Dybdahl is further convinced that, in order to make what she calls the "person-setting interaction" the focus of investigation, anthropologists and psychologists need to combine their efforts and that the developmental niche "might be a fruitful concept for this purpose." For a more recent report on this research, see Dybdahl and Hundeide, 1998.

In follow-up studies, the author used some of her experiences from this study in the design of a successful psychological intervention program with young children (mean age 5.5 years) and their mothers in the ecological context of war-torn Bosnia and Herzegovina. Participants were interviewed and tested to obtain information regarding their exposure to the war, psychosocial functioning, intellectual abilities, and physical and mental health. Findings revealed severe trauma with wide variations in displays of distress that were greatly helped and reduced by means of a simple and inexpensive intervention program adapted to their needs and to an understanding of the developmental niche in which they lived (Dybdahl, 2001, 2002, 2005).

Source: Adapted from "The Child in Context: Exploring Childhood in Somalia," paper presented by Ragnhild Dybdahl at the Twenty-Sixth International Congress of Psychology, Montreal, August 1996. Reprinted by permission.

---

force in development and why the authors' expanded cultural perspective on the environment is becoming increasingly important, see Super and Harkness (1999, 2002a, 2002b; Harkness & Super, 2003; Harkness, Hughes, Muller, & Super, 2004). Some of their suggested research methods and approaches are discussed later in this chapter.

Piaget's Theory of Cognitive Development

Jean Piaget (1896–1980), the Swiss-born psychologist, first developed an interest in cognitive development while working with Alfred Binet on intelligence testing in Paris. Piaget became curious about children's thinking and problem

TABLE 2.2 Piaget's Periods of Cognitive Development

PERIOD	APPROXIMATE AGE	DESCRIPTION	COGNITIVE MILESTONES
Infancy	Birth to 2 years	Sensorimotor	Object permanence
Early childhood	2 to 6 years	Preoperational	Egocentric thinking, use of symbols
Middle childhood	6 to 12 years	Concrete operations	Conservation
Adolescence	12 years and older	Formal operations	Abstract thinking

solving and why children of the same age made similar mistakes when trying to solve problems. For years, he carefully recorded the cognitive changes he observed in his three children in their home in Geneva. From these and other observations, he theorized that individuals learn by actively constructing their own cognitive world. To Piaget, development is a dynamic process that results from an individual's ability to adapt thinking to meet the demands of an ever-changing environment and, as a result, to formulate new ideas.

According to Piaget's view, normal cognitive growth passes through four distinct periods: infancy, early childhood, middle childhood, and adolescence (see Table 2.2). Each period is highlighted by the development of age-typical cognitive skills. Although Piaget provided age ranges for these various developmental periods, he recognized that the exact age at which a particular individual enters a specified period could be significantly affected by that person's physical, cognitive, or cultural experience—what Bronfenbrenner has referred to as the *ecological setting.*

It was Piaget's belief that cognitive development occurs as a result of children's attempts to adapt to their environments and to make sense of the many experiences taking place around them. The ability to do this requires the systematic development of progressively more complex mechanisms or structures. At the center of this activity lies the scheme. A **scheme** is *an organized pattern of thought or action applied to persons, objects, or events in an effort to make sense of them.* In short, it is a mental picture of the world and the things in it. For example, infants develop a wide variety of schemes during the first few months, including schemes for mother, breast, bottle, and father's voice. Over the years, increased interactions with the environment result in these schemes becoming more sophisticated and better coordinated, so that by the time an individual reaches formal operations, they are capable of thinking about behaviors and imagining their consequences.

According to Piaget, cognitive development and the ability to adapt to the environment depends on the processes of assimilation and accommodation.

Assimilation is *the process by which new information and ideas are incorporated or fitted into existing knowledge or schemes.* **Accommodation** is *the process of adjusting or modifying existing schemes to account for new ideas and information.* Anyone who has traveled abroad and attempted to make sense of new surroundings or tried to explain new objects or words to a foreign visitor has engaged in assimilation and accommodation—sometimes with success, sometimes with failure, and sometimes with humor! For example, what happens when Hakon from Norway tries to explain the making of a snowman to Yang, who lives in Malaysia and has never seen or touched snow? In this situation, Yang must make use of accommodation and adjust an existing scheme with which Yang is familiar (perhaps shaved ice) or create a new scheme (snow) to explain this new idea of a snowman.

It is through active and open interaction with one's environment or surroundings that individuals learn to balance these twin processes of assimilation and accommodation. In terms of Bronfenbrenner's ecological systems approach, these cognitive processes can be said to begin in the family (microsystem); gradually extend to increasingly complex situations that arise in the neighborhood, at day care, or at school (mesosystem); and eventually, as the individual moves into adolescence and adulthood, operate in the workplace (exosystem) and the culture at large (macrosystem).

While there is no doubt that Piaget's theory has had a significant impact on the study and understanding of cognitive development in mainstream Western psychology, his ideas have been challenged on several points. First, some have criticized his emphasis on individual activity occurring apart from social interaction. Such a focus reflects a more individualistic cultural perspective, such as that found in North America and Western Europe, and thereby fails to consider similarities or differences in cognitive development in traditional collectivistic cultures (e.g., China, Japan, and the islands of the South Pacific). Second, some have suggested that Piaget may have overestimated the contribution of motor activity and underestimated the ages at which children are capable of learning and performing a variety of behaviors by themselves. Third, Piaget's claim that once a person moves to a new period of cognitive development, the competencies mastered at that level will be exhibited in other phases of that individual's thinking, does not appear to be fully supported by cross-cultural research findings. While advances may be apparent in some domains of a person's thinking processes, this may not be true in other domains (Wellman & Gelman, 1992).

In the beginning, when Piaget was developing his theory and conducting his early studies, he paid little attention to cultural factors and the effects differences might have on cognitive development. However, as Thomas (1999) has noted, "In later years, Piaget did admit some influence of variations in environments, but still considered genetically controlled maturation to be the primary force behind mental development" (p. 65). Whatever one's position is regarding Piaget's theory, it continues to have considerable influence on contemporary research and practice and, as we see in Chapter 5, has been applied to the study of cognitive development in many cultures throughout the world—with varying success.

Vygotsky's Sociocultural Theory of Development

As we have just noted, Piaget's position was that cognitive development is largely an individual accomplishment, directed and shaped, in part, by the environment (and, in part, by genetics). However, he said little about the importance of the social context in learning. This view was challenged by the Soviet psychologist Lev Semyonovich Vygotsky.

Lev Vygotsky (1896–1934) was one of several children raised in an orthodox Jewish family in Russia. As a young man, he frequently wrote critically about Soviet government policies, with which he did not agree. As a result, his scientific writings were banned, although his highly acclaimed and influential book *Thought and Language* was finally published in 1934, the year he died of tuberculosis. (For an interesting, and generally ignored, view of how Vygotsky's Marxist orientation influenced the development of his psychological principles and also affected his life, see Gielen and Jeshmaridian, 1999.)

Vygotsky suggested that development is the result of interaction between cultural and historical factors. He believed that the key feature of development lies in matching a child's demands with the requirements of her culture. Vygotsky suggested that there were three major components in this process: the role played by culture, the use of language, and the child's zone of proximal development (Kozulin, 1990). Briefly, the **zone of proximal** (nearby) **development (ZPD)** refers to the distance between a child's actual developmental level and the higher-level potential (Vygotsky, 1978). It is *the difference between what children can achieve independently and what their potential level of development might be if given help or guidance.* This concept of the ZPD emphasizes Vygotsky's view that social influences contribute significantly to children's development of cognitive abilities and that mentoring or guidance strengthens their growth.

To tie this into several of the major themes already discussed, let us consider the case of twelve-year-old Dabir, a young Saudi adolescent. We might say that the process of learning, which takes place through mentoring in a number of Dabir's diverse ecological settings (home, mosque, school), defines his developmental niche at a particular time in his life. As Vygotsky would view it, Dabir does not have his own ZPD but participates in a shared ZPD with those around him (e.g., siblings, parents, teachers, and peers). This is also true with regard to Deratu (introduced in the opening vignette in Chapter 5), who does not go to school but learns the important cultural and practical lessons necessary for living in rural Ethiopia from the daily guidance provided by her mother.

While much of Vygotsky's work has been praised for its originality and usefulness, like the pioneering ideas of Piaget, it, too, has its critics. For example, some argue that the zone of proximal development is vague and cannot be adequately measured. Others believe that parts of Vygotsky's theory have been lost or misunderstood in translation and therefore are confusing and incomplete. Nevertheless, the theory still represents an increasingly important contribution to cross-cultural human development, with Vygotsky's zone of proximal development appearing more frequently in educator's teaching methods (Thomas, 1999). As an example, Thomas points out that "Rather than waiting for children to display a particular form of reasoning before attempting to teach skills and knowledge that depend on that form, teachers who follow Vygotsky's lead will attempt to teach the new learnings somewhat before the time children might exhibit their readiness spontaneously" (p. 48).

Interestingly, Bronfenbrenner (2005) points out that Vygotsky, along with others, ". . . served to redefine our conceptions of what a child is, what an environment is, what the nature of interaction is, and what development is—except that we have resisted any effort to think through and be explicit about exactly what these new conceptions are" (p. 63). He even goes as far as to point out that aspects of his model were foreshadowed by Vygotsky's theory and "With respect to the macrosystem, once again it was a Vygotskian concept that paved the way" (p. 100).

Erikson's Psychosocial Theory

Erik Erikson, a German-born psychoanalyst and student of Sigmund Freud's daughter, Anna, was the first person to propose a developmental theory encompassing the entire lifespan. Beginning with Freud's stages of psychosexual development, Erikson, a student of anthropology, modified and expanded them to focus greater attention on the social context of development (psychosocial) and less attention on biological and sexual development (psychosexual). Unlike Freud, his emphasis was on the growth of normal or healthy (rather than abnormal or neurotic) personality development, and he was particularly interested in cultural similarities and differences in the socialization of children and the development of identity during adolescence.

Erikson's theory provides a useful framework for attempting to define and unravel some of the major changes in social behavior that take place at various points in the lifespan. As shown in Table 2.3 on page 38, he proposed a sequence of eight stages ranging from infancy to later adulthood, each accompanied by a psychosocial crisis requiring resolution if one is to move successfully from one stage to the next. These crises or periods of increased vulnerability and heightened potential involve conflicts between newly developing competencies and a desire to maintain the status quo.

TABLE 2.3   Erikson's Stages of Psychosocial Development

STAGE	CRISIS	PSYCHOSOCIAL TASK
Infancy	Trust vs. mistrust	Develop first social relationship with primary caretaker(s); develop a fundamental trust in life and the world
Toddlerhood	Autonomy vs. shame and doubt	Explore the social environment outside the primary relationship; recognize self as an individual being
Early childhood	Initiative vs. guilt	Negotiate one's place within social relationships; learn about the impact of one's social behavior on others; develop a sense of power
Middle childhood	Industry vs. inferiority	Learn the importance of social norms and the personal consequences of conformity and nonconformity; develop a sense of competence
Adolescence	Identity vs. role confusion	Find social roles and social environments that correspond to one's identity and principles; form one's own identity
Young adulthood	Intimacy vs. isolation	Negotiate one's own identity within the context of intimate relationships
Middle adulthood	Generativity vs. stagnation	Make a contribution to the larger society; acquire a sense of accomplishment and a place in the world
Late adulthood	Integrity vs. despair	Become an integral and active part of one's family and community; come to terms with one's life and choices

When applying Erikson's theory, as we do at different points throughout the book, there are several points to keep in mind. First, although he assigns an age range to each of his eight stages, these should be considered only as a guide because of differences among individuals. Second, successful resolution of a crisis will depend on how a particular culture views the crisis, the sequence in which a particular stage occurs, and the solution evolving from it. Third, while many of Erikson's original ideas were based on development in Western societies, we attempt to modify some of these to show their increased applicability in other cultural and ecological settings.

Kohlberg's Theory of Moral Development

The study of moral development is closely identified with the work of Lawrence Kohlberg, who completed his first research as part of his doctoral dissertation. Responses to a series of moral dilemmas (hypothetical incidents involving a conflict between an individual's desires or needs and the rules of society) by seventy-two boys, ages ten, thirteen, and sixteen years, were analyzed to determine how moral reasoning developed. For each dilemma, subjects were asked to evaluate the morality of a specific act mentioned in the dilemma. On the basis of these findings, Kohlberg (1981) identified three levels of moral development with two stages in each level, representing a more sophisticated and complex orientation toward justice and normative moral principles (see Table 2.4).

Most children nine years of age or younger are in the preconventional level, but so are many adolescent offenders and adult criminals. Most adolescents and adults are in the conventional level. The postconventional level is not generally reached before the age of twenty, and then generally only by a minority.

One of the main assumptions underlying Kohlberg's theory is that these six stages are universal and are present in cultures throughout the world. However, Kohlberg concedes that the stage at which individuals complete their development and the time it takes to be completed may vary from one culture to another.

TABLE 2.4   Kohlberg's Stages of Moral Development

LEVEL	STAGE	BEHAVIOR
I. Preconventional	1. Punishment and obedience orientation	Obeys rules to avoid punishment
	2. Instrumental orientation	Obeys rules to receive rewards
II. Conventional	3. Good-child orientation	Conforms to rules to avoid disapproval by others
	4. Law and order orientation	Conforms to rules to maintain social order
III. Postconventional	5. Morality of contract, individual rights, and democratically accepted law	Accepts and follows laws for the welfare of the larger community
	6. Morality of individual principles and conscience	Believes in and follows self-chosen universal ethical principles

There have been several criticisms of Kohlberg's theory. First, it is sex-biased because it was originally based on studies of male subjects (without the inclusion of any women) in one American city—Chicago. Second, his stages are culturally biased because they are largely dependent upon Western philosophy, and efforts have been made to apply them to nonWestern cultures, which may have very different moral viewpoints. Nevertheless, his contribution to the understanding of the development of moral reasoning is important, and we will attempt to modify some of his ideas to show how they might be made more relevant and applicable to other cultural and ecological settings.

As we move through the rest of the chapters in this book, we refer back to each of these theories and show how they help to explain various aspects of human development within a wide range of cultural settings and niches. From time to time, we also indicate how these theories might be expanded and modified to better understand and explain cross-cultural similarities and differences in behavior. We now look at some of the methodological issues and approaches related to the study of cross-cultural human development.

◇ METHODOLOGY IN CROSS-CULTURAL HUMAN DEVELOPMENT

As we noted in Chapter 1, there are many different definitions of culture; therefore, it should not be surprising that there are an almost infinite number of ways to approach and measure cultural differences and similarities. For example, psychologists generally tend to focus on individual behaviors, while anthropologists typically tend to look at the behavior of groups. Those doing cross-cultural research in human development frequently make an effort to look at both individual and group behaviors. This is not always easy to do because each culture and those who live within it, including parents, peers, teachers, and others, have their own ideas and beliefs about children and the ways in which they should develop (Harkness & Super, 1996).

Imagine you are a social scientist (e.g., psychologist, anthropologist, or sociologist) interested in studying the effects of childrearing practices on children's personality development. Looking at your own culture, you find the range of behaviors limited. So, it seems like a good idea to seek out other cultures, which may have different practices, such as swaddling (found among the Hopi Indians in the American midwest and many Russian and Chinese families), severe independence training (characteristic of certain African tribal groups), or strict dependence training (often noted in Japanese families). Taking this approach offers several benefits. First, you are able to increase both the range of independent variables (childrearing practices) and their effects on the dependent variable (children's personality development). Second, this approach allows (perhaps) for a clearer distinction between biological and environmental influences. For example, if developmental sequences or processes are found to be similar across a variety of diverse cultures, it might suggest that genetic or biological factors are a significant contributor. If, on the other hand, there are wide differences among the cultures, it is more likely that environmental factors play a larger role. Finally, by conducting cross-cultural research in another culture, one becomes aware of his or her own ethnocentric biases that could influence the design, conduct, and interpretation of the results.

Carrying out a cross-cultural study may sound easy. However, here is the heart of the problem: jumping on and off planes in far away and often exotic places can be exciting, rewarding, and great fun, but it's not all beer and curry! Think about the young undergraduate student, Justin Tyme, in our opening vignette, and consider some other possible difficulties—getting required visas to visit certain countries is often difficult, time consuming, and expensive; you may not be allowed to conduct your research once you get there; you and the local food don't always agree; and you can become frustrated and lonely. In short, you have a great many challenges to meet and resolve. But as Dr. Kitty Litter, the anthropologist in our other vignette, demonstrates, with careful preparation and training, an individual can survive the culture experience and return with important research data. As we see in the next section, although there may be problems in doing cross-cultural research, there are also solutions.

Studying Development Cross Culturally: Some Methods, Problems, and Solutions

Our intent is not to cover all possible methods, problems, and solutions in this section—besides being impossible, much of this work has been done very well by others. Our aim is twofold: (1) to familiarize you with some of the important information in this area, so that you gain an appreciation for what cross-cultural researchers have to deal with, and (2) to prepare you to understand methods and findings you encounter as you journey through the remainder of this book.

When conducting research in cross-cultural human development, researchers are interested in discovering principles that are universal to all (or most) cultures, as well as principles that are unique or specific to certain cultures, such as the emic–etic distinction we made in Chapter 1. At the same time, they are concerned that the methods they employ are (1) **objective** (*unbiased and not influenced by a researcher's preconceived notions*), (2) **reliable** (*findings are observed consistently and accepted by independent observers*), (3) **valid** (*behaviors and findings are what the researcher claims them to be*), and (4) **replicable** (*other researchers using the same methods report the same or very similar results*).

In this regard, cross-cultural methods are firmly rooted in basic psychological methodology involving the use of experiments (experimental and control groups to test hypotheses), cross-sectional designs (one-time testing of separate age groups), longitudinal designs (repeated testing of same individuals over time), sequential designs (combination of longitudinal and cross-sectional designs), and correlational studies (measurement of relationships between and among variables).

While cross-cultural psychology shares with its sister social sciences a number of similar needs in designing research (e.g., selecting subjects, defining variables, and choosing appropriate measures and methods), it has to deal with unique issues, for example, the complexity of culture, interdependence of culture and self, indigenous (or native) psychology versus universal psychology, communication across cultures, and interpretation of cultural findings. For detailed discussions of some of these issues and approaches to their resolution, see Berry, Dasen, and Saraswathi (1997); Berry, Poortinga, and Pandey (1997); Cole (1998); Kim, Park, and Park (2000); Lonner (2005); Matsumoto and Juang (2004); Smith (2004); and van de Vijver and Leung (2000). For more specific discussions of issues related to measurement in cross-cultural human development, see Friedman and Wachs (1999), Keller and Greenfield (2000), and Super and Harkness (2000). For information on conducting fieldwork studies, see the recent book by Hobbs & Wright (2006).

Matsumoto (2000) discussed some of the critical questions and issues in this area (pp. 130–134); and because many of these also apply to the conduct of cross-cultural human development research, they are summarized here: (1) *theories and hypotheses*—can the theories under investigation be appropriately applied to all cultures in the study, and do the hypotheses have the same meaning for all subjects independent of their cultural backgrounds? (2) *methods*—are the subjects representative of their culture and are they equivalent for comparative purposes, and are all measures (e.g., scales, items) reliable and valid in all cultures under investigation and do they have linguistic equivalence (determined through the method of back translation from original language to target language and back to original language until all meanings are equivalent)? (3) *data and analyses*—are there any unique cultural responses operating and have they been controlled? and (4) *interpretations and conclusions*—are findings and interpretations free of cultural bias and value judgments based on the researcher's own cultural background? These serious and complex questions must be carefully considered and adequately answered if research across cultures is to make significant contributions to our knowledge about similarities and differences in human development.

Due to the seriousness of one of the issues mentioned above—linguistic equivalence—additional comments regarding the translation and adaptation of instruments and materials from one culture to another deserve special attention. The International Test Commission, consisting of members from a number of international psychological organizations, has prepared a set of twenty-two specific guidelines for conducting multicultural studies that anyone interested in conducting cross-cultural research should take into account before designing and carrying out a particular study (see van de Vijver, 2001, for a complete listing of these guidelines). These are divided into four categories: (1) context guidelines focusing on general principles for test translations), (2) development guidelines for enhancing equivalence, (3) administrative guidelines for attaining comparability of administration in the use of different language versions, and (4) guidelines for documentation or score interpretations.

One technique widely used to achieve linguistic equivalence when a researcher is unfamiliar with or not fluent in one or more of the languages to be used in a project is **back translation.** This procedure involves *translating material (instruments, surveys, etc.) from a "source" language, (for example, English), into a "target" language, (for example, Arabic) by a bilingual translator fluent in both languages.* The target translation (Arabic) is then translated by another bilingual translator back into the source (English) language. This continues until there is agreement that the translations are linguistically equivalent. Because this technique often relies on literal translation of the material, ignoring such issues as comprehension and readability, a second procedure involving a group or committee with expertise in a variety of areas (language, culture, psychology, anthropology) carries out the translation process until there is agreement that all language versions are equivalent.

As for the use of specific methods, there are numerous ways in which these can be categorized. One approach is to consider four possible types of cross-cultural studies: (1) investigation of theories and concepts originally developed in Western countries as they may (or may not) apply in non-Western settings (e.g., Piaget's stages of cognitive development and Kohlberg's levels of moral development); (2) replication in one culture of studies previously conducted in another culture (e.g., children's acquisition of language skills, peer pressure during adolescence, and expression of emotion in toddlers); (3) collaborative research in which researchers from two or more cultures participate equally in the design and conduct of a study (e.g., assessment of personality in five cultures, a cross-national study of children's behavior with their friends, and exploration of ethnic identity in Russia, Finland, and South Africa); and (4) administration of test materials designed and standardized in one culture but used in other cultures (e.g., tests of intelligence, personality, and socialization).

Matsumoto (2000) draws attention to two other approaches used with some measure of success by psychologists doing cross-cultural research. The first is the *"bottom-up approach,"* in which a psychological phenomenon, observed in one culture, is then studied "across many other cultures to examine and refine theories about it" (p. 11). An example might be the willingness of mothers to seek childrearing advice when raising their first child. The second is the *"top-down approach,"* in which investigators "begin with a theory about behavior and incorporate aspects of culture in testing its limitations and broadening its domain" (p. 11). An example might be studying the implications of social cognition theory for understanding behavior in individualistic and collectivist cultures.

A popular approach among psychologists, as well as some sociologists, is **cross-cultural comparisons** in which *individuals from at least two different cultural groups are measured and compared on some aspect of behavior* (e.g., European and Asian attitudes toward the criminal justice system). As for individual methods, a technique widely used by anthropologists in their cultural studies is **ethnography.** Typically, a researcher lives for a time in a culture observing, interviewing, and sometimes testing its members, and produces *a detailed description of a society's way of life, including its attitudes, customs, and behaviors.* The early work of Margaret Mead, Ruth Benedict, and others are examples. More recently, some interesting work has been done in "the ethnography of speaking," in which sociolinguists studied variations in conversational language in different social contexts (Hymes, 1996, 1999; Nelson, 1992). Information contained in hundreds of these reports has been classified and indexed in the **Human Relations Area Files (HRAF)** and is frequently used in **hologeistic research,** *projects in which hypotheses about such topics as gender differences in aggression or preference for breast versus bottle feeding can be tested on a worldwide sample of more than 340 societies.*

Another approach that has been around for quite awhile but is receiving increased attention from researchers today is the narrative method which, depending on the researcher, looks at a variety of narrative materials including stories (oral or written), diaries, letters, etc., and their analyses. For a description and discussion of this approach, see the book *Narrative methods* by Atkinson & Delamont (2006).

Matsumoto points out that "In recent years, there has been an interesting merging of research approaches across disciplines, with an increasing number of scientists adopting comparative techniques for use in single-culture immersion research, and comparative researchers adopting qualitative ethnographic methods to bolster their traditional quantitative approach" (p. 39). We see this as a positive sign that these social science disciplines, often at odds, may be showing signs of understanding and learning from each other.

Keller and Greenfield (2000) look more specifically at some of the contributions developmentalists' research make to cross-cultural psychology—methodologically, theoretically, and empirically. For example, in terms of methodology, they point to the use of "contextualized procedures, such as naturalistic observation, suitable for studying behavior in its cultural context" (p. 52). Theoretically, "developmentalists point to the fact that the culturally constructed behavior of adults can be viewed as an endpoint along a developmental pathway, and that adults provide cultural socialization to the next generation" (p. 52). Finally, empirically, they point out that "a developmental approach leads researchers to investigate the culture-specific shape of developmental stages" (p. 52).

American anthropologist Margaret Mead, who frequently used ethnographic methods, smiles at a Balinese infant. (© Ken Heyman/Woodfin Camp & Associates)

In an impressive work, particularly relevant to this discussion, van de Vijver and Leung (2000) comment on the extent to which methodological tools can be used to correct for the overemphasis on fact finding and, thereby, speed up the slow theoretical progress in cross-cultural psychology. It is their contention that, in the future, there will be two different types of cross-cultural researchers: "*natives* (whose emphasis is on culture and the methodology for the study of culture), and *sojourners* (who make brief, sporadic excursions into cross-cultural research)" (p. 48—italics added).

They point out that as a result of clearly different interests, each will take different methodological paths. For example, "Sojourners will be mainly interested in psychological-differences studies and generalization studies . . . [while] . . . Natives will carry out research that is central to our understanding of cultural differences and the influence of culture" (p. 48).

Van de Vijver and Leung conclude that when greater emphasis is placed on the development and testing of theories, and appropriate methodological tools are used in carrying out research, the replicability of cross-cultural findings will improve—a point Gardiner stresses elsewhere in this book. They believe that "impediments to progress in cross-cultural research . . . all derive from what could be called *partis pris* (preconceived opinions, prejudices) of cross-cultural psychologists" (p. 34). We might add this would apply to any researchers—psychologists, anthropologists, sociologists, or others.

For those who want to know more about cross-cultural research methodology, from a primarily psychological viewpoint, including additional problems and solutions, we recommend the volumes by Segall, Dasen, Berry, and Poortinga (1999), and Berry, Poortinga, and Pandy (1997). Cross-cultural research methodology, as practiced by anthropologists, is discussed in a volume by Ember and Ember (2000).

Let us now take a closer look at some of these issues and several of the research methodologies used in the cross-cultural study of human development, particularly those associated with our two major theoretical viewpoints—the ecological model and the developmental niche.

Methods for Assessing Components of the Developmental Niche

Super and Harkness (1999) have presented, in extensive detail, their suggestions for successfully measuring and assessing the components of the developmental niche. In this section, we provide an overview of their methodology, which, as can be seen in Table 2.5, involves a combination of psychological and anthropological research techniques. Anyone with a serious interest in the developmental niche approach is advised to consult this important work that blends theory and methodology in a way seldom done in the study of cross-cultural human development. It stands as a model for others in the field and as an example of the effort to bring closer together anthropology and psychology that we hope to see more of in the future.

Looking at Table 2.5, we find several ethnographic, observational, and formal methods (column one), the component to which a particular method contributes qualitative understanding (column two), and, finally, the component for which a method can furnish quantitative information (column three).

According to Super and Harkness, the first group of methods (participant observation and ethnographic interviewing) are indispensable for selecting and understanding important components or units of the developmental environment, and for providing the foundation for determining what should be measured and how to create hypotheses that will demonstrate how various components of the developmental niche are related to each other. They point out that **participant observation** (*a technique in which an investigator lives for a time with or near a group of people and observes its daily life, activities, and rituals*) and **ethnographic interviews** (*asking group members to describe their culture's typical behaviors, attitudes, beliefs, and values*), if carefully carried out, can help identify elements within each of the three developmental niche components (see Table 2.1). An example of their use in actual research is in a study by Levy (1996), in which he reports that differences in parental beliefs and practices about learners and teaching in Tahiti and Nepal

TABLE 2.5 Methods for Studying the Developmental Niche

METHOD	COMPONENT	
	Identified	*Measured*
Participant observation and ethnographic interviewing	Settings, customs, and caretaker psychology	—
Spot observations and diaries	Settings, customs, and caretaker psychology	Settings (and customs)
Behavior observations	Customs and caretaker psychology	Customs
Semistructured interviews and focus groups	Customs and caretaker psychology	Customs and caretaker psychology
Structured questioning	—	Caretaker psychology and customs
Passive enumeration	Caretaker psychology and customs	Caretaker psychology and customs
Formal methods: free listings, clustering, multidimensional scaling, and consensus analysis	Customs and caretaker psychology	Caretaker psychology and customs

Source: From "The Environment as Culture in Developmental Research" by C. M. Super and S. Harkness, 1999, in S. L. Friedman & T. D. Wachs (Eds.), *Measuring Environment Across the Life Span*. Washington, D.C.: American Psychological Association. Reprinted with permission.

may be a result of differences in the level of societal complexity in these two cultures.

Other techniques useful in identifying important aspects of all three components, but settings in particular, include spot observations and diaries. Results from **spot observations** (*a series of random unannounced observations of a group, sufficient in number to allow for statistical analysis*) and **diaries** (*written accounts of changes in daily activities kept by participants over varying periods of time, such as a full 24-hour day*) are useful for "describing the physical and social settings of daily life not only in terms of their particular qualities but also in terms of their empirical distributions . . . [and] . . . provide a basis for identifying regularities in settings and activities that may differ between groups, or that one wants to relate thematically to other elements in the niche, or to developmental trends" (Super & Harkness, 1999, p. 304).

Measuring customs (the second component of the developmental niche), according to Super and Harkness (1999), requires (1) a qualitative approach, in which behavioral consistencies are identified either through

direct observation of a cultural group or by means of **ethnographic descriptions** of its everyday attitudes, beliefs, and behaviors, and (2) a quantitative approach producing "measures of individuals' views on the nature and importance of the custom or measures of the frequency of occurrence of the identified practice, or both" (p. 308). They assert that the ideal approach to assessing and measuring the customs component "demonstrates their existence, documents their occurrence, and explains their relationship to the settings of daily life and to the psychological theories that guide them" (p. 308).

Measuring caretaker psychology or parental beliefs and values (the third component of the niche) also requires a combination of qualitative and quantitative approaches. These may include **structured questioning** (frequently based on findings obtained from the methods previously discussed) and **formal methods** originally employed in the cognitive sciences (see Borgatti, 1992, for additional information).

Truly understanding culture and the critical role it plays in human development requires an appreciation of qualitative, as well as quantitative, findings. In the words of Super and Harkness (1999), "Findings in one domain suggest further exploration or reexamination in another, and replication of patterns suggests salient cultural themes" (p. 312). Their unique organizational scheme provides answers to many questions about culture and development while setting forth even more challenges for the future.

Studying Ecological Systems

Unlike Super and Harkness, who constructed their approach to human development and conducted much of their own research in support of it, Bronfenbrenner has primarily been the developer of ideas and hypotheses, while others have carried out research to show the validity of his approach. To illustrate this, let us briefly look at some examples of representative research carried out on each of the four ecological systems.

First, Brown, Lohr, and Trujillo (1990), in an effort to show how the peer microsystem of adolescents becomes increasingly differentiated and influential in one's behavior, reported on the ways in which both positive (acceptance, friendship, status, and popularity) and negative (drinking, smoking, stealing, cheating) behaviors are associated with different adolescent lifestyle decisions. Second, Muuss (1996) has stated, "A mesosystem analysis examines the quality, the frequency, and the influence of such interactions as family experiences on school adjustment" (p. 325). An interesting example of this is Epstein's study (1983) of the longitudinal effects of family-school-person interactions on student outcomes, which, unexpectedly, reported that the interaction of family and school was of far greater importance and influence than the variables of race and socioeconomic status. Noted among the findings was a continuing influence of the family and school environments far beyond the early childhood years, lending support to the interaction effects among systems proposed by Bronfenbrenner. As an example, the author pointed out that students experiencing the greatest change in independence were those initially scoring low on this behavior (and whose families failed to emphasize decision making), but who attended schools that placed a strong emphasis on student participation.

Third, as you may remember from our original comments, Bronfenbrenner has asserted that decisions made in the exosystem (e.g., in parents' workplaces) can have an extremely important influence on the life of a child or adolescent (even though they are not a part of that setting). Flanagan and Eccles (1993) effectively demonstrated this point in their two-year longitudinal study of changes in parents' work status and their effects on the adjustment of children before and after their transition to junior high school. Results indicated that of four family types identified (based on patterns of change or stability in parental work status), children in deprived and declining families were less competent than their peers in stable or recovery families. Although most of the subjects experienced some difficulty in school adjustment, the transition was shown to be especially difficult for those whose parents were simultaneously dealing with changes in their work status.

Fourth, although the macrosystem, in many ways, is removed from the daily life of an individual, it does consist of extremely important societal influences (political, religious, economic, and other values) that clearly affect human development. Bronfenbrenner (1967) demonstrated the influence of macrosystem values in an early comparison of peer group and adult pressures on children in the United States and the former Soviet Union. At that time, in the Soviet Union, a cohesive core of socially accepted and politically endorsed values left little room for differences in expectations between the adults or peers in one's environment. In the United States, on the other hand, there were frequently unmistakable differences between these significant people, with the result that children and adolescents often found themselves being pulled in different directions. With the breakup of the former Soviet Union, the situation that once existed in the United States (and to a large extent, still appears to) now is much more characteristic of the former Soviet Union as well.

As we close this discussion, it seems only fair to give Bronfenbrenner the last word on the challenge of operationally defining elements of his evolving bioecological model as well as efforts to scientifically measure them. As he states, "Thus far, I have accorded more attention to the conceptual rather than to the operational aspects of this challenge. I did so for a reason; namely, most of the research designs and methods of measurement currently in use in developmental science are not well-suited for what I have referred to elsewhere as 'science in the discovery mode' (Bronfenbrenner & Morris, 1998). To be more specific, these designs and methods are more appropriate for verifying already formulated hypotheses than for the far more critical and more difficult task of developing hypotheses of sufficient explanatory power and precision to warrant being subjected to empirical test. . . . In summary, most of the scientific journey still lies ahead" (Bronfenbrenner, 1999, p. 24). For those interested in reading more about these issues, see any of the several references mentioned in this discussion.

◇ SUMMARY

This chapter focuses on theories and methodologies used in the conduct of cross-cultural research in general and developmental research in particular. We began with reasons for studying human development—to *understand, explain, predict, and* (in some instances) *control behavior.* To successfully achieve these goals, we need to use theories which, simply stated, are *sets of hypotheses or assumptions about behavior.* We discussed, in detail, six approaches that will receive significant attention throughout this book—Bronfenbrenner's ecological model, Super and Harkness's developmental niche concept, Piaget's theory of cognitive development, Vygotsky's sociocultural theory of development, Erikson's psychosocial theory, and Kohlberg's theory of moral development. We discussed some of the ways in which cross-cultural methods might be classified, distinguished between different types of cross-cultural researchers (natives and sojourners), and commented on specific techniques including ethnographies, cross-cultural comparisions, "bottom-up" and "bottom-down" approaches, and hologeistic studies. We concluded with a discussion of methods for assessing components of the developmental niche as well as ecological systems.

◇ STUDY QUESTIONS

Explain the purpose of theories in the study human development.

Describe and discuss Bronfenbrenner's ecological model of human development.

Describe Harkness and Super's developmental niche model.

Compare and contrast the human development theories of Piaget and Vygotsky.

◇ FURTHER READINGS

Urie Bronfenbrenner. (2005). *Making Human Beings Human: Bioecological Perspectives on Human Development.* Thousand Oaks, CA: Sage Publications.

> The culminating work by the author, consisting of twenty-three articles written over six decades that describe the historical development of his groundbreaking model. Contains recommendations for future research and applications for the design of social programs and policies for promoting positive development of children and families throughout the world.

Douglas Raybeck. (1996). *Mad Dogs, Englishmen, and the Errant Anthropologist: Fieldwork in Malaysia.* Prospect Heights, IL: Waveland Press.

> A lively account of the author's adventures and misadventures while doing fieldwork, with vivid descriptions of Kelantanese society and culture, kinship, linguistics, and gender relations. Provides a real sense of how an anthropologist conducts and gathers reliable information in cultural settings where often "things go awry."

Susan Goldstein. (2000). *Cross-Cultural Explorations: Activities in Culture and Psychology.* Boston: Allyn and Bacon.

> This book contains nine chapters with ten activities each revolving around case studies, self-administered scales, mini-experiments, and a collection of content-analytic, observational, and interview data allowing "hands-on" experience. Of particular interest is a chapter on "Culture and Psychological Research" that explores major issues and techniques in the conduct of cross-cultural research.

Walter J. Lonner & Roy Malpass. (1994). *Psychology and Culture.* Boston: Allyn & Bacon.

> Each of the forty-three short (five- to six-page) easy-to-read chapters on various aspects of cross-cultural psychology provides personal insights into the ways in which the authors carried out their research, often with revealing comments on the mistakes they made.

Theodore Singelis. (Ed.). (1998). *Teaching About Culture, Ethnicity, & Diversity.* Thousand Oaks, CA: Sage.

> A book of easy-to-use classroom exercises intended for use in teaching about culture, ethnicity, and diversity. A practical tool for those who want to learn more about these topics and have fun doing it.

F. J. R. van de Vijver. (2000). Types of cross-cultural studies in cross-cultural psychology. In W. J. Lonner, D. L. Dinnel, S. A. Hayes, & D. N. Sattler (Eds.), *Online Readings in Psychology and Culture* (Unit 2, Chapter 6), (http://www.wwu.edu/~culture), Center for Cross-Cultural Research, Western Washington University, Bellingham, Washington.

> This easliy accessible on-line article classifies cross-cultural studies along three dimensions and provides examples and illustrations of cross-cultural methodology.

◇ DEVELOPMENTAL ANALYSIS

INTRODUCTION

Throughout the remainder of this book, you will have the opportunity to explore your own development. By finding ways to apply important concepts to your own life, you will not only better understand them but will also become more aware of whom you are and the various influences (cultural, familial, biological, and social) that have contributed to your unique development.

(continued)

One difficulty with organizing the large amount of material in a book like this is that most research is not collected in a longitudinal manner. As you read through Chapters 3–10, you will become familiar with these eight areas of focus: socialization, physical growth, language and cognition, self and personality, issues of gender and sexuality, social behavior, family, and health. As you explore each of these, we recommend you take time to examine how each area has contributed to your development and, in many cases, continues to play a role. Try to relate the many concepts to your own life by jotting down brief examples from your experiences.

To help you in this self-exploratory effort, you will find in each chapter a developmental box presenting the fictionalized life of "Maddi" Skelton, who will be followed throughout the book as she describes her life in terms of the material presented in each chapter. Her life will be described in the first person from infancy through the later adult years. This will help to provide continuity among the various topics presented.

These developmental boxes, beginning with socialization in Chapter 3, will serve as examples of how you might reflect on your own life. Begin by first describing your culture and the ecological system and developmental niche in which you grew up. Subdivide your notes into sections labeled Infancy, Childhood, Adolescence, and Adulthood. Within each section, describe your development in terms of culturally influenced behaviors, such as sleep, feeding patterns, food preferences, attitudes toward caretakers (parents, teachers, siblings), early learning (formal and informal), rites of passage characteristic of your culture, family relations, and any other important aspects of the socialization process that had an effect on the person you are today. Be sure to use concrete examples from your own life. By the time you reach Chapter 10, not only will you understand these concepts better, you will also have authored your own autobiography—something you will likely treasure and add on to as you make your way through additional life stages.

Enjoy!

CHAPTER THREE

CULTURE AND SOCIALIZATION

Kamuzu Mathebula is fourteen years old and lives in Diepkloof, a section of Soweto, an all-black township outside Johannesburg, South Africa. He lives with his mother, aged grandmother, two brothers, and a sister in a shack made of discarded plastic sheeting and wood with a corrugated iron roof. There is no electricity or running water. Diarrhea and tuberculosis are common here. His mother, a widow, works as a maid for the Martins, an Afrikaner (white South African) family, five miles away. Kamuzu has attended poorly funded segregated schools most of his life. With the end of apartheid (the white-government-enforced system of "separateness") in 1990, his future has been looking better. Rather than working long hours for meager wages in one of the local textile factories, Kamuzu hopes to attend the University of Witwatersrand in Johannesburg and become a doctor and help his people.

Hendrik and Patricia Martin, the Dutch-descended Afrikaner family that Kamuzu's mother works for, have a son named Jeremy who is also fourteen years old. He and his younger sister, Yvonne, live in a wealthy neighborhood of large, well-kept homes. Jeremy's father is president of an import–export company, started by his grandfather, and his mother teaches science at the exclusive private school he and his sister attend. His goal, like Kamuzu's, is to attend the university in Johannesburg and study medicine.

Two young South African boys—the same age, residing just a few miles apart near the tip of the African continent—supposedly live in the same society but have been raised in clearly different environments (developmental niches) by very different families; yet they share a common desire of becoming doctors.

How can we account for the similarities and differences in the development of these two young adolescents? While it is true that Kamuzu and

Jeremy share a number of characteristics, in large measure, they are a reflection of two distinct cultures—different social contexts, parental belief systems, societal values, and cultural perspectives. Every one of us, like each of them, is influenced by a unique combination of factors, including the genetic material inherited from our ancestors, the family in which we are raised and the style of parenting to which we are exposed, the friends we make and the schools we attend, the historical period in which we are born, and (of pivotal importance) the culture and ecological context in which we live out our lives. As Sigel and colleagues (1992) noted, "Since it is a culture which serves to define values, beliefs, and actions of families, it is imperative and in fact a virtual necessity for the applied developmental psychologist to develop a knowledge base of cultures" (Roopnarine and Carter, 1992b, p. ix.).

Indeed, while this is essential, a knowledge of cultures is not enough. To genuinely understand and explain cultural differences in development, we first need to look at the way in which a culture defines these values, beliefs, and actions; and this requires an understanding of the crucial process of socialization.

◇ WHAT IS SOCIALIZATION?

Like many concepts in developmental psychology, socialization can be variously defined. For our purposes, we will view **socialization** as *the process by which an individual becomes a member of a particular culture and takes on its values, beliefs, and other behaviors in order to function within it.* According to Elkin and Handel (1989), it is this process that "helps to explain how a person becomes capable of participating in society . . . [as well as] . . . how society is possible at all" (p. 4). It is through the process of socialization that society teaches desirable behavior while inhibiting undesirable behavior, prepares individuals to become successfully functioning members in its principal institutional settings (family, school, community, and workplace), and guarantees that important traditions (although sometimes modified) will be passed to future members of the culture.

It is far from easy to describe or explain cultural socialization. Chamberlain and Patterson (1995) put this dilemma into focus when they state that "in a very real sense . . . socialization . . . is something that emerges from thousands of exchanges between the child and family members spread out over a period of many years. During these exchanges, the child is altering the behavior of the parent at the same time that the parent is presumably 'socializing' the child. It is this mutuality of effects that makes it very difficult to analyze cause and effect relations" (pp. 211–212).

With the steady increase in cross-cultural findings, our understanding of socialization has undergone significant change over the past several decades. For example, contemporary theories of socialization place greater stress on the interactive exchanges between parent and child as contributors to behavior.

In addition, explanations have become more complex and multidimensional than those offered by earlier approaches (Grusec & Hastings, 2006).

Edwards (1996) has noted that socialization theories have also undergone substantial revision, as theorists and researchers have recognized the cultural limitations of these theories. For far too long, theories and their proponents were ethnocentric (e.g., proposing that explanations of behavior in one society applied equally well in others). As we frequently note throughout this book, such theories relied heavily on research and assumptions based in Western societies, with the result that theories were either nongeneralizable to other cultures or failed to take into account the richness of human diversity. In a sense, theorists were victims of their own socialization and were promoting a Westernized view of the world that they frequently imposed on the cultures they were studying, rather than letting indigenous behaviors emerge and be recognized. As evidence, Edwards (1989) cites some of her own earlier work in which Mayan children in Zinacantan, Mexico, learned toilet training and other self-care skills by means of imitation, and thereby made a relatively easy transition from infancy to early childhood, compared with other cultures in which these activities are characterized by resistance and great difficulty. There would appear to be an entirely different cultural context operating in this Mayan culture than what we tend to see in North America and some cultures of Western Europe. Values important to the successful functioning of these Mayan children are being transmitted in a way that provides a foundation for the development of infants and toddlers, who closely observe and carefully imitate and respond to their elders and others, rather than expecting others to respond to them (Greenfield, Brazelton, & Childs, 1989).

A researcher who has made significant contributions to our understanding of socialization, particularly in the area of cognition, is Barbara Rogoff. Her book *Apprenticeship in Thinking* (1990) is recommended in Chapter 5 as a source for additional reading in this area. Rogoff's approach to this topic has been greatly influenced by the work of the Soviet psychologist Lev Vygotsky, whose work on culture and cognitive development is discussed in detail in the same chapter. Rogoff developed the concept of *guided participation* to expand on Vygotsky's concept of the *zone of proximal development*, "in order to draw attention to the opportunity to learn through participation in nonverbal and tacit forms of interaction as well as through societal arrangements, not just from instruction or scaffolding" (personal communication). Guided participation emphasizes the bidirectional, or two-way, nature of socialization and the fact that children are active participants in their own socialization. In describing this concept, Brislin (1993) provides an example familiar to those who have lived in or conducted research in many of the countries in South and Southeast Asia—namely, the cultural requirement that children learn that the right (clean) hand is for eating and the left (unclean) hand is to be used for personal hygiene. If children do not learn this behavior through participation in daily home activities, parents, other adults, or even older siblings will guide the children in the appropriate way. For example, while eating, one of these "teachers" might be seen inhibiting use of the left hand while gently guiding the right toward the food. The point, Brislin says, is "that the children's behavior directs the teacher's behavior. If children learn through simple observation, there is no need for the more active intervention of holding down and guiding hands" (p. 130). Contrast this more directive approach with the observational approach of Mayan child training cited above.

Let us now consider how the socialization process relates to two of our major themes: the ecological model and the developmental niche.

◇ ECOLOGICAL MODEL AND THE DEVELOPMENTAL NICHE

As we have already noted, socialization is a lifelong process, occurring within a variety of environments or social contexts in which we live, influencing the activities in which we participate, and significantly contributing to our development across the lifespan.

In Chapter 2, we introduced two important themes that are interwoven throughout this book: Bronfenbrenner's (1979, 2005) **ecological model** and the concept of the **developmental niche** (Super & Harkness, 1994, 1999, 2003). The ecological model allows us to look at human development as it occurs in its real-world settings or ecology and is composed of five categories of interrelated systems. It is within these interconnected contexts that socialization takes place and in which we begin to see the development of "lives across cultures."

This model, combined with certain elements of the developmental niche (a theoretical framework for looking at how a child's daily life is culturally shaped), creates a useful structure for better understanding the bidirectional nature of socialization and its effects on human development.

The various aspects of the ecological model and the developmental niche are illustrated in Box 3.1, which describes some of the ways in which Japanese children become socialized into their culture. To further illustrate this point, we provide three brief examples that will receive detailed attention later. First, if a child is doing poorly in school, this can have an impact on behavior within the family and affect the parent–child relationship in a variety of ways (e.g., neglect or abuse). Baca Zinn and Eitzen (1993) have pointed out that a home situation involving neglect or abuse can have effects on a child's relationships with parents, peers, teachers, and other family members. In addition, a child's temperament within a particular cultural context (e.g., Malaysia or Japan) may affect the way parents interact with that child and, in turn, influence the development of personality and self-concept. Finally, a sick, fussy, or light-sleeping child may keep parents awake at night, making them less effective at work or in their relationship with each

BOX 3.1

BECOMING JAPANESE: AN ECOLOGICAL VIEW OF SOCIALIZATION

In her insightful book on Japanese culture, Joy Hendry (1986) provides a delightful picture of the organization and function of three of the most important microsystems of early childhood development: family, neighborhood, and preschool. Using everyday examples, she shows how these contexts are connected with some of the most important cultural values found in the mesosystem, which, in turn, have significant effects on the surrounding exosystem. In addition, Hendry discusses the strong emphasis the culture places on cooperative behavior; academic achievement; indulgent attitudes toward infants; and the hierarchical nature of parent–child, sibling, and neighbor–child relationships. These fall within the setting of the macrosystem and deepen our understanding of how, accompanied by a traditional respect for age and seniority, these behaviors effectively combine to produce characteristics that are uniquely Japanese.

Hendry describes the family microsystem and the influence of those within it in this way: "The child . . . is in close contact with one set of grandparents and possibly one or two sets of great-grandparents, as well as its parents. . . . Other close relatives are likely to be frequent visitors . . . [and] may well play quite an important part in their early rearing" (p. 36). However, unlike recent developments in Western societies, Japanese fathers tend to play a relatively minor role in early childrearing because "many men [return] . . . home each evening after the children are asleep, and [leave] . . . in the morning before they get up" (p. 38).

According to Hendry, relationships within the neighborhood microsystem are much more institutionalized than in many other countries. For example, "Informal aid is usually given between houses popularly delineated as 'the three opposite and one on either side' (*mukosangen ryodonari*). . . . In this context, mothers of young children meet at the local swings, discuss problems with each other, and occasionally look after each other's children" (pp. 40–41). These neighbors are frequently the first people outside the family with whom the children interact and from which they acquire their first friends. When they enter school, children are organized into a children's group (*kodomogumi*) based on neighborhoods, which arrange "sporting activities, outings and school disciplinary groups [and] . . . gather at a meeting point every morning in order to walk to school together. Thus, the relations established informally at an early age are likely to continue, and even for children whose families move, there are similar groups for them to join in other areas" (p. 42).

The third microsystem, that of the kindergarten or day nursery, is also a highly structured setting in which children are separated according to age

(continued)

BOX 3.1 CONTINUED

"so that most of their contact with other children will be with peers, great emphasis being placed on the ideal that all children should be friends (*tomodachi*) and get on well with one another. . . . Conflict and competition is discouraged [and] . . . every child has a turn eventually to serve and to discipline the others" (p. 43). Later, "after-school classes in English and music provide excellent opportunities for kindergarten classmates to maintain their friendships throughout their school lives" (p. 45).

This short excerpt provides only a glimpse into the complex but interrelated ecological world of Japanese children and their families; we highly recommend that the reader look at Hendry's book for a fuller picture.

Source: Adapted from "Becoming Japanese: The Arenas and Agents of Socialization" by J. Hendry (1993) in R. W. Wozniak (Ed.), *Worlds of Childhood Reader* (pp. 34–47), New York: HarperCollins.

other. (Variations in sleep patterns and their relationship to the approaches mentioned above are discussed in the next section.)

With (hopefully) a clear understanding of the ecological model, the developmental niche, and the cross-cultural theme, we are now prepared to look at some cultural variations in socialized behavior.

◇ SOME CULTURAL VARIATIONS IN THE SOCIALIZATION OF BEHAVIOR

As pointed out in Chapter 1, in a book of this type, with its major focus on cultural similarities and differences, it is impossible to provide as comprehensive a view of human development as do more traditional developmental books. For a general overview of human development principles, we direct the reader to one of these books. Our goal is to consider selected topics for which a large or growing body of cross-cultural research evidence exists and discuss these topics chronologically—from the early beginnings of infancy through the later years of adulthood. Another aspect, unique to this discussion, is the incorporation (and suggested modification) of Erik Erikson's psychosocial theory of development in an effort to place these behaviors within a cross-cultural perspective. (See Chapter 2 for a review of the major aspects of this theory.)

We begin our discussion of selected topics, which are followed in a similar fashion in subsequent chapters, with a consideration of some of the principal behaviors socialized by most parents across cultures. We turn first to socialization during infancy.

Infancy

When a newborn arrives in the world, independent of its particular culture, it has many basic needs that require immediate attention. How these needs are met and the manner in which infants are socialized varies considerably across cultures and often among ethnic groups *within* a single society. In fact, as we shall see frequently throughout this book, there is often more variability in certain behaviors within cultures than between or among cultures.

It is clear that culture influences patterns of parenting from the first hours of infancy (e.g., when and how parents care for infants, the extent to which they allow them to explore their surroundings, how nurturant or restrictive they might be, and which behaviors they value and socialize). Bornstein (2002) expressed it succinctly when he says, "With the birth of a baby, a parent's life is forever altered. Those changes, in turn, shape the experiences of the infant and, with time, the person he or she becomes. Linked, parent and child chart that course together. Infancy is a starting point of life for both infant *and* parent" (p. 33)

Sleep

While all babies require sleep, psychological, anthropological, and even pediatric literature reveals considerable variation in cultural sleeping arrangements (McKenna, 1999, 2002; Super & Harkness, 1997). According to Harkness and Super (1995), the way sleep is organized, including where and with whom, is an intriguing aspect of culture because, although it is a private rather than public behavior, it is highly structured by different societies and tends to be relatively resistant to change. As these researchers point out, "Parents play a primary role in the assignment of settings and routines for sleep, thus perpetuating a cycle of culture transmission within the privileged context of the family" (p. 227). For example, in a 1981 study of Kipsigis farming families in the highlands of rural Kenya in East Africa, Harkness and Super noted that, although the next-to-youngest child continues to sleep with its mother and other siblings after the birth of a younger child, it no longer sleeps at the mother's front but rather at her back. This change, along with the termination of breast-feeding and back-carrying, results in a "fundamental shift in the child's physical and social settings of life" (1995, p. 227).

Sleep management is one of the earliest culturally determined parent–child interactions and may provide a useful framework for interpreting cross-cultural differences in the varying emphases placed on such behaviors as autonomy and dependence. Others have made a similar argument with regard to the development of interdependence and sensitivity to the needs of other people.

In a somewhat related effort, aimed at studying development as adaptation, Chisholm (1983) conducted an extensive investigation among Navajo

Indians in North America of their use of the cradleboard (a small wooden frame to which an infant is strapped) to determine if it might cause disruption in mother-infant interaction. (See p. 94 for a photo of a Hopi Indian cradleboard.) The Navajo cradleboard, or literally "baby diaper," has several purposes, such as infant transport, baby-sitting device, and regulator of infant states including level of physiological responsiveness or arousal and sleep. According to Chisholm, a child is asleep most (as much as 85%) of the time he or she is on the cradleboard, but the numbers of hours on the board may vary from only a few to as many as twenty-three, with fifteen to eighteen being normal. Chisholm concludes that cradleboard use seems to have no lasting effect on a child's behavioral development, and any observed group differences between Navajo and Anglo children is likely a result of social-cultural differences within the infant's environment—what we would attribute to the child's ecological settings and the developmental niche.

While it is common practice among middle-class families in the United States and Canada to put young infants in their own room to sleep (in part, to give them an early start down the road to independence), many Mayan mothers (American Indian peoples of Mexico and Central America) view this custom as equivalent to child neglect. On the other hand, interdependence—a prominent personality and cultural characteristic among Japanese—can be attributable, at least in some measure, to the fact that Japanese children (sometimes due to an overcrowded microsystem) frequently sleep with their parents until the age of six or even, in some cases, to the beginning of puberty, when independent sleeping marks a culturally recognized change in one's developmental niche. Similar findings have been found in China, where "all-night co-sleeping" during infancy and early childhood is the norm, decreasing in prevalence with increasing age, and unusual after puberty (Liu et al, 2005). In urban China, the prevalence of regular bed sharing has been found to be 18.2% and as high as 55.8% in 7-year-olds (Liu et al, 2003), and in Korea 73.5% of mothers approve of bed sharing between 3 to 6 years of age (Yang & Hahn, 2002).

The parent–child relationship and its effect on the development of dependence, independence, or interdependence can also be viewed within the framework of Erikson's psychosocial theory. According to Erikson's model, which, as we have cautioned, tends to present a predominantly Westernized perspective, social maturation during the first year of infancy is reflected in the development of a feeling of *trust versus mistrust* (e.g., the world is good and comfortable—trust—or threatening and uncomfortable—mistrust). Whichever view develops will depend largely on the parent–infant relationship. For example, many infants learn to trust that if they cry because they are hungry, someone will pick them up and feed them. Parents, on the other hand, learn to trust that their infants will be quieted and comforted when they are fed because the pattern of interaction is consistent.

Similar patterns develop near the end of infancy (during the second and third year) with regard to the second crisis of *autonomy versus shame and doubt*. For example, children will either begin to explore their surroundings on their own (sometimes getting into trouble) and decide for themselves what they want to wear, eat, or do, or they will obediently follow the demands of parents and develop doubts about their abilities and feel incapable of making decisions and governing their own behavior.

If we look at trust and independence, as illustrated in the Kipsigis and Japanese examples mentioned earlier, the Western bias inherent in Erikson's theory becomes obvious. In these cultural contexts, social maturation is not associated with increased independence, but rather with increased interdependence within the family. In both cultures, infants first develop trust and attachment as a result of sleeping with parents. Some degree of autonomy in Kipsigi infants is achieved when breastfeeding ends, and the older child is moved from the mother's front to her back to accommodate the arrival of a new baby. In the Japanese culture, in which a mother sleeps with the child for an even longer period, interdependence would appear to be even stronger than in Kipsigi society. Consideration of these examples strongly suggests that we may need to make adaptations in Erikson's theory when attempting to apply it in another cultural context.

The practice of **co-sleeping** (*a child sleeping with the parent*) is, in fact, routine in most of the world's cultures, and was the practice in the United States until shortly after the beginning of the twentieth century. Studies have suggested that the United States and other parts of North America are nearly alone in their expectation that children sleep in their own beds, in their own rooms, apart from their parents (McKenna, 1993, 2002). The well-known pediatrician Benjamin Spock, to whom generations of American

Japanese children often sleep with their parents for the first several years. (© Karen Masmauski/Matrix International)

Western infants often begin to develop independence by sleeping alone in their cribs. (Courtesy of authors)

parents have turned for advice on raising their children, stated that "it's a sensible rule not to take a child into the parents' bed for any reason" (Spock & Rothenberg, 1992, p. 213). Super and Harkness (1982), on the other hand, have suggested that the expectation that infants will be able to sleep through the night without some contact or involvement with parents may be "pushing the limits of infants' adaptability" (p. 52). Again, we see the importance of cultural as well as individual and familial differences in the determination of a particular behavior such as sleep patterns.

When considering sleep practices among parents in different cultures, it may not be the specific practice itself, but rather the cultural context and values that are the most important consideration. This view supports the ecological and developmental niche themes expressed throughout this book and leads us to another basic infant need requiring socialization—feeding.

Feeding

When infants are not sleeping, much of their time is spent eating. Just ask any new parent! How, what, and when to feed a child is another socialized behavior heavily influenced by the developmental niche, social context, parental beliefs, and values of one's culture.

Children need adequate nutrition, before birth as well as during infancy, if they are to grow properly and develop into healthy children and adults. The first two to three years are critical for physical development of the brain. The effects of nutritional deficiencies in infancy can be carried into adulthood and even affect another generation in terms of a mother's poor diet, inability to carry a baby to full term, or delivery of a low-birth-weight infant. According to figures gathered by the United Nations International Children's Emergency Fund (UNICEF) and released in *The State of the World's Children 2003* report, more than 150 million children in developing countries under the age of five are malnourished. This malnutrition contributes to more than half of the nearly 12 million under-five deaths occurring in developing countries each year. It can have an impact on an individual's resistance to disease, as well as normal development of intellectual or cognitive abilities. In fact, Pollitt, Gorman, Engle, Martorell, and Rivera (1993), in a study conducted in Guatemala, report finding a link between inadequate nutrition in infancy and cognitive functioning in adolescence, notably among those living in poor socioeconomic circumstances. In a study among low-income Nicaraguan mothers, findings revealed a clear relationship between maternal beliefs about infant feeding and a child's nutritional level during the first year (Engle, Zeitlin, Medrano, & Garcia, 1996). The authors conclude their study by stating that "behavioral encouragement to eat as observed here did not reflect the sense of responsibility of the mother about feeding [and that] . . . further work is needed to determine the ways in which mothers translate their belief in helping children to eat into feeding behaviors" (p. 443). On the positive side, UNICEF reported that over 300,000 children were saved from malnutrition in Niger in 2005, but that long-term programs were needed to address the issue.

For a long time, mothers around the world have been told that breastfeeding is the ideal method for providing nourishment to babies. The reasons most frequently mentioned include the fact that breast milk is more easily digested than other types of milk (e.g., milk from goats or cows), it protects against disease by providing natural immunization, and it is (obviously) immediately available. In most nonWestern cultures, it is the method most preferred by mothers, although one study has suggested a decline among mothers in Third World countries and an accompanying increase, at least on a short-term basis, among mothers in the United States (Ryan, Rush, Krieger, & Lewandowski, 1991). This topic receives additional attention in Chapter 4.

It should be noted that recent findings suggest that long-term breastfeeding may have additional benefits for the mother as well (e.g., significantly reducing the risk of developing type 2 diabetes). Using data from two Nurses' Health Studies of more than 150,000 women who had given birth, Steube and her colleagues (2005) found a 15% decrease in risk for each year of breastfeeding in the first study and 14% decrease in the second. Although not able to explain precisely how breastfeeding may help to protect mothers against diabetes, they suggested it improves insulin sensitivity and glucose tolerance and may help maintain blood sugar balance.

As you might expect, cultural attitudes play a significant role in whether babies are breastfed or bottlefed (Miller, Van Esterik, & Van Esterik, 2004; Talukder, 2000; Van Esterik, 1989). Some cultures, many of them in the West, tend to make a woman feel embarrassed about engaging in this natural function in public. When mothers return to work shortly after their child's birth, as many tend to do in North American and European countries, they may be unable to continue breastfeeding. On the other hand, if bottlefeeding is the method of choice, more fathers are able to participate in feeding and bonding with their infants. The United Nations estimates that improved breastfeeding practices could save the lives of almost 1.5 million children a year. Unfortunately, few of the 129 million infants born each year receive optimal breastfeeding (e.g., breast milk with no other foods or liquids for the first six months of life, followed by breast milk and solid or semisolid foods from about six months of age on, and continued breastfeeding for up to at least two years of age along with complementary foods), and some babies are not breastfed at all (UNICEF, 2001). In fact, in 2005, UNICEF stressed that the world has a major opportunity to reduce the toll of HIV/AIDS on infants by supporting exclusive breastfeeding.

At this point, we would like to emphasize that research findings have not yet clearly demonstrated that one method has long-term benefits over the other (Van Esterik, 1989). If both options are equally available, we would support the opinion of most experts and recommend breastfeeding for the reasons mentioned above. However, we stress that the method is not as important as what happens during the feeding process. The feeding situation provides an excellent opportunity, through socialization, for parents to establish an emotional connection with their infant (attachment or bonding) that has been shown to have important implications for interpersonal relationships throughout the remainder of the lifespan. (For an excellent overview of this topic, see Virginia Colin's 1996 book.)

As one moves through the lifespan, these early cultural experiences with food strongly influence what, when, and how much an individual will eat. For example, which would you rather eat right now—a hamburger with french fries, a bowl of rice with spicy flavored beef, snake on crackers, octopus, grasshoppers, or (perhaps) nothing? Depending on your cultural training, the mention of any one of these meals might make you hungry or completely suppress your desire to eat. While hunger and the feeding process begin biologically, they are individually socialized by cognitive, learning, and experiential factors deeply rooted in the culture and often within the immediate family. As with other behaviors, eating preferences may show greater variability within families or within cultural subgroups than they do across cultures.

Crying

All babies cry. But what does their crying mean, and is it responded to in the same or similar way in all cultures? Crying is the newborn's earliest form of communication with those in its immediate surroundings—the world of the micro- and mesosystems. Through crying, a baby lets others know that it is hungry, is not feeling well, has a wet diaper, wants attention, would like its older brother to stop annoying it, or conveys other information about its condition. In a sense, when newborns and infants cry, they are bringing their parents and others into their world and socializing them into understanding what their feelings are when they have no other way of expressing them. Although most parents in diverse cultures around the world can clearly differentiate these cries and distinguish one from another, it is almost impossible to teach this skill to others; experience seems to be the best teacher.

In addition, studies have shown that infants with various disorders (cystic fibrosis, Down syndrome, and others) cry differently than normal babies, and that individuals across cultures can recognize and differentiate among these various cries (Molitor & Eckerman, 1992; Zeskind, Klein, & Marshall, 1992). Recent studies have shown that mothers can discriminate different types of crying in low-birth-weight premature and full-term infants (Worchel & Allen, 1997); that cry analysis can successfully detect effects of prenatal alcohol exposure in newborn infants who do not show clinical signs of abnormality (Zeskind, Platzman, Coles, & Schuetze, 1996); and that crying among hearing-impaired infants differs from those with normal hearing abilities due to the lack of auditory feedback (Moeller & Schoenweiler, 1999). In a new development, Green, Irwin, and Gustafson (2000) have started to synthesize findings from several different approaches into a framework that one day could be used to relate crying to early health and development. Research also shows that fathers and other males respond in as nurturing a way to an infant's crying as do mothers and other women (Rosenblith, 1995).

When and how often should a caregiver respond to a child's crying? If it is responded to frequently, will the child be spoiled? If crying is ignored, will insecurity be the result? These are difficult questions, and not all experts agree on the answers. Bowlby (1988) believes that crying should be responded to frequently, especially during the first year, and will not result in spoiling but rather will greatly assist in promoting secure attachment. In terms of Erikson's theory, frequent responding to crying appears to promote attachment as well as assist in resolving the crisis of trust versus mistrust mentioned earlier.

Childhood

When we use the term **childhood,** we are referring to *the period extending from the end of infancy, about one and a half to two years of age, to just before the beginning of adolescence, typically about the age of eleven or twelve,* depending on the particular culture.

Edwards (1996), in a discussion of the parenting of toddlers, has outlined the developmental tasks she believes children are confronted with during their second and third years. We view each of these as an area of behavior in need of socialization and indicate, in parentheses, the chapters in this book in which they receive extensive discussion. These include, but are not limited to, learning to function independently or interdependently to become a functioning member of a society (discussed in this chapter), developing the beginnings of a self-concept (Chapter 6), understanding sex roles and establishing gender identity (Chapter 7), developing a moral conscience and the handling of aggressive behavior (Chapter 8), and taking a place in the larger family grouping (Chapter 9).

Some children experience difficulties and get "hung up" in the transition between childhood and adolescence. (© Joe Oppedisano)

Edwards (1996) points out that "although socialization processes in the field of toddler development are by no means fully understood . . . bidirectional, multicausational, and transactional models have become the goal" (p. 59). She goes on to say that "toddler development cannot be adequately described without introducing further theoretical perspectives based on Vygotsky's (1978) writings and using naturalistic observations that clarify the meaning systems and communication processes involved in socialization" (p. 49). Because these topics, in fact, provide the basis for a large part of the discussion on culture and cognition covered in Chapter 5, we will forgo any further mention of it and direct your attention to that chapter.

When older children enter elementary school, they come under the influence of two very different socialization agents—teachers and peers. In the school setting, the socialization process teaches children more about themselves (their personalities, abilities, and roles) and how to develop social relationships with adults who are not their relatives (teachers) and peers (other students), as well as ways to master some of the challenges of everyday life.

For the remainder of this section, let us consider the effects of socialization on formal and informal learning, as well as academic achievement in classroom settings.

Formal Versus Informal Learning

Most of the socialization experiences of children in nonindustrialized countries take place in informal settings (e.g., within the family or among peers and siblings) and are a fundamental part of one's daily activities. **Informal learning** is not characterized by a defined curriculum and is *generally picked* *up by means of observation and imitation.* According to Cushner (1990), "The responsibility for learning falls mainly on the learner, making it rather personal, with extended family members often playing a critical role in the act of instruction. . . . Change, discontinuity, and innovation are highly valued" (p. 100). For example, in certain African and South American tribal groups, young boys learn hunting and fishing skills as well as methods for navigating their way through jungles and rivers by observing and imitating adult males in their culture. Girls learn cooking and child-care techniques, not in school, but by helping their mothers, aunts, and other women in the daily activities of family and village life. Traditions change very little in some cultures; this is the way it has been for centuries and the way it is almost certain to be long into the future.

In other countries, the majority of children learn important cultural skills as part of their society's formal education system. As Cushner (1990) points out, **formal learning** is *"set apart from the context of everyday life and is typically carried out in the institution we know as school [and is characterized by] . . . an explicit and highly structured curriculum [in which] . . . material is learned from a book that may or may not be useful at a later time"* (p. 100). For a particularly insightful discussion of the failures of formal schooling in African societies, see Serpell's (1993) work on Zambia.

The issue of formal versus informal schooling gives us another opportunity to look at the two crises Erikson says are characteristic of the stage of childhood. As shown in Table 2.3, these are *initiative versus guilt* and *industry versus inferiority.* To put these crises into perspective, let us consider the case of Tamiko and Alexina. Tamiko, age ten, lives and goes to school in Akita, Japan. Like most children in her country, her success or failure depends more on her effort and character than on her innate ability. She is learning and working productively and harmoniously in mixed-ability groups similar to what she will encounter when she is an adult. Cooperation is seen as essential to the success of the group as well as the individual, and formal instruction occurs with this in mind. In this case, the developmental niche in which early learning takes place will share certain characteristics with the adult niche in which Tamiko will later live and work. The Japanese believe that parents and teachers must coordinate their efforts so that there is a high level of contact between the school and the home throughout a child's formal schooling. For Tamiko and her parents, academic work comes before everything else and involves long hours of study. There is a Japanese expression—"Pass with four, fail with five"—referring to how many hours of sleep are needed in order to succeed.

Tamiko's education actually began prior to entering formal preschool when her mother taught her to read, write, and perform simple mathematics. She spends more hours in school each year than almost any other children anywhere else in the world. This includes her regular classes, followed by several hours in a "juku" (cram school), and finally studying and doing homework at home until the early morning hours. While the latter is not formal in the strict sense of the word, it is nevertheless very serious and regimented. Alexina, also ten years old, lives in Minnesota in the midwestern part of the United States and is equally serious about her education. However, in her case the focus is more on independence and self-expression. She has learned that autonomy and individual achievement are valued over group collaboration. Getting ahead is a personal goal, as characterized by Alexina's ability to take the initiative to complete assignments on her own. As with Tamiko, there will be a certain consistency between the values and behaviors present in the developmental niches of childhood and adulthood. Unlike the Japanese, Americans believe education is to be provided in the school, not in the home. This again points out the distinction between formal and informal schooling mentioned earlier. If you think about the opening chapter vignettes, Kamuzu's educational experience, while not as rich in opportunities, would be similar in many ways to that of Tamiko (e.g., more cooperative or group learning and more informal home schooling). Jeremy, like Alexina, would be expected to show greater independence, autonomy, and self-expression. Again, in the case of Jeremy and Kamuzu, we observe more variability in their individual educational experiences within the South African culture than we do between the experiences of Jeremy in his culture and Alexina in the United States.

How might we apply Erikson's model and resolution of crises to these four children? In Tamiko's case, *initiative* and *industry* are achieved only after successfully recognizing the need for others to assist in the learning process. The same is somewhat less true in Kamuzu's situation, because his school is underfunded and he had to learn more in the informal settings of his home and community. In Alexina's case, industry is achieved when she is able to take initiative independently and become a "self-starter." Her success in this area is reflected in her school report card, which has a category for "industriousness." In this respect, Jeremy behaves similarly to Alexina. In short, Alexina's culture and Jeremy's subculture view initiative and industry in independent terms, whereas Tamiko's culture and Kamuzu's subculture, to a lesser extent, look at these qualities in interdependent terms. Again, when applying Erikson's theory to nonWestern cultures, it is of crucial importance to consider the relevance and cultural definitions of his concepts (e.g., independence and autonomy, initiative and industry). If this is not done, a researcher is liable to make serious misinterpretations of cultural behavior.

Before leaving the topic of learning, let us look more closely at the related issue of culture and educational achievement, particularly as it relates to the socialization of mathematical skills.

Cultural Influences on Academic Achievement

As noted earlier, learning and a significant portion of cross-cultural and cross-ethnic differences in educational achievement may be attributed to cultural factors, such as educational resources, Socioeconomic Status (SES), parental education level, and pedagogical systems and practices (Goh & Gardiner, 2004). Perhaps no education system, except that of the United States, has been more intensely studied than that of Japan. In an excellent and well-balanced presentation of the Japanese model of schooling and its similarities and differences with those of the United States, Tsuneyoshi (2001) characterizes the American approach as one that places an emphasis on competitiveness, individual attention from teachers and individual student accomplishment, development of cognitive abilities, and separation of teachers in terms of their disciplines. The Japanese approach, on the other hand, focuses on the whole child, with teachers and pupils closely interacting for extended periods of time in cooperative settings with attention to collective tasks, goals, and rewards, along with efforts to provide similar treatment for all students. One advantage of the American approach, seriously missing in the Japanese approach, is its attention to diversity as well as a sensitivity and concern for minority rights. At the same time, the Japanese approach has a clear advantage in its ability to concentrate on the whole child with a community structure designed to provide close, cooperative, face-to-face, student–teacher relationships.

What about the recurrent argument that American school children lag far behind children of other nations, particularly Japan and China, in math achievement (Gardiner, 1994; Ginsberg, Choi, Lopez, Netley, & Chao-Yuan, 2000; Randhawa & Gupta, 2000)? Unfortunately, research literature reports very few well-designed and carefully conducted cross-cultural studies of this topic. Most notable are those carried out by Stevenson and his colleagues (Stevenson & Stigler, 1992; Stigler & Fernandez, 1995), almost all of which show American students lagging behind their peers in other industrialized countries. In their classic study of math achievement among Chinese, American, and Japanese children, *Contexts of Achievement*, Stevenson and Lee (1990) attribute American children's poor performance to several factors, including a lack of emphasis on academic activities; the absence of shared goals in academic achievement; an overestimation of accomplishments by parents and children themselves; low parental achievement standards and little direct involvement by them in their children's schoolwork; and a widespread belief that all children, with the exception of those who may be seriously disabled, should be capable of learning and doing well in elementary school. Along these lines, Gardiner (2001a) pointed first to the dominant role in this process played by mothers and second to cross-cultural evidence strongly suggesting that informal learning styles, like those mentioned above and found in many Asian cultures, focusing on building interest, are more effective in teaching children a variety of skills, including math.

Support for this last statement, particularly with reference to informal math learning, can be found among some of Brazil's more than two-hundred thousand "Mennios de Rua" and Columbia's "Gamines" or "Chupagruesos"—street children (Aptekar, 1989). Many of these children survive by selling fruits and vegetables on street corners. Most of them dropped out of school by the time they were ten, before learning good math skills. Although they conduct scores of informal financial transactions each day without making a mistake, the majority of them are unable to complete a formal, written math problem requiring them to calculate change (not unlike what they do every day) without making numerous errors. Their school (ecological setting) is the street, and it is here that they have been socialized and have learned functional math skills that allow them to survive in the street culture of large Latin American cities where they live. For an interesting discussion of these different cultural practices and the advantages and disadvantages of each, see the book *Street Mathematics and School Mathematics* by Nunes, Schliemann, and Carraher (1993).

Adolescence

We know that adolescence begins in biology, when hormones that bring about physical changes and prepare the body for sexual reproduction are released into the bloodstream. But adolescent development ends in culture, where one's status is defined by the new role played in society and the transition to adulthood begins. From an ecological or cultural contextual perspective, adolescence is seen as a developmental stage in some, but not all, cultures (Burbank, 1988; Hollos & Leis, 1989). According to Cole and Cole (1996), its distinctiveness as a stage depends in large measure on whether "young people reach biological maturity before they have acquired the knowledge and skills needed to ensure cultural reproduction" (p. 629). For example, in the United States and Canada, there sometimes are young adolescents (ages twelve and up) with children of their own who, without a job or educational training, are totally incapable of providing for the welfare of their children or of themselves. Contrast this with the !Kung San living in the Kalahari Desert in Botswana and parts of Namibia and South Africa. Even before reaching the years of adolescence, older children have learned through socialization to hunt animals and gather wild plants as part of their nomadic life. They, like their North American counterparts, are biologically capable of reproduction but already know their developmental niche and have the skills to economically support themselves and a family if necessary (Draper & Cashdan, 1988).

Adolescence provides another opportunity to dramatically illustrate how the major themes of this book can be used to describe and explain how cultures structure and teach the kinds of activities that Cole and Cole (1996) say need to be mastered in order to "carry out the full process of human reproduction [and how these] . . . shape the psychological characteristics that one develops at the end of childhood" (p. 629). It is at this point in the lifespan that we can again clearly observe the development of "lives across cultures." For example, compare two fourteen-year-old girls growing up in cultures separated by both time and space. Mankushai is a member of the Masai tribe and lives on a flat grassy plain in southern Kenya. Her days are spent in her husband's village working side by side with her mother-in-law cooking and taking care of her young daughter, Consolata. Far away, in the United States, in California, Alisa spends her days in school studying chemistry, calculus, and world history, so that she will be able to attend college and prepare for a career as an economist. Each lives in a developmental niche within an ecological system, surrounded by family, peers, and teachers, learning her culture's values, and being socialized into an adult role. But how different their lives are and how different they will continue to be as they move through the lifespan.

Before leaving this topic, let us consider the socialization process from the perspective of immigrants and how they sometimes give up many of the values and customs of their native culture and take on those of their adopted culture, and the effects this might have on their behavior. This can be seen in studies involving first, and second-generation American Chinese adolescents who were compared with Chinese adolescents from Hong Kong, others whose parents had immigrated to Australia, and to European and Anglo Australian adolescents. For example, (Chiu, Feldman, & Rosenthal, 1992), found that first and second generation Chinese American adolescents, in terms of their adolescent problems and the severity of them, were similar to non-immigrant adolescents. On the other hand, immigration appeared to result in reduced perceptions of parental control, which was unrelated to adolescents' views of their parents' warmth towards them. However, across generations, Chinese American adolescents were found to place less value on the family as a "residential unit," consistent with the values expressed by European and Anglo Australian adolescents, and yet the authors indicated they still differed from the other groups on this particular value.

Much of an adolescent's time is again spent in the school setting where he or she come under the influence of even more socialization agents, such as involvement in various school organizations, music activities, or sports endeavors. During this period, at least part of their development will be influenced by the presence or absence of rites of passage.

Rites of Passage

In many cultures, the transition from childhood to adolescence is marked by some sort of public recognition. Called **rites of passage,** these are *ceremonies or rituals that recognize or symbolize an individual's movement from one status to another.* These "coming-of-age" experiences vary significantly from one culture to another but, according to a study by Schlegal and Barry (1991), are found in most nonindustrialized societies where nearly 80 percent of girls and close to 70 percent of boys go through some form of initiation.

In eastern Africa, ten- to twelve-year-old boys in the Kaguru tribe are led into the bush, stripped of all clothing, and ritually circumcised while being taught the sexual practices of adulthood by male members of the community. Later, they return to their village, are celebrated at a large feast, receive new

Masai men conduct an initiation ceremony bringing boys into manhood. (© Adrian Arbib/Anthro-Photo file)

names, and are expected to become responsible adult members of their society (Beidelman, 1997). Passage for a Kaguru girl is not as complex as for boys and occurs when she experiences first menstruation and is taught the ways of womanhood by her grandmother or older women in the tribe. She is fortunate in escaping the very painful and widespread practice of female genital surgery (called "circumcision" by some and "female genital mutilation" by others) already experienced by as many as 114 million women in twenty-eight countries in Africa, India, the Middle East, and Southeast Asia (Kelso, 1994). The practice is legally outlawed in only three countries—Belgium, Sweden, and the United Kingdom. For more on the prevalence and effects of these practices, see Obermeyer (1999).

The transition from adolescence to adulthood in North America and many other Western countries is not marked by such clearly defined rituals. In fact, many would say there are no true rites of passage experienced by all members of these societies at this particular stage in the lifespan, and if there ever were, they have disappeared. Among certain ethnic groups within the larger society, there may be some commonly experienced ceremonies, such as the Bar or Bat Mitzvah for Jewish boys and girls, that may come close to being a rite of passage. On the other hand, while not experienced by all adolescents at the same time, or by many at all, the following are frequently mentioned as possible rites of passage in North American society: graduation from high school or college, successfully passing a driver's test, marriage, or the first job. The lack of commonly accepted rites of passage in these societies may be attributed, in part, to a lack of conformity in developmental niches, for example, two families living next to each other may have significantly different backgrounds, cultural origins, ethnicity, values, and traditions than those found in more homogeneous societies.

Age certainly is not a very helpful marker in cultures like the United States, since there are several criteria by which individuals are considered adults (e.g., age sixteen for driving, eighteen for voting, and twenty-one for drinking). American adolescents, and their counterparts in many other countries, often linger in a "cultural limbo" between the ages of twelve to the early twenties when they may (or may not) one day be considered adults.

An exception to the comments made above is the **Vision Quest,** an experience common to many of the more than five hundred culturally diverse Native American tribes in North America. Performed primarily as a rite of passage for adolescent males, it begins with the taking of a boy, age fourteen or fifteen, into a "sweat lodge," where his body and spirit are purified by the heat given off by burning cedar. Sitting with the boy is a medicine man, who advises him and assists him with ritual prayers. Later, he is taken to an isolated location and left alone to fast for four days. He prays, contemplates the words of the medicine man, and waits for a vision that will reveal to him his path in life as a member of his tribal culture (Delaney, 1995). As another example, Navajo girls at the time of menarche take part in a rite of passage that involves morning running and the baking of a ceremonial cake.

It is clear from this discussion that different cultures treat their young people very differently. Some provide a clearly defined niche within the microsystem of the family where the parents, elders, and others initiate and prepare their young people to move into the wider realms of the mesosystem, exosystem, and macrosystem and to deal with the challenges and opportunities available to them as recognized adults. Other cultures, such as many Western societies, could do more to prepare their young people for the often difficult transition to adulthood.

In discussing rites of passage, it is important to keep in mind that each culture uses these as a way of helping their adolescents arrive at an understanding of their **identity,** or *self-definition as a separate individual in terms of roles, attitudes, beliefs, and values.* In the case of the Kaguru mentioned earlier, adult male identity is achieved when young boys undergo circumcision, and adult female identity is attained when young girls experience their first menstruation. Identity and adulthood are defined and achieved in terms of tribal customs and beliefs. In North American societies, identity is achieved when adolescents demonstrate some measure of independence, initiative, and industriousness, although these qualities are not always clearly defined.

The differences between these cultures can be considered in terms of Erikson's fifth crisis—*identity versus role confusion.* Failure to achieve identity in these cultures results in what Erikson refers to as role confusion. The difficulty in terms of this crisis lies in how each culture defines identity and marks the onset of adulthood. In many respects, achievement of identity is less ambiguous in traditional, nonindustrialized societies because rites of passage are clearly defined and adolescents know what is expected of them in order to become an adult. Conversely, in many industrialized societies, true rites of passage (which apply to all members of a given society) do not exist; consequently, there is ambiguity in how identity is defined and achieved. The result is that many adolescents do not know who they are or how they are supposed to behave as adults. Erikson refers to this dilemma as role confusion.

Some theorists and researchers imply that Erikson's theory also applies to preindustrial societies. However, when used to explain such behaviors as identity versus role confusion, the theory contains Western biases (e.g., viewing successful identity achievement as rooted in autonomous judgments). (For an extended discussion of identity formation, see Chapter 6.)

Adulthood

Developmentalists have historically devoted most of their attention to the earlier part of the lifespan, particularly the years from birth through adolescence. As a result, there is a great deal of research, many findings, and a host of theories describing, explaining, and predicting the events during the first two decades of life. A similar situation applies to cross-cultural human development: only recently have the last three quarters of the lifespan received serious attention. Even so, treatment of topics has been sparse and inconsistent (Zarit & Eggebeen, 2002). Cole and Cole (1993) explain it well: "Since psychologists are sharply divided over the relative roles of biology and culture in the process of development, it is only natural that they should be sharply divided on the question of whether development continues into adulthood and old age" (p. 656).

We know from casual observation that the experience of adulthood varies dramatically across and even within cultures and depends on a variety of factors, including age, gender, socioeconomic status, occupation, family structure, and timing of life events (e.g., marriage, parenthood, grandparenthood, and retirement).

Many psychologists (whose research you will become familiar with in subsequent chapters) have paid little attention to developmental changes, including socialization, after adolescence. For example, G. Stanley Hall, who wrote the first book on adolescence in 1904, believed that senescence (old age) began shortly after adolescence ended, generally when one reached the late thirties or early forties (Hall, 1904, 1922). Of course, he based this assumption partly on the fact that life expectancy was much shorter at that time. Jean Piaget, in his theory of cognitive development, proposed that individuals reached the final stage of formal operations during their late adolescence or early adulthood years. Only recently have attempts been made to explain cognitive changes in later adulthood, through the establishment of a stage of post-formal operations (see Chapter 5).

Two psychologists who did attribute significant developmental changes to the years of adulthood, and some of whose ideas have been subjected to cross-cultural examination, are Lev Vygotsky and Erik Erikson. Vygotsky, a Russian psychologist and one of the founders of the cultural-historical viewpoint, made some of the earliest contributions to our understanding of cognitive development within social settings, or cultures. (His ideas, many of which are similar to those expressed in our major themes, were introduced in Chapter 2.) Erikson, as we have previously noted, is one of a small number of theorists who emphasize cultural and social development across the entire lifespan, separating the years following adolescence into early, middle, and later adulthood. It is in this area that his views coincide most closely with those of the ecological, or cultural context, approach. Limited findings from anthropological, sociological, and cross-cultural studies, particularly those looking at adolescence, tend to support his theoretical assumptions (Erikson, 1963, 1982; Ferrante, 1992; Ochse & Plug, 1986).

Early and Middle Adulthood

During early adulthood (early twenties to mid-thirties), in cultures throughout the world, a majority of adults are dealing with the crisis of *intimacy versus isolation* (see Table 2.3 on page 38). Decisions are made about establishing a close, intimate relationship with another person, or individuals go their way alone and fail to achieve an intimate relationship. Chapter 7 looks in detail at intimate relationships in a variety of cultures and at the impact of this crisis on one's life.

Lefrancois's comment (1996) that age ranges be used only as descriptive guidelines is relevant here in terms of the cultural example we provided in the section on adolescence. Confronting the crisis of intimacy versus isolation usually requires that the individual has achieved a sense of identity, probably is self-supporting, and is involved in a long-term and interdependent relationship. With this in mind, consider fourteen-year-old Mankushai of the Masai tribe in Kenya, East Africa, mentioned earlier. Mankushai lives in her husband's village, cooks his meals, and takes care of her daughter, Consolata. Except for her age, she would appear to be in the stage of early adulthood. What about other cultures, like those parts of India where child marriages are common? In which stage do we put these individuals? Compared with earlier stages of development, there is less cross-cultural research on this stage and the crisis contained within it. This raises additional questions and problems about applying this theory beyond Western societies. We clearly need more critical analysis of ideas and concepts, as well as additional research to extend the cross-cultural usefulness of theories such as these.

For example, consider Catholic nuns and priests, Buddhist monks, or Hindu holy men, all of whom choose a religious life involving vows of chastity and, in some cases, isolation in cloistered settings. Have they failed to resolve the intimacy versus isolation crisis in a positive way? According to

Erikson, they have done so only if they have resolved the earlier identity crisis. But we need to look further. Erikson might suggest that these individuals are not necessarily isolated, but rather that they have defined intimacy differently. For example, Catholic nuns or priests who have devoted their lives to the service of others in the name of Christ would see themselves as married to and intimate with God. In fact, nuns are considered "brides of Christ." Buddhist monks experience intimacy with nature, Buddha, and the Sangha (membership of monks). In applying Erikson's theory, it is clear that additional cross-cultural research and modification is not only necessary but highly recommended.

When one reaches middle adulthood (mid-thirties to mid-sixties), a new crisis appears that involves *generativity versus stagnation* (see Table 2.3 on page 38). Middle-aged adults make work and career decisions, raise children, and show concern by guiding the next generation, or they become stagnant, self-absorbed, and self-centered. Some of our earlier comments regarding the role parents play in socialization would appear to be relevant here. It is through socialization within their ecological settings that individuals have the kinds of experiences that help them as adults find a balance between their self-interests and the interests of others. Unfortunately, as with some other areas, there is a lack of cross-cultural findings related to this stage crisis; the need for additional theorizing and research is clear. For the latest in contemporary thinking and research on the psychological, social, and cultural aspects of generativity in the lives of adults, see de St. Aubin, McAdams, & Kim, 2003.

Finally, looking once again at socialization, it is in this period of adulthood, as individuals move into the working world, that "globalization" and a clear understanding of cross-cultural differences in business practices becomes increasingly important. In certain occupations and careers, employees must be socialized to operate within a global organizational culture, or they will not be successful. In addition, some people form relationships with, and often marry, mates from different cultures. In such situations, they encounter differences in the assumptions and values in their own socialization and confront decisions about how they will socialize and raise their own children in multicultural and multiethnic contexts. Discussion of this latter topic will also be expanded upon in Chapter 9 ("The Family in Cultural Context").

Late Adulthood

During the last period in the lifespan (mid-sixties and after), older adults find themselves dealing with the crisis of *integrity versus despair* (see Table 2.3). According to Erikson, when individuals reach this stage they tend to reflect on their lives. They find that they are either generally happy and satisfied with their choices, having fulfilled many of their goals and having made their best efforts (integrity); or they find themselves filled with despair over missed opportunities or mistakes made, which leaves them unhappy and dissatisfied.

Considering the example of the nuns, monks, and holy men in the last section, will these individuals look back at their lives from this final crisis and feel unhappy and unsatisfied? Unlike Erikson, who would take this position, we suggest the opposite. In our thinking, most of these individuals will, in fact, feel their lives have been very satisfying and fulfilling and will have feelings of hopefulness and integrity.

In the final analysis, the manner in which this crisis is resolved and the reasons for the outcomes appear to involve a significant cultural component. Consider a nonindustrialized, collectivist, and extended family-based culture, in which respect and recognition are given the elderly for their wisdom and accomplishments. For example, most Native American tribes have a hierarchy of elders, who are held in high respect for their knowledge of tribal rituals and ceremonies, and who pass this heritage on through socialization of the future generation of tribal members.

We hypothesize that a negative outcome to this crisis might be more often found in some Western societies, which place great emphasis on economic and career success and in which nuclear families are the norm. In these cultures, parents or other relatives in their later years are sometimes seen as burdens to be moved from the microsystem of the family to rest homes in the mesosystem or exosystem. In societies in which young people

A Hispanic family enjoys an afternoon of music and multigenerational storytelling.
(© Tony Freeman/PhotoEdit)

Isolation and loneliness frequently characterize the later years of many of North America's elderly who live in institutionalized settings rather than within extended families. (© Mark Richards/PhotoEdit)

enjoy the greatest status, the elderly are more often rejected. Contemporary North American society is currently such a society, but given rapid increases in its older population, the ecological setting will soon undergo dramatic changes. An ecological setting that focuses on youth rather than age places an older person in a developmental niche, where either they have few contributions to make or their contributions are not highly valued. In these circumstances, individuals might well feel despair and regret about the past and a real fear of aging. Contrast this with an Asian or African culture, in which intergenerational families are the norm and older relatives are looked after by their family or by the village community. These differences are sharply distinguished in the photographs on pages 77 and 78.

It is interesting to note that when Erikson reached the eighth decade of his life, he reviewed his theory and suggested that increases in life expectancy might require a rethinking of his ideas, especially those related to development during adulthood (Erikson, Erikson, & Kivnik, 1986). We encourage others to begin this careful rethinking and, in the process, attempt to apply these new ideas to cross-cultural human development.

◇ SUMMARY

It should be clear after reading this chapter that universally accepted generalizations about the complex relationships among family, culture, and socialization are sometimes difficult. Numerous variables contribute to cultural differences, including cultural contexts, societal beliefs and values, individual views of children and their place in society, rural versus urban living, family structure, and parenting styles, to mention only a few. However, cross-cultural research on human development also shows that we are gaining a much better understanding of the significant role culture plays in socialization at all levels, from birth through the last years of the lifespan. Traditional, primarily Western, theoretical explanations of human development are, in large part, obsolete and were never very accurate when transported to other cultures in an effort to describe, explain, and predict behavior for which they were never intended.

You are reading this at a time when many societies are undergoing dramatic change in the way they and their family structures operate. In China, the "one-child policy" is having striking effects on traditional family practices; in the former Soviet Union, political and social changes are affecting parental goals and behavior; in Sweden, children's rights have taken center stage; in the United States, high divorce and remarriage rates and large numbers of working mothers are reshaping family relationships. In countries throughout the world, we have seen major changes in the roles played by children and their parents, and yet, as Roopnarine and Carter (1992a) have pointed out, "Perceptions of children and how a culture manages to mesh those perceptions with children's own birthright and value to members of a society, its rituals, functions, and expectations, are not well understood" (p. 251). We have only started the journey toward understanding; much lies ahead of us.

◇ STUDY QUESTIONS

Define the term *socialization* and explain its importance to understanding cross-cultural human development.

Discuss the components of the developmental niche and give examples from your own experience.

Explain what is meant by *rites of passage* and the role they play in adolescent identity.

◇ FURTHER READINGS

Virginia L. Colin. (1996). *Human Attachment*, New York: McGraw-Hill.
> Without question, the most comprehensive, introductory review of attachment research and its implications for development throughout the lifespan. Easy to read and containing a cornucopia of cross-cultural studies and findings related to the topic.

Joan E. Grusec and Paul D. Hastings (Eds.) (2006). *Handbook of Socialization*. New York: Guilford Press.

    Almost all you want to know about socialization, including historical and methodological perspectives, its effects across the lifespan (within and outside the family), and relationship to gender, cognition, emotional competence, and prosocial development.

John Loughery. (1995). *Into the Widening World: International Coming-of-Age Stories*. New York: Persea Books.

    An edited anthology of twenty-six short stories from twenty-two countries focusing on the adolescent experience and emergence of adulthood. Visit the sun-baked alleys of Cairo, the terrifying forests of war-time Nigeria, a hidden grove in Jamaica, a turkey farm in Canada, a young woman facing an arranged marriage in Malaysia. Fascinating, insightful, and informative reading.

Mothering Magazine Special Issue: *Sleeping With Your Baby: The World's Top Scientists Speak Out*. J. McKenna (guest Ed.). Vol. 114, September–October 2002.

    A series of articles by some of the world's leading scientists on the subject of co-sleeping, including "Breastfeeding and Bedsharing," "Solitary or Shared Sleep: What's Safe?," "Researching Cultural Effects," "Bedsharing among Maoris: An Indigenous Tradition," and "Sleeping Like a Baby: How Bedsharing Soothes Infants."

Meredith F. Small. (1998). *Our Babies, Ourselves: How Biology and Culture Shape the Way We Parent*. New York: Anchor Books/Doubleday.

    A fascinating introduction to ethnopediatrics—the study of parents, children, and childrearing across cultures and the way different parenting styles affect the health, well-being, and survival of infants. Includes material on attachment, feeding, sleeping, crying, and more. Written for general audiences as well as parents.

Y. Nipoda. (2002). Japanese student's experiences of adaptation and acculturation of the United Kingdom. In W. J. Lonner, D. L. Dinnel, S. A. Hayes, & D. N. Sattler (Eds.), *Online Readings in Psychology and Culture* (Unit 8, Chapter 5), (http://www.wwu.edu/~culture), Center for Cross-Cultural Research, Western Washington University, Bellingham, Washington.

    This online chapter discusses cultural factors affecting Japanese students' adaptation to British society. It focuses on four main points: differences in language, communication styles and educational systems, motivation and pressures, and the effects of students' insecure status in the host country. Each point is illustrated with easy-to-understand examples.

Dennis O'Neil. (2005). *Cultural Anthropology Tutorials*. http://anthro.palomar.edu/tutorials/cultural.htm.

    This online website offers tutorials on a variety of topics related to socialization, including culture, language, social control, culture change, social and political organization, and processes of socialization.

◇ DEVELOPMENTAL ANALYSIS

SOCIALIZATION

My name is Matilda Skelton, but everyone—thankfully—calls me "Maddi." I was named for my great grandmother, who immigrated to the United States from England in 1847. I was born on September 17, 1938, in Elfville, Pennsylvania a small farming community settled by Irish immigrants (population 1,734). The town consisted of a feed and grain store, post office, small grocery store, Catholic Church, school, railroad depot, barber shop, gas station—and not much else! The person I am today was very much influenced by my early socialization experiences in Elfville and with my family. Let me explain.

In terms of my developmental niche, I lived in a rural setting, in a nuclear family, consisting of my two parents, a younger sister, and a younger brother. I spent my early years establishing relationships with members of my family and playmates. I learned to deal with feelings of dependence, independence, cooperation, and competition. My early caretakers were my parents, relatives, or other mothers in town. We didn't have a day care center or preschool when I was young—it was typical of the era for mothers to stay at home while raising their children.

As an infant, I slept in a crib in my parents' room for a couple of months and was then moved to my own room. I was breastfed for nine months. When I cried, my parents picked me up and comforted me. Like most American children, I was part of a formal school system. My siblings, friends, and I walked to a small school consisting of kindergarten through eighth grade, with most classes held together in the same room and taught by the same teacher. My parents and teachers worked together to ensure I had a good education. I did chores on the farm and enjoyed learning about the animals. When I was fourteen, I began traveling eight miles by bus to attend high school; my ecological system was expanding. In terms of informal learning, my mother taught me to cook and take care of my siblings; my father taught me to drive a tractor and play a guitar. My parents were Catholic, although my mother took religion more seriously than my dad.

As I was entering adolescence during the 1950s, America was characterized by malt shops, rock'n'roll music, the hula hoop, and "hot" cars. Television was just arriving. At the same time, the nation was plagued by racial injustice, anti-Communist paranoia, and the fear of nuclear war. The closest event to a rite of passage for me was getting my driver's license at the age of sixteen. Like most of my friends, I struggled to establish an identity and often felt confused. After high school graduation in 1956, most of my girlfriends decided to be secretaries, teachers, or nurses.

I decided to go to college and chose an unusual major for girls at the time—business. My first contact with another culture was during my junior

(continued)

year, when I spent a semester in Italy. I was the first in my family to travel abroad or even outside Pennsylvania. It was a wonderful experience and really opened my eyes to the world. In 1962, I traveled to England for graduate work in economics. It was there that I met my future husband—Giorgio Carlo Conte—a student from Italy. He asked me to go out with him seven times before I finally accepted! Socialization can work in surprising (and wonderful) ways.

Giorgio and I were married on March 9, 1968, at my grandparents' home in Coudersport, Pennsylvania. We combined American and Italian traditions. We moved to Minnesota, where I was an economics professor at a wonderful liberal arts college. Giorgio worked at an international bank. Our daughter, Elizabeth Lucia, was born in 1969, and our son, Alexander Donato, was born in 1970. When they were young, we frequently traveled to Italy so they could spend time with their grandparents and relatives.

I have many fond memories from my childhood, adolescence, and adulthood. I can recall our 1940 Chevrolet sedan, my dad serving in WW II, riding my bicycle to the grocery store, our icebox, a large Philco radio around which we would gather to listen to radio programs, visiting grandparents, and going to the movie theatre on Saturdays to see two films, two cartoons, news, and previews of coming attractions. For 25 cents you got all of this, a candy bar, and a bag of popcorn! Each of these experiences had a socializing effect on me in one way or another. I am now 67 years old and continue to go through socialization changes. I'll tell you more about this and other events in my life in the next chapter. Ciao for now!

CHAPTER FOUR

 CULTURAL ASPECTS OF
PHYSICAL GROWTH
AND DEVELOPMENT

*Madam Foo Mei Yin is approaching seventy years of age and lives with her eldest son,
Kit Seng, in Petaling Jaya, a suburb of Kuala Lumpur, Malaysia. A widow of twenty-
five years, her husband, Boon Seng, died of heart failure at the relatively young age of
fifty. Madam Foo, as matriarch of the family, is much respected and well-cared for by
her four sons and two daughters. She receives frequent visits from her eighteen grandchildren, six great-grandchildren, and other relatives. Since old age is seen as a welcome milestone denoting wisdom, knowledge, and experience, preparations for her
birthday celebration have been taking place for months, and almost two hundred relatives and friends are invited. A troupe of Lion Dance performers will arrive to the
sound of banging drums and firecrackers, bringing prosperity and good luck to the
family. Food will be offered to the household gods, and a red cloth will adorn the en-
tryway, symbolizing good health and prosperity and warding off evil spirits. Each
member of her extended family will wish her good health and a long life. After a din-
ner, which includes long-life noodles and sweet bean paste dessert, everyone will toast
"Yum seng"—"To your health and success"—to Madam Foo.*

*On Saturday night, Sarah Lawson will turn seventy in Melbourne, Australia. She is
planning her own birthday celebration and hopes her two sons, three grandchildren,
and great-granddaughter will be able to come. She lives alone in a three-bedroom
house her husband built forty-five years ago. Five years ago, her husband, Patrick,
died after a long battle with cancer. Her two sons, who live in the adjoining state of
New South Wales, try to visit as often as they can, although distance prevents them
from doing so on a regular basis. Mrs. Lawson is very independent and is actively involved in her church and senior citizens' association. She enjoyed good health until a
recent stroke left her in need of a cane. Each Tuesday, she drives thirty miles to get her
allergy shots and to volunteer at the regional Red Cross office. She also swims every
other morning on the advice of her physical therapist. It's been a tradition in the Lawson*

household to celebrate birthdays with a barbie (barbecue) in the backyard. A few neighbors and long-time friends will be there to help Sarah usher in the new decade. She has bought the meat; prepared the salads and vegetables; made sure there's plenty of beer, soda, and iced tea; and bought party favors for the guests. Her best friend, Mildred, who lives next door, has promised to bake a cake. Sarah is looking forward to seeing her old friends, some of whom she hasn't seen in years. Eventually, the guests will gather around the piano and retell stories of growing up in the outback.

Madam Foo and Sarah are both approaching their seventieth birthdays, but the way in which each has lived her life up until now, and will live the remainder of it, differs in many ways. Their developmental niches, family settings, relationships, and health concerns illustrate the many ways in which lives are lived across cultures.

◇ANOTHER PIECE OF THE DEVELOPMENTAL PUZZLE: THE HUMAN GENOME

In recent years, findings from the neurosciences have begun to significantly influence the study of human development. It is becoming increasingly necessary to take into account the role of genes and biological principles and their interaction with one's environment and psychological experiences. As Segalowitz & Schmidt (2003) point out, "While we see both cognitive and affective development—the mainstay of developmental psychology—as having interesting parameters being set by neurological factors, new discoveries in developmental neuroscience also highlight the plasticity and adaptability of the system. Patterns of development are both biologically rooted in our brains and heavily influenced by experience. And the biological influences are manifested through experience" (p. 65).

In addition, with the completion of the thirteen-year Human Genome Project (1990–2003), we have seen an explosion in the study of genetics and the discovery of specific genes that may be responsible for a variety of physical illnesses and psychological conditions, including cancer, diabetes, heart disease, multiple sclerosis, asthma, depression, and many others. There are even those who believe this knowledge could lead to the ability to double the lifespan through a variety of new treatments and therapies. The project's goals of identifying all the approximately 20,000–25,000 genes in human DNA, determining the sequences of the 3 billion chemical base pairs that make up human DNA, storing this information in databases, improving tools for data analysis, and transferring related technologies to the private sector have largely been accomplished. However, analysis of the data, its application to specific situations, and implications of the legal, ethical, and social issues arising from this project will last long into the future. Nevertheless, its findings are exciting and, in many ways, will change the way individuals and their descendents across cultures will live their lives in the generations yet to come.

Another important step in this direction has been taken by the National Institute for Child Health and Human Development as part of its *NICHD Strategic Plan 2000: From Cells to Selves: Biobehavioral Development* (see online reference in "Further Readings" at the close of this chapter for access to this report). The strategic plan is divided into several documents, which provide the framework and goals to guide the Institute's long-term planning process. Separate research agendas, in various stages of production, are presented, with new plans being posted for public access as they become available.

Advances in genetic engineering and biotechnology raise serious questions in terms of culture and human development. For example, in this chapter we look at topics related to physical development. What if you had a child who was born with a growth hormone deficiency? Would you (if you could afford it) pay large sums of money, perhaps as much as $1,500 to $2,500 or more, for a series of injections to increase the height of your child at critical stages of his or her development? Would you allow genetic engineering to increase the number of neurons in the brain during fetal development in order to have a potentially "smarter" baby?

Carey (2003) points out that in the past, the greatest effect of culture on humans has been to alter the frequency of alleles (paired genes, alike or different, that affect a trait) and/or genotypes (the genetic makeup of an individual, containing both expressed and unexpressed characteristics). Further advances in genetic engineering could allow scientists to create *new* alleles ". . . thus, changing mutations from a random phenomenon into a deliberate, scientifically guided enterprise" (Carey, p. 216). The result would be individuals with entirely new and unique genotypes that are not now a part of the human genome. We can only imagine (and even that is difficult) what the effect might be on human development and culture.

Physical and cultural changes in human development have always been intertwined. For example, we can observe the many ways in which a culture's attitudes and beliefs about birth control, abortion, and related topics influence its members' social and religious attitudes, as well as its concern with the physical factors of reproductive fitness. A culture's attitudes towards marriage—who and who will not make appropriate partners—affect the ways in which dating and mating are structured. Advances in international travel (and internet communication) have increased contact among different cultures, sometimes resulting in an increased number of cross-cultural relationships, intermarriages, and bi-cultural children, with a subsequent reduction in "the reproductive isolation of human populations" (Carey, 2003, p. 215).

Only the future will determine how far the genetic revolution will take us. For the time being, let us consider what we know about the present state of physical growth and development and its relationship to culture.

◇ CROSS-CULTURAL PERSPECTIVES ON PHYSICAL DEVELOPMENT

When we talk about **physical development** we are referring to *changes in an individual's size and body structure* (e.g., variations in height and weight, increases in muscle size, specialization of brain and sense organ functions, improved motor skills, and various effects of nutrition and physical health). Changes such as these do not take place in a vacuum separate from one's cognitive experience, social and emotional development, or cultural context. Each realm interconnects with the others and influences one's development throughout the lifespan. For example, when studying child development, we explore the maturation of gross and fine motor skills together with cognitive abilities, social and emotional development, and cultural orientation. While muscle coordination is taking place, a child is also acquiring the language skills necessary for improvements in perceptual and memory processes. At the same time, social and emotional development are laying the foundation for the development of the child's interactions with others in the increasingly complex ecological settings in which we live. While there are many similarities in the manner in which these skills and abilities develop, the timing of changes varies across cultures and depends, in part, on the norms prescribed by each society. We begin with the prenatal period following conception.

The Prenatal Period

While we do not discuss prenatal development in great detail (you can find this information in many good developmental books), let us point out that **conception,** or **fertilization,** *takes place when a sperm and an egg unite and form a zygote,* or *fertilized egg*. The zygote then goes through a process of rapid cell division, duplicating the genetic composition provided by the mother and father. This cluster of increasing complex cells moves down the Fallopian tube into the uterus, where it penetrates the uterine wall and becomes implanted. It will progress through the embryonic and fetal stages until birth takes place.

The **prenatal period,** *the time between conception and birth,* generally lasts about 266 days, or thirty-eight weeks. Yet, the physical growth and development at this time can influence individuals' behavior for the remainder of their lives.

Physical development during the prenatal period is critical, and any number of environmental factors can adversely affect this development and increase the odds of giving birth to a child with birth defects. Environmental toxins (aluminum, lead, carbon dioxide) or **teratogens** (*agents such as chemicals or diseases*) can contribute to the development of prenatal abnormalities. For example, recent research suggests that even a small amount of alcohol consumed during a critical period of pregnancy may increase chances of giving birth to a child with physical and cognitive abnormalities. Known as **fetal alcohol syndrome (FAS),** these abnormalities include an unusually small head, low birth weight, facial deformities, neurological impairments, and signs of impaired intellectual functioning. While it is difficult to know the precise number of cases of FAS throughout the world, Abel and Sokol (1987) report that in comparative studies conducted in Australia, North America, and several European countries, approximately one in every five hundred infants is born with the disorder. The result is that FAS contributes significantly to the number of children suffering from mental disabilities. Along these same lines, other studies have shown that if an expectant mother uses **crack cocaine** (*a concentrated form of cocaine*) or another addictive drug such as heroin or methadone, it will have the same effect on her fetus that it has on her. The developing fetus is most vulnerable to teratogens during the third to sixth week after conception (the critical period), when the central nervous system, heart, arms, and legs are developing.

As many of the world's cultures move toward increased industrialization, the dangers of pollution to pregnant women and their children can sometimes be carried to horrifying extremes. A particularly graphic example comes from the former Soviet Union, where Tamara Kapanadze, the mother of a child with a birth defect, made a shocking discovery. Acting on her own, she put together a map using data derived from hospital records and a factory producing artificial limbs. She found that over a twenty-year period, at least ninety children in Moscow had been born with the same birth defect as her child—namely, terminal-limb deficiency, which consists most often of a missing forearm. Her figures showed that more than half the children lived in neighborhoods heavily contaminated by industrial emissions. While no definitive link could be made between the incidence of the birth defect and pollution, the number of children with the deformity was higher in these areas than in Russia as a whole (Edwards, 1994).

Turning to another aspect of this topic, two widely studied concepts discussed in cross-cultural psychology are **individualism** and **collectivism.** In the last chapter, we pointed out that *in individualistic cultures, the individual frequently pursues autonomy, independence, and personal achievement, often at the expense of the group.* On the other hand, *in collectivist cultures, emphasis is on group success, and individual ambitions are generally set aside for the attainment of group goals* (Hofstede, 2001).

You might be asking "How are these cultural concepts related to the issue of prenatal care?" In traditional collectivist countries such as Malaysia, Singapore, Indonesia, the Philippines, and Thailand, where childbirth is more family-centered, expectant mothers can rely on a large number of individuals to ensure the safe delivery of a healthy child. In a sense, the entire

Russian children from two Moscow neighborhoods, born with terminal-limb deficiency, possibly the result of industrial pollutants. (© Gerd Ludwig/National Geographic Image Collection)

extended family acts as a midwife preparing a woman for childbirth. In fact, in such cultures, it is customary for a young mother to yield to the elders in the family when it comes to decisions regarding diet and other matters. In contrast, in individualistic cultures such as the United States and Canada, childbirth is a more private affair, and precautions taken to avoid environmental hazards are the primary responsibility of the expectant mother.

Interestingly, more babies die at or soon after birth in the United States than in many western European countries (which, like the United States, are individualistic) and Pacific Rim countries (which have collectivist cultures). One possible explanation for reduced infant mortality in these two different cultures may lie in the additional assistance given by extended family members in Pacific Rim countries during the prenatal period and at birth, and in the fact that pre- and postnatal health care is provided without cost in both western European and Pacific Rim countries (see Figure 4.1. for statistics on infant mortality). These cultural and medical practices appear to significantly reduce rates of infant death, low birth weight, and other birth complications.

While this seems to be a straightforward explanation, a recent study demonstrates that the socioecological factors contributing to infant mortality may be a bit more complex. Landale, Oropesa, and Gorman (2000) found that, when compared to native and U.S.-born Puerto Rican women, infant mortality was lowest in Puerto Rican mothers who had recently immigrated to the United States. Certainly, in this study, more accessible health care or family and community support were not the dominant factors, as the nonmigrant groups had those advantages but still suffered higher rates of infant deaths. The authors speculate that better infant health among the immigrant

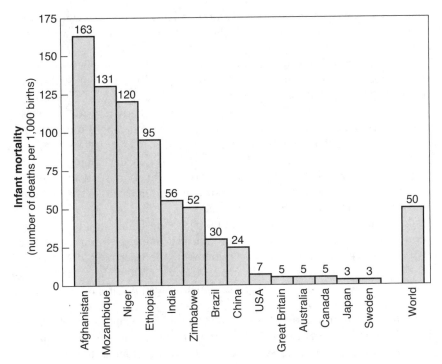

FIGURE 4.1 Incidence of Infant Mortality in Selected Countries

Data Source: CIA World Factbook 2005.

group may be the result of the selective migration of healthier or more economically advantaged mothers to the United States.

Infancy and Early Childhood

During infancy, enormous changes take place in physical growth and development. In just two years, many infants make the transition from dependent, almost helpless babies to independent, curious children. As their bodies grow and respond to social and cultural cues, their nervous systems mature, and their cognitive experiences are enhanced. They quickly adapt to the world outside the womb, slowly begin to imagine a future involving themselves and others, and discover methods for storing away memories of past and present events.

Physical Growth and Change

The most observable changes during the early years of life are in height and weight. Typically, if well-nourished, babies triple their birth weight by the time they are one year old and increase their height by nearly 50 percent in the same period. However, differences do exist. For example, by the time they reach four years of age, some children in Africa and Asia weigh as much as thirteen pounds less than their European and American counterparts, and may be as much as seven inches shorter (Hendrick, 1990).

In this regard, the importance of nutrition during infancy cannot be overemphasized. Nutrition affects changes in physical stature, brain development, and motor skill mastery, as well as other developments. Most of us have seen news reports of chronic malnutrition in many parts of the world. Just a little over ten years ago, one in every three deaths throughout the world involved a child five years of age or younger (Grant, 1994). According to UNICEF (2006), 30,000 children die each day in developing countries from infection and malnutrition due to poverty. This is more than 10 million children each year. In fact, the major cause of child mortality is the malnutrition and dehydration caused by diarrhea.

The incidence of malnutrition among young children, and the short-term and long-term effects of physical and psychological trauma associated with it, received worldwide attention following the December 2004 tsunami in Asia and the conflict in Sudan, where nearly 12,000 children with severe malnourishment were admitted to therapeutic feeding programs in Darfur since May 2004.

In industrialized countries, bottlefeeding is frequently preferred to breastfeeding, in part, because it allows women to pursue individualistic goals and to engage in professional activities. As developing nations become more technologically advanced and increasingly industrialized, there is a reduction in breastfeeding. In some situations this has resulted in many mothers, especially those living at the poverty level, diluting baby formulas and contributing to their infants' already deficient nourishment.

The nutritional status of children and the effects of poverty on physical growth and development have been studied in a number of countries, and the United States ranks fairly high in comparison to other countries (see Figure 4.2).

In the United States, some of the gains in this area have been attributed to federal programs, such as Food Stamps; the Supplemental Food Program for Women, Infants, and Children (WIC); and the National School Breakfast and Lunch programs. Even so, instances of inadequate nutrition are still found among low-income families and children.

On a more positive note, the early effects of malnutrition can, in some cases, be lessened and even turned back. For example, Barrett, Radke-Yarrow, and Klein (1982) conducted a follow-up study on a group of Guatemalan children who had been participants in an earlier investigation carried out by the Institute of Nutrition of Central America and Panama (INCAP). These children, suffering from the effects of severe malnutrition, were provided with caloric or nutritional supplements during the first several years of their development. As a result, they were significantly more active, physically as well as socially, than children who did not receive such supplements. In a related study involving malnourished Colombian infants, those

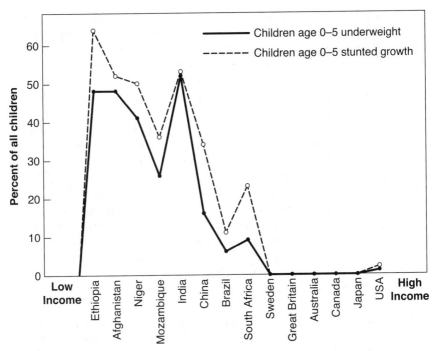

FIGURE 4.2   Impact of Poverty on Physical Growth and Development

Data Source: CIA World Factbook 2000.

who received regular food supplements along with home visits were taller and heavier than a comparable group who had not been given such treatment. The former group also demonstrated slightly higher ability in cognitive and social areas. The same reversibility of the effects could be observed in children who spent their first years of life in Romanian orphanages, suffering from physical neglect and malnutrition (Rutter & the ERA Study Team, 1998). The children had been adopted by families in Great Britain, where their environmental conditions improved dramatically. Researchers studied the children's physical and cognitive development at age four and found that most Romanian children had caught up physically with their British counterparts. This was especially true for children who had been adopted before the age of six months. During early childhood, young children also show improvements in the development of gross motor skills, especially as a result of their mastery of play.

Motor Skill Development

While parents help their children to develop many of the fundamental motor abilities, individual styles of parenting can vary considerably from one culture to another, and infants raised in these differing ecological settings sometimes show significant variations in physical development. For example, it has been well documented that the motor skills of African infants in such activities as sitting, walking, and running develop several months before they do in Caucasian infants. In Uganda, for example, infants begin to walk at about ten months (earlier than in most countries); in France, fifteen months is more typical; in the United States, the average is around twelve months.

What accounts for these differences? In most cases, it is likely to be the result of a combination of factors, including genetics, activity level, body type, and physical maturation. Genetic factors obviously play a major role in this early motor development. However, cultural and environmental factors (e.g., interactions between the child and others in his micro- and mesosystems and his unique developmental niche) are also extremely influential. For example, in many African and West Indian cultures, parents and extended family members place considerable importance on sitting and walking and actually provide early "formal handling" experiences that stimulate these behaviors. Examples of formal handling practices used by West Indian mothers in Jamaica for helping their infants develop their motor skills are shown in Figure 4.3.

Beginning with stretching exercises shortly after birth, parents gradually introduce other activities (e.g., placing infants in a sitting position or playing games that allow them to practice jumping and walking skills) (Hopkins & Westra, 1988; Super, 1981). !Kung infants of the Kalahari Desert also walk earlier than Western infants. In this case, it may be because they spend a great deal of time in slings that keep them upright and give them considerable freedom of movement (Konner, 1976).

Several of these handling practices have been found to be associated with maternal expectations. For example, in a study of Jamaican mothers and their infants, Hopkins and Westra (1990) asked mothers to estimate when they felt their one-month-old infants would be able to sit, crawl, and walk without assistance. Most reported that they planned to provide their infants with a variety of formal handling routines ranging from gentle massage to vigorous bouncing and stepping exercises. Results were compared with those of English mothers, who provided no formal handling for their infants. Findings supported a self-fulfilling prophecy—that is, when handling practices were conducted daily, Jamaican mothers' predictions were accurate as to when these motor skills would develop. English infants, on the other hand, learned to sit and walk somewhat later than did Jamaican infants. Time of crawling did not differ significantly between the two groups.

Dennis and Dennis (1940), in a classic study of infant motor development, disclosed that Hopi Indian children, though traditionally strapped to a cradleboard for much of their first year, still walked at approximately the same time as did children in other countries (e.g., early in their second year). In related research, infants reared in several European cities generally started

FIGURE 4.3 Handling Practices Used by West Indian Mothers

Source: From "Maternal Handling and Motor Development: An Intracultural Study" by B. Hopkins and T. Westra, 1988, *Genetic, Social and General Psychology Monographs, 14,* pp. 385, 388, 389. Adapted with permission of the Helen Dwight Reid Educational Foundation. Published by Heldref Publications, 1319 Eighteenth St., NW, Washington, DC 20036-1802. Copyright © 1988.

walking at about twelve to fifteen months, in spite of any significant differences in the assistance they received for this activity.

Lack of stimulation or encouragement may also result in a delay in walking. For example, Dennis (1973) observed orphans in two Iranian institutions who spent the majority of their time lying on their backs in their cribs and were never propped upright. The infants rarely interacted with adults, and when taken from their cribs were usually placed on the floor and left by themselves. Findings indicated that very few of them ever crawled in the typical hands-and-knees fashion. Instead, they tended to move themselves along the floor in a sitting position. None of the one- and two-year-olds could walk, and among the three- and four-year-olds, only 15 percent were able to walk at all without help.

Play and Physical Development

While play may look like a simple activity to adults, it is a highly complex and intricate achievement for a young child. For example, physical play

Native American children strapped to cradleboards during their first year walk at about the same time as other children. (© Lionel Delevingne/Stock Boston)

builds on the relationship among a child's cognitive abilities, social experiences, and cultural context. The simplest, least developed form of play is called **functional play** and consists of a child making *simple, repetitive movements with or without an object.* In **constructive play,** children learn how to *physically manipulate objects in order to construct or create something.* In most cultures, young children are encouraged to play with blocks or similar objects; in addition to being fun, this play also teaches children how to approach and solve problems.

In a study of Kpelle children in Sierra Leone, Lancy (1980) noted that families found a variety of ways to combine constructive play with physical work involving *nee-pele* (make-believe), *sua-kpe-pele* (hunting play), *mana-pele* (dancing and playing musical instruments), and *kppa-kolo-pele* (adult play). As in many other countries, play was used by adults to teach children the importance of play and work, while stimulating coordination, encouraging imagination, and fostering interpersonal relationships.

It is apparent that play is a necessary part of a child's normal physical development and an important expression of cultural heritage. In addition to developing gross motor skills through play and other activities, children also acquire fine motor skills (e.g., tying shoelaces, buttoning shirts, making towers out of blocks, cutting paper, coloring within the lines, and putting together simple jigsaw puzzles). Play is also a critical part of a child's social development and receives extended treatment in Chapter 8.

Handedness

Another topic associated with the development of fine and gross motor skills during infancy and early childhood is hand preference. **Handedness** refers to *the tendency to use one hand in preference to the other in writing and other activities*. Most children tend to show such a preference by about six months, with this tendency becoming stronger in early childhood.

Right-handedness appears to be historically dominant in most of the world's cultures. In fact, ultrasound images and intrauterine photographs have vividly demonstrated that even before culture and parental training can possibly have an effect, more fetuses suck the thumb on their right hand than on the left. In addition, the fact that infants between the ages of five months and two years show a universal preference for the right hand suggests a strong genetic factor.

Annett (1985) developed a model that demonstrated that handedness is associated with a single gene believed responsible for both right-handedness and the lateralization, or specialization, of language in the left cerebral hemisphere of the brain. The Human Genome Project, cited at the beginning of this chapter, is expected to add even more information to our understanding of the relationship between genes and handedness.

In addition to the universal genetic predisposition for right-handedness, there seems to be a strong cultural preference as well. When we look at different languages, we find that many meanings for the word *left* involve negative connotations or stereotypes. For example, the French word *gauche* means both "left" and "clumsy." People in many countries are deliberately discouraged from using their left hand at all. In Africa, the Middle East, India, and Asia, there is strong social pressure against using the left hand for many activities, because it is used in personal cleansing and other use is viewed as unhygienic. Thus, it would be considered rude to extend one's left hand to a merchant when waiting for change or to pass a drink to a friend or relative with the left hand. Likewise, in some of the areas of the world just mentioned, it would be unwise to use your left hand to pass your driver's license to a police officer about to cite you for a traffic violation. Such insensitivity may cause your fine to increase substantially! Yet, these cultural preferences can change over time, as a study by Takeshi Hatta (1994) demonstrated. Hatta found that the rate of left-handedness was greater among young Japanese women whose parents had been born after World War II compared to women whose parents were born before World War II. The author of the study concludes that Japanese society has become more tolerant of left-handedness among girls and women, perhaps because of increased Western influence after World War II.

Because most people are right-handed, and on the basis of the approach we take in this book, we suggest that ecocultural systems (including physical settings, family customs, and cultural traditions) tend to establish developmental niches that nurture a genetic predisposition toward left hemispheric dominance, or right-handedness. This perspective receives some support from a thorough review of studies on identical and fraternal twins (Laland, Kumm, van Horn, and Feldman, 1995). The review suggests that variation in handedness results from a combination of both cultural and genetic factors. In this regard, Janssen (2000) has proposed a theory of human handedness that takes into account various factors in the development of individual left- or right-handedness. Imitation and social learning as well as cultural childrearing practices play a role. If a parent or sibling is left-handed and left-handedness is culturally acceptable, the chance to observe and imitate left-handed behaviors influences a child's hand-preference to some extent. Moreover, Janssen suggests that the interaction between childrearing style, cultural values, and the child's physical predisposition for handedness may not only influence the child's motor skill development but extend to neurological, language, social, and personality development. This ecological view certainly presents an interesting area for future cross-cultural investigation.

Middle Childhood

Throughout the world, individuals passing through **middle childhood** (*approximately ages four to eleven*) experience changes in physical development that seem slower and less uneventful than in some periods of the lifespan (e.g., early childhood and adolescence). In most societies, school occupies most of children's time and energy, enabling them to build on existing patterns of physical and motor development. However, this does not mean they are any less active. Just watch children between the ages of six and eleven in almost any city or village in the world as they leave school at the end of the day. You will see young people running onto playgrounds, riding bicycles, climbing trees, wrestling, and playing tag and other games. Outside of school, they often take private lessons to learn how to play musical instruments, dance, swim competitively, or participate in group sports like soccer, baseball, and badminton. While possessing a seemingly unlimited supply of energy and excitement, their rapidly growing and changing bodies soon move them from the isolated world of the nursery and day care to the world of the school child.

Physical Growth and Change

During middle childhood, the growth rate begins to slow down a little. Baby fat gradually disappears, and children become slimmer and more muscular. They can run faster, fly a kite higher, and throw a ball farther and with greater accuracy than they once did. As a result of mastering new skills, children are able to compete more effectively against their peers in such board games as chess, backgammon, and mah-jongg.

The average six-year-old child adds about fourteen inches and thirty-five pounds by the age of twelve. For both boys and girls, this results in an average gain of two to three inches in height and seven pounds in weight per year during middle childhood. This pattern continues until the adolescent growth spurt, which typically begins at about age ten or so for girls and twelve for boys.

In addition, in middle childhood growth rates vary with ethnicity and socioeconomic level. For example, in a worldwide sample of eight-year-olds, the mean height of the shortest children included those primarily from Southeast Asia, Oceania, and South America, and the tallest were those most notably from Northern and Central Europe, Eastern Australia, and North America (Meredith, 1978). Although genetic differences account for some of this diversity, environmental influences also appear to play a role. While underweight and malnourished children encounter considerable health risks and obstacles to normal physical, social, and cognitive development, overweight children experience unique problems too, particularly as regards childhood obesity.

Childhood Obesity

Over the past three decades, health care professionals in the United States have become alarmed about the growing problem of obesity in middle childhood. This topic has important implications for the consideration of physical growth and development.

Obesity in middle childhood can lead to serious physical and emotional problems later in life. It can cause considerable respiratory and cardiovascular problems and can trigger excessive dieting and consequent complications. In addition, children often reject and ridicule their overweight peers, which negatively affects their self-esteem. **Obesity** is generally considered to be *body weight that is 20 percent or more over the recommended weight for one's age, gender, and body type.* Even with all the attention given to the importance of keeping one's weight under control, research shows that the incidence of obesity among children has increased dramatically within the last several decades. Cole and Cole (2001) point to a 50 percent increase among six- to eleven-year-old children and almost as large an increase among twelve- to seventeen-year-old adolescents. The greatest increase for children in the United States has been among Mexican American and African American children and for those living in low-income families.

What causes obesity? Many researchers believe it is caused by a combination of genetic and sociocultural factors as demonstrated in the Human Genome Project. However, this genetic explanation cannot explain obesity entirely; various social factors must also be taken into consideration. For one thing, children often get mixed signals in their culture. In North American society, there is a preoccupation with physical appearance, and being tall and slim are seen as acceptable forms of beauty. Furthermore, children are likely to observe their parents worrying about overeating and gaining weight. This, in turn, can add to children's confusion about how much food they should eat. There is also a tendency in some cultures for parents to overfeed their children in infancy and early childhood. This is often done in an effort to pacify restless children and as a way to cope with parents' busy schedules. Given the amount of food served in many family restaurants—the "all you can eat" specials—it is not surprising that many overweight children exist, particularly in North America.

Another social factor that contributes to obesity is lack of exercise. This may seem paradoxical, since we think of children as running around and being involved in the activities mentioned earlier. But while many children are active, a substantial number of children stay at home spending many hours taking care of younger siblings, playing video games, watching television, or, more recently, "surfing" the Internet. As a result, many school-age children do not get nearly enough exercise. Kimm and her colleagues (2005), in a nine-year long longitudinal study of over 2000 white and African American girls, from ages 9 and 10 to ages 18 and 19, reported that they had a pronounced decline in physical activity while their rate of overweight and obesity doubled. The authors recommended that even modest amounts of activity during adolescence could help prevent obesity development and the onset of adult chronic diseases. They also stressed that this problem is not confined to North America but, in fact, represents a "global obesity epidemic."

Refining Motor Skills

During the school years, children become better coordinated. They are able to master many of the skills they could not manage when they were younger. This is due, in part, to increased levels of myelin in the brain, which is manufactured at a faster rate between the ages of six and eight. Thus, in many Western societies, eight- and nine-year-olds are able to ride a bike, skip rope, draw, write or print, type at a computer keyboard, and play a variety of sports. In other parts of the world, a particular child's ecocultural system and developmental niche emphasize different skills. For instance, in Malaysia children engage in many of the same activities just mentioned but are also taught how to perform ethnic dances, weave intricate baskets, spin colorful tops, build and fly their own kites, and play soccer, cricket, or *sepak-takrow* with a bamboo ball.

Are physical activities like these dependent on age, experience, and gender—or a combination of all three? Does culture influence the types of motor skills taught to children of one gender or the other? Unfortunately, there is relatively little cross-cultural research focusing on such questions; this suggests the need for future investigation.

Adolescence

Much of the change associated with physical development during adolescence centers on **puberty,** *a period of biological transition between childhood and adulthood lasting approximately one to two years.* The physical and physiological changes during puberty are dramatic and have psychological and social consequences.

In the previous chapter, we introduced the topic of rites of passage and how cultures use these to prepare young people for the responsibilities of adulthood. In many traditional societies, these rites of passage are the public recognition of physical changes marking the transition from childhood to adulthood. Rites of passage also have important cultural and social functions. For instance, passage into "physical adulthood" often means that the individual is now deemed mature enough to take his adult place in the community, to marry, and/or to engage in sexual behavior. In short, with the onset of puberty, a person's ecological system changes at any and all levels.

In boys, transition from child to adult may be marked by several physical events, such as change in voice, emergence of pubic and facial hair, nocturnal ejaculation, or a sudden growth spurt and muscle development. The age at which a boy is granted "adult status" varies greatly by culture, mostly depending on which physical "marker" is used as indicator of physical adulthood. Nonetheless, recent research suggests that human sexual development, regardless of cultural context, may begin as early as age 10 (Herdt and McClintock, 2000).

The "landmark event" for girls marking the end of childhood is **menarche,** or *first menstruation.* The importance of viewing menarche within the cultural context and the ecocultural system is illustrated in a study of young girls living at low and high altitudes in Peru. Gonzales and Villena (1996) compared ten- to nineteen-year-old Peruvian girls living in the mountainous regions of Lima with girls of similar age in Cerro de Pasco. Results indicated that those living at higher elevations, where food sources are more limited, experienced the onset of menarche later than those living at sea level in Cerro de Pasco. The authors concluded that although nutrition is an important factor in determining the age at which menarche occurs, one's physical surroundings and developmental niche also need to be considered. Another example of this close interaction between environment and physical development is a study by Proos, Hofvander, and Tuvemo (1991). They observed that the drastic change in environment experienced by Indian girls adopted in Sweden led to an earlier onset of menarche. This earlier onset may affect the women's overall height by cutting short the period of physical growth.

Some cross-cultural researchers have focused on the extent to which exposure to modernization alters the menstrual experience of young girls. In one such study, Fitzgerald (1990) examined three Samoan communities as part of an ongoing stress and health project at the University of Hawaii. One community consisted of residents living in remote traditional villages on the island of Savaii in Western Samoa. A second community, experiencing rapid modernization, was made up of seven villages on the southern coast of the island of Tutuila in American Samoa. The third community was composed of individuals living in affluent neighborhoods in Honolulu, Hawaii. Ninety-three young girls reported on their family medical history, menstrual symptoms, menstrual beliefs and practices, and menstrual experiences. According to Fitzgerald, although the literal translation of the Samoan word for "menstruation" (*ma'imasina*) means "monthly illness," most Samoans view menstruation as a natural part of life—something given to them by God to prepare them for motherhood—over which they have no control. Findings revealed that the more exposed Samoans were to the influences of modernization, the more likely they were to report severe menstrual symptoms. This suggests that as cultures come into greater contact with each other, the values and beliefs of one tend to influence the behaviors of the other. In this case, the values and beliefs characteristic of the more modern society (Honolulu) tended to affect the menstrual experience of the Samoan islanders. Once again, this tends to support the validity of studying behavior from the perspective of the recurring themes of the ecological model and the developmental niche.

Early and Middle Adulthood

Although the process of aging actually begins early in the lifespan, physical growth nears completion by the end of adolescence or the beginning of the early adulthood years. As we have seen in earlier periods, biological processes occur slowly at first but then advance more quickly. For example, around the age of twenty-one, slow, continuous changes begin to affect the functioning of the human body. Muscular strength, reaction time, sensory acuity, and heart function approach their peak through the mid-twenties and then, depending on diet and exercise, slowly decline thereafter. By the time people reach their forties, they are well aware of the age-related changes affecting them and their bodies. (Doesn't this discussion make you feel good?)

The Experience of Menopause

A major event for women during these years is the experience of menopause. Since menopause, like menarche, is a universal event, it would be easy to assume that all women experience it in the same way. However, based on our earlier discussions of Bronfenbrenner's ecological model, we would expect that cultural values, expectations, and context would contribute strongly to shaping the experience—and they do. For example, in previous decades, Europeans and North Americans, among others, frequently described menopause as a "change of life." Many early television programs stereotyped elderly and middle-aged women as moody, unpredictable, and depressed. The picture of menopause as presented in contemporary print media does not seem to have significantly improved. While the frequency of articles on menopause has increased, the information is often insufficient, treated as a negative experience or disease needing medical treatment, frequently containing contradictions and inconsistencies, and ignoring or giving little attention to such factors as race and ethnicity, lifestyle differences, stress, or aging.

Today, most North Americans and, in fact, people in many other countries view menopause very differently. Women's own expectations have changed, and for some, menopause is seen as a liberating experience. Part of this new view can be attributed to changing cultural views of aging. For research that views menopause from a contextual analysis, see Anderson (1999).

In Israel, interviews conducted among five groups of Israeli women reveal different reactions to menopause (Datan, Antonovsky, & Moaz, 1984). These researchers interviewed four groups of middle-aged Israeli women from central Europe, Turkey, Persia, and North Africa and a fifth group of Moslem Arab women. The women from European and Arab cultures reported experiencing the fewest problems, viewing menopause as simply one more event in their lives. By comparison, women raised in the three remaining cultures reported greater stress related to menopause.

In a cross-sectional study of Japanese women between forty-four and fifty-five years of age, Lock (1991) indicated that only about 12 percent reported experiencing hot flashes, compared with 47 percent of Canadian women. Less than one fifth of Japanese women had experienced a hot flash, compared with nearly three quarters of Canadian women. In fact, there is no specific word or phrase in the Japanese language for "hot flash." However, Japanese subjects reported more physical discomforts (e.g., headaches, ringing in the ears, dizziness, and other complaints not usually associated with menopause).

In an interesting cultural interpretation, some Japanese government officials have suggested that such complaints occur more often among women with little to occupy their time (e.g., no children or work), and even went as far as proposing that caring for elderly parents would fill this idle time and thereby minimize such complaints (Lock, 1991). This topic would certainly make an interesting cross-cultural study.

More recently, Robinson (2002) reviewed cross-cultural studies conducted in Israel, North America, Japan, Peru, the Yucatan, and the Greek island of Evia. Results indicate that there are enormous differences in the experience of menopause among women in the same culture and among women in different cultures. The author concludes further that, indeed, menopausal symptoms are the result of not only physical factors but also psychological and cultural influences. From these examples it becomes clear that it is not only the physical change during menopause itself but also the cultural view of menopause that shapes a woman's experience. Is menopause just another "developmental stage" or is menopause an "illness" that can be treated (e.g., with hormone therapy)? If menopause is an "illness" that warrants treatment, should we begin to consider hormone treatment for puberty as well, with its many discomforting symptoms (e.g., acne, mood swings, and change in body shape)?

Later Adulthood

The term **senescence** is used to describe *the process of biological change associated with normal aging.* While the rate of senescence varies individually, socially, and culturally, few people (if they live long enough) can escape the aging process.

A better understanding of lifespan development, along with advances in medical technology, has helped to expand the life expectancy of the world's people. For example, in the United States, nearly 14 percent of the population is sixty-five or older. In addition, the first of 77 million "baby-boomers" (those born between 1946 and 1960) turned sixty in January of 2006; and by 2030, one in five Americans will be sixty-five or older including as many as 380,000 people over the age of one hundred. The fact that they are among the largest, healthiest, and best educated group of Americans ever to move through and beyond their fifties will present many challenges as well as opportunities to families, businesses, policymakers, and health care providers, and have significant impact on American culture and values for many years to come.

Cultural Images of Aging

What images do we have of people when they grow old? What role does culture play in shaping the way we think about aging? Certainly in many Western cultures, notably North America, stereotypes have portrayed the elderly as frail individuals, usually in poor health and unable to take care of themselves. We now know that these stereotypes do not fit the current population of elderly, many of whom remain active, independent, and in good health well into their eighties and nineties and beyond.

It is interesting to note how North American stereotypes of the elderly have influenced societal views of the aging process, especially when we consider how the elderly are perceived and treated in other countries. For example, in Brazil, Colombia, Japan, China, and many other collectivist societies, elderly people are revered and given high social status. Family members look to them as wise and knowledgeable members of the society with much to offer. Rather than attempting to push back the aging process and appear young, many look forward to aging. In traditional Native American culture, old age represents an important time of life, when a number of milestones have been attained. Old age is given prominence; elders teach tribal customs to children through the use of campfire stories, songs, games, and dances.

Aging—A Positive View

People are living longer than ever before, many, as we have just noted, over the age of one hundred. In fact, several remote areas of the world have become known for having large numbers of people who live unusually long lives. In parts of China and the former Soviet Union, senescence is postponed well into late adulthood, and a disciplined, highly active lifestyle is routine. Why do these people live to such advanced ages? Some commonly cited reasons for longevity include diet (lots of fresh vegetables, little meat and fat), mutual interdependence, family and neighborhood cohesiveness, genetic predisposition, and regular exercise. Whether it be regular morning tai chi exercises, meditation, walks, or hobbies, maintaining an active lifestyle is a way of life for most of these elderly persons.

Tse and Bailey (1992) designed a study to investigate the value of tai chi in promoting postural control (balance) among elderly, but healthy, adults. Tai chi is a Chinese method of exercise and self-defense emphasizing

Tai chi, the popular Chinese method of exercise and self-defense, emphasizes coordination, balance, and effortlessness. (© Fritz Hoffman/The Image Works)

balance, coordination, and effortlessness. Their subjects consisted of six men and three women (aged sixty-five to eighty-four), who practiced tai chi, and a similar group of six men and three women (aged sixty-six to eighty-six), who did not practice the Chinese method. Each participant completed a series of balance tests and a questionnaire concerning wellness issues and was measured for posture control. The tests included being able to maintain one's balance while standing on a single right and then left leg with eyes open, standing on a single right and then left leg with eyes closed, and doing a heel-to-toe walking exercise with both eyes open. Findings supported the researchers' hypothesis that those who practiced tai chi would perform better on the tests than those who did not practice such exercises. The better performance was attributed to a long-established connection between tai chi, improved balance, and self-control. The study suggested that tai chi practice might have therapeutic value in helping to fight disease, lethargy, and listlessness.

It is easy to see how a preferred type of exercise is shaped by cultural practices and traditions. The previous example describes tai chi as a method of exercise that is deeply rooted in the tradition of Eastern martial arts. Similarly, the bicycle is a common and practical form of transportation for people of all ages in the Netherlands. At the same time, it provides daily exercise. Aside from providing the opportunity for exercise in older age, the cultural environment may also provide the motivation for participation in physical activity. A study of older Australian-born and overseas-born Australians found a surprising difference between the groups in their motivation to participate in exercise. Overall, overseas-born adults were more motivated to participate in a community exercise program. Specific motivators for this group were factors such as the opportunity to socialize with peers and the feeling of accomplishment (Kirkby, Kolt, & Habel, 1998), whereas these factors were of little or no importance to Australian-born participants. The authors do not speculate about the cultural factors that may account for differences in exercise motivation in older adults. Nonetheless, at the very least, these results imply that not having been born in Australia is related to greater motivation to exercise in older age.

In a study of Chinese "oldest old" (ages 80 to 105) Yi, Yuzhi, and George (2003) identified social and economic factors that seemed to account for difference in physical performance, cognitive function, and self-reported health between men and women. Chinese females (more often widowed, illiterate, and economically dependent on family than their male counterparts) showed a dramatic decline in both physical and mental activities. This relation between social factors and physical and mental fitness is underlined by Silverstein and Parker's (2002) study with Swedish older adults. The authors found that maximizing activity participation by older adults is an adaptive strategy to compensate for social and physical deficits in later life. The authors point out that this strategy seemed particularly successful for older adults who had suffered physical impairments.

Studies like these and others suggest that contrary to many myths, aging is not synonymous with disease. We should not assume that illness is a necessary outcome of living longer. What is important to remember is that each culture has its own prescription for growing old, and that although it may be different from our own, no one particular approach is necessarily right or wrong, it's simply different. If we look closely at other cultures and the way in which their societies function, we may learn many lessons that could be positively applied to our own lives.

◇ SUMMARY

In this chapter we discussed the Human Genome Project and cultural similarities and differences in physical development at various stages of the lifespan. We gave attention to important issues of prenatal care, including exposure to environmental toxins and to alcohol (fetal alcohol syndrome), as potential causes of birth defects. Cultural differences in the role of nutrition and its relationship to health and physical development were also considered. Special emphasis was devoted to the interactions between culture and the development of motor skills, play, and coordination, including hand preference, in early childhood. The physical changes of adolescence, especially puberty and menarche, were viewed from a cross-cultural perspective. Finally, we explored cultural reactions to changes associated with the transition to middle and later adulthood, including menopause and senescence. As in previous chapters, our discussion placed these topics within the context of our recurring themes: the cultural-ecological model, developmental niche, and individualism-collectivism.

◇ STUDY QUESTIONS

Describe the Human Genome Project and its importance to understanding human development.

Explain how the ecological model and the developmental niche combine to account for physical development across the lifespan.

Discuss varying views on menstruation and menopause, and explain how cultural views affect later physical, cognitive, and social development.

◇ FURTHER READINGS

Michael Brannigan. (Ed.). (2004). *Cross-Cultural Biotechnology*. Rowman & Littlefield. Fifteen essays from international academics and practitioners address a broad range of legal, ethical, and social issues in biotechnology, underscoring the relevance of cultural values. Topics include the International Human Genome Project and research ethics in East Asia.

Susan Garrett (1998). *Miles to Go: Aging in Rural Virginia.* Charlottesville, VA: University of Virginia Press.

This narrative account describes the lives of elderly families and individuals in rural Virginia. The author describes the physical, economic, social, and psychological challenges these elderly encounter in their specific ecological systems.

Daniel B. Kessler and Peter Dawson. (Eds.). (1998). *Failure to Thrive and Pediatric Undernutrition: A Transdisciplinary Approach.* Baltimore, MD: Paul H. Brookes.

A variety of contributions from different disciplines address issues related to infants and children who fail to grow according to age and gender standards. Chapters discuss underlying issues, such as nutrition, medical aspects, developmental issues, community services, and social policies. The interdisciplinary structure of this book nicely demonstrates the interrelation of levels within the ecological system.

Jaipaul L. Roopnarine, James E. Johnson, and Frank H. Hooper. (Eds.). (1994). *Children's Play in Diverse Cultures.* Albany: State University of New York.

An extremely interesting and engaging illustration of children's play around the world. An added feature is the way the authors relate play to the cultural-ecological concepts in Bronfenbrenner's model.

James Shreeve (2006). *The Greatest Journey.* National Georgraphic, 209, 3, 60–73.

A very readable account of genes, DNA, migration, and the origins of modern human life and culture.

The Human Genome Project.

For information about this project—its history, research, publications, educational resources, and new programs based on data and resources from The Human Genome Project, The Microbial Project, and systems biology—go to this website: http://www.ornl.gov/sci/techresources/ Human_Genome/home.shtml.

NICHD Strategic Plan 2000: From Cells to Selves: Biobehavioral Development.

Detailed information is provided on (1) the institute's goals, including an understanding of the biobehavioral bases of developmental continuities and discontinuities from birth through parenthood and development of individuals with disabilities and chronic diseases, (2) research techniques and strategies, including data collection and analysis related to neural networks and dynamic systems for analysis of development, animal models, functional neuroimaging, and brain tissue banks, and (3) training and education programs. Can be ordered free of charge from Government Printing Office, Washington, D.C.

◇ DEVELOPMENTAL ANALYSIS

CULTURAL ASPECTS OF PHYSICAL GROWTH AND DEVELOPMENT

Of course I don't remember much about my prenatal period or even my early infancy, but my parents told me it was quite normal and healthy. My height and weight were above average. My motor skills were quite good, and I began to walk earlier than my peers, at about nine months. This meant I was continually exploring my environment and often getting into places I shouldn't have been. For example, my parents once found me stuck behind the furnace and the basement wall when I was eleven months old! My brother and sister walked later—at about twelve and fourteen months, respectively—and didn't get into as much trouble early on. My parents were both right-handed, but I have always used my left hand for most things, including writing. My teachers tried to change this while I was still young. However, I was stubborn and am still a "lefty."

Living on a farm, my mother prepared hearty meals. When I entered middle childhood, I wasn't obese, but I was what some might call "chubby." However, as I entered high school and began playing sports, as well as going through my adolescent growth spurt, I lost much of this excess weight. As an adult (and as a mother), I've tried to prepare and eat well-balanced meals. I also make every effort to exercise regularly.

I experienced menarche a little earlier than my girlfriends (at around eleven-and-a-half years of age), and went through the early stage of menopause at age 49. Other than irregular menstrual cycles and occasional insomnia, it wasn't a difficult experience for me.

As I said earlier, I am now 67 years old and in the early years of later adulthood. My husband and I are quite healthy. We both look at this stage of life very positively. We are retired and spend a lot of our time doing activities we enjoy, such as volunteering, traveling, and visiting with our children and grandchildren. We recently took three of our grandchildren to Disney World and just returned from a photo safari in Zambia. We enjoy our travels to other cultures and countries—eating the local foods, interacting with people, and learning about their lives. My husband's parents are no longer with us, but I help care for my aging mother, who you will read more about in Chapter 10.

CHAPTER FIVE

CULTURE, LANGUAGE, AND COGNITION

Deratu lives in one of the oldest nations in Africa—Ethiopia, a Greek word meaning "sunburned faces." Like almost 80 percent of the people in this nation in northeastern Africa, she lives in a rural village where her family grows sugarcane and raises goats and chickens. Deratu, like more than half the children in the country, does not attend school nor does she have many toys. What she needs to know, she learns in an informal manner from the work she has been assigned according to her age and gender, since this is the way new members of each generation learn what is expected of them. At five years of age, she helped her mother fetch water and gather wood for the fire. Now, at the age of eleven, she helps with the cooking and cares for her younger brothers and sisters. In just a few years, at about fifteen, she will start a family of her own. Deratu's learning is very much a social activity guided by her mother, who teaches her the important cultural and practical lessons she will need in order to survive in her rural Ethiopian village.

Maria, two weeks away from her twelfth birthday, lives in Brazil, in São Paulo, the seventh most populated city in the world. Brazil is the largest country in South America, occupying almost half the continent. She has attended the country's free public schools since she was six years old. Maria's parents and teachers have always described her as a naturally curious and inquisitive child. Learning how to read and write came easily to her. As a newly emerging adolescent, she is beginning to look more abstractly at the world and is using more logical problem-solving skills than she would have been able to use just two years ago. Now, Maria spends much time with her elderly grandmother. Although the girl sometimes gets impatient with the grandmother's deliberate speech, she enjoys the stories of the "old days" and admires her grandmother's excellent memory of even small details.

Deratu and Maria live worlds apart, physically as well as psychologically. In this chapter, we look at culture, cognition, and language and their effects on development. We consider two opposing theoretical viewpoints and some of the cross-cultural evidence that supports or refutes these views. As you progress through this chapter, you will be better able to understand and explain the cognitive and linguistic behavior of these two young women, using key concepts from these theories.

First, let us explain what we mean when we use the terms *language* and *cognition*. **Cognition** can be thought of as *the act or process of obtaining knowledge, including perceiving, recognizing, reasoning, and judging* (Gander & Gardiner, 1981). Cognition involves thinking, knowing, remembering, categorizing, and problem solving. **Language** refers to *a system of symbols that is used to communicate information and knowledge.* How does thinking affect language? How does language affect thinking? How do they influence each other? Later in this chapter, we discuss the links between cognition and language as they occur throughout life. Two of the major theoretical frameworks discussed in Chapter 2 will guide us in this discussion: Piaget's cognitive developmental theory, and Vygotsky's concept of the "zone of proximal development."

◇ THE LANGUAGE–COGNITION–CULTURE LINK

One of the early debates linking culture, language, and cognition surrounds the question "Do people who speak different languages think about and experience the world differently?" If so, are these differences in thinking due to the structural and lexical (language or vocabulary) differences in the languages spoken? Linguists Benjamin Whorf and Edward Sapir are the original proponents of this line of thought, which is known as the "linguistic relativity hypothesis." Elgin (2000) provides an example by comparing the sentence "I was riding a horse" in English and Navajo. She asserts that the most likely translation in Navajo would result in "The horse and I were moving about." It is easy to see that these two sentences describe the relationship between horse and rider rather differently. The English version portrays the rider as the active subject of the action and the horse as the object that endures being ridden. In Navajo, the act of riding is a joint endeavor without expressed subject–object relation. A Whorfian would conclude that Navajo speakers perceive and experience relationship with animals (horses, in this case) differently than English speakers. If people's thinking really is relative to their language, perhaps we could explain cultural differences in cognition by looking at the differences in the languages spoken in different cultures. Unfortunately, research results on the linguistic relativity hypothesis are not that clear-cut. A few supporting findings exist, but there are seemingly just as many findings that contradict Sapir's and Whorf's ideas.

Researchers have come to agree on a less absolute version of the linguistic relativity hypothesis. They believe now that thinking is not entirely
determined by the language we speak. Rather, *how* we talk about people,
objects, or events may make us pay more or less attention to certain aspects
of these events, people, or objects. In different languages, we find different
linguistic elements that make it easier to communicate about certain events
or objects. For example, English has a progressive form that allows English
speakers to distinguish between ongoing events and events that have concluded ("I worked all afternoon" versus "I have been working all afternoon").
Some languages (e.g., German and Hebrew) do not have a progressive form.
Speakers of these languages are still able to communicate about the temporal
sequence and duration of events, but they have to make a greater effort to
do so. A Whorfian may argue that distinguishing between the duration of
events may not be as important in German- and Hebrew-speaking cultures
but is more important in English-speaking cultures. In other words, if something is encoded in a culture's language, it must be important. This milder
form of the linguistic relativity hypothesis led many institutions in the United
States, in recent years, to establish "politically correct" language. Many view
this as a well-intended effort to change cultural meaning by changing language;
others disagree.

What is Vygotsky's position on these issues? He claimed that cultural
influence, mental processes, and language are dynamic processes that occur
simultaneously. This means that constant social interaction with those
around us helps shape the quality of mental abilities and language at various
ages. With this theoretical perspective in mind, Vygotsky coined the expression, *"talking to learn."* By this he meant that as children verbally interact
with others, they internalize language and use it to organize their thoughts
(Vygotsky, 1978).

Other researchers go even further and suggest that as parents interact
with their children, the children learn language and become socialized into
a particular set of cultural values and beliefs (Greenfield & Cocking, 1994;
Budwig, Wertsch, & Uzgiris, 2000). For example, in her extensive studies of
language acquisition in a Samoan village, Ochs (1988) showed the presence
of two major ways of speaking the language: "good speech" and "bad
speech." The latter contains fewer consonants and is mainly spoken in informal contexts. Good speech is used when speaking to strangers or in formal
settings, such as schools, church services, and when talking to a person of
high status. Along with learning both "good speech" and "bad speech," Samoan
children learn about the social contexts in which using each "language" is
appropriate. An interesting ongoing debate in the United States surrounds
what used to be called "Black Vernacular English" or "Ebonics." Ebonics is
spoken almost exclusively among African-Americans and is learned in informal contexts rather than in formal schooling (for an overview, see Fasold,
1999; Green, 2002).

A mother using scaffolding to help her child learn a new skill.
(Courtesy of authors)

Consequently, as children pass through Vygotsky's zone of proximal development in their language learning, they also acquire specific cognitive skills and they are becoming enculturated into a way of life. An effective method for achieving this is **scaffolding,** which refers to *the temporary support or guidance provided to a child by parents, older siblings, peers, or other adults in the process of solving a problem.* In construction, scaffolding is placed around a building to provide temporary support. Once completed, the scaffolding is removed, and the building is left to stand on its own. Similarly, the amount of scaffolding a child may need, in the form of guidance and support, depends on his or her ability to solve a problem alone. When the problem has been solved, the parent or others can remove the temporary scaffold (guidance) until help is again needed. An example of this guidance, or scaffolding, is illustrated in the photo.

Here a mother is shown mentoring her young son as he learns shapes of objects and how to place them in the right arrangement. As with reciprocal socialization, parents carefully observe their children's behavior to determine how much help they may need in completing a task or activity. As the activity continues, parents become increasingly sensitive to their children's needs, with the result that children do better on subsequent tasks.

In conclusion, the original question "Is cognition dependent on language or vice versa?" has lost some of its relevance. In shifting from studying language(s) to studying language and culture, researchers acknowledge that both language and cognition are cultural phenomena. Consequently, language and culture are both part of a person's ecological system, where they contribute jointly to an individual's experience.

◇ INFANCY

Early Cognitive Development in Cultural Contexts

Piaget's and Vygotsky's interest in children's intellectual development as a focus for understanding how ideas change over time has drawn attention to several important issues related to the study of cultural differences. Over a period of thirty years, hundreds of researchers throughout the world have subjected these theories to careful scrutiny. The result is that the cross-cultural literature is immense and cannot be given here anything approaching the full attention it deserves. However, there are a number of excellent reviews that we recommend to those who would like to pursue the topic further. These include the work of Rogoff and Chavajay (1995), Bronfenbrenner (1993), and Segall, Dasen, Berry, and Poortinga (1999).

Of all Piaget's periods, the sensorimotor (occurring during infancy) has been the least studied from a cross-cultural perspective. A major reason is that observation methods and data-collecting techniques based on Piagetian concepts have only recently been standardized (Cole, 1995). One of the first cross-cultural studies of sensorimotor intelligence, using a scale developed by Corman and Escalona (1969), was conducted in Zambia (Goldberg, 1972). In general, while minor differences in behavior were noted (a slight advance for African infants over American at six months and a slight lag at nine and twelve months), Goldberg's findings tend to support Piaget's observations. A later study, conducted by Dasen and his colleagues (1978) on the Ivory Coast, suggested that African infants are advanced in their development of object permanency and other object-related cognitive behaviors. In yet another African study, this one conducted in Nigeria, Mundy-Castle & Okonji (1976) reported that while early manipulation of objects is similar for English and Igbo infants, important differences emerge in later interactions. What they have to say about these differences lends support to our emphasis on the importance of looking at cognitive behavior from an ecological point of view. Specifically, Mundy-Castle (1974) proposed that, after a certain age, European and American infants develop increased experiences in the handling of objects, with their attention "more often deliberately focused on objective properties of reality," whereas "African babies receive more social stimulation and early emotional support than European babies. The issue here is whether in the long run this divergent stimulation brings about a differential patterning of cognitive development, with Africans acquiring an intelligence that is more socially oriented, while Europeans acquire one that is more technologically oriented" (pp. 19–20). Although not specifically mentioned, since this was not the concern, the microsystem (family) and macrosystem (cultural values) have an important effect on the development of these cognitive behaviors.

In an early review of the cross-cultural literature, Dasen and Heron (1981) recognized that differences in the ages at which the substages of this period are attained do occur. However, they go on to stress that "in emphasizing these cultural differences, we may overlook the amazing commonality reported by all these studies: in fact, the qualitative characteristics of sensorimotor development remain nearly identical in all infants studied so far, despite vast differences in their cultural environments" (p. 305). Werner (1979), however, concluded that "even in the first stage of cognitive development, that of sensorimotor intelligence, culture seems to influence the rate of development to some extent, although admittedly, the similarity of structure and process is more striking than the differences. Content seems to have little relevance to the activation of sensorimotor schemata" (p. 216).

Language Acquisition

Along with these astounding cognitive developments, infancy is also marked by the first attempts to produce speech and language. Prominent linguist Noam Chomsky believes that language ability is "hardwired" into the human brain. When born, infants have the entire range of human language possibilities available to them. Which language(s) they acquire depends on the languages to which they are exposed on a regular basis. Recent research has shown that the babbling sounds of infants show remarkably similar patterns across many languages (MacNeilage & Davis, 2000). That means that all infants produce basic sounds such as "ma," "da," "fa," "ba," and so on. At this point, parents and others in the child's social environment begin to play a crucial role in language development. If the infant produces a sound that is part of the language spoken in her environment, this sound is acknowledged and celebrated as an attempt to communicate (those of you with children or young siblings can remember the excitement surrounding the first utterance of "Dada" or "Mama"). In contrast, any sound that is not part of the language environment is dismissed as babbling. Soon, due to lack of encouragement, the infant stops producing these nonrelevant sounds and focuses on combining relevant sounds into meaningful words. This account of language acquisition demonstrates Vygotsky's concept of scaffolding as well as the developmental niche. The caretakers, with their specific language characteristics, gently guide the child in developing the tools for communication within a specific cultural environment. Once the child has learned language to communicate, the basis for facilitating further cognitive and language development through social interaction is set.

Cross-cultural studies of language development show that the acquisition of certain linguistic elements, such as nouns, verbs, and grammatical structure, may vary (Casadio, Casadio, & Bates, 1999). A variety of studies examining the child's understanding and use of these language markers in Mandarin, Italian, and English showed the following general results: an overall bias in infancy to use nouns; no differences among children in these cultures in the time they begin to use nouns; and as the use of verbs varies across languages, so does the complexity of grammar and vocabulary.

These examples clearly demonstrate Vygotsky's claim that culture plays an active role in directing cognitive activity, even in infancy. Uzgiris and Raeff (1995), in a study of parent–child play interactions, stated that the variety of activities involved in play (e.g., talking, touching, and interacting) help children to learn skills that will enable them to be active participants in later cultural interactions. You can probably see how these ideas fit into and support our major themes. For example, it is within the family context (mesosystem) that early parent–child interactions take place. It is here that infants are introduced to activities (e.g., play and the use of language) that help prepare them for successful participation in the broader cultural contexts of the workplace (exosystem) and understanding of important values and attitudes (macrosystem).

Along similar lines, Bornstein and his colleagues (1992, 2000) looked at the various ways in which young infants in Argentina, France, Japan, and the United States were engaged in conversation by their mothers. In each of these cultures, mothers were more conversant with older children (thirteen-month-olds) than they were with younger children (five-month-olds), and exhibited a variety of cultural differences in interactions and speech patterns when talking with them. For example, expressive speech was employed more often by Japanese mothers than it was by French, Argentinean, or American mothers. Japanese mothers also were more responsive to their children when they were engaged in play with them, while American mothers responded more quickly and favorably to their children when they were playing with physical objects. This behavior on the part of Japanese mothers is compatible with their culture's stress on interdependence as an important value. (You may recall our earlier discussion in Chapter 3 of interdependence and Japanese childrearing practices, the second component of the developmental niche, as they relate to socialization.)

French, American, and Argentinean mothers, on the other hand, gave greater attention to speech that communicated information to their infant or child. This is consistent with other findings in cultures characterized by individualistic behavior, such as the three Western societies represented in this study. Still, not all of these mothers communicated the same kind of

Family playtimes provide opportunities for language acquisition and development.
(Courtesy of authors)

information to their children. For example, American mothers asked lots of questions, reflecting, in part, the view within American society that children are active participants in the learning process and often (as we saw in our earlier theoretical discussion) construct their own knowledge. In contrast, French mothers provided their infants and children with less stimulation but greater emotional support. Finally, Argentinean mothers appeared to be the most direct in their interactions with their children, which is indicative of a more authoritarian approach to dealing with children (Bornstein et al., 1992).

Early Second-Language Acquisition and Bilingualism

Contact between individuals who do not share the same language has become commonplace in today's world. For example, immigrants may share neighborhoods with natives, international business people may spend months abroad, and refugees may seek an escape from war in their own countries. The need to communicate in a new ecological system often makes it necessary to acquire a second language—to become bilingual. We raise this discussion on bilingualism in this chapter because it illustrates the dynamics of the language–cognition–culture link within a developmental framework. Questions such as "Do children learn a second language faster or better than adults?" or "Does the age at which a person learns the language affect how the language is learned?" have been at the center of bilingualism research for many years.

Developmental Factors

A popular view claims that before a certain age, children learn a language naturally and easily. This supports the idea of a "critical period" for second-language acquisition. The "critical period" lasts a specific number of years during which a second language can be learned as easily and as well as the first language. However, after this critical period, a language learner will have greater difficulty being able to acquire a second language to the same extent he or she did with the native language.

The age at which this critical period is supposed to occur is one of several points debated by those interested in language. Penfield and Roberts (1959) set the first ten years of life as the critical years for language acquisition. Others suggest that no distinctions in language learning can be found until after puberty. However, more recent studies contradict the "critical period" assumption entirely. In particular, Birdsong and Molis (2001) found that postpubescent learners were not always less proficient than younger learners, and, in fact, some late-learners spoke the language as well as native speakers. This should not be the case if a true "critical period" for language acquisition exists. Hakuta, Bialystok, and Wiley (2003) report similar results in their analysis of data from over two million Spanish and Chinese immigrants. They observed a decline in second-language proficiency among older immigrants, but the decline was not as steep as might be expected outside a "critical period."

Although research does not completely support the claim that second language acquisition is limited by a "critical period" of development, we can reliably assume that "younger is better" when it comes to learning a second language. After a thorough review of existing research, Ellis (1994) concludes that (1) children learn a second language faster than adults in the long-run, and (2) early second-language learners are more likely to have a nativelike pronunciation and proficiency than late-learners. Does this mean that taking language classes in high school or at the university are useless, as students cannot expect to become proficient in a second language? We now turn to the ecological model for additional insights on bilingualism.

Ecological Factors

An easily identifiable ecological factor that influences second-language acquisition is the learning context itself. Sociolinguists distinguish two types of situations in which a second language can be learned, including (1) natural settings and (2) educational settings. Examples of "natural settings" might include learning a second language as a native language, while living in a country—a setting familiar to most immigrants. A natural setting is also present when learning a second language that serves as the "official language" of a country. For example, India maintains English as one of two "official" languages (Hindi being the other), which makes it necessary for many Indians to learn English as their second language. "Official" languages other than the native languages can also be found in Zaire (French) and Nigeria (English). Yet, even in "natural bilingual settings," the ecological system may shape the mastery and fluency a child can achieve in both languages. Recall the story from the introduction of this book (p. 1), in which Harry Gardiner's three-year-old daughter, Alisa, becomes aware of speaking two languages. She explains: "I thought it was all one big language and Mommy understood some words and you understood others and I understood them all!" Clearly, the parents provided Alisa with an environment that fostered bilingualism. Kasuya (2002) agrees when stating, ". . . there are some socialization circumstances which almost always produce bilingual children, and other socialization circumstances that produce monolingual children. . . ." (p. 295). For example, such circumstances include how many family members communicate regularly in one or both languages and how accepted both languages are in the larger community.

Educational settings, on the other hand, are those in which formal second-language instruction takes place. The traditional "foreign language classroom," a common high school or college experience for many readers, comes immediately to mind. In addition, other educational settings might include bilingual education programs (for immigrant students in the United States) or education of ethnic minority children (in mainstream classrooms) as is common in Britain, Germany, and the Unites States.

A widespread assumption is that a second language is learned differently in different settings but that the patterns are somewhat unclear. We do know that it is not always the natural setting that leads to successful mastery of a second language. In fact, it is more likely that educational settings provide better opportunities to learn a second language, but only if they involve immersion in both the native and the second language. (e.g., bilingual programs). Speaking in "ecological terms," being immersed in a second language means language is used within multiple levels of the ecological model (e.g., school, work place, sports club, grocery store, and the media).

Related to these settings are important social and psychological factors. For example, there is general agreement among researchers that attitudes towards the target language and culture, as well as motivation to learn the language, have an enormous influence on second-language learning. In an illustrative study, Scully (2000) collected data from Filipinas (who married into Japanese households) about their attitudes towards Japanese culture and their success in learning Japanese. The author found that immersion in the culture and family life, as well as positive attitudes towards Japanese culture, predicted successful mastery of Japanese. See Table 5.1 for a depiction of the relationship of attitudes, motivation, and potential language learning outcome.

A possible answer to the question posed earlier in this section could be as follows: individuals who wish to learn a second language at an older age may indeed develop near-native proficiency if they can choose a favorable ecological system and have a positive attitude!

TABLE 5.1   Attitudes towards Native and Target Culture and Potential Outcomes of Second-Language Learning

ATTITUDES TOWARDS		POTENTIAL LEARNING OUTCOME
Native Culture	*Culture Target*	
+	+	Strong motivation and high proficiency in both languages
−	+	Strong motivation to learn target language, losing competence in the native language
+	−	Failure to acquire the second language, maintaining native language only
−	−	Failure to learn second language, and losing native language competence

+ positive attitudes
− negative attitudes

Source: Based on material from *The Study of Second-Language Acquisition* by R. Ellis, 1994. Oxford, U.K.: Oxford University Press.

◇ CHILDHOOD

As we move from the infancy and early childhood periods to the school-age period, the majority of cross-cultural Piagetian studies have focused on the transition from the preoperational period to the concrete operational period and the attainment of conservation (Gardiner, 1994). These studies show great variability in their findings (Rogoff, 1990). Fishbein (1984) points out that the research literature on these topics, published during the 1960s and early 1970s, reports consistently more advanced development in children from Westernized cultures when compared with children from developing cultures. However, Kamara and Easley (1977) have drawn attention to what they feel are three serious faults with the majority of this work. They express the following criticisms: (1) the study of thinking in both of these periods depends heavily on the use of language, yet most of the researchers who conducted these early studies had little knowledge of either the culture or the language of their subjects; (2) although Piaget favored the use of clinical interviews for gathering information about children's thinking processes, many of these investigators attempted to employ various types of standardized measures that required little use of language; and (3) accurate birth dates of subjects were not always available, and attempts to approximate ages were frequently off by as much as two years. These are serious criticisms still deserving of further attention on the part of cross-cultural researchers.

Stages of Knowing and Learning

In an extremely interesting and creative cross-cultural study, Nyiti (1982) attempted to avoid the pitfalls mentioned by Kamara by varying the languages used and by employing three of Piaget's well-known conservation tasks for substance, weight, and volume. Subjects consisted of ten- to eleven-year-old Micmac Indian children from Cape Breton Island in Canada and white English-speaking European-Canadians. The European-Canadian children were interviewed in English by an English-speaking European, while the Indian children were divided into two groups. In the first group, children were initially interviewed in English by an English-speaking European and later in Micmac by a Micmac-speaking Indian. In the second group, the order of interviewing was reversed. When the white European-Canadians and Micmac Indian children were tested in their native languages, their performances on conservation tasks were nearly identical and were comparable to those of other European, Canadian, and American children. However, when tested in English, Micmac Indian children performed at a significantly lower level than the other two groups. More important, the results indicated that nearly twice as many children at both age levels, when interviewed in their native language, were more capable of solving each of the three conservation tasks than were the Micmac Indian children interviewed in English. Nyiti concludes his study by stating that "it appears that cognitive structures described by Piaget are universal and represent a necessary condition for any successful acculturation [and] . . . while children in different cultures may have to deal with different realities, they all apply the same operations or processes of thought" (p. 165).

In an important and exhaustive review of cross-cultural findings on conservation task performance, Dasen (1972a) sorted results into four types, each supported by several studies. These included (1) cultural groups in which conservation appears at about the same time as it does in American and European children (i.e., Nigerians, Zambians, Hong Kong Chinese, Iranians, and Australian Aborigines), (2) groups in which conservation generally develops earlier (i.e., Asians), (3) cultures in which conservation appears as much as two to six years later (i.e., African and lower-socioeconomic-status Americans and Europeans), and (4) groups in which some individuals fail to engage in concrete operations even when they reach adolescence (i.e., Algerians, Nepalese, Amazon Indians, and Senegalese). What can we conclude from this vast amount of cross-cultural data? First, support for the universality of the structures or operations underlying the preoperational period is highly convincing. Second, whether or not these structures become functional and the rate at which this might take place appear strongly influenced by factors within one's culture—further validation of the importance of looking at cognitive development from the ecological systems approach.

Finally, it appears that although the rate and level of performance at which children move through Piaget's concrete operational period depend

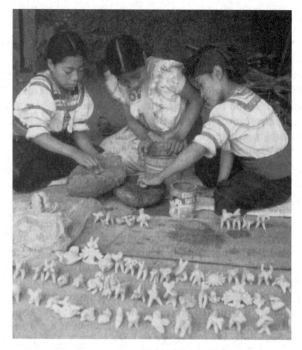

These young Zinacantean girls take great pleasure in making traditional pottery figures. (© D. Donne Bryant Stock)

on cultural experience, children in diverse societies still proceed in the same sequence he predicted (Mwamwenda, 1992; Segall, Dasen, Berry, & Poortinga, 1999). An early study by Price-Williams, Gordon, and Ramirez (1969) supports this view. For example, in one of their studies, conservation tasks were administered to two groups of Zinacantean children—half from pottery-making families and half from non–pottery-making families. Those children who had helped their families by working with clay showed signs of conservation at earlier ages than those without such experience.

Language Skills and Language Socialization

Jean Piaget's theory of cognitive development also provides clues as to how cognition and language might be related; that is, the ability to understand and use symbols requires certain cognitive skills. According to Piaget, a child first demonstrates the cognitive skills necessary for language use in the preoperational stage of cognitive development. The child needs to understand that different sounds and gestures do not simply stand alone but can serve as symbols for actual objects. Once grasping the concept of "symbols," she has acquired the necessary cognitive tools to use language as a form of communication about actual objects.

Suzuki (1998) gives another specific example of a particular cognitive skill and language competence. According to Piaget, one of the characteristics of preoperational thought is the inability to take another person's perspective. Instead, the child's thinking is guided only by how the world relates to him or her; for example, a child might answer the question "Why should you not hit your brother?" by saying "So that I won't get in trouble" instead of "Because he might get hurt." Suzuki argues that the ability to use passive construction in Japanese is closely related to a child's ability to go beyond preoperational egocentric thought. The results show that children in this study, between 3.4 and 6.9 years of age, interpreted passive sentence construction very differently, depending on their age and on their ability to adopt nonegocentric world views.

Childhood is the age in which socialization through language is most prominent. A good example of language socialization is a linguistic study by Brooks, Jia, Braine, and Da Graca Dias (1998). These researchers examined the ages at which Portuguese-, English-, and Mandarin-speaking children learn to distinguish between quantifiers such as "all" and "each" in their respective languages. The study shows that Portuguese and Mandarin Chinese speakers had learned to distinguish between "all" and "each" conceptually and linguistically by the time they were five years old. English speakers, on the other hand, were much less discriminating in their use of these quantifiers.

Once again, it is important to keep in mind the larger ecological systems in which languages are embedded. For example, China and Portugal can be considered as cultures with more collectivist belief systems (macrosystem) than the United States. The words "all" and "each" refer to objects or activities that are either collectively shared or not shared. Children in these cultures may learn words and concepts representing a relationship between "individual" and "collective" earlier than children in more individualistic societies. Eventually, through learning language and using language in social interaction, Portuguese and Chinese children also learn about social relationships that are considered important in their collectivist societies. Although certainly a simplified explanation, it may clarify the idea of language as a contributing influence to both cognitive development and socialization.

Another cognitive and linguistic challenge that faces many children between the ages of three and ten is learning how to read and write. If we consider the vast array of languages and how they are expressed in oral and written form, we can guess that the difficulties confronting children in their quest to become literate also vary greatly. For example, many European languages are phonetically based, meaning that a symbol primarily represents a sound rather than a meaningful word. Words are combinations of symbols and, therefore, sounds. Individually, the symbols and sounds d-e-s-e-r-t are not meaningful. However, when combined, they obtain meaning. This specific attribute of language allows the novice reader who knows the symbol and each sound associated with it, to find the meaning of the word by "sounding" out each symbol. This is difficult to do in languages such as

A young Chinese boy practices calligraphy. (© Joseph Sohm; Chromosohm Inc./CORBIS)

Chinese, which uses a combination of phonetic symbols and logographic symbols. Logographs are symbols that primarily represent a meaning; its sound is secondary. Novice readers have to know the meaning of the symbol to understand it. Good examples of logographs in European language use are Roman numerals. The symbol "X" has a specific meaning, namely the number "ten." Sounding out "X," no matter in what language, will not help find the meaning.

Considering all of this, it should not be surprising to learn that many studies of early literacy show that learning how to read and write are affected by the characteristics of the children's language. For example, a comparison between American and Chinese first graders revealed a different pattern of literacy (Stevenson & Stigler, 1992). English students had learned to break down words into sounds. This enabled them to figure out words that they had not yet been taught. Students who did not have this skill often were unable to read even the words they had already been taught. In contrast, Chinese first graders were able to read almost all the words they had been taught, but very few of the words not yet taught.

Speakers of phonetic languages can hardly imagine what is involved in learning to read and write Japanese, a language with basically three language systems: Kanji, Katakana, and Hiragana. Kanji consists of over 2,000 logographic characters, often with multiple sounds. Katakana and Hiragana are different forms of a phonetic system in which each character represents a syllable. Katakana is a "simplified" form, while Hiragana is the elegant cursive form of this symbol system. Almost all preschoolers pick up the basics of Hiragana at home or in kindergarten, while Katakana is taught in the first three grades. Instruction in Kanji is slowly introduced in the first three grades and continues through sixth grade. This example of Japanese learning to read and write shows very nicely the interaction of different levels of the ecological system in this aspect of language acquisition. Specifically, family and peers in the microsystem, aid the learning of Hiragana, as do extended family and families of peers in the exosystem. In combination, these systems assert a combined influence in the mesosystem. When learning Katakana, school and peers are the driving influence in the microsystem, while government-designed curricula (in the exosystem) and the cultural value placed on literacy (in the macrosystem) exert additional influences as one moves to the outer levels of the ecological system. An ecological system vastly different from the Japanese is described by Pretorius and Naude (2002). In their study of children (5.5–7 years old) in South African townships, they showed that the children's literacy and numerical skills were very poorly developed. The authors speculate that this may be because of the relative lack of emphasis on literacy both in the larger culture (child rearing practices that do not facilitate parental involvement in literacy development) and in the family (little exposure to reading and writing experience in the home).

◇ ADOLESCENCE AND EARLY ADULTHOOD

Formal Operational Thinking

Piaget's stage of formal operations also has been studied cross culturally, and it is the view of some researchers that individuals in many societies never achieve this type of thinking. In fact, a study conducted among Nigerian adolescents by Hollos and Richards (1993), using Piagetian tasks, revealed little use of formal operational thinking.

One of several tasks frequently used to measure cognitive development in the stage of formal operations is the pendulum problem. In the pendulum problem, individuals are shown several pendulums of different weights that are attached to different lengths of string. When the pendulums are swung, individuals are asked to figure out what determines the speed at which the pendulums swing back and forth. For example, is it the weight, the height from which it is dropped, the force with which it is pushed, the string's length, or perhaps a combination of all of these? According to Inhelder and

Piaget (1959), children in the stage of formal operations should be able to solve the pendulum problem through the process of elimination. Several cross-cultural studies have utilized this problem to observe cognitive changes in formal operations. For example, in studies carried out among adolescents in New Guinea, no subjects performed at the formal operational level (Kelly, 1977). Similarly, few adolescents showed formal operational thought when tested in Rwanda (Laurendeau-Bendavid, 1977). On the other hand, among Chinese children exposed to the British education system in Hong Kong, formal operational performance was found to be equal to or better than the performance of American or European children (Goodnow & Bethon, 1966). Some formal operational thinking was also found among schoolchildren in Central Java and New South Wales (Philip & Kelly, 1974). Based on these and similar findings, Piaget (1972) proposed that development of formal operational thinking is influenced by experience as well as by culture (Rogoff & Chavajay, 1995). As we have seen before, events taking place within one's ecological niche frequently determine how one will perceive and behave in a particular ecological setting.

These examples provide added impetus for considering the ecological setting in understanding why behavior, including cognitive activity, is expressed as it is. For example, Cole and Cole (1996) point out that "a lawyer might think in a formal manner about law cases but not when sorting the laundry . . . a baseball manager might employ formal operational thinking to choose his batting lineup but [not when doing] . . . the combination-of-chemicals task" (p. 674). As evidence, they cite a study by Retschitzki (1989), showing that when African men and older boys play a popular board game involving the capture of seeds from opponents, they make use of complex rules, complicated offensive and defensive moves, and skilled calculations. Interviews with skilled Baoule players from Cote d'Ivoire revealed that their strategies in playing this game used the types of logical thinking we usually attribute to formal operations.

The inability to show evidence for the universality of formal operational thinking among adolescents and adults is not confined to nonWestern areas. In fact, earlier studies demonstrated that not all adolescents or adults living in Western technological cultures achieve this type of thinking, and that they frequently show low levels of success on formal operational tasks. Even earlier studies conducted by Kohlberg & Gilligan (1971) with subjects in late adolescence reported that only between 30 and 50 percent of such individuals perform successfully on formal operational tasks. Werner (1979) sums this up by stating, "Formal-operational thinking might not appear at all or might appear in less-generalized form among cultures and individuals whose experience is limited to one or a few specialized or technical occupations. In other words, survival in a particular culture may not call for, nor be influenced by, formal logical thinking. Thus formal thought processes are probably cultural alternatives that can be learned. Humans have the capacity for it, but may not have realized it in order to 'get by' in their particular society" (p. 224). Shea (1985) has suggested that formal operational thinking (i.e., scientific reasoning) may not be valued in all cultures. For a review of fifty years of formal operational research, see Bond (1998).

Finally, in a discussion of the socialization of cognition, Goodnow (1990) concludes that Piagetian theory can be effectively applied to the conservation of weight, amount, and volume. However, she goes on to say that "if one's goal is to go beyond these domains—to construct an account of cognitive development that cuts across many domains or that takes place in everyday life—then classical Piagetian theory will certainly need some additions" (pp. 277–278). This, of course, is a position with which we certainly agree and which we encourage other researchers to take into account when conducting future cross-cultural studies of cognition.

Analytic Thinking and Problem Solving

Most of the research in cross-cultural human development has emphasized cognitive growth in childhood and adolescence. By comparison, few cross-cultural studies have examined cognitive development in adulthood. Piaget believed that formal operational thinking represented the highest level of cognitive development and proposed no additional stages in adulthood. He believed that an adolescent and an adult would think in the same way. However, some developmental psychologists have challenged this belief, arguing for a post-formal stage of cognitive development in adulthood. For example, Labouvie-Vief (1986) has suggested that in early adulthood, a change in thinking occurs, in which individuals begin to recognize cognitive limitations and may adapt their thinking to the demands of their environment. This process is called **adaptive logic** and involves *balancing critical analyses of objective observations with one's subjective reactions to these observations*. For example, when performing a memory task, older subjects may make a conscious decision to exclude much of the detailed information they remember, believing it may be uninteresting to the researcher or to other listeners. If this is the case, Salthouse (1987) suggests that when measuring cognitive abilities of middle-aged adults, we need to employ strategies different than those used with young adults (e.g., experience and expertise). This represents one more challenge for researchers interested in the study of cognitive development.

According to some theorists, the highest level of post-formal cognition is what is called dialectical thinking. **Dialectical thinking** *suggests that for every viewpoint there is an opposing viewpoint and these two can be considered simultaneously*. The ability to synthesize and deal with such opposing ideas in order to resolve contradiction represents a new level of cognitive flexibility and a deepening of thought, which, in turn, facilitates developmental growth (Peng and Nisbett, 1999). Whether this "higher form of thinking" is shaped by culture is up for debate (Ho, 2000), but considering the discussion in this chapter of ecological influences on cognition, we would argue that this question is worth further exploration.

◇ MIDDLE AND LATER ADULTHOOD

As one gets older, one supposedly gets wiser. At middle age and late adulthood, one has greater experience, becomes more sensitive to inconsistencies, and responds differently to social, political, and economic changes. These are generally the years of greatest productivity and self-satisfaction in career, avocation, or family.

Studying and understanding cognition during the middle and late adult years presents unique challenges, in part due to a confounding or intermingling of age and experience. Since the majority of research efforts have been conducted in Western cultures, which are youth oriented, the focus has tended to be on cognitive development among children and adolescents, not on the later years of adulthood. As a result, we know very little about changes in cognitive abilities among adults and even less from a cross-cultural perspective.

Intelligence

In their efforts to investigate changes in cognitive development during middle and late adulthood, Horn & Cattell (1967) proposed a distinction between fluid and crystallized intelligence.

Fluid intelligence involves *the ability to form concepts, reason abstractly, and apply material to new situations.* It is thought to be biological or intuitive and to be uninfluenced by culture. It is reflected in an individual's ability to make inferences, draw analogies, solve problems, and understand relationships among concepts. **Crystallized intelligence** refers to *an individual's accumulated knowledge and experience in a particular culture* (e.g., ability to react to social situations or respond to classroom tests).

Previous research in developmental psychology indicates that these two types of intelligence unfold in different directions. While fluid intelligence stays the same or declines somewhat throughout adulthood, crystallized intelligence may actually improve (Horn & Hofer, 1992; Lerner, 1990). Over the years, this view has been disputed on the basis of research conceptualization and methodology (Baltes, 1987; Schaie, 1984).

How might the ideas of fluid and crystallized intelligence apply across different cultures? To apply this view would require an understanding of how different cultures value speed, experience, youth, and age. While the speed of cognitive functioning tends to slow down in late adulthood, it is important to consider other factors when addressing this issue cross culturally. It is not clear how the cultural environment will react to or even notice an individual's cognitive slowdown. In some cases, a lack of speed might be compensated for by experience. Individuals who are admired for their experience (or wisdom) are often expected to be more reflective in matters requiring wise decisions. For example, Yang Tsu, an eighty-four-year-old master of martial arts in China, exhibits great discipline and patience (which took many years to cultivate), when teaching his young, impulsive apprentice, Low Chi Tho, who wants to learn everything very quickly. After some time, Low Chi has come to admire Yang Tsu and to realize the need to develop a more reflective approach to learning. In short, what might be negatively viewed by some cultures as a slowdown or decline in cognitive response is positively viewed in this case as a necessary quality for achieving success. Our familiarity with cross-cultural research suggests that there are many instances in which a behavior in one culture is viewed quite differently in another. This richness of differences (as well as similarities) provides many opportunities for those interested in pursuing the study of behavior from a cross-cultural, ecological, or sociocultural perspective.

In Western societies, speed is often more highly valued, and the ability to think quickly and make rapid decisions is seen as an indicator of high intelligence. In many nonWestern societies, time and speed are less valued, since individuals are encouraged to first view themselves as part of a group and to concentrate their efforts on the well-being of the family. In these societies, experience is more valuable than quick action. For example, when asked what advice he would give incoming American managers, a Japanese executive who had worked in Tokyo for fifteen years replied, "I'd tell him not to do anything for the first six months." He continued, "I've seen a lot more problems caused by Americans trying to do things too quickly than waiting too long to act." In America, it is often said, "Don't just stand there, do something." In Japan, they say, "Don't just do something, stand there" (Condon, 1984, p. 62).

Also in Western societies, youth is idolized, and displays of fluid intelligence are often synonymous with quick-mindedness. This attribute is often preferred over experience, or crystallized intelligence. Today, many corporations in the United States actively look for young employees who possess a fresh perspective and demonstrate the characteristics associated with fluid intelligence. At the same time, many senior employees, who have devoted several decades to their employers and have years of accumulated experience, find themselves confronted by the loss of their jobs or by offers of early retirement.

The issue of accumulated experience over time has been associated with wisdom. But does age alone make an individual wiser? Not necessarily. Smith and Baltes (1990) investigated sixty German professionals and divided them into three age groups of twenty-five to thirty-five, forty to fifty, and sixty to eighty-one. Each group was presented with four made-up examples

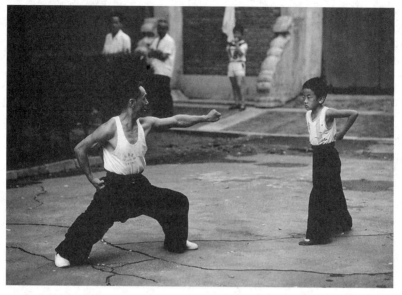

A martial arts instructor patiently teaches his young Chinese apprentice. (© Michael K. Nichols/National Geographic Image Collection)

of demanding situations and was asked to prepare solutions for these problems. Their approaches and solutions were rated by a panel of human services professionals. Of the 240 respondents, eleven scored in the "wise" category but were not necessarily older. In fact, they were found in almost equal numbers in each of the three groups. Wisdom, then, would not appear to be characteristic of any particular age group. In short, individuals do not become wiser simply because they get older. Wisdom takes many forms and varies according to each culture's orientation. In this study the criterion for determining what constituted wisdom was set by the researchers, who represent a specific cultural orientation that may or may not apply to all cultures. Replication of this study in a variety of other cultures might produce some interesting findings.

More recent research on this topic has led Baltes and his colleagues to propose several general characteristics associated with wisdom, including the ability to focus on important issues and to exercise good judgment, the development of a broad base of experiences, and recognition of one's wisdom by others (Baltes & Staudinger, 2000; Kunzmann & Baltes, 2003). In addition, Ardelt (2004) suggests that "wisdom-related knowledge has to be *realized* by an individual through a reflection on personal experiences to be called wisdom and that the wisdom-related knowledge that is written down in texts remains theoretical or intellectual knowledge until a person re-transforms it into wisdom. From this perspective, wisdom is a characteristic of people and not of texts" (p. 305).

In the final analysis, it is important to realize that although some aspects of cognitive functioning decline with age, how this change is viewed and evaluated depends largely on one's culture, ecological surroundings, and developmental niche.

Communicating in Later Life

Similar conclusions can be drawn with regard to language use and comprehension in later life. Undoubtedly, some actual changes occur in language with advancing age, particularly when there is a decline of cognitive functions, such as memory. For example, older speakers are a little slower and use different strategies in comprehending sentences, and they use less complex sentence structure. On the other hand, grammar, vocabulary, and speech production are relatively consistent across the lifespan. Despite these findings, there is the pervasive stereotype that older people are impaired in their communication. In a society in which aging is associated with negative expectations, older adults are confronted with physical changes of aging (e.g., hearing loss, voice quality, slowness of movement), and these are often interpreted by others as loss of competence. As a consequence, caregivers and others communicate with the older person in a simplistic and patronizing way. This, in turn, leads to diminished self-esteem, social withdrawal, and, ultimately, to a decline in communicative competence. Here, negative cultural expectations actually lead to a self-fulfilling prophecy. Consider, once again, the ecological systems approach. Although scientific evidence is lacking, it is conceivable that older adults in cultures that hold their elders in higher esteem will not experience the situation described above.

Just as cultural expectations differ in important ways, so do languages. Perhaps aging affects speakers of different languages in different ways. Research on cross-language differences and aging is very sparse and is certainly an area open to further investigation. Kemper (1992) shares a few-interesting observations. Some languages are very strict in their structure. For example, English has a fixed word order of subject-verb-object. Other languages, such as Russian and informally spoken Japanese, rely heavily on contextual cues and word order may vary. Kemper points out that the more "contextual" languages may make it easier for older people to comprehand and speak because they do not have to follow complex, strict language rules. This means that older adults who may have problems processing complex sentence sturcture can still understand and convey the meaning of a spoken sentence by interpreting the larger context. Overall, research on cross-language differences and aging is very sparse and is certainly an area open to further exploration.

◇ SUMMARY

Cognition is a general term referring to thinking, reasoning, decision making, remembering, categorizing, and problem solving. Cultural factors and beliefs found in the interaction among Bronfenbrenner's ecological systems, the developmental niche, and the sociocultural orientation contribute in a variety of ways to cognitive development across the lifespan.

The theories of Piaget, Vygotsky, and others provide a useful framework for conceptualizing cognitive growth and development and its relationship to language and culture. The linguistic relativity hypothesis states that different languages provide us with different frameworks within which we understand and communicate our experiences.

Vygotsky's sociocultural theory emphasizes the strong influence of social and cultural factors on both cognitive and language development. He introduced the zone of proximal development, which refers to what a child is presently capable of doing and what he or she could potentially do if guided by adults or capable peers. Vygotsky argued that cognitive development is enhanced when instruction is focused on an individual's potential rather than on the level of actual development. According to Vygotsky, the development of egocentric speech, inner speech, and external speech are grounded in one's social and cultural orientation. Vygotsky also emphasized the need for guided instruction (scaffolding), in which adults provide assistance (scaffolds) for children as they attempt to solve difficult problems. Vygotsky's view of language acquisition and sociocultural influences is mirrored in the learning of a second language. Along with a strong developmental influence, we have identified multiple ecological, social and psychological factors that account for the successful learning of a second, nonnative language.

According to Piaget, children's thinking differs significantly from that of adults, which is acquired only after successfully passing through a series of discrete stages. These stages have been studied from a cross-cultural perspective, and research evidence suggests that some aspects (the sequence of stages) may be universal, while others (the stage of formal operations) may not.

Cross-cultural investigations of human development have tended to focus primarily on children and adolescents and devote less attention to middle and late adulthood. At the same time, research in adult cognition has revealed that a fifth stage of cognitive development (post-formal thought) may emerge after formal operations. This new thinking allows an individual to move beyond abstract conceptualization and to integrate diverse reasoning abilities with pragmatic problem-solving strategies. The work of several researchers suggests that adult cognition is characterized by adaptive logic and dialectical thinking. The ability to synthesize new ideas and to realize that there are at least two sides to every point of view provides adults with more flexibility, effective problem-solving skills, and a broadening of thought.

Cognitive development in middle and late adulthood follows a different pattern than in childhood and adolescence. Horn and Cattell have suggested that a distinction be made between fluid and crystallized intelligence. Fluid intelligence is a person's ability to solve problems, think abstractly, and to apply new material in creative ways. Crystallized intelligence is learning that is based on experience. Early cross-cultural research indicates that as we get older, fluid intelligence declines, whereas crystallized intelligence increases. More recent research by Baltes and Schaie disputes this claim and suggests the need to consider cultural and contextual factors when attempting to explain individual differences in cognitive decline during late adulthood.

While some cognitive decline may influence communication in older age, other factors also influence language competence. Negative views of the elderly embedded in culture leading to perceived incompetence may be much more influential than actual loss of language competence. Moreover, changes in language competence in older age may be more or less relevant, depending on the characteristics of the language spoken.

◇ STUDY QUESTIONS

How was the original linguistic-relativity hypothesis (Sapir and Worf) revised, and how do they differ?

Which developmental and ecological factors play a role in language acquisition and early second-language acquisition?

Cross-cultural research testing Piaget's stages of cognitive development has shown that some aspects of the stage-theory describe universal patterns of development. What aspects of the developmental stages are seemingly universal?

What are "fluid" and "crystallized" intelligence, and how do they develop and change with age?

How does use of language and communication change in later life, and how might different ecological settings help people to adapt to those changes?

◇ FURTHER READINGS

J. Altarriba (2000). Bilingualism: Language, memory, and applied issues. In W. J. Lonner, D. L. Dinnel, S. A. Hayes, & D. N. Sattler (Eds.), *Online Readings in Psychology and Culture* (Unit 4, Chapter 4), (http://www.wwu.edu/ ~culture), Center for Cross-Cultural Research, Western Washington University, Bellingham, Washington.

Bilingualism, or the knowledge of more than one language, is prevalent throughout the world. However, much of the cognitive literature on language processing and memory retrieval has included participants who are monolingual speakers. This online chapter introduces the ways in which bilingualism has been investigated in the areas of autobiographical memory, memory recall, and communication in applied settings, and offers suggestions for further research.

S. H. Elgin. (2000). *The Language Imperative*. Cambridge, MA: Perseus Books.

In a conversational style, this book addresses many issues of culture and language. It discusses the linguistic relativity hypothesis, debates about multilingualism, and the power of language in different social and cultural contexts (business, family, medicine, religion).

Sandra G. Kouritzin (1999). *Face(t)s of First Language Loss*. Mahwah, NJ: Lawrence Erlbaum Associates.

This book contributes to the understanding of first language loss in both immigrant and indigenous communities in (at least) 3 ways. First, it provides insight into the process of first language loss and the factors contributing to it. Second, it attempts to define, from an insider perspective, what it means to "lose" a language. Third, it analyzes the perceived consequences of first language loss in terms of social, academic, emotional, and economic factors. Moreover, the book gives voice to 5 different story tellers who relate the histories of their first language while learning English. (From the cover.)

John Korte. (1995). *White Gloves: How We Create Ourselves Through Memory*. New York: Free Press.

Drawing on the latest research on cognition and clinical psychology, the author, in an intriguing, readable, and jargon-free manner, illustrates the nature of memory from childhood to old age. Using personal narratives, he covers such topics as first memories, photographic memories, memories of dreams, and repressed memory.

John Naisbitt. (1996). *Megatrends Asia: Eight Asian Megatrends That Are Reshaping Our World*. New York: Simon & Schuster.

One of the world's leading trend forecasters describes the significant political, social, business, and cultural values and beliefs that will change the world as we know it. A "new Asian way" of thinking is emerging that reflects increased individualism and urbanization and a more modern role for women.

Barbara Rogoff. (1990). *Apprenticeship in Thinking*. New York: Oxford University Press.

This book overflows with examples of parents leading their children through rough and calm cognitive seas to new levels of thinking. Illustrations of daily activities performed in scores of cultures fill almost every page of this book, which was written by one of the most prominent proponents of the cultural context perspective.

◇ DEVELOPMENTAL ANALYSIS

CULTURE, LANGUAGE, AND COGNITION

I have often reflected on the differences between my own upbringing and that of my children. While there are similarities, there are also some striking contrasts—particularly related to language acquisition. I grew up in a predominantly Irish, Catholic community. We all shopped at the same grocery store, attended the same church, and spoke the same language—English. I learned to speak while at home with my mother and honed my language skills when I entered kindergarten. My peers and I all exhibited an ability to sound words out according to the arrangement of letters. Once I had acquired this skill, I felt as if I had gained magical powers! I remember trying to teach my younger sister to speak shortly after she was born. It was extremely frustrating to me that this new little person (who had invaded *my* home) could not even talk.

It was not until I struggled through Latin in the eighth grade that I was exposed to another language. Staring at the letters on the page, trying to make sense out of these new patterns did not come easily to me. Sure, I could sound out some of these words (often incorrectly), but what did it all mean? After barely passing the first term's exam, I vowed to stay away from foreign languages. I kept my vow until I ventured off to study in Italy during my junior year in college. I met many people who spoke three, four, and five languages. Quite impressive compared to my one. Fortunately for me, English was often one of the languages spoken!

I began taking Italian language classes shortly after I returned from my study abroad program. It was not easy for me. But, I continued learning throughout the courtship with my Italian-born husband, Giorgio. It certainly came in handy when I met my future in-laws for the first time! Between savory mouthfuls of wonderful Italian food, I could effortlessly tell my mother-in-law how delicious her manicotti was. Benissimo!

Giorgio and I made the decision to raise our children in a bilingual environment by exposing them to both English and Italian. Regardless of whether a true "critical period" for language acquisition existed, we both agreed that as children, it would be best for them to learn Italian along with English. Therefore, Giorgio and I spoke both Italian and English in the home. When my mother-in-law came to visit us from Italy, she spoke only Italian. Both of our children now speak Italian fluently and have gone on to learn other languages as well. They thank Giorgio and me for our efforts to raise them in a bilingual environment. They often marvel at how Giorgio and I knew what to do as parents. I tell them that while we had some basic idea of what we were doing, much of our parenting was based on the experiences we had as we went along. Each experience helped us to shape our knowledge and parenting approach. Although I think we did a fine job, I often wonder if we could have done better knowing what we know now. I guess that is consistent with the idea that "older is wiser." I definitely feel as if I am *wiser* today—fortunately I do not feel much older!

CHAPTER SIX

CULTURE, SELF, AND PERSONALITY

Sergej was happy, agreeable, and easy to care for as a child. He grew up on a kolkhozy *(collective farm) in the Ukraine, one of the fifteen republics in the former Soviet Union. Sergej was quiet, and even his adolescent years were not characterized by the confusion and psychological turmoil experienced by so many young people. Sergej did well in school, completed an apprenticeship, and, following the breakup of the Soviet Union, now works on his family's small farm. He has been married for several years, and his wife Tamara describes him as a "good husband" who works hard, stays at home, and cares for his family.*

Yuen, born in Guizhou province in south central China, was what her mother considered a difficult child. Her moods were unpredictable and when upset, she took a long time to calm down. Yuen never developed a regular sleeping and feeding schedule, making it difficult for her mother to coordinate her work and childcare. Her adolescent years were equally challenging. Yuen had few friends and struggled with discipline problems at school. Now in her mid-thirties, she has assumed a leadership position in her work. Occasionally, she has to be reprimanded for her creative and sometimes radical ideas.

Sergej and Yuen clearly are very different people and showed very distinct character traits as children and as adults. Were they born with different personalities? Are these differences due to innate cultural patterns of personality? How much do cultural expectations about the course of one's life influence adult personality? We address these and other questions in this chapter by examining issues of personality, self, and individual differences and their embeddedness in a cultural context.

◇ INFANCY AND TEMPERAMENT

Many of the childhood behaviors exhibited by Sergej and Yuen can be explained according to differences in **temperament,** or *a person's characteristic behavioral style or typical pattern of responding to events in the environment.* Individual differences in temperament can be observed in the earliest hours following birth. For example, while some newborns and infants are irritable and cry frequently, others appear to be good-natured and calm. During the first few months of life, some infants are extremely expressive and react to people and events by making sounds and waving their arms; others are less active, may hardly respond to their environment, and appear withdrawn and uninvolved. Frequently, the differences we see in temperament among infants tend to be characteristically consistent throughout individual lives. In fact, some researchers maintain that infant temperament reliably predicts adult personality. The infant who is shy and anxious around strangers is more likely to be a shy adult than is an infant who curiously approaches strangers. The potentially powerful relationship between infant temperament and adult personality has led many researchers to the conclusion that traits of temperament are, to a significant extent, inherited. They argue that environment and socialization can influence temperament only within the limits initially defined by heredity.

The concept of heritability of temperament has received support from careful studies of twins (identical and fraternal) reared together and apart (DiLalla & Jones, 2000). These studies are based on the hypothesis that identical twins share 100 percent of their genes and, therefore, should be identical in their temperamental dispositions at birth. In contrast, fraternal twins, like other siblings, share only 50 percent of their genetic makeup and, therefore, should be less similar in their temperament. Yet, like identical twins, they share a very similar environment. Studies such as these should be able to provide answers to such questions as the following: (1) Are identical twins more similar in their temperament than fraternal twins? (2) Are identical twins raised in different environments more similar in temperament than are fraternal twins reared together? and (3) Are fraternal twins (who share half of their genes) more similar to each other than are adopted siblings (who do not share any genes)?

If the answer to all of these questions is "yes," we can conclude that genetic disposition, rather than environment, is responsible for the differences in temperament observed among people. However, to accurately assess the results of twin studies, it is important to understand the way heritability is measured. In general, the degree of heritability is expressed by the **heritability quotient,** which is *an estimate of the percentage of the variability in a given trait that can be attributed to genetic differences.* For example, a heritability quotient of 50 percent for trait X means that approximately half of the variation, or individual difference, found in a sample is due to genetic differences among those subjects in the sample. The remaining half of the variation is assumed to be the result of complex environmental factors or, possibly, unexplained errors in measurement. With this in mind, let us consider some twin research and what it tells us about the inheritability of temperament.

In general, twin studies have produced moderately high heritability quotients. For example, a study of 13,000 sets of Swedish twins showed a heritability quotient of about 50 percent for the traits of extraversion and neuroticism (Floderus-Myrhed, Pedersen, & Rasmuson, 1980). Similarly, a study of 350 twins in Minnesota revealed that approximately 40 percent of variability among subjects in such traits as stress reaction (related to neuroticism and general anxiousness) and aggression could be attributed to genetics (Bouchard, Lykken, McGue, Segal, & Tellegen, 1990).

While results like these suggest that certain temperamental traits are genetically transmitted, they also suggest that in specific instances other traits are heavily influenced by socialization within the family environment. In fact, most explorations in the field suggest that individual temperament is influenced by nutrition (Wachs, 2000b). After all, a heritability quotient of 40 to 50 percent also means that 50 to 60 percent of variation is due to environmental rather than genetic factors. The issue of environmental and genetic influences on temperament continues to be controversial, and researchers are not yet able to provide a definitive answer as to which plays the most significant role in determining differences in temperament. Most researchers recognize the existence of an intricate relationship between individual temperament and the larger sociocultural environment. In the next section we will discuss some theoretical perspectives that attempt to explain that relationship.

Temperament, Ecological Systems, and the Developmental Niche

As we pointed out in Chapter 2, a child's developmental environment consists of four basic subsystems: (1) the microsystem, consisting of interactions between the child and her immediate environment (e.g., home or daycare center); (2) the mesosystem, made up of individual microsystems (e.g., family and preschool); (3) the exosystem, consisting of influential social settings (e.g., parents' place of work); and (4) the macrosystem, consisting of customs, values, and laws important to the child's culture. Together, these subsystems provide the individual child with her developmental niche, or unique combination of socialization experiences. Each of these subsystems is influenced by, and in turn influences, a child's individual temperament. A child's behavior will initiate a specific response from a caretaker in a particular setting (home or preschool). However, these responses differ from one environmental setting to another. For example, a mother's reaction to a child who exhibits irregular sleep and eating patterns differs from North America to East Africa. A North American mother typically pays more attention to an infant who is unpredictable in eating and sleeping patterns, and she arranges her schedule to take care of the child's needs. In contrast, Super and Harkness (1994a) report that mothers in Kokwet, a small farming town in Kenya, interact more with children who operate on a regular daily schedule. Knowing when her baby will be awake and alert, the mother can more easily arrange her many other duties and activities. Kokwet infants who are less predictable in their daily patterns are more often left to the care of an older sister or another caretaker.

This example illustrates how a child's temperament influences the environment. At the same time, however, specific patterns of response exhibited by others in the child's environment may facilitate or inhibit particular behavioral styles on the part of the child, thus making the child–environment relationship a two-way interaction. A fussy child receives more attention from the primary caretaker in most Western cultures, thus potentially rewarding and facilitating the child's dependency on the caretaker. In nonWestern cultures, dependency and emotional attachment to the mother are often less pronounced, because mothers may not be available to respond with immediate emotional attention to fussy children.

Temperament and "Goodness of Fit"

Another theoretical explanation that contributes considerably to the understanding of how temperament, development, and culture relate to one another is that of **goodness of fit**—*the quality of the adaptation, or "match," between a child's temperament and the demands of his immediate environment.* This concept was introduced by Thomas and Chess (1977) in an elaborate longitudinal study of children's temperament that eventually included a wide range of environmental factors. The researchers began by interviewing and observing middle-class families of European background living in New York. They were able to identify clusters of traits that characterized three different temperament types among infants: (1) the "easy" child, (2) the "difficult" child, and (3) the "slow-to-warm-up" child.

An **easy child** was *characterized by a good mood, regular sleeping and eating cycles, and general calmness.* Mothers considered these babies unproblematic and easy to raise. On the other hand, temperament traits of a **difficult child** included a *negative mood, slow adaptation to and withdrawal from new experiences and people, irregular sleep and feeding patterns, and high emotional intensity.* Moreover, these "difficult" infants were found in later childhood to be less well adjusted and prone to more behavioral problems. A **slow-to-warm-up child** generally *showed few intense reactions, positive or negative, and tended to be mild and low in activity level.* Thomas and Chess assert that it is not the individual child's temperament itself that is related to future maladjustment, but rather the match or mismatch of the child's temperament with the environment that predicts problematic behavior. If "difficult" temperament disrupts family routine and leads to negative parental reactions, negative developmental outcome is likely.

A follow-up study by Korn and Gannon (1983) with Puerto Rican families in New York provided additional support for the goodness-of-fit concept but sounded a note of caution as well. For example, early "difficult" temperament did not predict poor adjustment and behavioral difficulties in later childhood. The researchers point out that in these families, characteristics that were originally classified as "difficult" were not perceived as necessarily problematic and therefore did not disrupt family life or evoke negative parental reactions toward the child. These studies and others provide convincing evidence that culture is a critical determinant of the "goodness of fit" between an individual child (temperament) and her environment.

DeVries (1994) and DeVries and Sameroff (1984) further illustrate this concept by describing two individual cases encountered in the study of infants from different parts of Kenya. The case of Hamadi, a Digo boy, demonstrates how an "easy" temperament can lead to poor adjustment due to a mismatch between the boy's temperament and his environment. For example, as an infant, Hamadi was energetic and active and exhibited healthy approach tendencies. He was described as one of the most advanced infants in the entire study. However, after starting school, Hamadi began to withdraw, became shy, and showed clear signs of distress through acting-out behavior.

What caused this transition? The researchers interviewed Hamadi's parents and teachers and were told that Hamadi's temperament did not fit with the cultural expectations of how a Digo boy his age should behave. The efforts of teachers and parents to control his energetic temperament and discourage his curiosity, instead of rewarding his enthusiasm and challenging his intellect, led Hamadi to withdraw and become angry and fearful.

Differences in infant temperament can often be observed side-by-side within the same cultural context. (© Gary Buss/Getty images)

The second case reported by DeVries introduces Enkeri, a Masai boy born in the same year as Hamadi. According to traditional temperament measures, Enkeri scored as "difficult." He was the classic "fussy" child—very intense, persistent, overactive, irregular in his daily behavior patterns, and not easily distracted or consolable. In a Western culture, these temperament traits would place Enkeri at risk for future adjustment problems. However, the behaviors that Western mothers dislike and describe as undesirable and difficult are valued highly in Masai society.

The Masai are an agricultural society and often have to struggle for survival in an extremely hostile environment. In times of drought, when herds of cattle and goats are destroyed, infant mortality is high because families cannot rely on the usual supply of milk. Under these kinds of conditions, infants who show "difficult" behavior tend to survive at a higher rate than infants who are quiet and undemanding. Why? Because infants who cry are fed and attended to, whereas those who don't are assumed to be content. Consequently, infants who cry a lot are fed more and are in better physical condition, which contributes to their survival.

Finally, Meijer, Super, and Harkness (1997) have recently attempted to further clarify the nature of "goodness of fit" and find a systematic relationship between maternal judgments of "difficult" and specific dimensions of child behavior. In a comparative study of mothers in Bloemenheim, Holland, and towns near Cambridge, Massachusetts, the researchers reported that parents in the two different cultural settings systematically interpreted the causes of difficult behavior differently. For example, while more American parents viewed difficulty as inherent in a child, more Dutch parents viewed it as a result of environmental factors. Clearly, the interaction of culture and individuality are different in these two ecological settings, and the resulting behavior and the interpretation of it are strongly influenced by the presence of different developmental niches.

Canadian researcher J. Phillipe Rushton (1998) pursues the "goodness of fit" hypothesis even further and in a very controversial direction. He argues that there are consistent "racial" differences in temperament that result from the unique survival challenges diverse groups of humans faced during evolutionary history. In particular, Rushton focuses on three categories of humans described as Mongoloid (Asian), Caucasoid (European), and Negroid (African). He argues that his research supports differences between these three groups in activity level, aggressiveness, cautiousness, dominance, impulsivity, and sociability. Rushton hypothesizes that the farther the populations migrated out of Africa, the more their temperament evolved over time to fit the survival challenges these populations faced. For example, the populations migrating north (Caucasoid and Mongoloid) spent long cold winters in closely knit social groups, requiring social cooperation and impulse control. Over time, these positive temperament traits (goodness of fit in these ecological settings) were passed on and became part of the "racial" temperament characteristics. While this perspective accounts for neither individual differences nor for cultural influences and socialization, it does illustrate the principle of the "goodness-of-fit" idea and is, thus, worth mentioning.

◊ CHILDHOOD AND THE EMERGENCE OF THE SELF

If you were asked to draw a picture of yourself, what would your picture look like? Would it show a single figure in the middle of the page? Would you attempt to portray your most typical features (e.g., hairstyle, clothes, facial features)? Or would you show yourself at work, at home, with friends, or with family? The way we think about persons, as individual entities or in a social context, is influenced by the cultural understanding of what a person is and what characterizes her or him.

◊ CULTURAL VIEWS OF THE PERSON

After decades of research, anthropologists, psychologists, and sociologists have determined that cultural views of the person frequently fall into one of two main categories: cultures with either a collectivist view or cultures with an individualistic view of the person. Not surprisingly, the collectivist/individualist distinction coincides with the distinction between Asian and Western cultures. How does the Asian/collectivist concept of the person differ from the Western/individualistic view? Perhaps this distinction can be best understood by using several of our themes (cross-cultural perspective, ecological systems approach, and the developmental niche) as a way of looking at life within a number of culturally diverse environments.

Personhood in a Balinese Village

Anthropologist Clifford Geertz (1973) spent years studying the lives of people in a small Balinese village. Among his many observations were those involving cultural customs related to the manner in which individuals describe and address another person. He found that the Balinese use six distinct labels to address another person and to identify him as a unique individual: (1) personal names, (2) birth-order names (first child, second child), (3) kinship terms (sister, aunt), (4) tekonyms, (5) status titles or cast names, and (6) public titles or occupational titles.

Personal names are rarely used among the Balinese. These and birth-order names are principally applied to children or adolescents. Kinship names are also used sparingly. Balinese most frequently use tekonyms when referring to or addressing each other. **Tekonyms** *describe the relationship between two people, typically the relationship between older and younger family* *members.* Geertz points out that as soon as the first child is born and named, the parents are referred to as "mother-of" and "father-of" that particular child. These terms then take on the function of personal names. Only after the first grandchild is born are the parents addressed as "grandmother-of" and "grandfather-of" a child. This approach to identifying individuals is quite different from practices found in Western cultures and denotes a very different understanding of the person, emphasizing the connectedness of the individual with the family—what Bronfenbrenner would view as part of the microsystem. On the other hand, individuals in Western cultures are designated by personal names, and their personhood is not usually derived from their relationship to others. The only comparable practice in Western culture may be the custom of the bride giving up her personal name and taking on her husband's family name. She may then be referred to as "Mrs. John Smith," creating a new identity that reflects her relationship to her husband. However, this practice is not as common as it once was, and married women are finding new ways of both retaining their premarriage identity and denoting their new relationship. Some women continue to be known by their birth name, some place a hyphen between their birth name and their husband's last name, and many find other ways to express their individuality.

Personhood in China, Japan, and the United States

Hsu (1985) has presented an interesting description and analysis of the concepts of personality and self in three very different cultures—China, Japan, and the United States. We chose this exemplary study to illustrate some of the existing cultural differences in conceiving of what defines a "person." We should note, however, that Hsu's study is not exhaustive, and thus we cannot draw conclusions about many other cultural concepts that exist. Hsu emphasizes the similarities between the two Asian cultures and their dissimilarity with North American culture. The Asian concept of *jen* (Chinese for "man" or "person" used also in the Japanese language) is defined by a person's place within his system of relationships. According to Hsu, personal wishes, motives, and feelings are only important to the individual in relation to their consequences for interpersonal relationships.

In China, the immediate family provides a place for the person and a framework for his sense of personhood. Similarly, in Japan an individual's personhood is also tied to one's relationship with others and not to oneself as an individual. However, in Japanese culture it is not exclusively kin members that provide a consistent system of social relationships. Japanese families are more willing to accept unrelated individuals into their family circle. Hsu concludes that in general, Japanese tend to form larger social networks than do Chinese, because they have fewer ties to their kin and need to seek their social network outside the immediate kinship group.

In contrast, American culture subscribes to the belief that a person is defined by her innermost feelings, thoughts, and motives. The individual's behavior as it relates to others is only an expression of these personal attributes. Personal boundaries are generally defined by the physical body (i.e., a person ends and the environment begins at the outer layer of one's skin). Personhood, therefore, is not directly tied to relationships with others. People in the environment are not considered a consistent feature of the person and thus seem readily exchangeable. For example, Hsu points out that the parent–child relationship in Western cultures is more voluntary than it is in Asian cultures, particularly after an individual is recognized as an adult. An individual can decide whether or not she wants to continue a relationship.

This brief discussion of personhood raises an interesting question: "What impact do these cultural conceptions have on individuals' perceptions of themselves throughout life?" After all, when I speak about myself, I am speaking about a person. My understanding of what it means to be a person must also apply to the special case of myself as a person.

◇ CULTURAL VIEWS OF THE SELF AS A PERSON

Before discussing culture-specific aspects of the self, we should point out that there are considerable similarities among humans in terms of the development of their sense of self. For example, psychologists generally agree that in many cultures individuals develop an understanding of themselves as distinct and separate from others. In addition, some developmental researchers argue that the sense of oneself as distinct from others develops within the first year of life.

These processes help to lay the foundation for development of the **self-concept**—*the perception of oneself as a person with desires, preferences, attributes, and abilities.* The unique structure and content of the self-concept, as well as some of the psychological processes related to it, are largely influenced by one's developmental niche and the level of the ecological system (microsystem, mesosystem, exosystem, or macrosystem) in which one finds oneself at a particular time in the lifespan.

Culture-Specific Aspects of Self

As with the concept of the person, the concept of self differs, depending on the cultural context. Since the self can be seen as a special case of the concept "person," it is not surprising that cultural differences in self-concept parallel differences in the person concept. Those who write most frequently about the topic of self-concept tend to discuss cultural variations in relation to the dimension of individualism–collectivism.

Triandis (1989), who has written extensively about individualism–collectivism, suggests that culture-specific views of the self result from early exposure to differing values and beliefs about the person in general. For example, childrearing patterns in collectivist cultures tend to introduce and reinforce the welfare of the collective over the welfare of the individual. In contrast, parents in individualistic cultures teach their children that the individual's primary goal is independence and the establishment of a unique self. Based on these fundamentally different approaches, it seems logical that individuals in collectivist and individualistic cultures should vary in how they view themselves. Some authors make a distinction between interdependent and independent selves (Markus & Kitayama, 1991; Gardiner & Mutter, 1994), whereas others look at Asian and Western conceptions of self (Page & Berkow, 1991; Spiro, 1993).

While the concepts of individualism and collectivism may be useful in describing general differences among cultures, critics point out that they disregard within-culture differences and neglect the fact that any culture includes both individualistic and collectivistic beliefs, values, and motives (Turiel, 2004). Applied to the concept of self, this means that a person's self can contain individualistic and collectivistic elements at the same time. In fact, one of the students who read an earlier edition of this book was concerned that she should be relegated to an "individualistic" concept of self just because she grew up in an individualistic culture. For example, she argued convincingly that some aspects of her self-concept and the belief that she is a "good" person is tied to her charity work and helping others. Research confirms this more complex understanding of self. Raeff (2004) reports that late adolescents recognize themselves in relation to others. When asked to describe themselves, most adolescents in Raeff's European-American sample did use autonomous terms (e.g., I am insightful, I am athletic, I like to read). However, when they were prompted to explain why these self-characteristics are important, the answers revealed a clear connection between self-characteristics and social relationships. For example, one woman pointed out that being insightful ". . . is very important because communication's obviously a very important thing. . . . You know, and sometimes it's nice to have insight into what somebody else is thinking and feeling" (Raeff, 2004, p. 73). Equally poignant are Li and Yue's (2004) findings that Chinese adolescents can show strong individual goals and ambitions in the realm of learning, despite the generally more collectivistic values present in Chinese culture. The ecological model is a useful tool in interpreting these findings. Viewed from this perspective, individual and collective orientations of self can coexist at different levels of the ecological model.

Figure 6.1 depicts various conceptions of self as they may exist within a given culture and across many cultures. The individualistic/independent self concept (a) remains relatively stable and consistent because interrelations with others are not defining elements of one's identity. This is represented in the figure as a heavier circle that does not contact other individuals that

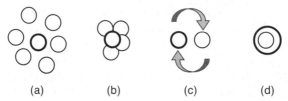

(a)	(b)	(c)	(d)

FIGURE 6.1   Independent, Interdependent, Relational, and Encompassing Concepts of the Self

Source: Adapted from M. F. Mascolo, G. Misra, and C. Rapisardi, "Individual and Relational Conceptions of Self-Experience in India and the U.S." in M. F. Mascolo and J. Li (Eds.), *Cultural and Developing Selves: Beyond Dichotomization,* 2004, pp. 9–26. New Directions in Child and Adolescent Development Series. W. Damon (Series Ed.). San Francisco: Jossey-Bass.

surround the person. The interdependent/collectivistic conception of self (b) is defined by the individual's relationship with individuals who are significant in that person's life. The heavier circle of self touches each individual illustrating the situational flexibility of the self-concept: the self must change if relationships change. These models of self are based on older work by Markus and Kitayama (1991) and Gardiner and Mutter (1994). The more recent findings we described above led Mascolo, Misra, and Rapisardi (2004) to propose two additional conceptions of self that could account for the coexistence of independent and interdependent elements within a person's self. In the relational understanding of self (c), self and other are neither entirely independent nor interdependent. Rather, aspects of the distinct self are defined in mutual relations with others. For example, self characteristics such as hostile, friendly, or gregarious can only be derived from relationships with others. How would one be gregarious by oneself? Finally, with the "encompassing" sense of self (d), Mascolo and colleagues account for a self that derives from relationships that are unequal in social status. Such relationships define one person as responsible, protective, and caring for the other person. In turn, the "subordinate" person sees himself as obedient, respectful, and appreciative. This type of self-experience may occur in parent-child relationships, and, in many cultures, between husband and wife or siblings. One would also find it in very hierarchically structured groups, such as the military or in organized religion.

◇ CONTENT AND CONTEXT OF THE SELF-CONCEPT

Numerous comparative studies have revealed distinct cultural patterns in the way individuals conceptualize the self, as well as in the content of the self-concept. In a cross-cultural study of self-concept in Japan and the United States, Cousins (1989) reported that subjects differed in the way they

BOX 6.1

THE SELF
IN BUDDHISM

The Singhalese monk Walpola Rahula (1959), explaining the role of self in Theravada Buddhism, has written: "Buddhism stands unique in the history of human thought in denying the existence of such a Soul, Self, or Atman. According to the teaching of Buddha, the idea of the self is an imaginary, false belief which has no corresponding reality. . . . To this false view can be traced all the evil in the world" (p. 51).

The self in Buddhism, which is more a psychological system than a religion, is thought of as an imaginary construct that limits the experience of total reality. Page and Berkow (1991) compare the sense of self to a "powerful belief" that results from the "desire to achieve an [illusory] sense of permanence within the ongoing flux of reality" (p. 89). The focus on "self" clouds a person's perception and experience of reality, because one organizes experiences

Phra Rajyanvisith, Abbot of Wat Luang Phor Sodh Dhammakayaram, Damnoen Saduak, Thailand, finds peacefulness and wisdom in meditation. (Courtesy of authors)

(continued)

BOX 6.1 CONTINUED

according to this limited belief (self) and is unaware of the reality beyond. Once this belief is abandoned and the self "ends," the perception and experience of reality are thought to be more comprehensive and unified. The loss of self, according to Buddhist teachings, is not the loss of identity. In fact, individuals continue to refer to themselves by name and are aware of themselves as individuals. Rather, the loss of self provides a new way of perceiving the world characterized by empathy, awareness, and deepened experience of reality.

These ideas are quite unlike what we find in Western thought, in which the self is viewed as a distinct and functional construct that psychologists have even succeeded in "assessing" and "measuring." Individuals are taught from an early age to become aware of, express, and satisfy their own wishes and needs. In fact, in Western societies, any significant or unusual change in the typically consistent and unitary entity called the self is considered pathological. When a person is "just not himself" or is "beside himself," he is frequently thought to suffer from disturbed perceptions, thinking, and behavior. Moreover, a person with multiple individual selves (or personalities) is considered severely mentally ill and highly dysfunctional.

Buddhist thinking exerts a very strong influence in many Asian cultures (Gardiner, 1995). How do Buddhist ideas regarding the self translate into the beliefs of the people in these cultures? Are conceptions of self the same in all Asian societies? Do individuals really deny the existence of self and strive to dissolve it in order to achieve a more complete understanding of reality?

Spiro (1993), while conducting field work in Burma, discovered that the cultural norm or ideal represents only one aspect of a culture's concept of self. Interviewing Burmese villagers, Spiro determined that the cultural ideal of the selfless person is not generally reflected in the personal beliefs of many people, nor does this ideal fit the personal understanding of their spiritual aspirations. In short, at least in Burmese Buddhist society, the ideal of the selfless person does not make sense to many people. For example, the idea of a selfless person appears to conflict with other strongly held beliefs, such as those related to reincarnation or rebirth in a different physical body. According to Buddhist thinking, the form rebirth takes depends on an accumulation of actions and behaviors performed in previous lives. Several of Spiro's subjects expressed the following reservations: If there is no self and it is not me who is reborn, then why should I be concerned about my actions in my present life? After all, it is not me who would benefit from my virtues or suffer from my misdeeds in the next life. The inference, from these statements, is that contrary to this particular society's cultural ideal, a very strong sense of self exists among individuals. Yet the selfless being remains an ideal and a norm in this culture. The occasional conflict of cultural ideal with personal beliefs is integrated into the person's identity without causing overt emotional distress or other psychological discomfort. Those familiar with

BOX 6.1 CONTINUED

Asian thinking do not find this unusual. In fact, Asians have generally been much more pragmatic in their thinking than Westerners and quite capable of resolving what for others would appear to be serious contradictions in beliefs or behavior. For example, in Japan, couples are married according to Shinto traditions (which celebrate life) but perform their funerals according to Buddhist practices (which celebrate death). In contrast, Western families often are seriously divided by issues centering on religious differences.

described themselves as individuals. Cousins used the Twenty Statements Test, which asks individuals to write twenty responses to the question "Who am I?" Results indicated that Americans used more psychological attributes, such as traits or dispositions, to describe themselves. In contrast, Japanese subjects frequently included the larger context when describing who they were. For example, Japanese subjects used more preferences and wishes, social categories, and activities in their self-descriptions.

Interestingly, the results from this study support several of the major themes we discussed in Chapter 1. For example, in terms of Bronfenbrenner's ecological model, Americans can be said to view the self as part of the microsystem. The individual selects characteristics derived from early interactions between the child and the immediate environment, most notably the family. This conception reflects the individualistic nature of the American culture. The Japanese, on the other hand, select characteristics that emerge from interactions in social settings or institutions—that is, in the exosystem or even the macrosystem—where they have come into contact with the customs, values, and laws of their culture. Such behavior reflects a collectivist society. This contrast can be seen in the examples of Sergej and Yuen in the opening vignettes of this chapter.

In another study using the same methodology (the Twenty Statement Test), Bochner (1994) reported similar results when comparing adults from Malaysia (a collectivist culture) with adults from Australia and Britain (individualist cultures). Interestingly, unlike Cousins's study cited earlier, Malaysians gave more responses referring to personal traits and dispositions than responses associated with social groups, and members of the two other cultures (Australia and Britain) gave more socially oriented responses. However, overall Bochner's cross-cultural comparison showed significantly fewer personal responses and significantly more group-related responses among Malaysians than in either the Australian or British samples.

In yet another study, Miller (1984) found similar differences in perceptions between Americans and Hindus in India. When adults in these two cultures were compared, Indians attributed their actions more to contextual factors, whereas Americans explained actions in terms of personal dispositions. Miller suggests that these differences are developmental in nature (another theme weaving through our topical discussions). For example, self-descriptions among young American and Hindu children (eight to eleven years of age) did not differ in any significant way; both groups referred more to context than to personal characteristics. This suggests that Americans, with age, may learn to focus more on the person than on the context when perceiving and evaluating behavior. This also casts some doubt on the definition of the individualism–collectivism dichotomy and its effect on actual behavior (in this case, self description). After all, it would be naïve to assume that cultural effects on self-concept and behavior could be reduced to two distinct categories of cultural values. This might be an interesting area for future research.

Additional evidence for the early influence of culture comes from a study conducted in the Netherlands (Van den Heuvel, Tellegen, & Koomen, 1992). Moroccan, Turkish, and Dutch children in grades six through eight were asked to describe five things about themselves, about one classmate who is like them, and about one classmate who is different from them. As hypothesized by the researchers, children from the two more collectivist cultures (Morocco and Turkey) used more social statements indicating group memberships, social activities, or clearly interpersonal traits (e.g., friendly toward others) when describing themselves or a similar classmate. Dutch children used significantly more psychological attributes, such as traits and personal preferences, in their description of themselves or a similar classmate. The authors conclude that the significant psychological differences found between individuals with an individualistic cultural background and those with a collectivistic background emerge at an early age and continue to develop across the lifespan.

Development of self-concept is greatly aided by language development and the words we use to describe ourselves. Pronouns such as *me, mine, you, us,* and *them* distinguish between self and others. Through the use of such words we learn to understand ourselves as unique and different from others. In an early study, Mead (1934) suggested that personal names were at the center of self-concept development. Personal names help identify the self and distinguish oneself from others who are not referred to by that name. In many cultures in which names are carefully selected for their meaning, the person is thought to adopt characteristics associated with that name. These attributes become part of their self-concept. How often have we met someone with the same name as someone else we know and compared the characteristics of the two individuals?

◇ SELF-ESTEEM AND SELF-EFFICACY

A recurring question in the study of self-concept is whether we can and should separate how we *think* about ourselves from how we *feel* about ourselves. Some contend that the content of the self-concept and its evaluation,

BOX 6.2

THE SELF AND PERSONALITY: SOME CULTURAL PERSPECTIVES

Personality and views of the self have most frequently been investigated from a Western perspective emphasizing the importance of the individual and the independent self in identity formation. Healthy and successful individuals in Western cultures are viewed as being self-directed and self-confident with high self-esteem, an internal locus of control, and a positive self-concept. However, to fully understand personality and the self, these concepts need to be examined more broadly from several perspectives and within a variety of cultural contexts.

Personality can be thought of as an individual's characteristic pattern of thinking, feeling, and acting. In Western cultures, it is typically viewed as a separate entity or an attribute of an individual. In China there is no equivalent Chinese word for personality. The closest translation is *jen*, standing for "person." As such, it includes the individual and his or her societal and cultural environment—very different than the Western view of a personal attribute.

The self, once it is shaped by culture, directs behavior and gives meaning to a person's life experience including cognition, emotion, and motivation. For example, people in individualistic cultures (e.g., those in North America and Europe) base their self-view on the characteristics that make them unique. They view themselves as distinct, autonomous, and self-reliant. People in collectivist cultures (e.g., Asia, Africa, and Latin America) base their self-view on their interdependence with others.

At the same time, there are universal aspects of the self that include (1) an understanding of the self as physically distinct and separate from others, or what some have called the "ecological self" and (2) an awareness of internal activity (e.g., dreams, thoughts, and feelings) that others cannot know about unless they are disclosed.

The following sections highlight several cultures that have a body of research focused on the concept of the self—Japan, China, and India.

Japan

Japan is considered to be a collective culture, where the Japanese place the group above the individual and tend to be other directed. The Japanese are extremely sensitive to and concerned about relationships and maintaining harmony (an influence from Confucianism) and stress such values as filial piety, shame (as a method of reinforcing expectations and proper behavior), self-control, emphasis on consensus, and fatalism.

The Japanese view the self as consisting of two parts—the inner self and the outer self, also known as the social self (what is typically shown to others). At the core of the inner self is the *kokoro*, a reservoir of truthfulness

(continued)

BOX 6.2 CONTINUED

and purity that remains private and is not shared with outsiders. Interestingly, the Japanese describe the self in concrete terms that are more contextual and relational than individuals in the United States. For example, while an American may say, "I am shy" (an abstract definition), a Japanese is more likely to say, "I am shy at work" (a contextual definition) or "I am shy with strangers" (a relational definition).

In addition, Japanese behavior often avoids direct communication and careful control over emotions and actions, allowing for the masking of feelings and the appearance of extreme modesty or shyness. The downplaying of one's performance may result in a nonthreatening atmosphere in which no one feels threatened, but the modesty displayed does not mean the person is not confident or he or she is shy. The individual may be extremely confident but, according to cultural expectations, is not to behave in an outwardly confident manner. Finally, the Japanese tend to be less unrealistically optimistic than Americans. Unrealistic optimism is the tendency for people to believe that, compared to others, they are more likely to experience positive events and less likely to experience negative events. The Japanese are believed to be less unrealistically optimistic, because the attention to the individual that self-enhancement engenders is not valued in Japanese culture.

China

An interest in understanding personality and the self is not new for the Chinese. An ancient theory held that personality is a result of the interaction of two forces—*yin* (passive, weak, and destructive) and *yang* (active, strong, and constructive)—and the Five Agents or *Wu-using* (metal, wood, water, fire, and earth), each of which has corresponding physical and temperamental characteristics. All of this is mediated by the Confucian Doctrine of the Mean, which states that there should be a balance of these forces and an avoidance of one-sidedness or extremity to maintain the Mean (moderation). This balance results in all things being in their proper order and thriving. If there is a balance, then the person is active or passive *according to the situation*. If the Doctrine of the Mean is violated, then the person is either extremely passive or extremely active.

A more modern Chinese theory of personality centers on Chinese social orientation or a person's tendency and desire to maintain harmonious relationships with others. An example is dedication to the family that results in Chinese merging their sense of self with the family and not focusing on personal interests, desires, or goals.

Beliefs about personality and the self are also influenced by Confucianism. Confucian personality is viewed as "the becoming process" and not an attained state of being. There is no fixed personality; rather, it is constantly

BOX 6.2 CONTINUED

evolving. A person becomes a personality by embodying a life worth living. At the same time, there is a belief in a "boundless" self, and the Chinese see the self as part of a larger vision of the universe

Finally, while the Chinese focus greater attention on the inner self than individuals in Western cultures, their self-presentation is similar to the Japanese. In other words, the Chinese downplay their successes, engage in self-effacement, are less likely to demonstrate self-serving bias, and mask their feelings in social interactions.

India

India is predominantly Hindu, with large minorities of Sikhs and Muslims. To understand India's views on the self, an awareness and understanding of Hinduism is extremely helpful. Hinduism is multifaceted and encompasses a body of beliefs, philosophies, worship practices, and a code of conduct. According to Hinduism, all individuals have four basic aims in life that form the basis of Indian values: (1) *kama,* pleasure or enjoyment, (2) *artha,* wealth or success, (3) *dharma,* righteousness, faithful duty or code of conduct, and (4) *moksha,* liberation or salvation. Of these, dharma is the most relevant for the concept of self, because it deals with righteousness, faithful duty, or the code of conduct. In India rights and duties are defined separately for various segments of the society divided by age and social category (i.e., caste). In fact, the primary term for personhood has been *purusa,* meaning *man,* and the term conveys the privileged status of men.

The Indian view of the self is also related to the "Law of Karma," the guiding principle that assumes lawfulness and order in the physical, biological, mental, and moral realms. According to the law, each person must face the appropriate consequences for his or her actions regardless of whether the actions are good, bad, or indifferent. Because India, like many other Asian cultures, is a collective society, individuals are not identified by individual traits, but instead are described in terms of social relationships. Responsiveness to the needs of others is viewed as a high moral obligation.

Source: Adapted from *Personality, the Self, and Culture* by Vicki Ritts, 2001, unpublished manuscript, St. Louis Community College. Reprinted by permission.

---

which results in self-esteem, are virtually inseparable. However, other self-concept research increasingly demonstrates that self-esteem may indeed be a distinct aspect of self-concept. From a developmental perspective, Harter (1982) has shown that a global sense of self-esteem (perceived self-worth), distinguishable from the descriptive aspects of self, emerges around the age of eight.

Watkins and Dhawan (1989) argue that the distinction or lack of distinction between self-esteem and self-concept may be a cultural phenomenon. In several studies, these investigators examined aspects of the self-concept and self-esteem of children and adults from diverse cultural groups. As before, they found distinct differences between members of Western and Asian cultures. For example, Dhawan and Roseman (1988) reported that 62 percent of responses of American young adults were classified as self-evaluations, compared with 35 percent of responses among Indians of the same age group. In addition, most of the self-evaluations made by Western subjects were positive rather than negative.

These results, along with others, suggest that the distinction between self-concept and self-evaluation is more pronounced in Asian cultures, whereas both aspects of self are intertwined in Western cultures. Once again, the explanation seems to lie in the individualistic or collectivistic orientation of the cultures involved. If an individual is independent and responsible for her success or failure, a focus on specific positive aspects of the self is an efficient protection against low self-esteem (Gardiner & Mutter, 1994). In contrast, in cultures in which individual success and enhancement are less important, personal attributes and accomplishments are not an immediate source of self-esteem and their value need not be emphasized.

As we noted previously, particularly in our discussion of the developmental niche and the ecological systems approach, childrearing practices and family environment are major contributors to cultural differences. These factors are also believed to be very influential in the development of personality and self-esteem, especially during the first years of life. Therefore, the fact that cultural differences in self-esteem are related to cultural differences in childrearing should not be surprising. Childrearing that emphasizes warmth and acceptance, together with consistent rules and achievement expectations, is clearly related to high self-esteem. For example, Olowu (1990) argues that many African children have higher self-esteem than children in Western countries because they enjoy the warmth and acceptance of an extended family. Such parental warmth can be provided by aunts and uncles as well as grandparents. Western children, on the other hand, frequently rely on one or two caretakers for their self-esteem needs.

Another example of the direct influence of the family atmosphere on self-esteem can be found in Jamaica. Phillips (1973) notes that it is common for Jamaican parents to separate and remarry several times. Children from previous marriages are expected to adapt to new environments and form relationships with new family members. While the family structures are very loose, children experience strict and authoritarian discipline from both parents and teachers. According to several researchers, this combination of unstable family dynamics and overly strict discipline results in a lack of self-esteem and self-worth in Jamaican children (Phillips, 1973; Smith & Reynolds, 1992).

In Burkina Faso, a senior Lobi man shows warmth and affection towards a young friend. (© Bertrand Rieger)

Social psychologists recently have argued that we cannot understand a person's self by only considering the general sense of ourselves as a person distinct from another person (self-concept) and our general sense of self-worth (self-esteem). Bandura (1997) explores the construct of "self-efficacy" as an important factor in the development of self. **Self-efficacy** refers to *the general sense of one's ability to master tasks and to direct one's behavior towards a goal.* Although highly correlated with self-esteem (Judge, Erez, Bono, & Thoresen, 2002), self-efficacy adds important insights to our understanding of the developing self.

According to Bandura, self-efficacy, unlike self-esteem, influences personal goals and behavior. When children learn that they can influence their environment through their behavior, and they succeed in doing so, they develop a sense of efficacy. This sense of capabilities allows and motivates them to set goals and achieve them. As their world and their ecological systems expand, from family to peers to school, they develop self-efficacy in different domains. For example, Bandura's Children-Perceived Self-Efficacy scales, or CPSE (Bandura 1990) measure self-efficacy in three domains: academic self-efficacy (capable to manage one's learning and master academic subjects), social self-efficacy (capable to form and maintain social relationships and manage conflicts), and self-regulatory efficacy (capable to resist social pressure).

In a study involving 10– to 15–year-old Italian, Hungarian, and Polish children, Pastorelli and her colleagues (2001) showed that some national differences in academic and social efficacy exist. For example, Hungarian children were more confident in their ability to master academic subjects, but had a lower sense of being able to take charge of their learning than Italians and Poles. The authors point to the differences in educational practices in the different countries. They suggest that students may develop high efficacy in subject mastery in an educational system that is highly structured and tightly controlled by teachers and parents. On the other hand, these students may perceive a lack of control in choosing and directing their own learning activities. Likewise, the explanation for the tendency of Italian children in this study to perceive themselves as more capable in the social domain than both Hungarian and Polish children may lie in the ecological system. The family exerts the earliest influence in a child's life and provides early opportunities to develop social efficacy. Italian culture is known for its emphasis on strong family relationships throughout life, so it might not be surprising to find that Italian children consider themselves socially competent. They may just have had more opportunities to develop social efficacy within their microsystem.

◇ ADOLESCENCE: THRESHOLD TO THE ADULT WORLD

Adolescence is a particularly interesting period of transition in the lifespan. It begins with biological maturation and ends with society's acceptance of the young person as an adult. Most Western societies have clear social markers that define when a young person is considered mature enough to assume adult responsibilities (e.g., voting in elections) and adult privileges (e.g., driving a car or consuming alcohol). In contrast to many nonindustrialized cultures, adolescence generally lasts several years in most modern Western cultures. Adolescents in nonWestern societies assume adult responsibilities much earlier, because these societies cannot afford to let their young people be "nonproductive" and engage in idle "self-discovery" for an extended time.

Identity Formation

During the adolescent years, young people encounter one of the most important developmental tasks of their lives—the establishment of an individual identity. **Identity** is *a person's self-definition as a separate and distinct individual, including behaviors, beliefs, and attitudes.* Simply stated, the individual is trying to answer the question "Who am I?" Finding the answer isn't always easy and involves many of those within one's various ecological systems, including family and friends, members of peer groups, and teachers. Some adolescents find the journey particularly difficult and have to deal with serious issues, including antisocial or delinquent behavior. These topics receive attention in the section that follows.

Psychologist Erik Erikson is generally credited with the first complete analysis of identity development (Erikson's stage theory is discussed in detail in Chapter 2; see Table 2.3). Furthermore, he proposed the integration of identity, social roles, and the broader cultural context (Erikson, 1963). In his cross-cultural research, he collected evidence for the universal existence of identity development, yet the exact process by which individuals achieve an adult identity is influenced by specific contextual factors. The basic premise of identity development across cultures is that it is rooted in the physical and psychological developmental changes an individual experiences during the adolescent period.

It has long been assumed, particularly in Western societies, and most notably in the United States, that the transition to adulthood is a rather painful and psychologically challenging event (Hall, 1904). However, other research shows that the experience of stress during adolescence varies cross-culturally (Offer, Ostrov, Howard, & Atkinson, 1988). Some writers suggest that adolescence is more stressful when individuals are confronted with a large number of choices, as they frequently are in Western cultures. In non-Western societies, in which roles are frequently more clearly defined and choices are more limited, the transition to adulthood appears to be much smoother. For example, if the firstborn child is expected to take over the family business and assume care of the aging parents, it is not necessary for him to explore a variety of social roles in order to find a suitable adult identity. The important decisions have already been made for him. In contrast, those societies that value independence offer adolescents numerous opportunities to explore a variety of different social roles, thereby making the search for identity more difficult and of longer duration.

One study serves as an example of the influences of specific contextual factors on identity development. Tzuriel (1992) was interested in knowing whether adolescents exposed to multiple (and sometimes conflicting) sets of norms and expectations experience more identity conflict than adolescents with a less ambiguous environment. Israeli Arabs, who represent a relatively small minority in Israel, grow up experiencing elements of both their traditional culture and the Jewish majority culture. In contrast, Israeli Jews know a more homogeneous culture, in which their values and beliefs are reflected and reinforced. Would Israeli Arabs have a more negative view of themselves or express more confusion regarding their identity as a result of their different cultural experiences? Among the six factors of identity examined in this study, Arab youths expressed more self-confidence, a stronger sense of ideological and vocational commitment, and more genuineness. In contrast, Jewish adolescents reported more feelings of alienation and discontent with their

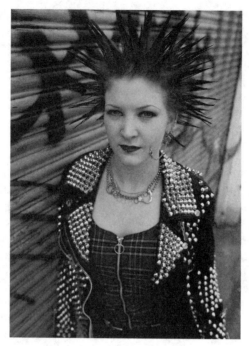

Personal identity is expressed in interesting ways throughout the world. (© PhotoDisc/Getty images)

appearance and behavior. However, they also recognized that others valued them and their abilities.

These findings suggest that Jewish adolescents experienced a somewhat different struggle in their identity formation than did Arabs. Tzuriel speculates that the ambiguous environment, especially among Israeli Arabs, may actually facilitate identity exploration and self-awareness in relation to identity issues. Thus, a seemingly ambiguous environment may have a more positive influence on identity formation than common sense would suggest. With the resolution of the identity conflict, most adolescents achieve an identity with which they are comfortable and adjust their behavior accordingly.

Social Identity Formation

We tend to think of identity as something that is very unique and represents the individual's personal history, experiences, and personality. However, our lives are inextricably connected with those around us—our family, our peers, our coworkers. Viewed from an ecological systems view, groups of people in a given context show a great degree of overlap. It is not surprising, therefore, that part of what we like to think of as our self results from what we share with others. Psychologists call these shared aspects of self "social identities." French psychologist H. Tajfel (1981) defines **social identity** as *"that part of an individual's self-concept which derives from his knowledge of his membership of a social group (or groups) together with the value and emotional significance attached to that membership"* (p. 255).

We tend to belong to multiple groups. Some are assigned to us (e.g., gender, nationality), while we choose others (e.g., political affiliation). Among these, ethnic or cultural identity has been singled out as particularly important to self-concept and the psychological functioning of ethnic group members. Phinney (1990) and others suggest that the formation of ethnic or cultural identity is similar to the formation of ego-identity as outlined by Erikson.

Ethnic or cultural identity formation appears to take place in three stages. The first stage, generally occurring in adolescence, is characterized by the lack of exploration of ethnic identity. The second stage involves becoming aware of one's ethnicity and actively exploring that ethnicity. At this stage, the person may engage in ethnic group activities, including reading and talking to people about the culture and participating in cultural events. The completion of this stage results in the final stage: ethnic identity achievement. This stage is characterized by a deeper understanding of one's ethnicity and the internalization of ethnic identity into the self. Because this understanding of ethnic identity varies from person to person, according to personal history and ecological systems, the implications for the self-concept and, ultimately, social behavior, may also vary. For example, one person may become deeply involved in the activities of her ethnic group by maintaining the language, wearing traditional dress, and practicing ethnic rituals and customs. For another person, ethnic identity achievement may result in an intrinsic confidence in his ethnicity and not necessarily require strong ethnic involvement.

Cultural Influences on Social Identity

Just as the larger cultural context influences the specific content of adolescents' self-concepts and personal identity, culture also plays an important role in the progression of social identity formation. With regard to ethnic identity as an example of social identity, the position an ethnic group holds in the larger society (minority or majority status) and relationships among ethnic groups are the most influential of these cultural factors (Phinney, Lochner, & Murphy, 1990).

Research in the West Indies shows how general cultural conditions and beliefs (i.e., macrosystem) shape the basis from which young people begin their ethnic identity formation. Gopal-McNicol (1995) presented black and white preschool children with black and white dolls. The investigator asked the children questions such as "Which doll would you like to play with?" "Which doll do you want to be?" "Which doll is rich, ugly, pretty?" Similar to research in the United States, nearly five decades earlier (Clark & Clark, 1947), most of the children chose the white doll in response to the positive questions. The author concludes that colonialism, along with the representation of blacks and whites in the media, has made a marked impact on attitudes toward and perceptions of ethnic groups in the West Indies. It is not unreasonable to assume that these attitudes and perceptions play an important role in the eventual ethnic identity formation of those black and white children who participated in the study.

Contemporary adolescents are growing up in a world much more culturally diverse than that of their parents and grandparents. This increased globalization has implications for adolescents in many societies as they attempt to develop and establish their cultural identities. Jensen (2003) suggests that adolescents increasingly form multicultural identities as a result of their exposure to diverse cultural beliefs and behaviors either from first-hand contact with people from other cultures or through the media. She further argues that the process of developing a cultural identity during adolescence in a global society has become more complex and presents more challenges than it did just a generation or two ago.

As an example, Jensen (2003) discusses the changing view of marriage in India. The cultural tradition of arranged marriage in India is deeply rooted in values such as obligation to one's family and conforming to social roles rather than pursuing individual preferences. In today's more global Indian society, young Indian women and men are also exposed to values that emphasize freedom of choice and individual rights. Multiple traditional and nontraditional cultural values and practices influence adolescents' conceptions of who they are and how they fit into the world. The words of a young Indian woman exemplify this process of negotiating multiple cultural identities: "I've always insisted that I've got to have the right man and I won't just be able to adjust to anyone . . . There have been pressures, if I can call them that, from family, but I've . . . not given in to it. I won't do that because I know the situation now . . . From the very beginning things foreign and imported were very glamorous to me. From those days onward [when I became familiar with things foreign], I was against having an arranged marriage. Arranged marriages in India are becoming obsolete, I think." (Jensen, 2003, p. 4)

As researchers have begun to recognizing increasing globalization of the adolescent world, they have come to adopt more complex models to interpret their research findings and understand adolescent identity development. In recent years, developmental researchers have pointed explicitly to ecological systems theory as a useful model to guide research and practice (Spencer et.al., 2003, Swanson et al., 2003). In fact, globalization is a good example of a sociohistorical force that is captured by the "chronosystem" in the ecological model (see Chapter 2). As we saw in the preceding discussion of identity formation, the globalization of values, beliefs, and practices permeates all levels of the ecological system, and greatly influences individuals' developmental paths.

◇ ADULTHOOD AND AGING: A TIME OF STABILITY AND CHANGE

Given a secure identity by the early to mid-twenties, along with a set of relatively stable personality dispositions (traits), one might assume that personality would not change much after adolescence. However, distinct patterns of personality development, related to temperament traits, continue to occur. In particular, adults become more agreeable, more conscientious, more emotionally stable, but less extraverted and less open to experience. Numerous studies examining these "Big Five" personality traits have shown this pattern to be surprisingly consistent across many age groups and cultures, such as the United States, Germany, South Korea, Italy, Croatia, and Portugal (McCrae and Allik, 2002; McCrae et al, 1999; McCrae and Costa, 2003). See Table 6.1 for a description of these traits.

The big five personality traits were "discovered" when researchers performed statistical analysis on adjectives that describe personality characteristics, as well as on existing personality tests (also based on language). They assumed that natural language, used to communicate differences and similarities between oneself and others, reflects the socially relevant dimensions of personality. Therefore, the analysis of natural language should reveal the characteristics that are important in describing oneself and others. Their analysis showed that all descriptors used in natural language, as well as

TABLE 6.1   The Big Five Personality Traits

TRAIT	DESCRIPTION
Agreeableness	Tendency to be compassionate, cooperative, generous, trusting, sympathetic, and altruistic versus suspicious, critical, and antagonistic toward others
Conscientiousness	Tendency to be well-organized, reliable, hardworking, persistent, ambitious, reliable, and responsible versus disorganized, negligent, and irresponsible
Extroversion	Tendency to be energetic, active, outgoing, and sociable versus quiet, deliberate, reserved, and less involved in the social world
Openness to experience	Tendency to be curious, imaginative, creative, and artistic versus conventional, unimaginative, and uncreative
Neuroticism	Tendency to be emotional, anxious, unstable, temperamental, and worried versus unemotional, calm, stable, even-tempered, and not easily upset

Sources: Ahadi & Rothbart, 1994; McCrae & Costa, 1990; McCrae & Costa, 2003; McCrae & John, 1992.

test items designed to measure personality, can be represented by five common dimensions—the "Big Five" personality traits. Further research indicated that these five traits are also found in different languages and different cultures.

Robert McCrae (2004), one of the main proponents of the Five Factor Theory, even goes so far as to suggest that humans, as a species, have a genetic predisposition to develop in basically the same way, regardless of life experiences or cultural influences. McCrae cites the universal occurrence of the five traits and the seemingly universal pattern of personality change as evidence of a biological basis for personality and personality change.

Are we destined by biology to become more agreeable, conscientious, emotionally stable, and less sociable and open to experience, relative to when we were younger? Are we bound to change in much the same way as our parents and grandparents did?

While other researchers acknowledge the seemingly universal pattern of adult personality development, they offer a different explanation. For example, Roberts, Wood, and Smith (2005) suggest that it is not genetic "hardwiring" that predicts universal patterns of personality development. Rather, it is universally occurring tasks of social living that lead to a shared pattern of personality trait development (Helson et al, 2002).

Roberts and his colleagues argue that "the majority of people in a majority of different cultures go through similar life transitions at roughly the same age" (p. 173). All cultures have defined times at which certain life events are supposed to take place. For example, at some point in their lives individuals in most cultures are expected to find a partner, start a family, produce offspring, work for a living, and contribute to one's community.

It has been suggested that these markers affect the adult personality in several ways. First, people adjust more easily to transitions that occur according to normative tasks than to transitions that are "not on time." The unexpected death of a child represents an "off-time" event, because parents are supposed to be survived by their children. However, the same event, while unexpected, is not considered "off-time" in societies with high infant mortality rates. Second, a new stage of life requires changes in behavior that frequently result in personality changes. Young adults who experience their first serious romantic relationship increase their emotional stability and conscientiousness (Neyer and Asendorpf, 2001). In turn, individuals who are more emotionally stable and conscientious tend to have relationships that last longer and are more satisfying (Roberts and Bogg, 2004).

Finally, certain personality traits appear to be associated with adherence or nonadherence to the normative tasks. Helson and her colleagues (1984) examined 141 women over a period of several decades and found that those whose lives followed the cultural expectations of women at that time (e.g., prescribed role of wife and mother) displayed an increase in tolerance, responsibility, nurturance, and self-control, but also a decrease in self-confidence and feelings of competence. Those women who chose a career path and departed from their prescribed roles as mothers adapted to this role by developing high levels of confidence, initiative, and intellectual independence.

◇ SUMMARY

This chapter discussed the development of individual, self, and personality across cultures and in specific cultural contexts. Some aspects of personality and behavior are clearly influenced by innate temperamental dispositions. The ways in which individual temperament is expressed and what is considered acceptable were shown to be largely dependent on cultural values and practices. Discussion also focused on cultural variations in the concept of person and self and their relationship to the early development of self-concept. While adolescents in most cultures experience the need to establish an identity, the manner in which they accomplish this and the specific issues and behaviors related to it show great cultural variation. Finally, we raised the question whether seemingly universal patterns of personality development in adulthood are the result of "hardwired" developmental processes or the result of universal socially prescribed "normative life tasks".

◇ STUDY QUESTIONS

Use the examples of Hamadi and Enkeri to describe how children and their environment shape each other and create a "goodness of fit."

Using the ecological model, explain why the concept "individualism/collectivism" is limited in explaining cultural differences in self-concept.

Proponents of the Big Five personality theory claim that our personality changes in a distinctly universal pattern as we get older. What is this pattern?

◇ FURTHER READINGS

A. T. Church and M. S. Katigbak. (2002). Studying personality traits across cultures: Philippine examples. In W. J. Lonner, D. L. Dinnel, S. A. Hayes, & D. N. Sattler (Eds.), *Online Readings in Psychology and Culture* (Unit 6, Chapter 2), (http://www.wwu.edu/~culture), Center for Cross-Cultural Research, Western Washington University, Bellingham, Washington.

This online chapter reviews the questions addressed by researchers who study personality traits across cultures, including whether traits are used in all cultures to understand persons and their behavior, the universality versus culture-specific traits, the validity of impoted and indigenous measures of personality traits, and the meaningfulness of trait comparisons across cultures. Evidence relevant to these questions is summarized for one collectivistic culture—the Philippines.

Sigmund Freud. (1961). *Civilization and Its Discontents* (Vol. 21). London: Hogarth.
One of the most important writings on the interaction between personality and culture by one of the most creative and influential contributors to the field of psychology.

L. E. Harrison and S. P. Huntington (Eds.) (2000). *Culture Matters. How Values Shape Human Progress.* New York: Basic Books.
A collection of essays that addresses the controversial question: Are some cultures better than others in creating conditions that offer a better quality of life to its people? This book provides an excellent starting point for a discussion about "cultural character."

R. R. McCrae (2002). Cross-cultural research on the five-factor model of personality. In W. J. Lonner, D. L. Dinnel, S. A. Hayes, & D. N. Sattler (Eds.), *Online Readings in Psychology and Culture* (Unit 6, Chapter 1), (http://www.wwu.edu/~culture), Center for Cross-Cultural Research, Western Washington University, Bellingham, Washington USA.
An online chapter discussing the Five-Factor model, its use across cultures, and some recent research findings.

Margaret Mead. (1973). *Coming of Age in Samoa.* New York: American Museum of Natural History.
The author's best-known book; compares the lives of Samoan adolescents with adolescents in Western cultures. The comparisons have been seriously challenged, causing anthropologists to give greater attention to multiple interpretation of findings gathered by field research. Nevertheless, this is a classic and worth reading.

The Big Five Personality Test.
If you are interested in learning more about the big five personality traits mentioned in this chapter, you can take a free, anonymous, online test that will help you to understand the traits as they relate to your personality by going to http://www.outofservice.com/bigfive/

◇ DEVELOPMENTAL ANALYSIS

CULTURE, SELF, AND PERSONALITY

As you read in this chapter, temperament, ecological systems, and the developmental niche all seem to be intertwined. This was certainly the case with me. At times my mother said I was an "easy child" because I was usually happy, outgoing, and slept fairly well. I certainly enjoyed my meals, especially desserts, even as an infant in a high chair. However, occasionally I could be a "difficult child," as when I would insist on climbing trees and jumping to the ground! My younger sister was more difficult than I was—maybe because she was the middle child, and my brother, the youngest, was more "slow-to-warm-up." It is not unusual for a family to have all these types of children.

(continued)

Just when my husband and I (like most parents) thought we had learned all we needed to know about successfully raising children, along came the next one who was so different, in many ways, from the previous child. Maybe this is true in your family, too.

Apparently, as a child, I was determined to establish my own personality. I didn't always conform to the norms in terms of clothes, play activities, and school interests. I felt confident in most of my emerging abilities (such as doing math and playing sports) and had a good self-concept—often to the point of being stubborn, especially during my adolescent years. I guess you might say I had high self-efficacy. Although our town didn't have the cultural diversity that many places have today, I found a large part of my cultural and ethnic identity in my Irish background (reflected in my red hair, freckles, and sense of humor).

In terms of personality, I have always tended to be extroverted and outgoing, agreeable and trusting, well-organized, hardworking, and ambitious (as reflected in my career accomplishments), curious, creative, and open to new experiences (demonstrated in my travels and efforts at cooking new foods). I see some of these same personality characteristics in our children and grandchildren.

As I approach the seventh decade of my life, I'm generally happy with the person I have become, and as I look back on my early life, I see the many influences that my family, culture, developmental niche, and unique ecological system had on the development of my self-concept and personality. Maybe I would have changed some things—but not many. It's been a good life so far.

CHAPTER SEVEN

CULTURE AND ISSUES OF GENDER AND SEXUALITY

Alisa and Alan are middle-aged adult siblings who grew up in a small town in the midwestern United States. As young children, they lived in a single-parent home with their mother, who worked as a secretary. Growing up, they experienced typical gender socialization for that time. Alisa, dressed in her favorite party dress, enjoyed playing with her dolls and stuffed animals in her room; while Alan, in his sturdy jeans and T-shirt, played rough and tumble games outside. During their school years, Alan was encouraged to study science and went on to become an engineer. Alisa, who did well in school, hoped to have a career too but was raised to see her future role as a wife and mother. Both Alisa and Alan married and had children. One of Alisa's daughters is an astronaut in the American space program and another is a surgeon. Now divorced, Alisa takes care of her elderly mother since Alan lives and works in Japan.

Harin and Tippa, also in their middle adult years, grew up in rural Thailand with their parents, two brothers, two sisters, and various aunts, uncles, and cousins. As children, they played the same games, took care of their younger siblings, and worked in the rice fields. They both went to the same schools and enjoyed studying together. After graduation from high school, they went to Chulalongkorn University in Bangkok, where Harin studied to be an elementary school teacher and Tippa became an electrical engineer. Both are married today with families of their own.

These two pairs of mixed-sex siblings experienced childhood in very different ways. Harin and Tippa shared most of their activities and interests; Alisa and Alan grew up in two different worlds. Did Alisa and Alan deliberately "choose" different interests, or were they "assigned" those interests? Was Harin and Tippa's experience really that similar? Did the upbringing experienced by these children influence the choices and preferences all four made in later life? How did culture contribute to these differences in upbringing?

Many introductory textbooks in psychology carefully differentiate the concepts "sex" and "gender." **Sex** is usually defined as *biological aspects of femaleness and maleness;* **gender,** as *acquired behavioral and psychological aspects of being a woman or a man* (Ashmore, 1990). This nature–nurture distinction provides the illusion of two nearly independent sources of behavior. However, on further review, it becomes clear that the two are not as independent as these definitions might suggest. Rather, it is essential to understand that the relationship between biological sex characteristics and gendered social behavior is much more complex.

West and Zimmerman (1987) argue that a person's sex is initially determined by applying culturally agreed upon biological criteria, such as external genitalia at birth. Depending on the evaluation of these criteria, the person is placed in one of two sex categories: female or male. This sex category represents the person's biological sex, even though the biological characteristics greatly vary from person to person, and sometimes the classification as male or female is ambiguous at best.

A person's sex is determined by four different criteria: chromosomes, hormones, gonads, and external genitalia. In most cases, all variables correspond with each other and with the designation of female or male. Yet, there are exceptions. For example, one female may carry the XY chromosomes usually occurring in males, yet show all "female" physical characteristics. In contrast, a female with the "normal" XX chromosomes may have a naturally occurring hormonal imbalance (e.g., adrenal hyperplasia) that causes her to develop muscle patterns and genitals similar to those of males (Nelson, 1994). In short, culture creates an artificial dichotomy of two mutually exclusive groups, "female" and "male," while disregarding the wide range and variety of biological variables. Once the nurse or doctor announces "It's a girl" or "It's a boy," the first major decision in a child's life has been made for her or him.

A great deal of social behavior is determined by one's assigned membership in one or another such exclusive category. For example, there are distinctly different sets of normative expectations associated with each category that guide the interaction between people in most situations. West and Zimmerman (1987) even suggest that gendered behavior is a necessary social requirement, since it helps identify a person as a member of one or the other gender, even if biological characteristics are ambiguous or lacking. For example, some traditional Islamic societies demand that women not reveal their faces to strange men. In this case, a woman needs to know if a stranger who approaches her is a woman or a man so that she may dress accordingly. Identifying another person as male or female provides us with one of the most basic social clues as to how this person is likely to behave toward us and how we are expected to behave toward that person.

Decades of psychological and anthropological research have produced evidence showing that differences between women and men appear in many known cultures. How many consistent differences exist and to what degree they can be rendered truly "universal" is the subject of much discussion in the field. In this chapter, we will discuss the developmental challenges involved in growing up female or male in different cultures.

Before we reflect on the role gender plays in every stage of a person's life, we will introduce some of the issues and theoretical perspectives relevant in gender research today.

◇ THEORETICAL PERSPECTIVES ON GENDER DIFFERENCES

Biological Perspectives

It is generally accepted that females and males of any species exhibit distinct biological and physiological differences. These include differences in chromosomes, hormonal production, and reproductive capabilities. It is unclear, however, how directly connected these physiological differences may be to differences in social behavior. For example, there is evidence that testosterone level is related to aggressiveness (Book, Starzyk, & Quinsey, 2001; Harris, 1999). Since men are known to have higher average levels of testosterone than do women, they should be expected to exhibit more aggressive behavior than do women. However, it is entirely possible that in cultures that encourage aggressive behavior in both genders, women will be more aggressive than men in cultures that discourage aggressive behaviors in general. In addition, there is clear evidence that females show more aggressive behavior than males in certain situations, for example protecting their offspring from predators. Consequently, we can only assume that physiological makeup may predispose women and men toward different behaviors.

The extent to which these behaviors are actually expressed depends in large part on environmental expectations and restrictions. Viewed from Bronfenbrenner's ecological systems model, the degree to which a child's behavior becomes gender appropriate in a given society depends heavily on the ecological system surrounding that particular child. The macrosystem (or larger outer ring) provides general customs and values regarding gender. For example, it is customary in most cultures for men and women to wear clothes and hairstyles appropriate for their respective gender. At the microsystem level, girls and boys may be assigned different roles in the family depending on their gender and may be given different rights and responsibilities (e.g., taking care of siblings, helping with household chores, or working in the garden).

Evolutionary Perspectives

Proponents of the evolutionary perspective suggest that many gender differences may be explained by an organism's motivation to pass on genes by producing offspring (Buss, 1994a, b; Low, 1989). The particular way in which this is accomplished appears to differ among men and women. Women, who have the ability to produce a limited number of children over a lifetime, put their energy into creating an environment that ensures the survival of a maximum number of children. To accomplish this, a large number of a woman's activities are directed toward the family and involve food preparation, home maintenance, and creation of a protective network of other people who will assist in larger tasks and also help protect against enemies (a part of the microsystem). In other words, the woman creates a developmental niche (or a microsystem) that will be most favorable for the development of her children.

In contrast, men can produce an almost unlimited number of children, given the availability of women. According to the evolutionary perspective, men strive to produce as many children as possible, because the more they have, the more will be likely to survive. To do this, they have to compete with other men. Under these circumstances, much of their energy is devoted to competing with other men for available women, and the focus is on physical strength and aggressiveness.

Despite these different reproductive strategies, women and men have a common goal; this ensures that their children have the greatest possible chance of survival. According to Darwin's "survival of the fittest" doctrine, children have a greater chance of survival if both parents have healthy genes. Consequently, men and women can increase the chances of their children's survival if they mate with a healthy partner. Both men and women enhance and display those characteristics that are evolutionarily attractive in order to be chosen as mates. According to this perspective, men tend to exhibit behavior that conveys strength and sexual prowess, such as engaging in challenging sports and games or displaying symbols of wealth and status—ranging from a Mercedes Benz in Europe to camels in Egypt (Chuang, 2002; Bereczkei, Voeroes, Gal, & Bernath, 1999). Women, on the other hand, tend to reinforce symbols of youthfulness and health, such as smooth skin, healthy teeth and hair, and a strong body, to communicate that they are young and fit enough to bear many children. If one accepts this evolutionary view of reproductive strategies, it may help explain those social behaviors that are considered specific to women and men in most societies. Regardless of the universality of reproductive strategies, culture-specific ecological systems determine the manner in which these behaviors are expressed.

Socialization and Learning Perspectives

Beginning at birth, individuals are socialized into their particular culture and taught the values, beliefs, and behaviors that will permit them to successfully function within it (see Chapter 3). From an early age, as part of the socialization process, children learn to conform to the roles that culture considers consistent with their biological sex. In general, girls are rewarded and praised for exhibiting behavior considered desirable for a woman in that culture and discouraged from showing undesirable, or gender-inappropriate, behavior.

In turn, boys are rewarded for male behavior and ridiculed if they exhibit behaviors reserved for girls or women.

By no means are "feminine" and "masculine" behaviors consistent across cultures. Occasionally, gender-specific norms may interact with cultural norms and modify gender roles. For example, while modesty and humility are viewed in China as culturally important values for all individuals, in other cultures these traits are more desirable, and more expected, in women than in men. For example, Chinese women have been found to be more self-effacing, modest, and less likely to take personal credit for accomplishments than are men, even though the cultural norm requires modesty from both genders (Crittenden, 1991). However, other sources suggest that these values, as well as gender socialization, are undergoing significant change in China and in other Asian countries (Ruan, 1991; Smith, 1992; Yi, 1993).

In addition to direct reinforcement and punishment, children in most cultures also observe same-sex adult role models and imitate the gender-appropriate behavior exhibited by these models. These behaviors are further reinforced and become internalized as attributes of gender-appropriate behavior patterns. In short, gender concepts are salient at many, if not all, levels of the ecological system and linked to gender differences as they occur in various cultures (Adler, 2001; Best, 2001).

As Gibbons, Stiles, and their associates (1996) have demonstrated, these cultural "systems" influence the gender socialization of children. In their studies, the researchers obtained drawings of the "ideal" woman and the "ideal" man from children and adolescents in several different countries (see Figure 7.1 a–d). Although they found a common tendency for the children to portray women as caring for children and the men as occupied in work roles outside the home, the researchers also found specific cultural differences. For instance, adolescents were more likely to draw the ideal woman in a nontraditional role as businesswoman in cultures with "masculine" work values, and the ideal man in a nontraditional role as caretaker in "feminine" cultures. The latter was the case in Norway, where adolescents more often expect the "ideal" man to participate in housework (Stiles & Gibbons, 1995). The researchers explain this finding by pointing out that Norwegians hold very egalitarian beliefs about the roles and status of women and men in their society and convey these beliefs to their children. Ideals may not always reflect social reality. Loscocco and Kalleberg (1988) point out that in highly "masculine" cultures such as Japan, positions of power are largely held by men, and women have only limited opportunity to achieve status and power and tend to remain in subordinate positions, both in the workplace and in private life. However, there is evidence that the role of Japanese women is slowly changing, affecting the image of women throughout Asia (Smith, 1992).

In summary, these different perspectives all propose a slightly different explanation for why some behaviors seem to vary with gender. The biological perspective considers gendered behavior a result of underlying biological and physiological processes. The evolutionary perspective describes gendered

a. Drawing by a fourteen-year-old girl from Mexico

c. Drawing by a thirteen-year-old boy from Guatemala

b. Drawing by a fifteen-year-old girl from the Netherlands

d. Drawing by an eleven-year-old boy from Spain

FIGURE 7.1   Drawings of Ideal Women by Children of Various Cultures

Source: From material from J. L. Gibbons and D. A. Stiles. Reprinted by permission.

behavior as the result of evolutionary processes. Gendered behaviors represent behaviors that have evolved as most adaptive, considering both biological attributes and environmental challenges. Finally, socialization and learning theories see gendered behaviors as the result of a person's individual learning history within a specific sociocultural context. None of these perspectives can explain the phenomenon of gender differences and how they originated. Nonetheless, they show clearly that gender, like many other concepts in this book, cannot be viewed just from one perspective. Keep that in mind when we now turn our attention to how issues of sex and gender relate to development in each of the stages of the lifespan.

◇ INFANCY AND CHILDHOOD

As we pointed out in Chapter 3, parents are the primary source of socialization in the lives of young children, and they introduce the important knowledge, values, beliefs, and expected behaviors of the culture. One aspect of this concerns society's expectations regarding appropriate behavior for women and men, or gender-role stereotypes.

Gender Socialization

One of the most exhaustive investigations of gender stereotypes and attitudes was conducted by Williams and Best (1990), who found significant differences between male and female stereotypes in each of the twenty-five countries studied. In general, passivity, submissiveness, affiliation, and nurturance were seen as more typical in descriptions of women, whereas activity, dominance, achievement, and aggressiveness were more typical of men. In this study, Williams and Best also found fascinating evidence related to differences in the socialization of gender stereotypes among children five to eleven years of age. For example, across all age groups, children in most countries were more familiar with the male stereotype than with the female, suggesting that male stereotypes are more dominant in their lives and are learned earlier. Only in Brazil, Portugal, and Germany did five-year-old children clearly identify more items associated with the female stereotype. Overall, Williams and Best suggest that gender stereotypes are well-established in children by the time they are eight years old. After that age, they serve as powerful "blueprints" for behaviors that are reinforced throughout life. Gender-role stereotypes not only promote overt behavior and prescribe types of clothing and social rituals, but also influence the way in which men and women in a given society view themselves and others. According to these researchers, by the age of nine, children are already applying gender stereotypes in their descriptions of themselves. In the case of the midwestern siblings Alisa and Alan, both did well in school and both wanted a career. Yet, Alisa was raised according to the cultural stereotype of women as caretakers. She cared for her husband and two children, and even after her divorce she continued her role as the caretaker of her elderly mother.

Feminist scholars (Rhode, 1990) argue that these gender blueprints socialize women into lower-status roles and dependency due to the differential positions of power either group holds in society. Since, in most known societies, men tend to hold positions of power and to distribute available resources, they frequently have the opportunity to define social roles for both women and men. They also have the potential to use resources and status as rewards. To preserve male social dominance, younger men are rewarded for conforming to the behavior that later enables them to achieve positions of power in society. Among these desirable behaviors are competitiveness, aggressiveness, and dominance. If men conform successfully and "play by the rules," they will gain power, status, and access to resources.

Women, on the other hand, are usually discouraged from exhibiting behaviors that are reserved for men. Instead, an entirely different set of normative behaviors is defined for them. In many cultures, they are expected to be submissive, nurturing, and weak. This feminine ideal is defined by men in order to preserve male privilege. The idea is that weak and submissive individuals are not likely to compete for resources and power. By conforming to this feminine ideal, women become attractive and gain the recognition of powerful men. In turn, they may be rewarded by receiving indirect access to power and resources. Women who refuse to conform to the female gender role will be denied these resources and status. In this case, the differing social status and power of women and men represent an important part of the ecological system in which children grow up. Power differences between women and men are related to their differential treatment by society, as well as gender differences in behavior.

Low (1989) examined the training of children in relation to different reproductive strategies prevalent in several cultures. In polygynous societies, in

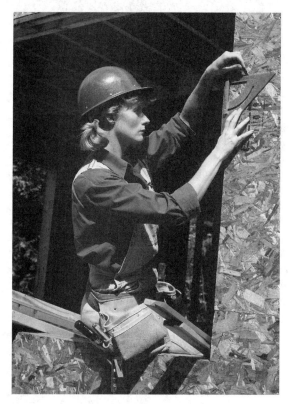

Being a "homemaker" takes on a new meaning in today's society. (© CoCo/Rainbow)

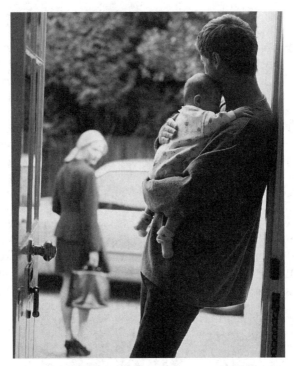

More fathers are staying at home to care for their children while mothers enter the workforce. (© Ronald Mackechnie/Getty images)

which it is customary for men to have multiple reproductive partners, the competition among men for women is very strong. In polygynous societies, like those of sub-Saharan Africa, young boys are taught to be aggressive and competitive. In societies in which monogamy or even polyandry prevails, the number of reproductive partners is restricted, and men are not engaged in competition to the same extent. For example, the role and socialization of boys in Nyinba, Tibet, are quite different. They are taught cooperation and sharing rather than competition and aggressiveness, since they will one day share a common wife and children with one or more men. In addition, polyandrous societies grant women more control over resources and more independence from one particular man. Consequently, socialization of girls focuses more on independence and assertiveness and less on obedience and submissiveness.

Cultural Influences on Female and Male Socialization

In spite of the widespread similarities in gender-role expectations across cultures, there are distinct differences in how gender-related behaviors are transmitted to young girls and boys (Maccoby, 1998). Depending on avail-ability of role models, displays of expected role behavior, or influence of so-cialization agents, children in different cultures experience their socialization differently. Examples of gender-role socialization from a variety of cultural perspectives, including Korean, Japanese, Islamic, Indian, Nigerian and Na-tive American, will serve as illustrations of this point. (See Box 7.1).

One cannot view the socialization of certain behaviors independently from the cultural context. Cultures define the basic values and ideals (macrosystems) as well as the agents who teach the values and the settings in which they are taught (microsystems). In turn, individuals growing up in this ecological system will shape their environment by adding individual characteristics to that setting, establishing a unique developmental niche. As a consequence, the socialization experiences of individuals in the various cultures described above have taken very different paths.

Gender Relationships in Childhood

Apart from parents and caretakers, the role of peers in childhood social-ization cannot be underestimated. In fact, Hartup (1983) points out that "in most cultures, the significance of peer relations as a socialization con-text is rivaled only by the family" (p. 103). Consequently, same-sex and mixed-sex peer groups provide an effective context for the observation and practice of gender-role behaviors. For example, it could be argued that early gender segregation indicates very large differences in normative expectations for women and men in that society; these differences need to be reinforced early. On the other hand, mixed-sex peer groups through-out childhood and the relative lack of differential treatment of the two genders may indicate greater equality between the genders in adulthood. The examples of our two pairs of siblings in the chapter vignettes may suggest that this is indeed the case. Harin and Tippa shared many of their childhood activities and did not experience much gender segregation. As adults, they have chosen professions that appear to contradict the stereo-type associated with many occupations, suggesting greater flexibility of gender roles. However, a look at different cultures shows that the rela-tionship between gender relations in childhood and adult gender-role be-havior is not always as linear.

Overall, there is a large range of cultural variation in the extent to which children's playmates are of both genders or predominantly of the same gender (Whiting & Whiting, 1975). Gender relations in play groups range from completely segregated, to segregated for part of the time, to inter-gender relations. The makeup of play groups can be more or less dictated by cultural conventions that include the gender constellation of the groups.

As an example, there seems to be clear evidence that even though most activities are not gender-segregated by definition in early childhood, children in North America prefer to interact with peers of their own gender

BOX 7.1

 CULTURAL PERSPECTIVES ON GENDER-ROLE SOCIALIZATION

Korea

In Korean society women observe the Confucian virtues of the *Rule of Three Obediences*, in which they are required to be obedient to their fathers, husbands, and sons. Parents stress the emotional development of girls, who are expected to be kind and nurturing, and the strength and intellectual development of boys, who are expected to be strong and courageous. The division of responsibilities in the Korean household is segregated by gender, with men providing the financial support and women tending to the house.

Schools are also gender-segregated, but both sexes have the opportunity for education. Elementary school attendance is compulsory for both boys and girls, with more boys attending high school and college. Korean schools stress different curricula for males and females, and teachers hold differential expectations based on gender. For example, the curriculum for females is designed to foster feminine traits, and students must take mandatory courses in home economics and subjects geared to women as consumers and childbearers. The male curriculum promotes masculine traits, and male students are required to take technology-type courses.

Marriage is viewed as a stage that everyone should experience. Adult identification depends on getting married, starting a family, and gaining status in one's profession. While modern marriages are no longer solely prearranged to continue the family lineage, this does occasionally still occur. Contemporary Korean society views marriage as a way of fulfilling individuals' happiness.

In Korea, the law states that fathers have rights and obligations over their children in case of divorce, and, although some legal action has been taken to reduce paternal rights, they almost always receive custody. As a result, many women who fear losing their children remain in unhappy marriages.

Japan

Modernization has begun to alter Japan and has affected many areas including gender. For example, more Japanese women remain single or work outside the home than ever before. However, some traditions remain strong. For example, traditionally the eldest male child was responsible for carrying on the family lineage and entitled to an automatic inheritance of the family property. Today, while the oldest son is no longer automatically entitled to the inheritance, he is considered responsible for supporting and caring for aging parents, although, in reality, the daughter-in-law generally provides such care.

Education is extremely important, and, like Korea, there is a gender difference. For example, females are under less academic pressure than males.

BOX 7.1 CONTINUED

Later, most Japanese men gravitate toward the occupational role while women become committed to the domestic role. The "homebody" or "professional housewife" is idealized even though 60% of women are in the labor force. Childrearing remains the most important aspect in Japanese women's lives, and, although more women are working outside the home, this commitment continues to exist today.

Finally, women and men both exert a considerable amount of influence but in separate spheres. For example, women tend to control almost all household duties, including home finances and children's educations and, similar to American women, do a disproportionate share of household labor; while men more often spend long hours working and commuting.

Islamic Culture

While Islam emphasizes the complementary nature of the sexes, what Islam says about men and women may vary in interpretation and practice. Contrary to what some may believe, Islam does not say that women are naturally inferior. In fact, a Muslim woman is entitled to the following rights: (1) independent ownership, (2) to marry whom she likes and to end an unsuccessful marriage, (3) to education, (4) to keep her own identity, (5) to sexual pleasure, (6) to inheritance, (7) to election and nomination to political offices and participation in public affairs, and (8) to respect. However, because sons carry on the family name and daughters do not economically contribute to the family, there is a definite preference for male children. As children, girls help their mothers with the house (an activity discouraged in boys) and have more restrictions placed on them than boys with regard to their behavior.

Marriage in Islam is viewed as a contract between two equal and consenting partners. The wife has a right to stipulate her own conditions and the dowry belongs to her. Islam considers marriage a lifelong commitment, and while divorce is allowed, it is discouraged. When women marry, they enter a new stage of life in which they are sending signals that they are good wives and mothers and this is a very important way of gathering respect.

While the *Qur'an* advocates equal partnership between husband and wife, the husband often assumes the role of authoritarian and the wife becomes submissive to his wishes and orders—a distinction between what Islam says and its actual practice. Females do have inheritance rights, but they often inherit one-half the portion that men do.

Although education is a basic right in Islam for both sexes, educating females has not always occurred. Recently, efforts have been made to improve female education in some Muslim countries; however, educational opportunities for women, especially in the Middle East, lag behind men. For example, the Islamic world, especially the Arab world, is one of the areas that

(continued)

BOX 7.1 CONTINUED

have the highest rates of illiteracy among women, the lowest level of schooling for females, and the smallest number of women in paid employment.

India

In India, both age and gender play an important role. Elders, especially elder males, have more status than younger people, and male children are valued more than female children, especially in North India. Marriage is optional for males but considered essential for all girls regardless of caste, class, religion, or ethnicity; and females are often viewed as visitors because they leave home and reside with the husband's family.

A Hindu woman's role is a series of role relationships as daughter, daughter-in-law, wife, and mother, and she achieves her highest status as mother of a son. A daughter-in-law's status is increased when she gives birth to a boy. Divorce is rare and is considered an admission of a woman's failure as a wife and a daughter-in-law. Brides have impressed upon them that walking out of a marriage for any reason disgraces her parental family. The supervision of daughters-in-law is delegated to their mothers-in-law, who wield considerable power. Thus, older women come under the authority of men, but younger women come under the authority of both men and older women.

Socioeconomic status plays a role in gender and beliefs about men and women. For example, upper-middle-class and upper-class women are likely to have an education and, thus, be exposed to modern (often Western) thought. School is considered essential for boys but not necessarily so for girls, although they are taught to read and write. Instead, girls are often kept at home to care for younger children, especially among lower socioeconomic-level families.

Nigeria

In infancy, there is little difference in the childrearing of male and female babies, but gender segregation begins in early childhood. The male child, after the age of six, is involved in secret societies that serve as models of adult society. Girls, however, are not allowed to join.

Children are sent to school when money is available, and boys are enrolled more frequently than girls. However, there has been, in certain parts of the society, a rapid growth in the number of educated females. While there are many institutions of higher education in Nigeria, a significant proportion of the population still views advanced education as unnecessary for females. The Igbo tribe has been more accepting of female education and changes in female roles than the Hausa tribe.

Women often marry early, usually in their teens, and have large families. Thus, childbearing occupies their fertile years. Nigerian marriage laws acknowledge that the husband is the head of the household and that he has complete

BOX 7.1 CONTINUED

authority over his wife and children. Nigerians often practice polygyny and, under Islamic law, a Muslim male can have up to four wives if he can support them. Inheritance is often difficult for women unless they can prove that they helped to acquire the material wealth. In some cases, widows are considered property and may be inherited by the husband's oldest male relative.

Finally, there is a difference in the division of labor, with men often involved in cultivating cash crops and blacksmithing, and women, in some areas, selling their weavings and pottery. The Igbo relies on market trade conducted primarily by women as a large part of their economic system. Thus, women's control over local trade helps to establish their independence in a culture primarily dominated by men.

Native American Culture
There are over 300 distinct tribes of American Indians who primarily live in California, Oklahoma, New Mexico, Arizona, Alaska, North Carolina, and Washington. The tribes vary in customs, language, and type of family structure, as well as in their degree of acculturation and whether or not they live on reservations or in urban areas. However, despite their great diversity, they are generally viewed as sharing a number of common values, including (1) sharing, (2) cooperation, (3) noninterference, (4) present time orientation, (5) extended family orientation, and (6) harmony with nature.

Traditionally, great value was assigned to the role of women in Native American society and they were frequently the primary educators and historians. Life was rooted in spirituality and the extended family, and traditional ideologies stressed the importance of balance and harmony between the genders and the equal contributions of both to maintain the household and the community. For example, men and women share in the work of grazing, agriculture, and crafts and have equal rights of inheritance.

The status of both women and men increases with age, and age and wisdom are revered in both sexes. The Navajo is a matrilineal society (i.e., the mother's clan is of primary importance and the father's clan is secondary). A Navajo belief is that the people were created from the Changing Woman, who represents the season and the earth, and children of both genders are equally welcomed.

The job of the Navajo father is to provide for his children and to serve as a role model in teaching skills, values, and good behaviors. Mothers teach small children and growing girls. If the father is absent, then the mother's brother assumes some obligations toward her children. Fathers and sons have a more direct relationship than father and daughter.

Source: Adapted from *Culture and Gender* by Vicki Ritts, 2001, unpublished manuscript, St. Louis Community College. Reprinted by permission.

(Maccoby, 1990; 1998). On the other hand, Harkness and Super (1985) report that rural Kenyan children are segregated by gender starting at about six years due to gender-specific duties expected from boys and girls. However, regardless of this culturally imposed segregation, the authors argue that there is evidence that children do not interact more with same-sex peers than with opposite-sex peers, even when more of them are present. According to an early description of Truk society in Oceania, children there associate with playmates of both sexes without distinction until the age of about six, when groups tend to become more structured according to gender (Gladwin & Sarason, 1953).

Another example of gender segregation in childhood and its consequences for gender relations later on is reported in an early study from Taiwan (Wolf, 1972). In childhood, relationships between girls and boys are characterized by competition, especially in schools that are coed but separate girls and boys in the classroom and during other activities. Interactions between girls and boys are characterized by heated exchanges in which it is the goal to insult the other group. Wolf reports that this hostile attitude is often carried into adulthood, when women and men are expected to cooperate in usually mixed-gender work settings. These examples demonstrate the different arrangements for gender interactions during childhood (and beyond) in various cultures. However, even when culturally determined arrangements are seemingly similar, there are variations in how gender relations develop. For example, even lacking cultural demands for gender segregation, younger children nonetheless may prefer to interact more with same-sex peers.

Eleanor Maccoby's research (1990, 1998, 2002) suggests that the preference for same-sex playmates is universal, regardless of cultural norms prescribing gender-segregated environments in childhood. Although cultural research on playmate preference is still scarce, a few studies conducted in nonwestern cultures seem to confirm Maccoby's claim. Munroe and Romney (2006) analyzed observational data from Belize, Kenya, Nepal, and American Samoa. These four cultures vary in their emphasis on gender differentiation. The Logoli of Kenya and the Newars of Nepal emphasize strict gender-specific roles, rituals, and activities, thus exposing girls and boys to very different socialization experiences. In contrast, among the Garifuna of Belize and in American Samoan society, gender-differentiated socialization is much less pronounced. For example, girls and boys are expected to contribute about equally to work around the house and there are no gender-specific initiation rites.

Munroe and Romney's results (2006) confirmed that children clustered in predominantly same-sex playgroups. This tendency was more pronounced in boys than girls and increased with age. Similar findings occurred in all four cultures studied and were not mediated by cultural norms regarding gender-segregation. In this regard, Salamone (1983) has described differences in the games played by girls and boys in Yauri, Nigeria. A popular girls' game is called *sunana bojo ne* (My name is Bojo). Ten to fifteen players, holding hands, form a half circle and move clockwise while singing and dancing. They dance around one girl in the middle, who serves as the song leader. Eventually, and without warning, this girl falls backward into the circle, trusting her playmates to catch her. Girls will take turns playing the role of the lead singer. In contrast, a popular boys' game is ring toss, where each boy tosses a rubber ring at a bottle or a stick with the goal being to get the ring to land around the neck of the bottle. This game involves a great deal of competition, since none of the players wants to be the last one to score and be teased by his playmates as the loser. The traditional games played by girls reinforce behaviors considered desirable for females in that particular culture. By playing *sunana bojo ne*, girls practice cooperation and interpersonal skills rather than focusing on their physical and motor skills.

The seemingly consistent phenomenon of same-sex preference in playmates lends itself to a biological explanation of gender differences. Due to their predisposition, boys might bond together through activities that facilitate physicality and competition. Girls' pattern of play, in comparison, emphasizes interaction and collaboration. However, biological predisposition towards gender-specific behavior and preferences may only serve as a partial explanation. Harkness and Super (1985) explain these differences in terms of the developmental niche, in which children actively explore and define gender relations within the parameters set by cultural expectations. In addition, unique group processes, inherent in the microsystem of the playgroup, may highlight the expression of gender-specific behaviors. Gauvain and Cole (2005) note that "gender-related behaviors are more evident when children are observed in groups than when they are tested individually."(p. 187).

◇ ADOLESCENCE

Markers of Sexual Maturation

In addition to clear biological markers of sexual maturity, such as menarche and development of breasts in girls and growth of facial hair and change of voice in boys, there are distinct cultural markers that indicate a readiness among women and men to find a sexual partner. Biological and cultural markers may or may not coincide, depending on cultural norms. For example, Hindus consider a girl sexually mature with the onset of menstruation. However, a sexually mature unmarried woman living in her father's house is considered unfortunate for all involved, and it is the duty of the father to marry off his daughter as soon as she reaches puberty or even before.

The transition from adolescence to adulthood is often considered a highly spiritual event that is celebrated with elaborate initiation ceremonies. These ceremonies often involve a ritual change of hairstyle, clothing, tattoos, or even circumcision in order to make the newly gained status as adult visible to all. However, transition to adulthood is not always marked by one single event. Mayan culture, for example, considers young women and men sexually mature and allows them to find a mate when they begin to feel sexual desire. Parents or other members of the community do not get involved in the young person's decisions about who or when to marry. Bertrand and others (1992) report that this generally does not happen until the ages of sixteen to eighteen for women and twenty for men.

Gender, Sexuality, and Cultural Taboos

Once young women and young men are considered sexually mature, they are prepared to experience their first initial sexual encounter. Across cultures, these experiences vary greatly in terms of how strictly they are guided by cultural norms and which forms they take. The expectation of chastity until marriage (particularly for women) is a norm among many cultures. Patriarchal societies and those based on traditional Catholic or Islamic values generally have very strict chastity norms. Consequently, young women have little or no sexual experience or instruction until they marry. In societies in which girls are allowed to explore their sexuality more or less freely, such as the Masai of Kenya or the Hopi Indians of North America, there are some legal or normative rules about the age at which a girl may become sexually active. Usually, the minimum age is no younger than thirteen or fourteen. Chastity norms rarely apply in the same way to young men. Instead, boys are frequently encouraged to engage in various types of activity in order to practice sexual behavior, satisfy their sexual desires, or express their virility and dominance. Young men's sexual experience is seen as preparation for a longterm relationship or marriage. It is the practice in some cultures for older women, frequently prostitutes or unmarried women in the community, to instruct adolescent boys in sexual matters (Ruan, 1991).

In some cultures, such as the indigenous societies of North and South America, communication about sexual matters is largely taboo and surrounded by myths, so that adolescents are left to explore their sexuality on their own. In their study of Mayan culture in Guatemala, Bertrand, Ward, and Pauc (1992) report that adolescents receive little education or information about sex. Young girls do not learn about menstruation until they experience menarche and also have few sources from which to learn about sexual matters. In contrast, boys learn about physical development in school, from friends, or even from television or movies. While these are informal sources of information, culturally sanctioned information about marriage is conveyed during a traditional religious ceremony. However, according to their findings, this ceremony is considered primarily a ritual and does not provide practical advice and instruction regarding sexual relations.

In addition to prohibiting sexual intercourse before marriage, some societies have strict taboos about sexual activities. In China "the only sexual behavior which is acknowledged to be legally and morally permissive is heterosexual intercourse within a monogamous marriage. Every imaginable variation is explicitly proscribed. Thus, prostitution, polygamy, premarital and extramarital intercourse (including cohabitation), homosexuality, and variant sexual behaviors are illegal" (Ruan, 1991, p. 159). Traditional Hinduism prescribes a very specific definition of sexuality, and following that definition is absolutely essential. Any unnatural sexual activity, including extramarital relations or homosexuality, results in losing one's caste, mutilation, or even death. It should be noted that these norms refer to the most strict followers of traditional Hindu teachings. In modern India, as in many other cultures, the norms themselves, as well as the consequences for breaking them, vary greatly.

Young adolescents in many other cultures are permitted to explore and express their sexuality in a variety of ways. For example, among the Maya in Guatemala, it is common to freely choose one's sexual partner. Parents do not have much to say regarding the selection of a mate or the age of marriage. Nonetheless, Mayan adolescents respect cultural traditions and generally abstain from sexual contact before marriage. Their interactions are typically limited to talking, holding hands, kissing, and embracing.

In cultures in which premarital relations between women and men are not prohibited by cultural norms, they are considered an expression of love and affection. Yet, how love and affection are perceived and expressed is, again, subject to wide cultural variations. In a comparison of college students of four different ethnic backgrounds, Dion and Dion (1993) found that Asian subjects of both genders view love relationships more in terms of friendship and caring than do women and men of European or Anglo–Celtic backgrounds. The authors argue that this view of love is consistent with the notion of self and others in cultures that emphasize collectivism (see also Ting-Toomey, 1991).

In most cultures, the concepts of gender and sexuality are closely related. The cultural norms about what men and women should look like and how they should behave extends to the realm of sexuality (Diamond and Savin-Williams, 2002). For example, gender appropriate behavior for women usually includes being attracted to men and engaging in sexual relations with men. Thus, a lesbian woman violates this female gender norm by being attracted to and sexually active with other women. By deviating from the female gender norm, she sheds doubt on her "womanhood." If she does not behave like a "real" woman, is she a "real" woman? Conversely, a heterosexual man, who happens to be feminine in his appearance or makes a career choice that is more typical for women in his culture, will likely be perceived as gay. If he is gender atypical in his behavior, he must also be gender-atypical in his sexuality.

Other sexual minorities, such as transgendered individuals and bisexual youth, face similar challenges. In adolescence, when issues of gender and sexuality become particularly salient, young people may struggle with the expression of their gender identity and sexuality. Deviating from gender norms and/or deviating from sexual norms may have serious social and psychological consequences. Interestingly, the extent of the consequences depends on how strictly gender deviation is viewed in a given cultural context. For example, in traditional Latino cultures that value and expect "machismo" from young men and passivity, subservience, and nurturance from young women, those who deviate from these ideals are stigmatized, ostracized, and sometimes the victims of violence (Parker, 1989). When strict gender norms are less pervasive in a person's ecological system, mild or temporary deviations from gender norms may be tolerated (Martin, 1990; McGann, 1999). This might be the case in some contemporary Northern European countries, in which people hold very egalitarian beliefs about the roles and norms for women and men in society (see Stiles and Gibbons, 1995, earlier in this chapter). Not coincidentally, Scandinavian countries have the most liberal laws concerning sexual minorities.

◊ EARLY AND MIDDLE ADULTHOOD

The life tasks individuals encounter in early and middle adulthood can be considered universal. In any culture, adults are faced with responsibilities related to childrearing and providing for themselves and their families. In short, they have to "make a living." How these responsibilities are distributed and what the settings in which people "make a living" look like depends, in large part, on the individual's ecological system. Cultural values, socioeconomic status, and family size are just some examples of ecological influences, as well as characteristics of the developmental niche. In this section, we look at the specific ways in which gender influences the lives of adults in different cultural environments.

Status and the Division of Labor Within the Family

Based on universal gender-role stereotypes and gender-role socialization, the adult roles of women and men are very different. Throughout history, and in almost all known societies, women take primary responsibility for childrearing and housework, while men are responsible for work outside the home. Industrialization and increasing economic pressures have brought about drastic changes that have affected the exclusive nature of this arrangement. Today, agricultural communities can no longer sustain all their families, and many men have to leave their villages and towns to find work in larger cities. As a result, traditional family structure is disrupted and, along with it, traditional gender roles. Women then find it necessary to seek work outside the home to fulfill some of the tasks the departed men leave behind. Also, in highly industrialized countries, technology has made housework much easier and less time-consuming, but sometimes more expensive. In many cases, these additional financial needs can only be met by an additional income provided by the woman.

Surprisingly (or maybe not so surprising to some), increased participation of women in the workforce has not led to a significant change in gender roles at home. Numerous studies show that men tend to participate more in housework when their spouse works outside the home. However, even if both spouses are employed full time, childrearing and housework are still the main responsibility of the woman. Similar patterns are found in families in the United States, Switzerland, Indonesia, the Philippines, Taiwan, and South Korea (Charles & Hopflinger, 1992; Sanchez, 1993).

Kerig, Alyoshina, and Volovich (1993) describe some psychological and social consequences of these changing demands and unchanging gender roles within some Russian families. Russian policies strongly emphasize equality of men and women in the workforce, and the large majority of families are two-income families. However, traditional gender-role socialization puts the burden of household chores and childcare exclusively on women, while men actively focus on their work and career. Women may request that their husbands take more responsibility for the family, but husbands are reluctant to become involved in gender-inappropriate activities and often respond by distancing themselves even further from the family. As a result, wives become more demanding and husbands withdraw more, causing great distress for all involved. The authors point out that "rates of divorce are higher in Russia than in any other industrialized nation except the United States, and that births among ethnic Russians have been rapidly declining" (p. 402).

Division of Labor in the Workforce

In addition to the gendered division of labor in the family, women and men are frequently segregated into different occupations in the labor force. Many occupational fields are either female-dominated or male-dominated. One possible explanation is that those occupations requiring female stereotyped attributes (e.g., nurturance) are female-dominated because women have better skills for that work or simply prefer it. For many women and men, these gender-stereotyped occupations represent an important aspect of their developmental niche. Not surprisingly, in many cultures women tend to be teachers, nurses, or caregivers. Similarly, occupations requiring physical endurance, strength, or assertiveness (e.g., laborer jobs or executive positions) tend to be dominated by males. However, stereotypic gender roles are only one possible explanation for occupational gender segregation.

Occupational fields are also frequently segregated by status. Female-dominated occupations generally have a lower status than male-dominated occupations, regardless of the work involved. For example, activities that involve interpersonal communication and interaction are often associated with women, because they tend to have stronger verbal and interpersonal skills. This helps to explain why more women than men become teachers, therapists, and social workers. Yet, few women are involved at the highest levels in international politics, business, or academia, all of which require a great

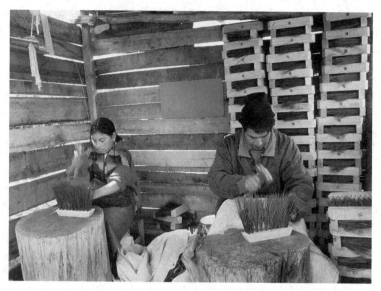

In Paslocale, Equador, a father and daughter work together making brooms.
(© Richard Lord/The Image Works)

deal of interpersonal and verbal skills. Harin, mentioned in our opening vignette, who prepared to be an elementary school teacher in Thailand, probably has many more female colleagues than male colleagues, unless this occupation is highly regarded in his culture.

High-status occupations typically are better paid and are associated with access to greater resources, resulting in frequent wage and status gaps between some women and men. As a consequence, women are often economically disadvantaged and dependent on their husbands or other men as financial providers. In fact, it appears that there is a consistent gender difference in how men and women view the relationship between status, money, and pay. Tang (1996) revealed that men in the United States with high money ethic endorsement (MEE—the psychological importance of money) allocated significantly more money to the highest position and less money to the lowest positions (creating a large pay differential and clearly linking status with money) than did those to whom money was less important. Women's allocation of money was not affected by their MEE. In a subsequent study, Tang and his colleagues (2000) conducted a cross-cultural comparison of pay differentials (in the United States, Taiwan, and the United Kingdom) as a function of the rater's sex and MEE. Findings showed that Taiwanese allocated more money to different positions than did their British and American counterparts. Men tended to have a significantly higher top/bottom pay differential than women. In another study focusing on the devaluation of women's work, England, Hermsen, and Cotter (2000) found that there is a "wage penalty" for working in occupations that have a higher percentage of women. The following section discusses how this societal stratification may, as part of the ecological system, affect interpersonal relationships in some contemporary societies.

Gender Relations in Social Status, Religion, and Public Policy

Social and economic stratification is deeply rooted in culture, contributes to gender inequality, and is reflected in relationships within the family. Assuming that economic power equals social power, the family member with the greatest social power will be most dominant within the family and thus be a powerful influence within the microsystem. Asserting this power can mean making financial and social decisions, asserting one's needs, assigning tasks to other family members, and yielding or denying access to resources. Since men generally have more economic and social power than women, they are likely to control and shape interpersonal relationships with a spouse and within the family. While women may manage everyday financial or social affairs, the ultimate power of approval or disapproval for decisions often lies with men, who may choose or not choose to exercise this power. Since these status differences are so pervasive, they are often reinforced by the religious and political institutions present within a culture's various ecological settings. Traditional Christian and Islamic religious teachings present arguments for the "destructiveness" of women as justification for the superiority and dominance of men.

Similarly, traditional Hindu religious texts assert that a woman represents an inherently dangerous spiritual force that needs to be controlled and restrained through all stages of her life. Thus, first the father and then the husband are assigned the religiously sanctioned task of subordinating and subduing the woman. In interpreting this philosophy, Kumari (1988) writes, "Thus, the ideal Hindu woman is one who sees her highest good in her husband, is devoted to him with a religious zeal and is good and chaste. In other words, she is under the control of her husband, and the wifely role is one of subordination and devotion whatever may be the circumstances. The woman's place is primarily confined to the home, her role limited to procreation and the bringing up of children and catering to the needs of her husband. Chastity and control of sexuality are the most important aspects of the role of a wife. The maintenance of chastity requires control of sexuality and a woman's sexuality should always be under the control of a man. Before marriage it is the father who controls her, and after marriage the husband" (p. 11).

Following these religious prescriptions is beneficial for women. Religious texts further command that the woman who meets this ideal is to be worshipped and held in the highest regard. Thus, her subordinate role to man is to be seen as an honorable subordination that contributes to spiritual salvation of both herself and the husband who successfully fulfills his task of controlling her "evil" powers. Demonstrating a certain ambivalence about "femaleness" in Indian culture, Bhogle (1999) points out the following: (1) the Indian constitution gives women and men equal rights, (2) India has had powerful women leaders (most notably Indira Ghandi, the former Prime Minister), and (3) an Indian temple contains as many goddesses as gods (wealth, learning, and power have been associated with goddesses rather than gods). Faced with this seemingly contradictory image of the ideal woman, when the modern Hindu woman, "due to economic reasons or from a psychological need for self-fulfillment . . . broadens the boundaries of her traditional sphere to include matters outside 'home and hearth,' she comes into conflict with her gender roles" (p. 282).

In cultures where there is an absence of support for working mothers, policies that prevent women from managing their own financial affairs, and neglect of health issues, women frequently find themselves in a position of dependency. Making changes in such policies would reverse these situations and contribute to greater gender equality and a reduction in gender-role stereotypes. For example, in contemporary China, the government's practice of assigning some individuals to selected work sites separates many married couples, who are only allowed to see each other for about two weeks in a given year (Ruan, 1991). As a result, husbands and wives have little opportunity to develop and practice traditional gender-role behavior in the home. In addition, China's one-child policy gives women the opportunity to make nontraditional career choices and increase their financial independence.

Furthermore, China has seen a dramatic change in sexual attitudes. Even though public policy explicitly prohibits any sexual relations between women and men outside of marriage, premarital and extramarital sexual activity has increased sharply (Ruan, 1991). While all of these factors may contribute to high divorce rates and marital dissatisfaction among Chinese couples, they also promote more egalitarian relationships between men and women.

Similarly, children's views of men and women have begun to change in countries where public policies have addressed gender equity. For example, in one study, when asked to draw their image of the ideal woman and the ideal man, adolescents in North America depicted women as working at a job and men as caring for children (Stiles, Gibbons, & de la Garza-Schnellman, 1990). Williams and Best (1990) found the same trend in Norway, a country in which the government has promoted gender equity for many years.

◇ LATER ADULTHOOD AND OLD AGE

In Chapter 9, we shall discuss cultural views on marriage. At this point, it may be sufficient to point out that men and women in later adulthood, in most cultures and religions, consider marriage to be one of the highest sacraments. However, in any society there will be a number of individuals who do not have a spouse, either because they never married or because they lost their mate through divorce or death.

Divorce and Widowhood

According to traditional Hindu beliefs, divorce is unacceptable. If men are not content in their marriage, they are allowed to take a second wife. After their wife's death, men are also permitted to remarry immediately. Widowhood for women, on the other hand, carries a strong social stigma. Without her husband, she is considered incomplete and even sinful. She is not allowed to remarry, becomes a social outcast, and simply awaits her own death. As a result, some women choose to burn themselves at their husband's funeral to attain spiritual salvation. **Sati,** or *widow immolation,* is a sacred practice (Kumari, 1988). Although the current Indian government strongly discourages this practice, a widow's memory is still held in high regard if she dies within a reasonable time after her husband's death.

Among the Hausa of Northern Nigeria, marriage also plays an important spiritual role. Adults who die while still married are expected to move on to **Lahira,** or *paradise* (Smith, 1965). Although divorced and widowed adults are stigmatized, they are not met with nearly as much resentment as adults who never marry. Previously married women can still acquire some status by becoming prostitutes and remarrying later, an option denied to women who were never married. Similarly, Wolf (1964) reports a surprisingly high number of divorced women who work as prostitutes in Hokkien society in Taiwan.

In many Native American societies, a widow secures her livelihood by marrying one of her husband's brothers or another close relative. Divorced women may return to their parents or marry another man. Divorce proceedings are relatively uncomplicated unless wife and husband share a great deal of property or the wife's relatives want to negotiate the return of the bride price paid to the husband. These examples of women in different societies show that even in adulthood, individuals create their own developmental niche in response to cultural norms and expectations associated with, in this case, divorce and widowhood.

When viewing divorce in the larger ecological context, it becomes clear that cultural beliefs about gender roles and gender-typical behavior (macrosystem) shape individual experiences within the family (microsystem). "Divorce is not merely behavior on the microlevel, but is associated with shifting cultures on the macrolevel" (Yodanis, 2005, p. 656). Yodanis argues that the option of divorce, when accepted in society, gives women the power to negotiate equal status in the family. Her study of 22 countries revealed that women and men experience more equality in their marriage when divorce is practiced and accepted in their society. In countries that, until recently, outlawed divorce (The Philippines and Ireland) or in which divorce is highly unaccepted (Japan), gender roles within the family tended to be more traditional and unequal in terms of work distribution and decision-making power in the home.

These findings are mirrored in Bulbeck's (2005) description of young people's understanding of gender relations within the larger cultural context.

Even though many of the young adults interviewed had not yet established their own family, the cultural beliefs about gender relations within the family were well-established. Respondents from Asian cultures (Japan, Korea, Thailand) tended to emphasize separate roles for men and women within the family. These beliefs were associated with the cultural belief that prescribed gender roles serve the family and society. In contrast, young adults from Australia, USA, and Canada showed strong support for gender equality in the home based on individual preference.

Gender Roles and Status in Old Age

In traditional societies, age is frequently associated with a gain in community status. Older adults are respected and accepted as leaders who bring with them a wealth of life experience. Furthermore, they are frequently thought to have supernatural powers, and they hold important spiritual and religious responsibilities. Finally, both female and male elders are considered important to the socialization process because they pass on the group's cultural heritage to the next generation. In societies in which status is based on age and role as much as gender, older women may actually gain considerable power, both within their families and in society, once they have broken through the "seniority" barrier. Lebra (1999) suggests that this may be the case in Asian societies more so than in Western cultures.

Sangree (1992) examined two societies, with a particular focus on older men and women. The Tiriki of Kenya and the Irigwe of Nigeria are two societies that view their elders with great respect and appreciate the wisdom they bring to the society. On closer examination, Sangree discovered it is not seniority alone that leads to status and influence among these elders. A necessary condition for being recognized as an elder is grandparenthood. In order to achieve the highest respect as an older person, one has to have at least three living children. Being accepted as an elder represents a gain in status, particularly for Tiriki women. According to cultural norms, Tiriki women cannot be initiated as adults and are denied important positions in the clan or the village. Moreover, their activities are limited to domestic work and farming. As elders, women achieve considerable power and influence by being involved in community affairs, although their contributions are not publicly recognized.

Among the Irigwe, elder status derives from the cultural belief surrounding a mystical relation between death and birth. The Irigwe believe that the soul of a deceased person will eventually be reincarnated as a newborn. The departure of one soul is essential for the creation of a new life. Elders who are approaching death are held in high esteem because their death ensures the continuation of life.

Although Irigwe women are not granted formal leadership in the form of a public office, they nevertheless play a critically important role in community life. In contrast to Tiriki society, women have more opportunities to excel in certain areas and gain public recognition (e.g., as healers or craftswomen). As grandmothers, they achieve even more status and are held in high regard.

With changes brought about by modernization, the gender roles and status of older adults, as well as of younger adults, have changed, particularly in Irigwe society. Sangree (1992) describes how young educated men are taking over community activities formerly conducted by the male and female elders. Such changes are not characteristic of younger women. They are often too busy with their family responsibilities or limited by their lack of education to compete with men for jobs and status.

Among the Tiriki, male elders retain their influence in some local affairs. The culture has preserved the elder males' role as an essential agent in the socialization and initiation of younger males. They are also more involved in their sons' lives, since they manage their sons' property while they are away from home working. The influence and status of female elders are gradually disappearing, and there are fewer opportunities for them to be involved within the community. Overall, the status of Tiriki individuals in late adulthood and how they are viewed increasingly resemble the view held by other modern cultures.

◊ SUMMARY

This chapter discussed the development of women and men across the lifespan. Whereas some gender differences can be viewed from a biological perspective (see Chapter 4), the emphasis here was on social and cultural forces that contribute to the psychological development of men and women in different societies. In early childhood, prevailing gender stereotypes already influence the socialization of gendered behavior. Cultural customs and arrangements determine the structure and content of social interaction between boys and girls. These interactions become increasingly important during adolescence, when young people are preparing for their roles as adults. Aside from biological maturity, cultural norms determine when a youth may engage in sexual activity. In addition, cultural rules may dictate mate selection as well as acceptable or unacceptable sexual activities. The years of adulthood are characterized by clearly stipulated roles and obligations, many of which are defined by gender. Although many of these roles show great similarities across cultures, the status of men and women and their relationships may differ depending on their cultural environment and their unique developmental niche.

◊ STUDY QUESTIONS

Define and distinguish between the terms "sex" and "gender."

Use biological, evolutionary, and social learning perspectives to explain gender differences that are considered universal (e.g., relative strength, body size, aggression, verbal skills).

Give examples of how factors at the micro-, exo-, and macro-levels of the ecological system explain cultural differences in gender equality during adulthood.

◇ FURTHER READINGS

Caroline B. Brettell & Carolyn F. Sargent (2004). *Gender in Cross-Cultural Perspective*, 4th edition. New York: Prentice Hall.
   This reader introduces learners to the most significant topics in the field of gender—drawing from classic sources as well as from the most recent, diverse literature on gender roles and ideology around the world. It features broad geographical coverage and the most current research available. An extensive range of topics.

John Colapinto. (2000). *As Nature Made Him: The Boy Who Was Raised as a Girl*. New York: HarperCollins.
   The story of a couple who arranged for one of their twin sons to undergo sex reassignment. The case, initially proclaimed a success, was considered a landmark in explaining the shaping of human sexual identity. However, thirty years later, the subject tells of his participation in an experiment in psychosexual engineering gone wrong. When informed of his medical history, at age fourteen, the subject decided to live as a male and shares his eventual triumph in asserting his sense of self against his medically and surgically imposed identity. Fascinating reading.

Joanne Eicher & Lisa Ling. (2005). *Mother, Daughter, Sister, Bride: Rituals of Womanhood*. Washington, DC: National Geographic Society.
   This book celebrates the defining connections among women, and honors their differences from Quinceañera parties commemorating a Hispanic girl turning 15, to pre-wedding henna ceremonies in the Middle East, to American traditions such as the debutante ball, as well as the coming-of-age rituals of Mende girls in Sierra Leone. Illustrated with photographs from the National Geographic archive. A fascinating look at the historical, cultural, emotional, and personal impact of women's rituals and ritual practices.

Leslie Feinberg. (1995). *Transgender Warriors: Making History from Joan of Arc to Ru-Paul*. Boston: Beacon Press.
   A historical look at the social and cultural constructions of gender. The author's discussion of gender issues, ranging from pink and blue to bathroom taboos to transexuality/transgenderism, opens readers' eyes to the ways in which gender shapes everyday experience.

D. P. Schmidt. (2000). Are Sexual Promiscuity and Relationship Infidelity Linked to Different Personality Traits Across Cultures? Findings from the International Sexuality Descrition Project. In W. J. Lonner, D. L. Dinnel, S. A. Hayes, & D. N. Sattler (Eds.), *Online Readings in Psychology and Culture* (Unit 6, Chapter 4), (http://www.wwu.edu/~culture), Center for Cross-Cultural Research, Western Washington University, Bellingham, Washington.

Over 17,000 participants responded to self-reported measures of sexuality and personality. Analyses across 58 cultures from 52 nations revealed that romantic relationship infidelity was significantly associated with disagreeableness and low levels of conscientiousness across most cultures. Sexual promiscuity was related to extraversion across many, but not most, cultural regions. Discussion questions focus on patterns of findings and why regional differences in sexuality–personality linkages seem to exist.

Suzzane LaFont. (2002). *Constructing Sexualities: Readings in Sexuality, Gender, and Culture*. New York: Prentice-Hall.

This collection introduces readers to a broad range of ideas and theories and encourages critical thinking about the relationships between sexuality, gender, and culture. The readings include descriptions of variations in sexual and gender ideologies, expressions of sexuality, gender diversity, and global issues. Gay rights, transgendered movements, female genital mutilation, male circumcision, AIDS, sex tourism, and other current issues are addressed.

◇ DEVELOPMENTAL ANALYSIS

GENDER AND SEXUALITY

My life would be very different had I been born a boy or even a girl in another culture with different expectations for women. I have had more freedom and opportunities than women in many other countries. However, as I was growing up, especially during adolescence, I often felt a sense of confusion and lack of direction. I think American society sometimes sends women different messages about what should be most important in life. This is especially true today. Should a young woman focus on marriage and childrearing or on a career? Can she find a balance among these competing interests? I believe she can but it certainly is not easy.

All cultures have gender stereotypes that are established early. Boys and girls are frequently expected to conform to them. This was certainly true when I was growing up. One example is the type of toys children are expected to play with. I had my dolls and cooking sets (to help prepare me to be a mother and housewife), and my brother had his doctor kit and chemistry set (to encourage him to experiment with science and think about a career). Today, boys' and girls' toys are less associated with gender, and everyone learns about computers, plays video games, and has their own iPod (and often cell phone, too).

On the other hand, when I was young, my father took me fishing and later taught me how to hunt. Sometimes I think he wished I'd been a boy, although he never said that. When I was 12, he had me take Hunter's Safety. I didn't want to because my girlfriends weren't doing it. This is an example of

(continued)

where peers influence gender stereotypes. I am also an avid football fan—unlike many of my female friends. In seventh grade I wore makeup and skirts. The following year I changed to jeans and sweatshirts. I was trying to find myself in both extremes and learned I could be both a lady and a tomboy.

My life growing up as a female was quite different from that of my mother. I've been able to do so many more things than she could. For example, I went to college, studied business, traveled abroad, married a man from a different culture, am a mom *and* a professor, and take students on foreign study tours to places like Guatemala, Egypt, China, and Norway.

My mother and father knew each other as children and married right after high school. Being raised with a strict Catholic background, she knew little about sex and her own sexuality. Although it was embarrassing at times, my girlfriends and I would read magazines, discuss what we read, and try to understand what was happening to our bodies and our changing attitudes toward boys. Naturally, I learned more when I went to college, and when I met my future husband and began to develop an intimate relationship, I learned there are cultural differences in the way people view dating, love, romance, and marriage.

The lives of my son and daughter underwent even more change than I experienced. The same will likely be true for our grandchildren. In terms of gender and sexuality, this is an extremely interesting time in which to live—as you know from your own experiences.

CHAPTER EIGHT

CULTURE AND
SOCIAL BEHAVIOR

Shula grew up in a kibbutz not far from Haifa, Israel, where she lived with her parents and two siblings. Shortly after she was born, her mother returned to her job on the farm, leaving Shula in the care of the kibbutz daycare. At daycare, Shula built close relationships with the three or four women who were assigned to take care of her. When she was older, Shula spent her mornings in school and her afternoons at the communal area, where she and the other children played and worked under the supervision of adult kibbutz members. Even though her family expected her to stay in the kibbutz, she could not wait to leave to be on her own. She now attends Ben Gurion University in Beer-Sheva, where she dedicates most of her time to her studies and her political activities.

Manami and her parents live in a small apartment on the outskirts of Sapporo, Japan. Even though her father is an engineer, his salary alone barely supports the family. Manami's mother, Midori, gave up her job as an architect when her daughter was born. As a woman who was raised in a traditional Japanese family, Midori decided it was best to stay at home and raise the child herself rather than leaving Manami in the care of someone else. Manami has no siblings, and the first year in school was very difficult for her. She missed the undivided attention of her mother and did not get along well with the other children. After a while she built a circle of friends with whom she stayed close all through college. Now in her early thirties, Manami is an independent woman with a career in the competitive business of real estate.

Manami's and Shula's social and cultural environments were very different from the day they were born. How did these aspects influence their development as social beings? Did the emphasis on collectivism in the kibbutz instill values such as sharing and cooperation in Shula? How do single children like Manami fare in a collectivist culture? In this chapter we examine psychological and cultural factors that influence how people relate to their social environment and develop as social beings.

◇ INFANCY

During the first year of life, children actively begin to explore their environment; their curiosity seems almost limitless. To ensure continued learning and growth, the caretaker must encourage this exploration. At the same time, the child must trust that the caretaker is nearby and provides a safe haven when needed. *The emotional bond between child and caretakers that allows children to feel secure and to know to whom they can turn in threatening situations is known as* **attachment.** Early studies with baby monkeys (Harlow & Zimmermann, 1959; Harlow & Harlow, 1962) showed that infant–caretaker attachment goes beyond the fulfillment of physical and security needs. In fact, Harlow and others argue that the social interaction that takes place within a secure infant–caretaker relationship is necessary for the development of healthy social behavior.

Child–Caretaker Relationships and Attachment Patterns

The process of attachment over the first two years appears to be similar across different cultures. It is assumed that children have developed an attachment with their caretaker if they show distress when separated from the caretaker.

Ainsworth and Wittig (1969) are credited with developing a standardized event (the **strange situation**) that makes it possible to observe the type of bond a child has with her primary caretaker—most frequently the mother. In the strange situation, a mother and child are placed together in a room equipped with toys. A stranger enters the room and sits quietly in a chair. The stranger begins a conversation with the mother, and after a while slowly approaches the child. The mother leaves the room while the stranger keeps interacting with the child. After a few minutes, the mother returns, reunites with the child, and the stranger leaves the room. Another few minutes pass and the mother leaves the room again. Shortly thereafter, the stranger reenters and tries to distract the child. Finally, the mother returns and reunites with the child.

The child's responses are recorded at specific times during the situation. How close does the child stay to the mother during the initial period? How does she react when approached by a stranger in the presence of the mother? How distressed is the child when the mother leaves the room? How does she react when alone with the stranger? Is the child happy when reunited with the mother? Specific responses indicate the type of attachment the child has with the primary caretaker.

Ainsworth and her colleagues observed that children could be classified according to three categories of behavior patterns when faced with the strange situation (Ainsworth, 1982). Children classified as *anxious/avoidant* will not pay much attention to whether the primary caretaker is absent or not. If they experience distress, they may turn to a stranger for comfort. On the mother's return, these children do not actively strive to reunite and be close. Children classified as *anxious/resistant* tend to stay close to their caretaker and become very distressed when she leaves the room. Even when comforted after the caretaker's return, these children will take a long time to settle down and remain anxious about the caretaker's whereabouts. Finally, *securely attached* children will be calm and not threatened by strangers in the presence of the caretaker. When the caretaker departs, the distressed child is unlikely to be comforted by a stranger. When the caretaker returns, the child is eager to reunite and will settle down and relax very quickly. Main and Solomon (1990) proposed an additional category—*disorganized*—to account for those children who appeared to have no specific pattern for coping with the discomfort created by the strange situation.

This approach to the study of attachment remains popular among researchers, with a significant number of recent studies (Lewis, Feiring, & Rosenthal, 2000; Waters, Hamilton, & Weinfield, 2000; Waters, Merrick, Treboux, Crowell, & Albersheim, 2000). Although cross-cultural comparability of the strange situation has been questioned, findings from numerous studies in Europe, Asia, Africa, the Middle East, and North America demonstrate that these attachment patterns occur in a wide variety of cultures (Miyake, Chen, & Campos, 1985). In recent years, the strange situation has been extended to the Indonesian caregiving context (Zevalkink, Riksen-Walraven, & Van Lieshout, 1999) and to East German and Russian family settings (Ahnert, Meischner, & Schmidt, 2000).

As illustrated by Figure 8.1, most children in the four cultures studied by Kagan and his colleagues (1978) did not show behavior indicating attachment until about their seventh month of life. This does not necessarily mean that they were not attached to their caretaker earlier. Rather, they may not have had the psychological and social abilities to interpret the departure of the caretaker as threatening and to translate their attachment into social behavior. Toward the end of the first year, social development interacts with development in other areas and accounts for a dramatic change in the child's social behavior. At about seven to nine months, children first acquire **object permanence,** *recognition that objects and/or persons continue to exist even when they cannot be seen.* At the same time, infants begin to communicate and respond more by means of language rather than facial expressions, and they actively check for their caretaker's responses to their behavior.

In addition to the similarities of attachment across cultures, there are also differences. Caretaker–child interactions and relationships are influenced by the environment in which they take place. From the two examples at the

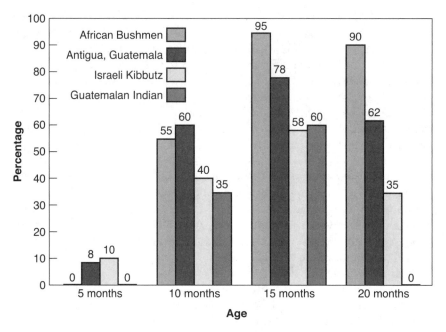

FIGURE 8.1 Cross-Cultural Comparison of Children Showing Distress in the Strange Situation

Source: Adapted from *Infancy: Its Place in Human Development* by J. Kagan, R. B. Kearsley, and P. Zealazo, 1978, Cambridge: Harvard University Press.

beginning of this chapter, one may conclude that Manami and Shula had very different relationships with their mothers during their first years of life.

Finally, a growing body of cross-cultural research has focused on three patterns of attachment (see Rothbaum, et al., 2000, for an overview). First, research in various cultural settings suggests that secure attachment requires a *"secure base,"* represented by a primary caregiver with whom the child feels safe when threatened or stressed (Bowlby, 1988; Posada et al., 1995). Second, secure attachment further requires that the primary caregiver is *sensitive to subtleties in the child's behavior and responds accordingly* (Van Ijzendoorn and Sagi, 1999). New mothers, for example, learn quickly to distinguish between their child's angry cry and its anxious cry. Third, attachment theorists predict that *securely attached children grow up to become socially competent, securely attached, and emotionally stable adults* (Wei et al., 2004, Mallinckrodt, 2000).We will discuss each of these cross-culturally examined themes in attachment.

The Secure-Base Hypothesis

The conditions under which a child experiences her first social attachment are often determined by the specific cultural setting. These conditions may influence the relationship between caretaker and child considerably. Two of these conditions involve (a) availability of the primary caretaker and (b) the number of other individuals involved in childcare. For example, parents' economic circumstances or the structure of the community may require them to work outside of the home, leaving the care of the children to family members or others in the community.

Sagi (1990) speculates that the high rate of insecurely attached children in the Israeli kibbutz may be a result of the specific childrearing arrangements. For example, caregivers in the kibbutz (metaplot) are often assigned to work with three or more infants during the day, while all of the infants are watched by a single caretaker at night (in kibbutzim with communal sleeping arrangements). Sagi argues that this "multiple mothering" leads to inconsistencies in maternal behavior and may result in different (possibly less secure) attachment patterns.

Tronick, Morelli, and Ivey (1992) describe the childrearing arrangement among the Efe in Zaire. Here, children also enjoy multiple social relationships with other children and adults. However, particularly during the first year, the mother is involved in more than half of the child's social activities. This also means that children spend half of their time with individuals other than their mothers. For example, during the time the mother works away from the camp, her child is left in the exclusive care of other adults or older children. Even when the mother is present, other family members, the children's peers, or other adults are continually engaged in social interactions with the child. In fact, the authors point out that at a given time about ten people are within sight or close hearing range of the child. Unfortunately, there are no data available from this culture describing specific attachment patterns resulting either from these continuous multiple relationships with others or from the close relationship with the mother. However, the authors suggest that the children benefit from this setting in that they develop a multitude of social skills early in life; this leads to better adjustment in social situations later on.

Similarly, Indonesian children not only enjoy much attention from their mother but also from their older siblings. For example, Farver and Wimbarti (1995) found that mothers and older siblings engage in different types of playing behavior with young children. In particular, older siblings were more active playing partners and facilitated pretend play more often than mothers, thus adding an important dimension of social interaction to the young child's microsystem.

In other settings, mothers keep their infants with them during work. Women in Madura, Indonesia, for example, systematically adjust their work patterns to accommodate their children (Launer, 1993). Several North American Indian societies utilize the cradleboard. Niethammer (1977) has written that "all [cradle boards] provide a firm, protective frame on which babies felt snug and secure (see photo on page 94). A baby in a cradle board could be propped up or even hung in a tree so it could see what was going on and feel part of family activities. After spending much time in their cradle

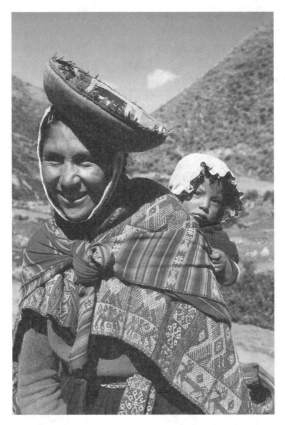

A Peruvian mother uses a manta pouch to keep her infant near her. (© Craig Duncan/D. Donne Bryant Stock)

board, Indian children became very attached to them. One Apache mother related that whenever her toddler son was tired or upset he would go and get his cradle board and walk around with it on his back" (p. 15).

Similarly, the Quechua use a **manta pouch** to carry their infants. This is a *backpacklike device that protects the infant from the harsh elements in the Peruvian mountains and provides a secure environment close to the mother* (Tronick, Thomas, & Daltabuit, 1994). These and similar devices allow parents to keep their infants near them and to provide the necessary restraint so that children's physical activity does not interfere with the mother's work.

In conclusion, a "secure base" for healthy attachment may express itself in different ways, depending on the general childcare arrangements that are part of the macro- or mesosystems in the child's ecological environment. In setting the stage for the microlevel aspects of parent-child interactions, the "secure base" is crucial in the development of social relationships and behavior in early childhood.

The Sensitivity Hypothesis

Both the infant and the caretaker bring certain characteristics to the caretaker-infant relationship that become a crucial part of the ecological system in which the child grows up. This happens when some of the behaviors and characteristics of the mother interact with the characteristics of her child to create a unique developmental niche. For example, Richman, Miller, and Levine (1992) studied the behaviors Mexican mothers showed in response to their infant's distress signals, such as crying and worried facial expressions. One factor that influenced mothers' responsiveness was their level of education. Mothers with more schooling tended to respond with more talking and facial expressions than mothers with less schooling, who tended to hold their infants more. In explaining these findings, the researchers pointed to earlier research suggesting that mothers with more education generally tend to initiate more verbal interaction with the children.

Caretakers also bring their unique cultural beliefs about parenting to the relationship. These beliefs may be culturally influenced, but they are also based on the caretaker's unique experiences. For example, Grossman and colleagues (1985) noticed that mothers in their German sample appeared quite unresponsive to their children's crying. Closer observations revealed that this behavior resulted from a shared cultural belief that infants should become independent at an early age and learn that they cannot rely on the mother's comfort at all times. In contrast, traditional Japanese mothers instill a strong sense of dependence in their young children by being available at all times (Miyake et al., 1985). These cultural variations in sensitivity to children's behavior illustrates that sensitivity may be a universal requirement for secure attachment, yet, the specific ecological systems define what the appropriate "sensitive response" might be.

Consistency and Inconsistency of Attachment over Time

What about Harlow's assertion (at the beginning of this chapter) that secure attachment in infancy is necessary for the development of healthy social behavior? Much of attachment research over the years has shown that attachment patterns can be stable over long periods of time. This means that a child who is securely attached in infancy is likely to show secure attachment patterns through adolescence and early adulthood (Waters, Merrick, Treboux, Crowell & Albersheim, 2000).

Yet, significant negative life events may disrupt the stability of attachment. For example, a securely attached child who experiences the loss of a parent, parental divorce, psychiatric parental disorder, or physical abuse may change to an insecure attachment pattern in adolescence (Weinfield, Sroufe & Egeland, 2000; Hamilton, 2000). Similarly, children who experience prolonged social deprivation may reach a point where it becomes difficult to establish secure or even meaningful relationships with others. O'Connor and colleagues (2003) studied Romanian children who spent much of their infancy and childhood in Romanian orphanages. Many of the children who had spent more than six months in an orphanage showed very inconsistent attachment behavior with their new adoptive families. These behaviors ranged from indiscriminant attachment to frequent switching between friendliness and suspicion.

On the other hand, as we discussed in the previous sections, the developmental niche plays a crucial role in initial infant attachment. Changes in caretaker characteristics (e.g., illness of a parent), specific setting of child-parent relationship (e.g., parental divorce), or general childcare conditions (e.g., lack of social support for single parents) are all related to changes in attachment. But these changes are not necessarily detrimental. A review of several studies of children (ages five to eighteen) in India (Sharma and Sharma, 1999) included street and working children, school dropouts, children of disabled parents, children in single parent families, and children with disabilities, low birth weights, or chronic disease. All of these children in "difficult circumstances" were deemed at risk for psychological and social maladjustment. However, the researchers conclude that "at risk" children who were "nestled or vicariously encircled in their family network, seemed to be coping and getting ahead" (p. 412). Although "at risk" from the outside, these children seemed to experience a resilience within their developmental niche that allowed them to develop and maintain a secure attachment, fostering healthy social and psychological development over time.

◇ CHILDHOOD

When children pass the stage of infancy, they begin to develop social relationships that extend beyond caretakers and the family context, even though the family remains very important. These relationships include children in the immediate neighborhood or at school and frequently become quite complex and multifaceted. Corsaro and Eder (1990) refer to these expanding relationships as children's "peer culture."

Peer Culture and Social Relationships

In their review of relevant research, Corsaro and Eder identify three central themes that characterize peer culture from early childhood to adolescence. These include (1) dealing with confusion, concerns, fears, and conflicts; (2) resisting and challenging adult rules and authority; and (3) sharing and social participation.

Dealing with Confusion, Concerns, Fears, and Conflicts

In the company of their peers, children learn to cope with everyday conflicts and fears through fantasy play (e.g., role playing the defeat of a monster).

Children also engage in fantasy play to deal with anxiety and violence. For example, children in several South African communities, where daily life was often interrupted by riots or police raids, played out the violence and aggression they saw around them. Kostelny and Garbarino (1994) explored the drawings of Palestinian children living in Israeli-occupied territories. The drawings of the five- to eight-year-olds frequently showed themes of victimization (e.g., large soldiers with guns threatening small children).

Resisting and Challenging Adult Rules and Authority

Corsaro and Eder (1990) maintain that challenging adult rules serves to establish a sense of independence from parents. At the same time, children strengthen their peer group identity by developing rituals and routines that make fun of adult authority or challenge adult rules. Corsaro (1988) observed frequent violations of Italian and American nursery school rules prohibiting children from bringing toys from home to school. Children attempted to break this rule by bringing in concealed toys or candy, which were then shared with other children who gladly became coconspirators in the violation. Similarly, Marshall (1976) describes a game called "frogs" played by !Kung children. In this game one participant poses as the "mother," and the others are the "children." While the "mother" pretends to prepare "frogs" as food, the "children" openly refuse to perform tasks, disobey the orders of the "mother," steal the frogs and hide them, and so on. The game ends by the mother chasing the children, who run away in all directions in an effort to avoid being caught.

Aside from challenging rules and authority, it is through games and play that children come to understand concepts of creating and enforcing rules as well as cheating and breaking rules. Schwartzman (1983) provides a thoughtful analysis of the socializing function of children's play and includes examples of children in the kibbutz, Australian Aborigine children, Kpelle children in Liberia, and several more.

Sharing and Social Participation

As they get older, children begin to seek the company of other children and enjoy social activities. In interaction with other children and without the presence of adults, they acquire a sense of **cooperation** and sharing. One of the most important settings in which social interaction takes place is that of play and games, which represent a crucial element of the ecological system during childhood. Games like tag, hopscotch, and jacks, as well as soccer and baseball, are played in similar forms in many cultures. All these games facilitate taking turns, cooperation, and negotiation, yet the rules or content may vary with different contexts. Children in the United States may play soccer (what most of the world refers to as football) in an organized league governed by adults and consisting of set teams, coaches, scheduled match play, and so on. Soccer may also be played without adult participation and with makeshift goals and changing teams in a back alley of São Paulo, Brazil, or in a farmer's field in Nigeria. The social interactions taking place in each of these settings may be quite different. For example, organized sports and games tend to focus on competition, achievement, rules, and success, whereas free play activities tend to focus on participation, equality of players, and adapting or creating rules in order to ensure everyone's enjoyment of the game.

Games and play also introduce children to concepts of competition and differential status. Observers of children's peer culture have noted the cultural variation in competitiveness and cooperation in children's play. For example, children in North America generally appear to be more competitive than children in many other societies. On the other hand, Domino (1992) found Chinese children to be more concerned than American children about group accomplishment. In this study, children were asked to complete a task in which tokens could be exchanged for various prizes. Depending on the task, tokens could be obtained by working alone or collaboratively. Most of the American children preferred to work individually, trying to accumulate as many tokens as possible for themselves. Chinese children tended to adopt strategies that emphasized collaboration with others rather than individual success.

In another example, Sparkes (1991) used a dyadic (two-person) marble game in which children had the choice to play cooperatively or to compete with each other. Findings showed that Chinese children were more competitive in this situation than American children in the comparison group. Sparkes points out that these differences may be due to the different teaching styles practiced in these cultures. She suggests that the Chinese emphasis on teacher-directed, large-group activities leaves little room for dyadic interactions. As a result, Chinese youngsters may have less experience in negotiating roles and taking turns with a partner. These selected examples demonstrate that cultural differences or similarities in competitive and cooperative behavior may depend on the definition of these concepts and the specific context in which the behavior takes place.

Studies in Africa provide additional cues for environmental factors that may influence cooperative and competitive behavior. Friedman, Todd, and Kariuki (1995) studied 120 Kenyan children from different backgrounds (a middle-class Westernized suburb of Nairobi, poor semiurban Kikuyu, and a poor rural mission village). Results showed that middle-class children behaved competitively, even when cooperation was the most adaptive strategy. Surprisingly, rural children also engaged in competitive behavior. Poor semiurban children from Kikuyu were the most cooperative of all groups. One could speculate that the degree of Westernization corresponds to the degree of individualism found in these settings (i.e., the more individualistic the environment, the greater the emphasis on competition).

Marshall (1976) reported a complete absence of competitive games among !Kung children living in tribal communities in Southwest Africa (tug-of-war being the exception because of its special historical meaning). The author suggests that the collectivist nature of !Kung society emphasizes group performance rather than individual achievement and success. Taken as a group, these studies suggest that the degree of collectivism–individualism may play a role in the social behavior of children since it is part of the ecological system in which social behavior develops.

Kagitcibasi (1990) has recently criticized the use of the collectivism–individualism dimension as a simplistic explanation of cultural differences in competitiveness. As an alternative, Searle-White (1996) proposes a Vygotskian approach. As you may recall from our earlier discussion, this framework emphasizes socialization and language as "psychological tools" for mental growth and development. Depending on how these tools are used, children and adults view themselves as being at a point along a continuum of interdependence, where cooperation reflects, in part, the inclination to stay socially connected to others.

This view fits in with our themes of the developmental niche and the ecological systems approach. When children cooperate with others, they work within their developmental niche and recognize that they are interconnected with others. Likewise, in terms of Bronfenbrenner's model, the child interacts with other people within her microsystem. At first, this system may be small, involving just a few caregivers. However, as children get older, they do more things with others, expanding their social world. As they become socialized within the mesosystem of the school and the neighborhood, they recognize the benefits of working together to accomplish their academic and personal goals. They learn the rules of cooperative play and practice social behaviors. Later, as children express the cultural values of cooperation and interdependence through language and social behavior, they begin operating within the cultural context of the macrosystem.

Moral Development and Prosocial Orientation

With increased social participation in early childhood, children begin to understand how to relate to others in socially desirable ways. As they acquire the foundations of moral reasoning and behavior, they begin to understand concepts such as "right" and "wrong." Developmental psychologists have proposed that moral development progresses in stages, each stage representing more mature reasoning about moral thought and conduct (for a detailed overview, see Shields & Bredemeier, 1995). Kohlberg's theory of moral development was introduced in Chapter 2. Generally, researchers understand morality as two-dimensional, one dimension describing "pro-social" judgments, actions, and behaviors that benefit others, such as helping, sharing, comforting (Tisak, Tisak & Goldstein, 2006, p. 611). The second dimension of morality refers to judgments, actions, and behaviors that may result in negative consequences for another person or persons. Aggression is considered an expression of this "anti-social" dimension of morality. In the next two sections, we will consider ecological systems and how they relate to pro-social and anti-social morality, particularly with regard to culture.

Cultural Influences on Caring and Justice Orientation

Kohlberg's definition and assessment of moral reasoning is not accepted by everyone and has been challenged by several researchers (Eckensberger, 1994; Snarey, 1985; Shweder, Mahapatra, & Miller, 1987). In fact, a number of studies suggest that individuals in many nonEuropean cultures, as well as women, exhibit moral reasoning equivalent to that of an adolescent in Kohlbergian terms. Critics argue that an Anglo male bias is built into the model because the highest level of moral development is based on interviews with a 1960s sample of Harvard male undergraduates. In addition, the hypothetical moral dilemmas Kohlberg created to elicit moral reasoning responses and the scoring of the responses may also be culturally biased. Carol Gilligan (1982) specifically pointed to the gender bias in Kohlberg's theory. In her own research, she learned that women's moral thought is *guided by caring and maintaining the welfare of others,* whereas men emphasize *more abstract principles of justice.* Gilligan concludes that women develop a different kind of morality altogether, due to their different socialization. Stack (1974) found a similar **caring orientation** (as opposed to a **justice orientation**) described as "what goes around comes around" in a midwestern African American community.

Different socialization, parental beliefs, and customs of childcare—that is, different aspects of the developmental niche—may explain many research findings in the cultural domain. For example, studies of Buddhist monks showed that young adolescent monks reasoned at stage 2 and even mature adults barely reached stage 4 in Kohlberg's schema (Huebner & Garrod, 1993). Can we conclude that the monks' moral reasoning is less highly developed compared with Western adolescent males? Huebner and Garrod argue that Kohlberg's model is only partially applicable in this context because the Buddhist conception of morality is different than the Western, Christian, liberal democratic view inherent in Kohlberg's theory.

According to the authors, the ideal moral person from a Western perspective is an autonomous individual with strong convictions who stands up for her own, as well as others', rights. She is an influential individual who uses her power to influence others in a "good" way. In contrast, among Buddhists, ideal moral individuals are those who are ultimately connected (to others, the environment, the cosmos) through their compassion and detachment from their own individuality. Buddhist morality is characterized by an understanding of interconnectedness and interdependence and is more reminiscent of Gilligan's caring orientation than Kohlberg's justice orientation.

Similarly, Bersoff and Miller (1993) found that people from India were more likely to forgive moral violations if there were extenuating circumstances or emotional hardship.

In a comparative study of adolescents from China, Hong Kong, and England (Ma, 1989), both Chinese samples showed a stronger orientation toward abiding by the law as well as being altruistic or affective toward others. Ma concludes that this cultural difference may result from the Chinese practice of rearing their children in a more authoritative manner than the English, encouraging them to obey authority and follow norms. At the same time, Chinese cultural values are inherently collectivist, emphasizing human relationships and interdependence.

This discussion of various cultural influences on aspects of moral reasoning demonstrates that moral development may not strictly follow a universal psychological script, as suggested by Kohlberg. Instead, the ecological system in which early social participation takes place shapes individual development of moral thought and behavior.

Cultural Influences on Distributive Justice

Based on Kohlberg's broad model of moral reasoning, Damon (1973) focused specifically on children's understanding of one aspect of moral reasoning that has important implications for the development of social judgment and social behaviors, namely **distributive justice**—*the judgment of what constitutes criteria for the fair distribution of goods and resources in society.* Damon's six levels of distributive justice reasoning development, which occur from early to middle childhood, are presented in Box 8.1 on pages 206–207.

In order to assess children's distributive justice capabilities, Enright, Franklin, and Manheim (1980) created the **Distributive Justice Scale (DJS),** which is *a pictorial instrument used as a tool in one-on-one interviews.* Researchers have since adapted the DJS for use in a variety of contexts. For example, Box 8.1 shows Solomon's (1997) Adapted Distributive Justice Scale, which is used to assess the thinking of children from different ethnic backgrounds within a sports context.

Cross-cultural studies have suggested that cultures may differ in their normative beliefs of what constitutes a "fair" distribution of resources. For example, Sweden is considered more of a need-based society (i.e., everyone receives according to his needs), whereas the Protestant work ethic (i.e., everyone receives according to his effort) still prevails in the United States (Enright et al., 1984). In another study men and women from Hong Kong considered distribution of goods fairer when based on merit than when based on need. Subjects from Indonesia believed the opposite (Murphy-Berman and Berman, 2002.)

The other two central concepts in Damon's model, reciprocity and equality, are also conceptualized differently depending on cultural context. In Damon's model, mature reasoning about the just distribution of goods and

BOX 8.1

THE ADAPTED DISTRIBUTIVE JUSTICE SCALE

The following example is from Solomon's (1997) Adapted Distributive Justice Scale:

All of these boys and girls are on the same baseball team. There is Clarice, the oldest one on the team; Jennifer, whose family is poor and does not have much money; Lamar, who is a hard-working ball player; and Matthew. One afternoon they thought it would be a good idea if they helped

BOX 8.1 CONTINUED

the younger children learn how to play baseball. When they were done, Clarice had helped for two hours, Jennifer had helped for two hours, Lamar had helped for four hours, and Matthew had helped for two hours. After they did this, the coach decided that the children were so nice to help the younger children that she gave them eight quarters. The children have to decide how to divide up the quarters. What is the best way to do this?

Answer options in the ADJS and Damon's corresponding levels of reasoning:

Answer Option	Reasoning guided by
Matthew gets the most quarters because he wanted the quarter more than anything.	The mere expression of a wish: "Whoever wants it most, gets it."
Clarice gets the most because she is the oldest.	External characteristics such as size or age: "Whoever is older or bigger gets the most."
All children get the same amount so there won't be any fights about who gets more.	Strict equality, regardless of other attributes or actions: "Everyone gets the same."
Lamar gets the most quarters because he helped more than the other children.	Reciprocity for behavior or actions: "Whoever works hardest gets the most in return."
Jennifer gets the most quarters because she is poor and needs them more than the other children.	Psychological or material need: "Whoever needs it most gets the most."
Both Lamar who helped most and Jennifer who needs the quarters get the most.	Compromise between need and equality: "Everyone should get what she or he deserves, which may differ by person and situation."

Source: G. B. Solomon, "Fair Play in the Gymnasium: Improving Social Skills Among Elementary School Children," 1997, *Journal of Physical Education, Recreation, and Dance, 68,* 22–25. Reprinted by permission.

resources in society is guided by two principles: equality and reciprocity. Equality refers to the judgment that people are equally deserving of receiving resources and goods. Reciprocity refers to the reception of resources, either in exchange for a behavior (e.g., work) or to meet a need. At the most mature level of reasoning, children are able to take both equality and reciprocity into account when making judgments about the fair distribution of resources.

FIGURE 8.2   Proposed Model for the Study of Cultural, Socialization, and Developmental Influences on Distributive Justice Reasoning

Source: Adapted from "Socilization and Cognitive-moral Influences on Justice Rule Preferences: The Case of Indian Culture" by L. Krishman in *Culture, Socialization, and Human Development: Theory, Research, and Applications in India,* T. S. Saraswathi (Ed.), 1999. Thousand Oaks, CA: Sage Publications.

Miller and Bersoff (1994) point out that in India, exchanging helping behavior for money is considered a personal choice, but exchanging helping behavior for previous helping behavior is a social obligation. In contrast, either type of reciprocity is considered a personal choice in the United States. Based on these differences in ecological systems, it would be easy to assume that developmental patterns of distributive justice reasoning may also vary for children in different cultures. Surprisingly, studies in Japan, Sweden, Germany, and the United States indicate that children show similar patterns of distributive justice reasoning corresponding to Damon's developmental model (Eisenberg, Boehnke, Schuhler, & Silbereisen, 1985; Watanabe, 1986). Other researchers found distinct patterns of distributive justice reasoning in India and Japan, both considered more collectivistic cultures. They found that distributive justice reasoning was guided by equality and need (Krishnan, 1997; Naito 1994). Even though the results are mixed, differences in ecological systems deserve consideration as a possible explanation for differences in moral reasoning development. For example, Krishnan (1999) proposes an adapted model for distributive justice development, a model that explicitly includes the influence of cultural factors through socialization. (See Figure 8.2)

Aggression

Most children in most cultures fight, argue, or aggress against one another (peers or siblings) as well as against adults (especially parents) at some time during the years of childhood. Learning the differences between appropriate and inappropriate behavior and how to handle hostility and aggression fall within the social realm.

Let us begin by distinguishing between two often misunderstood terms that are frequently used incorrectly to mean the same thing. **Hostility** is *a* *motive or desire to cause damage or injury.* If someone calls me a name or insults me, I may feel like I want to strike back by returning the insult or by taking something away from that person. I am experiencing hostility. **Aggression,** on the other hand, is *an overt action or behavior intended to cause harm, damage, or injury.* If I follow though on my hostile motive and actually use an insult, hit the person, or take something away, I am acting aggressively.

The form and extent to which such intentions and actions are exhibited depends on many factors, including culture and gender. Research generally shows boys, in most cultures, exhibiting more aggression than girls. Although there is not a great deal of agreement as to why this may be the case, socialization plays a major role, and differences appear to become particularly noticeable between the ages of two and three. At least one study (Fagot & Leinbach, 1989) has suggested that an observed increase in aggressive behavior among boys and a corresponding decrease among girls may be related to a greater awareness of one's sex role and a culture's rules regarding the expression of this behavior. (See Chapter 7 for a detailed discussion of the relationship between gender and the development of aggression.)

What causes a particular child to be aggressive? We wish there were a simple answer to this question, but none seems readily available. Some say the cause lies in the evolution of the human species; others, in a child's models (siblings, peers, and parents); still others, in the methods by which one's culture rewards or punishes the expression of aggression. We would certainly agree with Cole and Cole (2001), who suggest that social stressors and ecological factors contribute to some of the individual differences observed in aggressive behavior. Rather than attempt to do what others have been unable to do (adequately explain the causes of childhood aggression), we would prefer to view the topic within a cross-cultural context and discuss similarities and differences across cultures with some detailed illustrations.

Bourguignon (1979) gives an example of two children, a girl of seven or eight and a boy of about six, walking along a path in the mountains of Haiti. The girl is hitting the boy and calling him names. He complains loudly but makes no effort to hit back. Why? We learn that the girl's mother has put her in charge of her younger brother and, modeling her mother's behavior, she is punishing him for being disobedient. Bourguignon explains, "We are dealing with an example of child socialization. Children are beaten to enforce obedience toward elders, a central concern in this society. . . . Haitian society is based on a hierarchy of age and . . . places less stress on differences in sex" (p. 3). The girl is older and so her brother must obey her and pay her respect. She is permitted to hit him, if necessary, to discipline him, and he is not allowed to hit back. In another example, Bourguignon describes a quarrel between two boys in a village in southern France, who are seen insulting and threatening each other. One boy hits the other, runs away, but is not chased. According to Wylie (1974), who studied the village in which this incident occurred, "If two children start to fight they are immediately separated by any adult who may happen to witness the scene. . . . If it is relatives who separate fighting children, both children are punished. No inquiry is made into the question of which child started the fight or which was in the right. They are both fighting and consequently they are both guilty" (pp. 49–50). Wylie further notes that while French parents discourage physical aggression, they do permit verbal aggression (e.g., insults) as a socially accepted way to deal with anger. According to Bourguignon (1979), adults tend to model this behavior and may themselves "on occasion make a great public show of anger in words and threats, but physical fighting is said to be rare" (p. 2). More recently, researchers have found that children from Sweden, Germany, Indonesia, and the United States differ in their use of aggressive contents when telling stories. For example, stories told by North American children include more aggressive words, aggressive content, unfriendly characters, and aggressive situations compared to those told by children from the other countries studied. The authors suggest that the content of the children's narratives mirror their experience with and knowledge of aggression in their respective cultures.

As these examples illustrate, there are certainly considerable cross-cultural differences in the amount of aggressiveness various societies tolerate, first among its young people, and later among its adult members. With some effort, it would be possible to draw a continuum with the least aggressive cultures on one end and the most aggressive on the other. Among the least aggressive would be the Inuit of the North American Arctic, the Pygmies of Africa, and the characteristically tranquil and polite Amerindian tribes of Zuni and Blackfoot (Moghaddam, Taylor, & Wright, 1993). At the other end would have to be the Yanomamo, living in the Amazon region of Brazil and Venezuela, often described in anthropological literature as the "most fierce and violent people in the world."

According to Chagnon (1997), the first anthropologist to report on Yanomamo society and who has continued to research their behavior for over thirty years, aggressiveness is the major determinant of status within the group, and learning the aggressive ways of the society begins at an early age. He relates an example involving a four-year-old boy named Ariwari, whose father encourages him to "beat him on the face and head to express his anger and temper, laughing and commenting on his ferocity. . . . He has already learned that the appropriate response to a flash of anger is to strike someone with his hand or with an object, and it is not uncommon for him to give his father a healthy smack in the face whenever something displeases him [and he is] . . . rewarded by gleeful cheers of assent from his mother and from the other adults in the household" (p. 127).

Why are the Yanomamo so aggressive? According to Chagnon (1997), a great deal of conflict, aggression, and fighting centers around sex, infidelity or suspicion of infidelity, failure to deliver to a suitor a promised wife, revenge, accusations of sorcery, or "harmful magic that 'causes' death" (p.97).

In contrast, Ember and Ember (2003) cite an example from the Semai of central Malaya, a group known for its timidity, who say, "We do not get angry" (Dentan, 1968). The Semai raise their children to be nonviolent and, on the rare occasion that one of them may show anger, do not use physical punishment. As Dentan points out, with this kind of socialization, children are seldom exposed to aggressive models and, as a result, have no aggressive behavior to imitate. Robarchek and Robarchek (1998) have compared the Semai, one of the world's most peaceful cultures with the Waorani of Amazonian Ecuador, one of the world's most violent societies. The study is worth noting, especially because the two cultures are similar in their ecological contexts, ways of living, level of technology, and social organization; yet their attitudes toward violence and their patterns of behavior are at opposite extremes.

Finally, we would be remiss if we did not mention the findings of the six cultures study (Whiting, 1963; Whiting & Edwards, 1988; Whiting & Whiting, 1975). These classic studies examined, in great detail, a wide range of behavior in children ranging from three to eleven years of age in India, Japan, Kenya, Mexico, the Philippines, and the United States. In an analysis of this data, Lambert (1971) reported that American parents were fairly tolerant of displays of aggression against other children, and Mexican parents were the most punitive. Lambert attributes these differences, in part, to a higher level of interdependence within extended Mexican families, which leads, as we saw earlier, to more adult supervision and greater management of children's behavior. As far as American parents' greater tolerance of peer-directed aggression is concerned, Moghaddam and his colleagues (1993) quote one mother as saying, "If he can't get along with one child, he can always play with someone else. There are plenty of children around to choose from" (p. 126). They conclude with the observation that "this statement clearly reflects the attitude that interpersonal relationships are the product of choice and can be terminated. Given this element of choice and impermanence, it is less consequential to be aggressive against those around you" (p. 126). Once again, we see the intermingling of cultural and individual differences as influences on behavior.

We hope, after reading these examples, you are able to see how one's unique developmental niche and place within a culture's ecological system helps to determine the definition and expression of aggressive behavior. It is only by looking at a topic like this from a cross-cultural and developmental perspective that the richness and diversity of human behavior can be fully observed.

For an especially useful discussion and approach to studying aggression within a cross-cultural framework, see Chapter 9 in the book by Segall, Dasen, Berry, and Poortinga (1999). They end their presentation on a positive note, stating that, "because the evidence reviewed in this chapter does not support the view that it is inevitable that male adolescents will aggress, there is hope that the pervasive amount of aggression that presently characterizes the world may be reduced, but only if we become more knowledgeable about the experiential factors, rooted in culture, that presently encourage so many people to aggress" (p. 272). We can only hope that they are right.

◇ ADOLESCENCE

Family and Peer Influences on Adolescent Social Behavior

Although parents and family continue to play a central place in the lives of young adults, the importance of the **peer group,** *individuals who share certain characteristics (e.g., background, age, status, class) and interact on generally equal terms,* increases considerably during adolescence. The importance of peers is also discussed in Chapter 9 in relation to family structure; however, here we focus on the social relationships and social influence between peers. Adolescents look to their parents and other adults as models for adult roles and behavior. They look to their peers for opinions, lifestyles, and experiences that are different from those to which they have been exposed through their families. However, adolescents in different cultures seem to perceive their social networks quite differently. A comparison of adolescents in Zimbabwe and the United States showed that parents and friends have different functions in the two cultures (Harrison, Stewart, Myambo, & Teveraishe, 1995). In Zimbabwe, adolescents consider adults (including extended family and teachers) both as mentors and disciplinarians, whereas American youths perceive their relatives as primarily providers of emotional support. Second, Zimbabwean young people feel closer to their siblings, relatives, teachers, and fathers than do Americans, who feel closer to their friends. Finally, African adolescents experience more conflict with their teachers and best friends, while American adolescents struggle more with their mothers, fathers, and relatives.

Findings such as these indicate that both parents and peers have a strong influence on adolescents' prosocial as well as antisocial behavior, although this influence may vary from culture to culture. For example, the strong orientation toward family among traditional Puerto Rican male adolescents appears to lower their likelihood of engaging in interpersonal violence and illicit drug use (Sommers, Fagan, & Baskin, 1993). In contrast, young men who have acculturated to the majority culture in the United States are more likely to show violent behavior.

There is also some evidence that parental attitudes are related to adolescents' choice of peers. In their study of European-American adolescents, Durbin and her colleagues (1993) found that adolescents with authoritative parents tended to choose peer groups that conformed to the norms their parents valued. For example, these young people gravitated either to groups known as "brains" (the smart students), "populars" (socially active students), or "jocks" (student athletes), depending on parental values. Adolescents from households in which parents were not demanding and less attentive were more likely to engage with peers who did not endorse adult values (e.g., "druggies" or "partiers"). Smith and Blinn Pike (1994) also observed a relationship between social contact and the self-image and attitudes of Jamaican adolescents. Adolescents had stronger overall family relationships, were better adjusted, and had more positive career goals when they chose adults as their socializing partners, compared with adolescents who socialized primarily with their peers.

Parent's attitudes toward drugs and their own use of drugs and alcohol, as well as parent–child communication, were among the strongest predictors for the use of tobacco, alcohol, and other drugs among Spanish adolescents. Recio Adrados (1995) argues that parents and friends act as role models and that their use of and attitudes toward drugs and their relationships with the adolescents predicted drug use by adolescents.

On the other hand, peer group influence does not always facilitate delinquent behavior. Berndt and Zook (1993) have proposed that while antagonistic friendships frequently foster antisocial behavior, friendships characterized by closeness and prosocial behavior tend to facilitate social adjustment. In particular, peer groups provide social support in achieving social competence. For example, one study demonstrated that Costa Rican peer groups emphasize the generally cooperative and collectivist social attitudes necessary for functioning in the larger society (DeRosier & Kupersmidt, 1991). In contrast, American adolescents often stress the importance of having one "best" friend among peers, reflecting the cultural importance of individuality.

Clearly, young people's cultural definitions of acceptable and unacceptable relationships may sometimes lead to difficulties. Roberts (1994) describes the dilemma African American men experience. The dominant Euro-American culture defines male styles of relating to each other, disregarding the cultural context of relationships experienced by African American men. The white American relationship between men is typically highly competitive and characterized by power and control and a lack of emotion, trust, and connectedness. In contrast, the African American mode of relating emphasizes interconnectedness, caring, and the importance of community over individual needs. Roberts asserts that African American men must try to integrate two models of relationships that at times are quite incompatible. As a result, their relationships with male (and female) peers are often difficult and fail to provide much-needed social support. Roberts states, "It would seem that the statement 'like a brother' reflects a common expectation among Black men that their relationships with other men reflect the trust, caring, openness, and honesty associated with one's brother. Unfortunately, the majority of the evidence suggests that Black men are not getting (or giving) what they desire and expect in relating to each other" (pp. 387–388).

Cultural Influences on Adolescent Social Behavior

Arnett (1992) suggests a theoretical framework that is helpful in understanding why adolescent behavior is judged so differently in different cultures. He suggests that the socialization of adolescents is largely influenced by factors other than family and peers within the microsystem. The larger cultural influences include school, community, legal system, cultural beliefs, and the media (meso-, exo-, and macrosystems). According to Arnett, some cultures are characterized by **broad socialization** in which *independence and free self-expression are more highly valued than conformity.* Cultures such as these have no commonly accepted belief systems that judge right and wrong behavior, and deviations from cultural expectations are not severely punished. In these cultures, the range of behavior that falls within the norm is much greater than in so-called **narrow socialization** cultures. The latter clearly *prescribe an ideology that strictly sets forth the basis for right and wrong behavior.* These cultures value conformity and adherence to the standards of the community rather than autonomy, and severely punish deviations from community norms.

Arnett's framework is useful in explaining why behaviors considered delinquent in one society are merely frowned on or even acceptable in others. For example, drinking is unacceptable for adolescents in many kibbutzim in Israel, with the exception of some Jewish festivities, during which moderate alcohol consumption is allowed (Kaffman, 1993). In contrast, the attitude toward alcohol consumption by adolescents in Jamaica is casual, and few legal restrictions apply. In Jamaica, adolescent drinking is not a sign of delinquent behavior. Similarly, compared to the United States, adolescents in Spain are able to consume more alcohol per week before they are categorized as "drinkers." Among European countries, the prevalence of weekly drinking varies considerably. For example, adolescents in Greece and Italy drink about twice as much alcohol per week as their counterparts in Ireland. Possible explanations for these variations probably can be found in the cultural differences in beliefs related to alcohol consumption and adult drinking patterns.

An additional factor that needs to be taken into account when defining adolescent social behavior is the status of a given group within the larger culture and this group's attitude toward the majority culture. Gotowiec and Beiser (1993) found a much higher rate of school failure, substance abuse, and suicidal behavior among aboriginal Canadian adolescents than among majority culture adolescents. Similarly, drug consumption patterns of Australian aboriginal peoples differ significantly from that of urban Australians, who represent the majority culture (Fleming, Watson, McDonald, & Alexander, 1991).

Calabrese and Noboa (1995) closely examined Mexican American gang culture. They report that Mexican American adolescents may decide to join a gang as a way of retaining their culture of origin and of resisting the majority values found in American public schools. In this case, violence must be interpreted from the standpoint of the minority culture, since majority views are rejected. Another example of differential perception of delinquent behavior is the street-fighting code of a minority youth culture in Mexico (*cholo*). The mass media in Mexico choose to portray *cholo* youth as uncontrolled, violent, and destructive. In contrast, Cummings (1994) describes a complex system of *cholo* street-fighting rules based on fairness and honor. This social structure contains rules about who can fight with whom about which matters and under which circumstances. For example, fights only take place when the groups involved are perceived as equal in strength or number; women may intervene on men's behalf, but men never interfere with women's fights.

BOX 8.2

WHAT WERE ADOLESCENTS CONCERNED ABOUT IN THE TWENTIETH CENTURY?

The difficult psychological task of defining one's identity is frequently accompanied by many concerns and problems. Studies reveal that there are many concerns that are shared by adolescents and adults around the world. Some of these include questions such as: "What will my life look like in five years?" "What kind of person will I be then?" "Will I ever get along again with my parents?"

Gibson and others (1991) examined seventeen nations in Europe, North America, and Asia and found adolescents' primary areas of concern were family, education, and self-concept. Young people in Singapore reported that their worries revolve around succeeding in school, getting a high-status job, and general concern about the future (Isralowitz & Hong, 1990). Turkish adolescents are concerned about their personal future, relations with others, and their identity. However, they also think about local and universal issues and drug use (Sahin & Sahin, 1995).

Nurmi (1991) provides an extensive review of studies on adolescents' future concerns. This review includes thirty studies conducted between 1959 and 1989 in fourteen different countries. He concludes that there are three main domains of concern shared by adolescents in different cultures: (1) major normative life tasks (e.g., having a career and establishing a family), (2) nonnormative life events related to parents (e.g., death or divorce of parents), and (3) global events (e.g., nuclear war). In spite of these similarities, Nurmi also points out that adolescents from traditional cultures seemed to be more concerned about issues relating to family, whereas those in urban cultures worried more about future education and career.

Regardless of the specific parameters of their ecological systems, young people are faced with the difficult developmental task of identifying and establishing their place in the adult world. For some, this process may progress more smoothly; for others, it may be characterized by inner conflict and turmoil. Nonetheless, young people across cultures share general concerns about the world, their lives, and their future, as described in Box 8.2.

◇ ADULTHOOD AND AGING

While achieving a healthy adult identity is one of the most challenging life tasks, Erikson asserts that psychosocial development does not end with this task. The next challenge (or crisis) faced by adults involves finding intimacy and requires the individual to integrate his own identity with the identity of a long-term intimate partner. (The cultural aspects of this particular stage of development are discussed in detail in Chapter 9.)

Developmental Tasks in Middle and Later Adulthood

The two remaining psychosocial crises or challenges occur in middle and late adulthood and focus on **generativity versus stagnation** and **integrity versus despair** (see Table 3.1). The former refers to the *generation of something lasting that represents oneself.* A successful resolution of this developmental issue leads to a sense of accomplishment and achievement. Such accomplishments can be expressed in material wealth, artistic or intellectual creations, raising children, or having achieved status in the community. This developmental phase clearly influences individuals' attitudes and behavior in social and work-related situations.

Integrity versus despair reflects older adults' attempts to *integrate previous identity resolutions and make sense of life as a whole.* Successful resolution of this final stage is characterized by an acceptance of oneself and one's accomplishments and failures. Unsuccessful resolution, on the other hand, leads to bitterness, resentment, and, in extreme cases, may be accompanied by withdrawal from the social environment.

Work and Leisure in Middle Adulthood

Cultural beliefs and values influence how individuals come to judge their efforts and accomplishments. Hofstede's (1980) initial examination of more than forty countries revealed significant differences in how people in these countries viewed and interpreted work and approached their social relationships at work. In particular, cultures differed on the following four work-related values: power distance, uncertainty avoidance, individualism/collectivism, and masculinity/femininity.

Cultures low on **power distance** put *less emphasis on organizational hierarchy and status between people.* In some cultures, it may be acceptable for a president of a company and a warehouse worker to socialize outside of work. Examples of countries low in power distance are Denmark, Israel, and Austria. Countries high in power distance are Mexico, Venezuela, and India.

The workplace in cultures low in **uncertainty avoidance** tend to *have few rules, policies, and codes that guide workers' communication and interpersonal relations.* In these cultures, a worker's complaints may be handled by different people in a relatively informal way, rather than by an appointed person according to specific procedures. Cultures low in uncertainty avoidance are Singapore, Denmark, and Sweden. Countries with the highest uncertainty avoidance are Greece, Portugal, Belgium, and Japan.

Collectivism, according to Hofstede, refers to the *degree to which a culture facilitates conformity, compliance, and the striving for harmony in the workplace.* Peru, Pakistan, Colombia, and Venezuela score high on collectivism, whereas the United States, Australia, Great Britain, and Canada tend to foster individualistic work values.

Finally, work environments in **"feminine cultures"** *promote gender equality, interpersonal contact, and group decision making.* This dimension can best be described as "working to live" versus "living to work." Scandinavian countries rate the highest in "femininity," whereas Japan, Austria, Italy, and Switzerland tend to promote "masculine" values.

Furnham, Kirkcaldy, and Lynn (1994) studied forty-one nations with regard to seven work-related beliefs. Their results showed that people in North and South America scored highest on work ethic (commitment to work), mastery (need to master problems), savings (importance of saving money), and conformity (identification with the organization and its success). Asian and Eastern countries scored highest on competitiveness (motive to be better than others) and money beliefs (importance of money). In addition, European countries scored lower than non-European countries on all seven dimensions, including achievement (need for excellence).

These beliefs about the work environment are also related to the nonwork environment. Studies of leisure activities show that these are both similar and different across cultures. Beatty, Jeon, Albaum, and Murphy (1994) questioned adults in the United States, France, Denmark, and New Zealand about their participation in recreational activities. Findings revealed three consistent clusters: *aesthetic-intellectual* (e.g., reading for pleasure, attending the opera, ballet, or dancing), *sports-action* (e.g., attending sports events or individual sports participation), and *social-entertainment* (e.g., going to the movies, having drinks, and enjoying entertainment). Two additional dimensions that were also examined did not replicate across cultures: *outdoor-nature* (e.g., walking for pleasure or bicycling) and *passive-in-home* (e.g., watching TV and playing sedentary games). The United States and New Zealand were most similar in their leisure activity preferences, with both scoring higher than their European counterparts on the sports-action and social-entertainment dimensions.

Among Chinese adults (Hu, 1995) the first choice for a hobby is reading, followed by social and intellectual activities. Physical exercise is third, tied with other productive activities, such as knitting or crafts. One could speculate that leisure activities, defined as the antithesis of work (see Beatty et al., 1994), provide an environment or context that fulfills needs not met in the workplace. Therefore, one could possibly draw conclusions from predominant work values about the preferences for leisure activities. For example, individuals in cultures that emphasize collectivist work environments may choose to spend their leisure time in solitary activities, as is the case in China. On the other hand, people in individualistic societies, such as New Zealand, Canada, and the United States, where people work independently and often autonomously, may prefer leisure activities that are social and cooperative.

Sport as a Social Phenomenon

As we have seen earlier in this chapter, play serves multiple important functions in the lives of children. In the following section, we outline how play and games are a central part in the ecological systems of adults in many societies. Games and sport can consist of spontaneous activity or highly organized sport, and participation may range from passive spectator to participating spectator (e.g., referee, coach) to player. Anthropologists and sport historians have identified multiple functions of sport in society. We shall summarize these findings and illustrate how cultural settings shape sporting activities and, at the same time, are shaped by them (for an overview, see Calhoun, 1987). Two of the main historical functions are the practice of economic skills necessary to make a living and military training. The former is expressed in kayaking contests among Eskimos and rodeos among North American cowboys. Boxing, fencing, martial arts, and tug-of-war are classic examples of sports used for building strength, endurance, and skills in the interest of warfare preparation. However, sport and games also serve important social functions.

In many cultures, games or sport can have a ritual or ceremonial function. As such, the game or contest is dedicated to requesting help from, or expressing gratitude toward, a supernatural being. The Native American game of lacrosse or Japanese sumo wrestling are representative of this function. The origins of sumo were religious in nature. The first sumo matches

A traditional sumo ceremony. (© Michael Reynolds/epa/CORBIS)

were rituals dedicated to the gods. Along with dances and prayers, sumo matches expressed gratefulness for a bountiful harvest. This ancient sport dates back about 1,500 years and its ritualized character has survived to this day. As Hall (1997) describes, the ceremony preceding sumo matches is marked by strict traditional etiquette. The *rikishi* (participating sumo wrestlers) enter the ring in their colorful ceremonial aprons (*kesho-mawashi*) and perform a short sumo ritual. After they depart, the wrestlers scheduled to fight enter the ring. Over their *kesho-mawashi* they wear a large braided hemp rope tied in the back and decorated with patterned paper strips in the front. This kind of decorated rope is a religious symbol that can be found in many Japanese homes and in temples. Each sumo wrestler then performs the prefight ceremony with great dignity. He claps his hands to attract the attention of the gods. Then he extends his arms to the side, palms up to show that he does not carry any weapons. Finally, he lifts first one leg high in the air and brings it down with a thundering stomp on the ground. This move is repeated with the other leg. This maneuver is meant to symbolically drive the evil spirits from the ring. After this, the match begins. Throughout Japan today, sumo wrestlers are honored not only as successful athletes but also as representatives of a small group of individuals who preserve and celebrate religious and cultural traditions. In a culture that is characterized as a tight culture, high in uncertainty avoidance and high in power distance, the sport of sumo emphasizes these cultural values.

At the microsystem level, games and sport serve as recreational and communal activities. They also are an acceptable way of expressing rivalry and settling disputes. On the more distant level of the ecological system, sport expresses social identity and strengthens the sense of unity among members of a culture. Archetti (1999) provides a thorough account of the cultural meaning of sport in Argentina. He discusses football (soccer) as a cultural institution that permeates history, politics, and social and national identity. Archetti describes the evolution of the distinctive style of Argentinian soccer as a result of two main social forces: British imperialism and the ecological settings in which young Argentinian boys learn to play soccer. As opposed to the highly organized system of sport in Britain, most young Argentinian boys learn to play the game in the streets, in confined spaces with uneven surfaces. This setting lets them develop strong dribbling and ball-control skills, but little strategy. This led to a style of soccer much the opposite of the British style, which is very linear and strategic. Hence, soccer may be interpreted as a form of expression of independence from the British, and as such it has become part of Argentinian national identity and pride (macrosystem).

The Argentinian soccer player has also become an idealized role model for male social identity and behavior. The *pibe criollo* (ball-playing boy) represents one of the male ideals in this culture: he is spontaneous, free-spirited, and positive, feels responsibility toward family and society, and seeks to achieve. He remains imperfect, but imperfections are forgiven because he is, after all, only a boy. Young boys strive toward this ideal and are reinforced by family and peers (microsystem). In Argentina, as in many countries, spectators rally behind their national team in international competition. The unity of spectators is expressed by uniform colors, national anthems, the display of flags and other symbols of national pride (exosystem). Victory of the national sports team equals victory of the nation and fills the members of that nation with pride, reinforcing the loyalty and unity of the country at large. This phenomenon of social identification through sports is nowhere more clearly observable than during the Olympic games, which bring many nations together in competition.

These cultural examples of sport show that this social activity is an important element in the ecological systems of adults who participate (actively or passively). In that capacity, students of human development have to consider sport and games as central to adult social development. For example, as individuals age and make a transition from active to passive participation, their ecological system changes, which, in turn, influences their social behavior.

Social Support and Well-Being in Later Adulthood

The relationship between well-being and social support in later adulthood appears to be largely universal. Comparisons of diverse cultures show a remarkable similarity in patterns of social support from spouses, relatives, adult children, and friends and their influence on well-being (Lennartsson, 1999). At the same time, cultural differences can be found in the expectations or norms regarding social relationships maintained by elderly persons.

Normative expectations that children care for their elderly parents in Thailand result in the common arrangement that at least one adult child lives in the same household or very close by, thereby providing a minimum level of social support. Even if the caregiving is perceived as demanding, a deep sense of family obligation and emotional bond maintains this system of social connection in old age.

However, cultural change may affect the social support system of some elderly. For example, shifts in familial positions in Taiwan have recently produced situations in which the daughter-in-law gains more importance in some families than the formerly powerful mother-in-law. With decreased responsibilities, older women have begun to experience feelings of uselessness and reduced social support. This change in social relationships has been related to an increase in suicide risk among the elderly in Taiwan (Hu, 1995).

It is not merely the presence of a social support system that is relevant to well-being. Reciprocal relationships, in which individuals both receive and provide support, are related to greater life satisfaction. Such relationships seem to be more prevalent in France than in North America (Antonucci, 1990). For example, the elderly in France perceive their social relationships as more reciprocal than do both Caucasians and African Americans in the United States.

◇ SUMMARY

While virtually all social relationships and behavior patterns change over the lifespan, some aspects are more salient at different ages. The types of relationships and behaviors children develop with their primary caretakers early in life set the stage for many social relationships to come. Even though there appear to be universal patterns of "secure base," "caretaker sensitivity," and a correlation between secure attachment and social competence late in life, early attachment patterns are seemingly influenced by caretaking practices and general conditions under which children grow up.

As children learn to communicate, they begin to form more social relationships; these are initially built and later maintained through play. Social relationships require basic behavioral skills, such as conflict resolution and cooperation, which involve a general understanding of moral principles. Kohlberg's theory of moral development addresses some important aspects of morality, namely the understanding of normative principles of justice. However, Gilligan has demonstrated that individuals may also base their moral decisions on nurturance and caring. Though they represent interdependent elements of moral reasoning, the salience of either of these moral orientations may vary from culture to culture.

Along with developing prosocial reasoning and behavior, children and young adolescents are also facing the challenge of managing their own and others' aggressive social behavior. Once again, examples from various cultures illustrate that one's place within a culture's ecological system helps to determine the definition and expression of aggressive behavior.

Adolescent social development is marked by an increased influence of peers (in addition to family) on prosocial as well as antisocial behavior. However, cultural differences in values and beliefs about appropriate and inappropriate social behavior have to be taken into account when analyzing adolescent social development.

Middle adulthood is dominated by concerns of productivity, which manifest differently depending on values and expectations. As in childhood, the social functions of games and play continue to shape social development in middle and later adulthood. Active and passive participation in sports are part of the ecological system. Finally, social support and satisfying social relationships facilitate well-being and peace of mind in older adulthood.

◇ STUDY QUESTIONS

Show an understanding of early attachment and conditions in an infant's environment that serve as a basis for social development.

Compare and contrast theories of social development and be able to discuss their cultural implications.

Comment on cultural influences on parent-child and parent-adolescent relationships. Explain how and why play and games are a vital part of an adult's ecological system.

◇ FURTHER READINGS

Cheryl Bentsen. (1989). *Masai Days*. New York: Anchor Books.

> The author provides a closeup look at this traditional African culture. This book is not so much a scholarly account but an informative and lively view of Masai everyday life. Among other things, the reader learns about the concerns of two young boys torn between traditional and modern ways, young adult women and their social network, and young men who take great pride in their role as warriors.

Robert Kaminski and Judy Sierra. (1995). *Children's Traditional Games: Games from 137 Countries and Cultures*. Phoenix, AZ: Oryx Press.

> The authors provide practical educational activities based on folk games from more than 130 countries and cultures. Although the book is designed mainly as a practical reference book for teachers, it also discusses the function of games in childhood development, their cultural importance, the types of games found around the world, and the rationale for using folk games in the classroom.

H. J. Kornadt. (2002). Social Motives and their development in cultural context. In W. J. Lonner, D. L. Dinnel, S. A. Hayes, & D. N. Sattler (Eds.), *Online Readings in Psychology and Culture* (Unit 15, Chapter 6), (http://www.wwu.edu/~culture), Center for Cross-Cultural Research, Western Washington University, Bellingham, Washington.

> This online chapter deals with differences in social motives between cultures and with their development. After describing social motives as complex functional systems, aggressiveness and achievement motivation are dealt with as examples. Assumptions about biological factors are reported and cultural differences in early mother–child relations and in cultural norms and values are discussed.

R. V. Levine. (2003). Measuring helping behaviors across cultures. In W. J. Lonner, D. L. Dinnel, S. A. Hayes, & D. N. Sattler (Eds.), *Online Readings in Psychology and Culture* (Unit 15, Chapter 9), (http://www.wwu.edu/~culture), Center for Cross-Cultural Research, Western Washington University, Bellingham, Washington.

> This online chapter focuses on some of the special challenges and difficulties in conducting cross-cultural research including a series of studies in which helpfulness toward strangers was assessed in 36 cities across the United States and 23 large cities around the world. Situations included seeing if passersby would alert a pedestrian who dropped a pen, offer to help a pedestrian with a hurt leg, and assist a blind person to cross the street.

Robert R. Sands. (1999). *Anthropology, Sport, and Culture*. Westport, CT: Bergin and Garvey.

> This unique collection of current research on culture and sport discusses issues including ethnicity, identity, ritual, and culture change, as well as the effect of environment and genes. The book illustrates the importance of studying sport as a universal phenomenon that both shapes and is shaped by its cultural context.

◇ DEVELOPMENTAL ANALYSIS

CULTURE AND SOCIAL BEHAVIOR

As a young child, I grew up quite attached to my mother. While I also felt very close to my father, my mother was my primary caregiver. My first memory of being in a strange situation with the absence of my mother was in the local grocery store. I was just two years old and a boisterous walker. I did not want to sit in the cart, so my mother let me walk alongside her. Quite predictably, I began to wander off and soon realized that the flowered skirt I was staring at was not my mother's. The unfamiliar woman knelt down and asked me if I was lost. I began to cry. Nothing would comfort me until I felt the familiar touch of my own mother's arms. Needless to say, I was pleased to sit obediently in the cart during subsequent trips to the grocery store!

My own children grew up in a very different cultural setting. Both my husband and I had careers and were working full-time. Circumstances allowed me to stay at home with my daughter for 8 months—during which I was the primary caregiver. I was a new mom but did not want to admit that I needed any help. I was home alone with Elizabeth, tending to her every need. By the time my son was born, one year later, I had just started a new position as a professor and could not imagine taking leave for so long. We were faced with the question of whether we would put our son, Alexander, into daycare at a much earlier age than our daughter. I looked to our families for help. Fortunately, my husband's mother was able to come from Italy and stay with us for an extended period of time. In fact, she stayed for nearly the entire first year of my son's life. As you may know, it is quite common in other cultures for grandparents, aunts, uncles, and cousins to all live together. Many of my friends and colleagues could not imagine having their mother-in-law stay with them for more than a week! I was grateful for the opportunity to continue progressing in my career, while also keeping Alexander and Elizabeth at home with a loving caregiver. Although I was Alexander's mother, his paternal grandmother was his primary caregiver during his early infancy, and they have always shared a special bond.

Together, Elizabeth and Alexander learned about competition and collaboration. At the ages of four and five, I recall watching them struggle to put a puzzle together. They began by dividing up the pieces and racing to see who could put their pieces together first. Soon, they realized that the other sibling may have pieces each of them needed and it would be better to work as a team. Through experiences like this, they learned the importance of cooperation in pursuit of a common goal. However, put a basketball between them and it's an entirely different story! Their competitive drive is obvious during a heated game of hoops.

Our family had an interesting, life-changing, cultural experience many years ago. During one of our many vacations to Brazil, we met a family from Korea. They had just arrived in the country for a brief visit and were having

(continued)

difficulty getting to their hotel. My husband and I were able to help them and shared a meal later that evening. Each year, they send us a gift at the holidays to show their appreciation. When our daughter studied abroad in Korea, they insisted on having her to their home, feeding her, and taking her around the country. For our daughter, this was a wonderful experience. For them, this was their "social obligation." Because we had helped them years before, they felt the need to reciprocate. I was impressed watching their daughter and Elizabeth interact and find how many things they had in common. They were equally consumed with mastering their classes, selecting the right career, and worrying about finding a life partner! I remember being a young girl and sharing such concerns. I am proud to say that it has all worked out for me. I consider marrying Giorgio, raising our lovely children, and having a successful career among my greatest accomplishments.

CHAPTER NINE

THE FAMILY IN
CULTURAL CONTEXT

The sun is just beginning to rise in Boslanti, along the Saramacca River in central Suriname, the smallest country in South America. Sindy Sowidagkijm, twenty-four, and her husband David, twenty-six, surrounded by a midwife and several female relatives, including two grandmothers, are nearing the birth of their third child. The two older children, on the other side of the small wooden house, are lulled to sleep by the rhythmic sound of light rain on the corrugated-iron roof. Suddenly, a baby's cry fills the room, and little Jacob makes his arrival known to all. Sindy, exhausted but happy, will breastfeed her newborn and take a deserved rest. David will dream of the day when his new son will join him and his uncles on the family fishing boat. The others will proudly spread the word about the newest citizen in Boslanti.

At Mt. Sinai Hospital, in downtown New York City, Walter and Patricia Mezzanotti have just entered the brightly lit delivery room on the eighth floor. At thirty-eight, this is Patricia's first pregnancy and it has been unusually difficult. She is lightly sedated with an intravenous needle pumping a labor-inducing drug into her arm. Two hours later, following an emergency Cesarean section performed by two doctors and two nurses, she is sleeping quietly in the recovery room, awaiting the time she will see her new son for the first time. Just down the hall, relaxing in a rocking chair in a birthing room and talking with her husband John, five-year-old daughter sarah, other family members, and two close friends is Ruth Hazelton. In a half hour, she will give birth to a daughter in a quiet homelike atmosphere and begin the bonding process by immediately holding and feeding her newborn.

225

◇ CULTURAL VARIATIONS IN THE FAMILY LIFE CYCLE

In the words of William Kenkel (1985), *"Families have a beginning, they grow in numbers, their membership next declines, and eventually the original family exists no longer.* The individual is born, grows, enters a period of decline, and inevitably passes from the scene. The striking parallel between the life pattern of a normal individual and the history of a typical family gave rise to the concept **family life cycle"** (p. 375). Although not a literal analogy, this concept provides a framework that allows us to consider the shifting attributes that affect individual behaviors and interactions within the family, community, and cultural context. As we make our way through this chapter, we shall be looking at the family life cycle in terms of the developmental stages used in previous chapters and relating these to real-life examples of families living in a wide variety of ecological settings throughout the world. We begin with the selection of a mate and the process of marriage.

Mate Selection

Buss (1994b) begins his study of mate preferences in thirty-seven cultures with a statement that cannot be disputed: "Every person is alive because of a successful mating. People in the past who failed to mate are not our ancestors" (p. 197). Considering how much of a person's life might be spent with a partner and the impact this relationship has on one's social, emotional, and psychological development (as well as on one's children), selection of a mate is frequently one of our most important decisions. "How do we select a marriage partner?" "What characteristics do we consider important?" "Are there cultural differences in selecting a mate?"

In an effort to answer these questions, Buss (with the help of fifty other researchers) conducted an extensive study of more than ten thousand individuals living in thirty-seven cultures. The approach involved asking subjects to indicate how important each of eighteen characteristics was in selecting a mate and then to rank thirteen of these in terms of their desirability. Findings revealed that, across cultures, men and women looked for mates who were kind and understanding, intelligent, had an exciting personality, and were healthy.

Buss indicated that he and his team of researchers were surprised by some of the results, particularly cultural variations concerning the most variable characteristic—chastity or the lack of previous sexual experience. For example, they expected that men throughout the world would highly value this quality more than would women. It would be surprising if cultures did not vary in the value placed on chastity, since other sources on sexuality usually note cross-cultural variation in practices, values, and expectations (Hamon & Ingoldsby, 2003; Hatfield & Rapson, 2005). Such variation was indeed shown in Buss's study. While chastity was considered irrelevant or unimportant

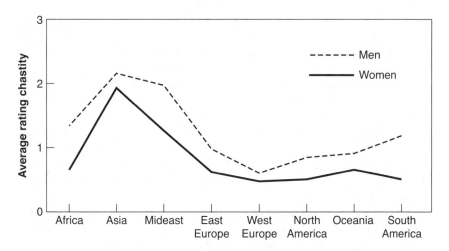

FIGURE 9.1 Cross-Cultural Differences in the Importance of Chastity

Source: From *Love and Sex* by E. Hatfield and R. L. Rapson; 2005. Lanham, MD: University Press of America, p. 124. Reprinted by permission.

in a prospective mate by both men and women in the Netherlands, Sweden, and Norway, it was viewed as indispensable in China and scored very highly by those from India, Taiwan, and Iran. Among those who viewed chastity as only moderately desirable were those living in Colombia, Estonia, Japan, Nigeria, Poland, South Africa, and Zambia. Yet, in an overwhelming majority of countries (two-thirds), chastity was desired in a marriage partner more by men than by women. (See Figure 9.1.)

Other categories showing large cultural differences in response were: "*good housekeeper* (highly valued in Estonia and China, little valued in Western Europe and North America); *refinement/neatness* (highly valued in Nigeria and Iran, less valued in Great Britain, Ireland, and Australia); and *religious* (highly valued in Iran, moderately valued in India, little valued in Western Europe and North America)" (Buss, 1994b, p. 199). Buss cautions that although these differences are important, there is undoubtedly much variability across individuals within these cultures. This once again reinforces our point that *there are often greater differences within cultures than between or among cultures.*

Looking more specifically at what each of the genders wanted in a mate, Buss found some interesting differences. As for women: "From the Zulu tribe in South Africa to coastal-dwelling Australians to city-dwelling Brazilians, women place a premium on good earning capacity, financial prospects, ambition, industriousness, and social status more than men—characteristics that all provide resources" (p. 199). Men were found to prefer women who are younger than they are—how much younger depends on the culture. For example, in those cultures where men often have more than one wife (e.g., Zambia and Nigeria), men prefer brides who are younger by as much as seven or eight years. In cultures where only one wife is permitted (e.g., Germany, Spain, and France), the preference was for brides only slightly younger. In all cultures, women had a preference for older men, since men tend to mature later than women and also tend to have greater access to more financial resources than do younger men. Finally, "in *all* known cultures worldwide, from the inner-continental tribal societies of Africa and South America to the big cities of Madrid, London, and Paris, men place a premium on the physical appearance of a potential mate" (p. 200). According to Buss, there is a good reason for men to favor youthfulness and physical appearance, even though they may not be fully aware that "these qualities provide the best signals . . . that the woman is fertile and has good reproductive capacity" (p. 200).

Research on mate selection has become increasingly complex and has begun to focus greater attention on a variety of new variables, including "sexual strategies theory" and the effects of context (Buss, 2003; Buss & Schmitt, 1993) and physiological factors, such as body type and hormones (Gangestad, 1993; Singh, 1993). Looking at such important contextual variables as one's age, family networks, and parental and kin influences on mating decisions, Buss and Schmitt (1993) have proposed a contextual-evolutionary theory of human mating strategies, in which both men and women are hypothesized to have evolved distinct psychological mechanisms that underlie short-term and long-term strategies. They outlined nine key hypotheses and twenty-two predictions based on this theory and submited them to empirical testing. According to the authors, some of the problems sensitive to context include sexual accessibility, fertility assessment, commitment seeking and avoidance, assessment of mate value, and parental investment. Singh, on the other hand, takes a different approach and examines the role of body fat distribution as measured by waist-to-hip ratio (WHR) on the judgment of women's physical attractiveness. According to Singh (1993), WHR appears to be correlated with a woman's reproductive status and long-term health risk. Three studies were conducted to investigate whether individuals have perceptual and cognitive mechanisms to utilize the WHR to infer attributes of women's health, youthfulness, attractiveness, and reproductive capacity. College students (aged 18–22 years) and 134 older subjects (aged 30–86 years) of both sexes ranked female figures with normal weight and low WHR as attractive and assigned to them higher reproductive capability. In another part of the study, college-age subjects of both sexes guessed the ages of female figures. Results showed underweight figures were assigned lower ages than normal weight figures. The author concluded that WHR is a reliable measure of a woman's reproductive potential.

Hamon and Ingoldsby (2003) have explored the processes of mate selection in a variety of cultures, including those in North America, the Caribbean and South America, Africa, the Middle East, Asia, and Europe. With contributions from twenty authors, using a common set of guidelines and formats, it is easy for readers to make comparisons between and among more than sixteen cultures spread throughout the world. For this reason the book appears in the "Further Readings" section at the close of this chapter.

Do men and women actually act on these preferences? Perhaps we'll get some answers when we look at the next topic—marriage.

Marriage and Other Long-Term Relationships

Children generally benefit from a stable system of primary caretakers, commonly including, but not limited to, the biological parents. Thus, heterosexual long-term relationships are facilitated, sanctioned, and protected in most societies. The motivation for marriage is to provide a stable environment for children. In fact, the cultural definition of "family" influences the ecological system on many levels. For example, it shapes the microsystem by ensuring (in many cases) that two parents are present, and regulates the macrosystem because it views this form of "family" as an important element of societal structure. It also affects all three components of the developmental niche in a variety of ways, such as determining family structure, presence or absence of parents and other relatives, customs of childcare, parenting styles, values, belief systems, and developmental expectations.

In addition to (hopefully) providing a good and healthy environment for children, individuals commit themselves to long-term relationships for other reasons. For example, Hindu religion considers marriage to be sacred and a symbol of the marriage between the sun goddess Surya and the moon god Soma. Without a wife, a man is considered spiritually incomplete (Kumari, 1988). The motivation for marriage is the striving for spiritual growth. Chinese cultural philosophy proposes that all objects and events are the outcome of two interacting principles: **Yin,** the *negative, passive, weak,* and *female,* and **Yang,** the *positive, active, strong,* and *male.* Harmonious interaction of the female and male principle, ensures the continuation of reality as we know it. Thus, in Chinese culture, long-term relationships between women and men are a spiritual necessity for the survival of humankind (Ruan, 1991).

Marriage may also be a means to gain or maintain status in one's society. In most cultures, simply the fact of being married gives married men and women a higher status than their unmarried counterparts (Kumari, 1988). Unmarried adults may be stigmatized and denied full adult status. In addition to social status, marriage may result in higher economic status. The pooling of resources of two families or a dowry paid by the family of the bride can mean considerable financial gain for both spouses. Finally, and certainly not to be forgotten, individuals may be motivated to share their lives out of a desire for love and companionship.

Anthropologists have demonstrated that marriage takes many forms in cultures around the world. These include **monogamy,** in which *one man is married to one woman;* **polygyny,** in which *one man is married to several women;* **polyandry,** in which *one woman is married to several men;* and **group marriage,** in which *several women are married to several men*. Polygyny is found on every continent. It is common in many Islamic countries, African societies, and parts of Asia, and it is also found in North America. An abundance of wives of different ages not only represents wealth and power, but it also ensures the reproductive success of the man. A verse from the *Qur'an* helps explain the practice in Islam: *"Marry women of your choice, two or three or four; but if you fear that you shall not be able to deal justly with them, then only one or one that your right hands possess. That will be more suitable, to prevent you from doing injustice."* (*Qur'an* 4:3). While some Muslim majority countries still retain traditional Islamic Law permitting polygyny, there are some movements within Islam that challenge its acceptability. Polyandry is much less common. In some regions of Tibet and Nepal, brothers may share the same wife. However, in most cultures in which polyandry is accepted, husbands do not share blood relations. In general, polyandry is associated with greater economic power of women. Men in polyandrous societies have to be more considerate of women's needs to prevent them from switching their attention to more generous and caring husbands. Thus, wives can rely on generous shares of their husbands' wealth or income and may acquire considerable wealth themselves (Sangree, 1992). Only a few societies allow both women and men to be married to multiple spouses. Sangree points out that these polyandrous–polygynous societies have been found only in some regions in Western Africa.

You may be surprised to learn that the most "favored" form of marriage across societies is polygyny. However, Kenkel (1985) points out that "if we were to judge solely on the basis of a preponderance of a given marriage form, then few, if any, societies could be classified as polygynous. . . . No society . . . could arrange for all its males to have plural wives unless . . . the sex ratio could somehow be upset" (Kenkel, p. 22). In other words, for each man married to two women, there would have to be a man who was not married at all. Therefore, only those cultures in which more than one wife is preferred are typically considered to be polygynous. Using this criterion, G. P. Murdock (1967), the pioneering anthropologist, in a study of a large sample of the world's societies, classified 721 as polygynous, 137 as monogamous, and only four as polyandrous. Kenkel states that while "monogamy is actually the preferred form in a relatively small number of societies . . . it [is] . . . the only form of marriage that is permitted and recognized in every society throughout the world, although it is not always the form of marriage that receives highest approval. . . . The great bulk of the world's married population, by lot or by intent, is monogamously wed" (1985, p. 23).

A number of cultures permit sexual relations of some sort between individuals of the same sex (Cabaj & Purcell, 1998). The very few studies that address the subject in a cultural context mainly focus on homosexual relationships between men. In reviewing research conducted in many different cultures, Carpo (1995) distinguishes two main forms of socially recognized long-term homosexual relationships: mentorship and pathecism. **Mentorship** *refers to relationships between partners of different ages and social status*. Sexual relations by no means occur in all mentorships, and when they do take place are only one aspect of the relationship. More importantly, the older man frequently serves as a socializing agent for the younger man and introduces him to the fundamentals of warfare, politics, and religion. **Pathecism** *involves partners of similar age and status who commit themselves to a long-term partnership* comparable to heterosexual marriage.

Because cross-cultural studies of homosexual relationships are limited in number, it is difficult to know with certainty what percentage of societies accept, tolerate, or even support same-sex relationships. Nonetheless, Bolton (1994) concludes from a review of anthropological studies that male homosexual relations are common in 41 to 64 percent of societies studied. By comparison, data on lesbian relationships are not as readily available, but Bolton argues that "societies which are tolerant of homosexuality are consistent in expressing that tolerance across age and gender categories" (p. 162).

The presence or absence of homosexual relationships in a given society once again illustrates the concept of the developmental niche, namely how certain behaviors may develop or be inhibited in response to cultural conditions. In societies that tolerate or even support relationships between people of the same sex, there are a greater number of gay and lesbian relationships. In contrast, societies that strictly prohibit homosexual relations report fewer instances of homosexuality. These differences do not occur as a result of a higher or lower percentage of gays and lesbians in the population, but as a result of differential opportunities to develop a certain preference and behavior within one's ecological surroundings and to express it as part of one's developmental niche.

How and why individuals are attracted to each other varies significantly across cultures. Another distinction might be referred to as the "Eastern versus Western ideal." In many Western cultures, perhaps best represented by the United States, marriage is often viewed as the culmination of romantic love. The belief is that each person has an "ideal" mate that he or she is destined to meet, fall in love with, marry, and live with "happily ever after." One of the authors (Gardiner) recalls a student telling him how her parents, living in Yugoslavia, met and married. One day, her father climbed a hill next to his village and watched a young woman washing clothes in the river below. He returned the next day and watched her again. On the third day, he walked down to the river, told her he had been watching her for three days and had fallen in love with her and wanted to marry her. She said "yes." They were now celebrating their twenty-fifth wedding anniversary! However, there are other people who find "true love" several times and have the marriage certificates to prove it.

The "Eastern ideal" continues to characterize many of the arranged marriages in Asia, Africa, and some other parts of the world. This ideal is based on the premise that each person has several possible mates with whom they could develop a successful marriage. Frequently, India being one example, families will discuss a possible future liaison between their infant children. Sometimes, the children are aware of this arrangement; sometimes, they are not. They are expected to marry (or bring shame and embarrassment to their families); if they are lucky, they may one day fall in love with each other. A female Indian graduate student, speaking in one of the author's (Gardiner) cross-cultural courses, related that she was returning home to Bombay to get married. When asked what her future husband did, she replied, "I don't know because I've never met him." The liberated young American women in class told her that she shouldn't marry someone she didn't know. Her reply, which makes an interesting point, was that she trusted her parents to make a wise decision regarding a future husband because they knew her and him and his family. In the meantime, she could concentrate on her studies while they (the American women) would have to search for their own husbands, go through the trials and errors of dating, and hope that in the end it would all work out.

Many of those who live in collectivist cultures view marriage as the coming together or blending of two families. For example, in northern Kenya, the creation of a new house is a significant part of the marriage ceremony. Once the wedding date is established, based on lunar calculations, the groom's family literally disassembles the new house, moves it to the bride's village, and rebuilds it. Prior to the wedding ceremony, the bride is taken through a rite of passage during which she is initiated into womanhood by the village's female elders and is taught what to expect from married life. Among the Mande, another African group, girls between ages twelve and eighteen attend clitoridectomy schools, where they have their clitorides removed and are formally taught how to be wives. They learn secret languages and codes that allow them to communicate with other married women. In Africa, as well as other parts of the world, wedding customs are undergoing change and reflect a mixture of the traditional as well as the modern.

Harry and Ormsin Gardiner's Thai wedding ceremony. (Courtesy of authors)

The same might be said of contemporary Japan, where love marriages have increasingly replaced the earlier practice of arranged marriages. Whichever practice is followed, certain traditional customs remain. For example, a *yuinou*, or ceremonial betrothal gift (often in the form of money), is first presented by the bridegroom-to-be, through a go-between, to the bride-to-be's household. In anthropological terms this represents the bride's price. The bride's parents are then expected to spend several times the value of the *yuinou* on a new home for the couple. Most wedding ceremonies in Japan are performed according to Shinto customs, followed by the drinking of sake (rice wine) as confirmation of the marriage and later by a celebration party.

In Thailand, couples tend to marry at later ages (late twenties to early thirties) as they continue their education and establish careers. According to Gardiner and Gardiner (1991), "While young people frequently reject arranged marriages in favor of making their own choices, they still observe the traditional ceremonies associated with marriage, including the morning blessing and chanting by monks, the pouring of lustral water, and a large evening reception for friends and relatives" (p. 180).

◇ THE BIRTH PROCESS ACROSS CULTURES

The vignettes that opened this chapter, Sindy and David Sowidagkijm in Suriname, Patricia and Walter Mezzanotti and John and Ruth Hazelton in New York City, illustrate that, although newborns arrive every day in cultures around the world, the birth experience depends very much on cultural traditions and is deeply embedded within an ecological setting influenced by family, community, and culture.

In some societies, having a baby is just another normal event in one's life and takes little preparation. This is illustrated in the following example taken from the !Kung in the Kalahari Desert of Africa: "The first labor pains came at night and stayed . . . until dawn. That morning, everyone went gathering. Mother and I stayed behind. We sat together for a while, then I went and played with the other children. Later, I came back and ate the nuts she had cracked for me. She got up and started to get ready. . . . We walked a short way, then she sat down by the base of a large nehn tree, leaned back against it, and little Kumsa was born" (Shostak, 1981, pp. 53–54). Similarly, in rural Thailand, pregnancy does not significantly change a woman's behavior, and she "generally carries on with her household chores until the time of birth—even, in some cases, up to the last few minutes before delivery. Rural children are usually born at home with the mother resting on a mat or mattress on the floor assisted by a non-medically trained midwife and older relatives or neighbors" (Gardiner and Gardiner, 1991, p. 183). A few hours later, the new mother is often up and participating in family activities.

In many parts of North America, including the United States, fathers-to-be are typically present during labor and encouraged to actively participate in the delivery of their child, whether it is at home or in a hospital. Not so in some parts of the former Soviet Union or in East Africa, where an expectant Ngoni mother is assisted by other women, while husbands and other men are completely excluded.

Clearly, not every culture approaches childbirth in the same way. In the next section, we look at the birth process in more detail and consider its variations across cultures.

The Ecology of Birth

For a long time, what we knew about childbirth practices came from a Western, largely American, perspective that viewed the procedure as a medical event. Interestingly, this was not always the case. In fact, childbirth in Canada and the United States, like most other countries, was handled exclusively by women until the middle of the nineteenth century, when physicians, almost all of whom were men, began delivering babies and made it a medical rather than a social event.

In the original edition of her now classic cross-cultural investigation of childbirth in four cultures, Brigitte Jordan (1978) anticipated the approach we take here when she noted that "we have paid little attention to the social-interactional and socio-ecological aspects of birth [which address] . . . what is biological and what is social and cultural in the process of childbirth" (Preface). In the Preface to the fourth edition of this book, Jordan and Davis-Floyd (1993) state that "an anthropology of birth must focus on

A Mayan woman, lying in her hammock, surrounded by her husband and a midwife, gives birth. (From *Birth in Four Cultures,* 4th ed., by B. Jordan, 1993, Prospect Heights, IL: Waveland Press, Inc. Reprinted by permission of Waveland Press, Inc.)

the study of birthing *systems* and not the comparison of individual and iso-lated practices. We know that birth is everywhere a socially marked crisis event that is consensually shaped and socially patterned [consisting of] . . . practices that make sense from the inside out, though not necessarily from the outside in" (pp. xi–xii).

In a section of her book titled "The Ecology of Birth," Jordan discusses the particular locations in which babies are born and how these reflect cul-ture-specific patterns (or ecological settings, as we would view them) within which individuals' lives are forever entwined. She also comments on the cul-tural implications of these specific arrangements.

Yucatan

Of the four cultures presented by Jordan and Davis-Floyd (1993), the Yu-catan imposes the least changes in the expectant mother's surroundings, maintaining its familiar and reassuring qualities by encouraging the Mayan woman to lie in the same hammock in which she sleeps each night "whose strengths and tautness she knows to exploit for maximum support and com-fort [thereby providing] . . . the kind of security that marks the event as a normal part of family life" (p. 68).

In Yucatan, there is a clear expectation that the father-to-be will be pres-ent during labor and birth, not only to take an active role, but also in order to observe "how a woman suffers." Frequently, if a child is stillborn, it is blamed on an absent father. In addition, the pregnant woman's mother should be present, often in the company of others from the family microsystem, includ-ing sisters, sisters-in-law, mothers-in-law, godmothers, and sometimes neigh-bors and close friends. According to Jordan (1978), all of these people make a contribution to a successful birth, and the intensity of their emotional and physical involvement is "mirrored in the strain on their faces and in the signs of fatigue that become evident in them as well as in the mother" (p. 38).

Immediately following birth, it is believed that the mother and her child are susceptible to the influence of evil spirits from the bush and must remain inside the house for one week before returning to normal activity. An infant girl will have her ears pierced within the first hour after birth and sometime within the next three days will receive her first earrings, often a family heirloom. Nearly all newborns are breastfed, with nursing beginning a few minutes after birth and continuing whenever the infant appears hungry or anxious.

Holland and Sweden

In Holland, like Yucatan, women generally give birth at home, assisted by a midwife or physician, and the country continues to maintain one of the lowest infant mortality rates in the world—5.04 deaths per 1000 live births (*World Factbook,* 2005). In Sweden, often cited as the country with the lowest infant mortality (2.77 deaths per 1000 live births), almost all babies are de-livered in hospitals with the help of highly trained midwives (*World Fact-book*, 2005). According to Jordan, what these two countries have in com-mon is a program of government-sponsored prenatal care for every woman as well as availability of abortion on demand, with the result that "for all practical purposes, all pregnancies are wanted pregnancies and all babies are wanted babies" (p. 46).

In both Holland and Sweden, the mother-to-be is usually assisted by a midwife and her assistant and sometimes by a husband, male or female friend, or relative, who is there to provide help and emotional support. Ac-cording to Jordan (1978), Dutch and Swedish midwives do not view the woman as a patient to be delivered but as an individual capable of giving birth on her own. Their role is to give encouragement, be prepared for com-plications, and take care of cutting the umbilical cord.

United States

In the United States, ranking forty-three in the world in infant mortality (6.50 deaths per 1000 live births) in 2005, the majority of births (approxi-mately 98 percent) continue to be in hospital settings under the control of medical specialists. However, unlike the three countries mentioned above, there is a wider range of options available. For example, while some families prefer to have their babies delivered at home with the assistance of a mid-wife, increasing numbers, like the Hazelton family in our opening vignette, are taking advantage of birthing rooms located in hospitals, where technol-ogy is available but a home atmosphere is provided.

In this regard, an experimental project cited by Jordan is of historical (and perhaps contemporary) interest. Over a period of three years during the early 1970s, two nurse-midwives conducted the majority of normal deliver-ies in a California hospital. During this period, there was a dramatic drop in the number of stillbirths, fetal deaths, premature births, and neonatal deaths. When physicians once again took charge, all of these types of incidents in-creased, with the prematurity rate going up nearly 50 percent and neonatal mortality more than tripling (Levy, Wilkinson, & Marine, 1971).

In the years since this 1971 experimental project, several other small-scale studies have confirmed the success rate of nurse–midwife assisted deliv-eries. In 1998, MacDorman and Singh reported findings from the first large-scale study to examine the infant mortality risks for *all* single, vaginal births at 35 to 43 weeks gestation delivered by nurse-midwives in the United States during the year 1991 (182,461 births or about 4.4% of all births that year). After controlling for a variety of social and medical risk factors, the authors compared the data for midwives with a random sample of 25% of physician-attended births in 1991. Results indicated that infant deaths were 19% lower for births attended by nurse-midwives, the risk of neonatal mortality (death during the first 28 weeks of life) was 33% lower, and the risk of delivering a low birthweight infant was 31% lower. Differences in these birth outcomes may be explained, in part, by the differences in prenatal, labor, and delivery care practices demonstrated by nurse-midwives, for example, more time spent with patients during prenatal visits, greater emphasis on counseling and education, and provision of emotional support before, during, and after delivery. Such findings lend support to Jordan's earlier contention that not only is the birth experience significantly influenced by who is allowed to be present during birth, but so is the outcome of the birth process itself.

Discussing the consequences of a culture's choice of birth setting (home, hospital, bush, or elsewhere), Jordan and Davis-Floyd (1993) make an intriguing comment when they note that when babies are delivered in hospitals, "responsibility and credit are clearly the physician's . . . visible in the handshake and 'thank you' [exchanged] . . . after the birth. . . . Typically, nobody thanks the woman [who] . . . has delivered rather than given birth" (p. 71). However, when babies are delivered at home, birth arrangements are the choice of the expectant mother and her family—"Their choice, their problem, their task, and . . . finally . . . their achievement" (p. 71). These may be subtle differences in language, but they represent significant differences in cultural views and belief systems that form a crucial part of one's experiences within different developmental niches and ecological surroundings.

Writing nearly thirty years ago, Jordan (1978) concluded her original birth study with the following statement: "What we need to keep in mind here is that birthing systems themselves are part of a larger cultural system . . . within an economic and political structure, via the socialization of birth participants" (p. 73). This point is even more relevant today, especially in light of our recurring themes, which focus on the cultural context in which development takes place.

In a sense, if you know a society's approach to childbirth, you will understand a great deal about the values and beliefs that are at the heart of its ecocultural system, how it socializes its members, and how it conducts its interpersonal relationships.

◇ THE TRANSITION TO PARENTHOOD

Kenkel (1985) puts the transition to parenthood in perspective when he states that "one of the significant features with regard to the parent role is a general lack of preparation for it. . . . Related to [this] . . . is the fact that the transition . . . is abrupt [and] . . . is largely irrevocable" (pp. 455–456).

Becoming a parent results in major life changes that affect not only the parents and their infant, but also many others within the ecological setting where this event occurs. For example, Heinicke (1995) writes that within a family system, "the personality characteristics of the parents as well as their relationship support systems (partner and extended family) to a significant extent define future parenting transactions with their child" (p. 277). We might ask "What about other niche influences such as the social and physical environment and customs of childcare?" These surely play an equally important role and are worthy of future research on the part of those interested in cross-cultural human development.

In this regard, Belsky (1985) hypothesizes that "supportive developmental experiences give rise to a mature healthy personality, that is then capable of providing sensitive parental care which fosters optimal child development" (p. 86). This again points to the importance of the ecological setting and the transmission from one generation to another of successful parental belief systems learned within a healthy family environment. In fact, Vondra and Belsky (1993), in a later study of the developmental origins of parenting, state that "by assuming an ecological perspective . . . and by adopting a longitudinal design, research has begun to provide a more adequate test of developmental and clinical theory on the origins of parenting" (p. 25). In a new volume devoted to the transition to adulthood and family relationships, Scabini, Marta, & Lanz (2006) analyze family relationships by gender and generation and offer new research questions.

◇ PARENTING INFANTS AND CHILDREN

Each day throughout the world, approximately 750,000 individuals become new parents (*World Factbook,* 2002). Contrary to what many of these parents may think, a newborn is not always the pretty, smiling, curly-haired cherub they have imagined or seen in pictures or television commercials. Rather, a newborn is frequently an unattractive little creature—sometimes very small (or very big), often bald, toothless, hungry, and complaining—that has come to live with the new family for many years. During the first few days and weeks, most new couples wonder if they are capable of nurturing this new person and attending to its needs. Fortunately, the majority of parents are capable and, with later additions to the family, often get even better at it.

On arrival, most **newborns** (the *term applied to babies from birth through the first two weeks,* after which the term *infant* is used) are well-equipped to deal with their new environment. For the most part, their senses work well, and they have a large repertoire of reflexes to help them adjust to the world beyond the womb. So effective are these reflexes, and so resilient are newborns, that following the devastating earthquake in Mexico City in September of 1985, babies were found alive in the ruins of one hospital nursery six days later.

In the initial days and months following birth, parents devote much attention and concern to satisfying their child's basic needs for sleep, hunger, and elimination (see Chapter 3). As Bornstein (1995) aptly observes, "Infants forever alter the sleeping, eating, and working habits of their parents; they change who parents are and how parents define themselves. . . . Parenting an infant is a 168-hour-a-week job" (p. 3). As children get older and move into the years of early, middle, and later childhood, development keeps pace. At the center of all this activity, largely determining the nature of the parent–child relationship, are parental belief systems.

Parental Belief Systems

In every culture, parents tend to develop shared ideas about the nature of children, their developmental processes, and the meaning of their behaviors. Strongly influenced by the cultural context, these ideas are entwined with other aspects of life, including time and place, meaning of self, family, and parenthood (see Box 9.1).

As Harkness and Super (1996) point out in an important contribution to the literature of culture and human development, these cultural under-standings are organized into categories referred to as **parents' cultural be-lief systems** and "relate in *systematic ways to action—including . . . styles of talking to children, methods of discipline, or seeking advice from experts.* Ultimately [these belief systems] . . . exert a powerful influence on the health and develop-ment of children, and they are a key component in the development of par-ents themselves" (pp. 2–3). Parental beliefs represent one component of the developmental niche—the psychology of the caretaker.

Developing a philosophy of childrearing is one of the major tasks faced by new parents (Francis-Connally, 2000; Kenkel, 1985). In a particularly in-teresting application of this idea, Richman and others (1988) observed mother–child interactions in five cultures (three industrial and two agrarian) and reported several prominent differences. Among the more interesting was the finding that Gusii mothers of Kenya hold their nine- to ten-month-old infants and engage in soothing physical contact more than do middle-class mothers in Boston, Massachusetts, but, at the same time, look at and talk to them less often. Why? According to Richman and her colleagues there are several reasons for this behavior, all of which make perfect sense once you understand the ecology of the cultures involved. For example, among the Gusii, (1) infant mortality rates are high, and holding and soothing provide a greater chance of survival, (2) there is a belief that language is not under-stood by children until about the age of two, and (3) the culture teaches that one should avoid making direct eye contact with others. On the other hand, in the American culture there is a belief that (1) language learning should begin early, and (2) placing infants in playpens where they can play by themselves begins the process of independence so highly valued in American society.

Ever since Sigel (1985) edited one of the first volumes discussing this concept, interest in parental belief systems as an approach to understanding cultural similarities and differences has grown rapidly (Sigel and McGillicuddy-DeLisi, 2002). This concept has also been fostered by the emergence of paral-lel trends in social anthropology, psychology, and new interdisciplinary

BOX 9.1

PARENTING AMONG
AFRICAN PYGMIES

There are about 150,000 Pygmies living in parts of several African countries, including Rwanda, Cameroon, Gabon, Congo, Burundi, and Zaire. The majority range in height from 4 feet to 4 feet 8 inches (1.2 to 1.42 meters). While no one is sure why they are so small, research studies suggest it may be a combination of factors, including a growth hormone deficiency and an evolutionary adaptation to their ecological setting that allows them to move quickly and silently through the forest.

One group, the Efe (who prefer to be known by their tribal name rather than the derogatory term emphasizing short stature), are hunters and gatherers living in the Northeastern region of the Ituri forest in the Congo, formerly Zaire. They are believed to be the oldest pure ethnic group in the world with a culture, language, and tradition at least ten thousand years old. They live in small, extended family groups (about twenty to thirty people), consisting of brothers and their wives, children, unmarried sisters, and perhaps parents. They live in temporary camps composed of leaf huts used for sleeping, food storage, and protection from the weather. These huts, moved when the food supply runs low, are arranged in a semicircle, creating a shared communal space where most day-to-day activities take place.

Sharing and cooperation among the Efe, in terms of food, work, and childcare, are essential to their survival. The workload is high, and many activities, such as foraging, are engaged in by both men and women, although only men hunt.

An Efe mother braids the hair of a child in the Ituri forest in the Congo. (© Anthro-Photo file)

BOX 9.1 CONTINUED

There is a strong belief among Efe that mothers *should not* be the first person to hold a newborn baby. This belief not only prevents an Efe woman from going off to give birth on her own, but it also introduces a child to multiple caregivers early. In fact, infants are frequently nursed by women other than their own mothers.

Fathers have an early presence in the child's life. For example, it is common practice for them to view the birth from the doorway of the hut. When not hunting, they and other men are often present in camp and often watch and hold the children (theirs and others), although most childcare is the responsibility of mothers.

The developmental niche of the Efe is intensely social. The continuous presence of others, along with early multiple care, helps prepare Efe children for their social world while protecting them from common dangers in the physical environment.

Source: Adapted from *Infusing Culture into Parenting Issues: A Supplement for Psychology Instructors* by Vicki Ritts, 2000, unpublished manuscript, St. Louis Community College. Reprinted by permission.

approaches to culture and human development (Dasen, 2003; Harkness & Super, 1996, 2002).

Also contributing to this unifying new concept are some of the approaches serving as major themes for this book. For example, the ecological model of Bronfenbrenner (1989, 1993, 2005) provides a dynamic, interactive paradigm of parent–child interactions as they occur within a continually expanding cultural context that shapes the development of effective parental beliefs and practices. The developmental niche framework proposed by Super and Harkness (1986, 2002) assists in "conceptualizing relationships among parental belief systems, customs, and practices of childrearing and the organization of physical and social settings for children's daily lives" (Harkness & Super, 1996, p. 5). The concept of an "ecocultural niche" integrates ideas from these approaches and connects parental belief systems and parental behavior with these beliefs and family and community ecology (Gallimore, Weisner, Kaufman, & Bernheimer, 1989). Parents in the ecocultural niche of the family and in the developmental niche of individual children play a crucial mediating role between children's experiences and the larger culture in which they live. In the words of Harkness and Super: "The conceptualization of parents in the child or family's niche leads naturally, in turn, to an interest in the cultural construction of experience from the point of view of parents themselves, in particular their cultural belief systems or 'parental ethnotheories' regarding children, families, and parenthood" (1995, p. 228).

In 2003, Dixie West, in collaboration with the Biodiversity Research Center at the University of Kansas, hosted a National Science Foundation funded international workshop on Ecocultural Niche Modeling. This study had the goal of applying data sets into a variety of modeling schemes that have proven successful using biological data. Finally, the developmental models emerging from the Vygotskian perspective (discussed in detail in Chapter 2) focus on the relationship between individual development and cultural meaning systems, as well as between parenting behaviors and symbolic systems.

After reviewing these and numerous similar studies, we find that the following questions have not been adequately answered by the research literature: "In general, are there relationships between specific parenting beliefs and parenting behaviors?" "Are there universals, as well as variations, in what we might call 'good parenting'?" "Do certain kinds of parenting lead to certain kinds of outcomes for children, both cross-culturally as well as within cultures?" "What form do parental cultural belief systems take in cultures where relatives, other than parents (e.g., uncles, aunts, grandparents, and in-laws) play critically important roles?" We offer these questions in the hope that those who might pursue future studies in these areas will help extend our understanding of human development within the context of culture. Throughout the remainder of this chapter, we will learn how parents' cultural belief systems influence the manner in which lives develop across cultures, beginning with mothering and fathering behaviors.

Mothering

In their research on mothering, Barnard and Martell (1995) note that cultures consider this behavior extremely important, especially since mothers are the primary day-to-day teachers of culture. The authors also point out that opportunities to view similarities and differences in the mothering role have been limited, because mothering generally takes place in the privacy of the family. Although these researchers do not use Bronfenbrenner's ecological model terminology, their thinking sounds similar. For example, they state that "the role [of mothering] . . . develops in relation to the family system wherein roles of father, siblings, and other extended family members are enacted as well. . . . Each person's role is connected with all others in the family system and because that is true there are always variations within cultures. [For example] . . . as the position of women changes, aspects of the mothering role will be assumed by others in the family or in the society" (p. 3).

According to Harkness and Super (1995), mothering has historically been associated with women, because in most cultures women have provided primary care for children. In this regard, and in light of our discussion of Japanese families in this chapter, it is interesting to consider Barnard and Martell's (1995) analysis of the Japanese words for *woman, mother, man,* and *father:* "The character for woman is a stick figure with a protuberance, resembling a

| Man | Woman | Father | Mother | Parenting |

FIGURE 9.2   Japanese Characters Related to Parenting

Source: Drawn by Alan V. Gardiner.

pregnant abdomen, whereas the character for mother resembles the chest with two breasts. The symbol for man, on the other hand, is the rice field illustrating work. The character for father is a stone axe symbolizing power" (p. 4). More accurately, the symbol for man is a combination of two characters, one representing a rice field and the other representing power which symbolizes hard work (Gardiner, 1996). *Parenting* is represented by three characters literally translated as "to stand," "a tree," and "to watch," which, when combined, can be interpreted as "watching over a growing child" (Gardiner, 1996). For a visual representation of these characters, see Figure 9.2.

Barnard and Martell also point out that these characters came from the original Chinese language and represent ethnic and intergenerational thinking about these roles within both these cultures. These character distinctions raise several intriguing questions: "Are mothering, fathering, and parenting distinct roles?" "Are birthing and nurturing unique characteristics of the mother's role, whereas support and family control are assigned to the father's role?" "Is parenting different than mothering and fathering?" Hopefully, with an increased interest in cross-cultural analysis, these and related issues will be answered in the not too distant future.

In a review of research on mothering, Barnard & Solchany (2002) discuss the concept of allomothering (or "shared mothering"), a term coined by Hrdy (2000), which includes all those people who help to care for a child, "including (but not limited to) the mother's mate, extended family, peers, and neighbors" (p. 21). These are all individuals we find interacting with and influencing a child's development as he or she moves among the micro-, meso-, and exosystems of his or her unique ecological environment. Examples of allomothering can be found in many African tribal villages, Israeli kibbutz, and even American daycare or childcare settings, in which the safety, nurturance, and responsibility for children's well-being is shared by a number of people. The authors also discuss the meaning of motherhood in the context of becoming a woman, preparation for motherhood, important functions of mothering (e.g., expected nurturing, monitoring and surveillance, and caregiving-social partner role), and explore some of the challenges of mothering.

Fathering

Research on the role of fathers is of relatively recent origin (Biller, 1993; Parke, 2002), and research on cross-cultural comparisons is still comparatively rare (Aldous, Mulligan, & Bjarnason, 1998; Gardiner, 1994; Lamb, 1987, 2003; Lykken, 2000; Yang, 1999). In fact, cross-culturally, only a minority of childcare is carried out by men. However, it is promising to note that when fathering is studied, it is being increasingly observed from both the ecological model and contextual approach (Day & Lamb, 2004; Parke, 2002; Sullivan, 2004) as well as the lifespan perspective (Elder, Modell, & Parke, 1993; Parke, 2000). Of interest is a study by Marsiglio and Cohan (2000), clarifying the basic features of a sociological perspective as it relates to the study of fathers' involvement with, and influence on, their children. The authors focus on the social, organizational, and cultural contexts of fathering, with particular emphasis on the interplay between social structures and processes at the macro, meso, and micro levels, along with social psychological issues.

In this regard, Parke (2002) stresses "the importance of examining developmental changes in the adult because parents continue to change and develop during adult years" (p. 28). He points out that the age at which an individual becomes a parent can significantly affect the ways in which men and women carry out their paternal and maternal roles, and that education, self-identity, and career tasks are related to the demands of being a parent. For example, the average age of marriage in Egypt and the Sudan is twenty-five to thirty-five years for men and twenty to thirty years for women in urban areas, twenty to twenty-five for men and sixteen to eighteen for women in rural areas (Ahmed, 1991).

In Nigeria, among the Muslim Hausa, a boy usually enters his first marriage around the age of twenty, often to a girl of thirteen or fourteen who has just reached puberty. For a Yoruba male, marriage typically takes place when the man is in his middle to late twenties and the girl is about sixteen to eighteen years of age (Okafor, 1991). Among the Southeast Asian Hmong, large numbers of whom have migrated to the United States, it is common for men in their twenties to thirties to marry young girls in their early to middle adolescent years. While many of these young people may be adequately prepared, as part of their developmental niche, to assume parental responsibilities at these relatively young ages, others are not; and, recently being children themselves, will find married life and childrearing difficult.

As Shwalb and his colleagues (2003) have noted, in a review of research on Chinese, Japanese, and Korean cultures, fathering is affected by many contexts, including history, changing families, work roles, and marital relationships. For example, while China has promoted gender equality at work and encourages both women and men to be active in childrearing, Japanese and Korean fathers have often reduced their involvement in

Father and son find mutual enjoyment during caretaking. (Courtesy of authors)

family matters to provide financially for their families. Chinese fathers appear to blend a combination of warmth, control and authoritativeness in their parenting style. Korean fathers, who historically focused greater attention on their sons, now spend more time with each child because of the drastic reduction in family size. The authors suggest that more research is needed not only on fathers' direct influence on their children but also on how they influence children indirectly through the husband-wife relationship.

One of the leading views of fathering or father involvement has been presented by Lamb, Pleck, Charnov, and Levine (1987), who consider three components to be of crucial importance: interaction, availability, and responsibility. They describe these in the following way: "Interaction refers to the father's direct contact with his child through caregiving and shared activities. Availability is a related concept concerning the child's potential availability for interaction . . . whether or not direct interaction is occurring. Responsibility refers to the role the father takes in ascertaining that the child is taken care of and arranging for resources to be available for the child" (p. 125). In addition, Radin (1993) has recommended that a distinction be made between absolute and relative involvement, as well as between a father's participation in childcare activities and in leisure, play, and related activities, since these are likely to be independent and have an effect on the way children and adults view the father's role.

In cross-cultural studies focusing on a variety of cultures (United States, Great Britain, France, Belgium, Israel, Sweden, and Australia), in which quantitative assessments were made comparing mother and father involvement with children of a wide age range (one month to sixteen years), on a large number of measures (basic care, holding, reading, verbal interactions), the overall pattern was the same: mothers spent more time and engaged in more activities with their children than did fathers.

In a recent review of research on fathers and families, Parke (2002) notes that substantial progress has been made in understanding the paternal role and its impact on fathers themselves, as well as on their children and others within and outside the family. Among his conclusions are that (1) while mothers still have the greater responsibility in raising children, the level of father involvement has continued to increase, (2) fathers can and do show qualities of competent caregiving, (3) cross-cultural findings point to the importance of cultural and environmental contexts, as well as possibly biological factors, in determining and shaping differences in play styles between mothers and fathers, (4) fathering roles show greater variability across cultures than do mothering roles, and (5) men's marital relationships as well as their "sense of self" are significantly affected by fathering activities.

Finally, Parke (2002) points out that studies of father–child relationships are now "a more fully contextualized issue. Fathers in the context of their social relationships both within and beyond the family are increasingly the appropriate point of entry for understanding the issue of both parental roles and their impact on themselves and others" (pp. 62–63).

This approach and the need for meeting the needs of fathers within an ecological perspective have been effectively presented in the work of Meyers (1993). In order to provide maximum benefits for fathers (and mothers), he proposes that parent education programs address issues such as the enhancement of child and marital communication skills, provide social support for parents, increase their involvement in childrearing, and provide authoritative childcare knowledge, while acknowledging diversity among parents in terms of their differing social and cultural backgrounds, including parents who are single, adolescent, low-income, or minority.

One last effort of note is a book by Flouri (2005), reviewing the effects of differing fathering styles on children's mental health, academic achievement, socioeconomic status, adolescent relationships, and delinquency. The research was based on more than twenty studies she conducted in the United Kingdom using data sources collected over a period of more than 40 years. Among her findings are those showing that father involvement protected against the experience of homelessness in adult sons, but not in daughters, from low, but not high, socioeconomic groups, and was associated with low risk for delinquincy in sons, but not in daughters. In addition, a father's interest in child education was related to a daughter's, but not a son's, educational attainment in adult life.

◇ PARENTING ADOLESCENTS

As a child makes the transition from childhood into adolescence, accompanied by a variety of developmental changes (e.g., physical, social, cognitive), seeking to find a balance between dependence and independence, as well as trying to establish an identity, parent–child relationships frequently undergo significant change, more in some cultures than others.

According to Holmbeck, Paikoff, and Brooks-Gunn (1995), parenting of adolescents has only recently become a topic of concern in the research literature. In fact, just two decades ago one author found so little information on family relationships during the adolescent years that it was impossible to write a very lengthy review of the topic (Adelson, 1985). While a significant body of relevant literature, as well as several useful reviews, have since appeared (Lerner, Brennan, & Noh, 1998; Steinberg & Silk, 2002), little detailed attention has been given to the study of adolescence in many cultures other than the United States and a few other societies around the world.

The lack of cross-cultural, parent–adolescent research from the standpoint of cultural context may be the result of several factors. First, many theories of adolescent development place greater emphasis on biological than on social or cultural factors as primary determinants of psychological characteristics. Second, there is continuing disagreement within the field as to whether adolescence represents a universal period of development. While some theorists take the viewpoint that it does, others argue that adolescence may be a developmental stage in some cultural settings but not in others.

Among those specifically interested in studying adolescence from the ecological perspective are Garbarino (1985, 2000) and Muuss (1988; Muuss & Porton, 1998). In the words of Muuss (1988), a strong adherent of this approach: "An ecological model goes far beyond what is presently known, opening up new perspectives and generating new hypotheses that are bound to move developmental research from the clearly defined, easily controllable research laboratory into the ecological field" (p. 300).

The Ecological Model and Adolescence

Employing the ecological model, let us look at the structures that influence the development of adolescents, irrespective of the cultures in which they live. First, various **microsystems** are involved, including the primary one of the family (parents, siblings, extended family members); the system involving friends, peers, and school; and perhaps other systems made up of neighbors and other social groups. As we learned in earlier chapters, microsystems are continually undergoing change, as are the individuals who move in and out of them. As Muuss (1996) points out, a healthy microsystem is one based on reciprocity, especially in the relationships between parents and adolescents: "If a microsystem is rich in information, it enhances learning and development by providing opportunities in which questions are asked and answered, exploration and experimentation encouraged, and guidance provided [and it] . . . will foster opportunities for success in later life" (p. 324).

Next, there is the **mesosystem,** which links the adolescent's various microsystems (e.g., family, school, and peers). In many cultures, conflicts exist between the parents' values and peer group values. This lack of agreement can result in family conflict, regardless of culture. White (1993) provides the following quote from a Japanese adolescent (which could just as easily have been made by a North American, European, or Latin American young woman): "When I'm with my best friend I feel safe. Talking to her gives me peace. She never gets angry, or tries to get me to change. And she never embarrasses me in public the way my mother does" (p. 144).

While an adolescent may not actively participate in the next ecological level, the **exosystem,** much of what goes on there (e.g., at local government meetings, in parents' workplaces, or in the mass media) may indirectly affect her (Muuss, 1996). For example, the school board in Salto, Uruguay, may determine that school enrollment will be down next year and be unable to hire fourteen-year-old Manuel Sacco's mother, Graciela, to teach for them. This will lower the family income and mean that Manuel and his brother and sister will have fewer new clothes and less food and may have to transfer to other schools.

Finally, there is the adolescent's **macrosystem.** Although of considerable importance, this is probably the least studied of all ecological systems; except for anthropological research, it almost never receives systematic investigation. As Muuss (1996) points out, "Although the macrosystem does not impinge directly on the life of the individual adolescent . . . it contains an overarching societal ground plan for the ecology of human development. [This includes] . . . a core of general cultural, political, social, legal, religious, economic, and educational values and, most important, public policy. As such, a macrosystem may be thought of as a societal blueprint" (p. 330).

These macrosystem values frequently find expression in social customs and what the culture considers fashionable at various times. For example, the macrosystem determines standards of physical attractiveness and what is appropriate and inappropriate behavior for each sex (Muuss, 1996). Physical attractiveness appears to be important to adolescents throughout the world, yet one culture's definition of what is considered physically attractive may differ from another's. As we will see in Chapter 10, in many Western countries, especially the United States, the media (television, movies, magazines) portray thinness as the female ideal. In certain African cultures, scarring of the face is considered physically attractive. In China, at one point in its history, binding a woman's feet to keep them small and dainty was a sign of beauty.

Cross-Cultural Differences in Adolescent Peer Relationships

The role of **peers**—*individuals of similar age and sometimes the same gender*—is very important in the microsystems and exosystems, as well as in the social settings component of the developmental niche of some adolescents. There are significant social and cultural differences in the specific influences peers and friends have on adolescents. For example, Muuss (1988) suggests that peer groups play a much greater role in Western societies, where extended education is the norm, than in more traditional societies, where schooling ends in the early adolescent years. In the latter, he points out, orientation becomes vertical in relation of one's elders, rather than horizontal in relation to one's peers. As evidence, he cites an early study by Hsu, Watrous, and Lord (1961) in which second-, third-, and fourth-generation adolescents of Chinese background in Hawaii were compared to a matched group of Chicago adolescents. Findings revealed that the Hawaiian group was more family oriented, less rebellious, and less troubled by adolescence than the Chicago group, which tended to be more oriented toward peers.

Along similar lines, Bronfenbrenner (1967) looked at the role of peer groups in the Soviet Union, his native country, and the United States, his adopted country. He noted that in the United States, a country whose macrosystem consists of pluralistic political and social structures, the distance between peer group and adult values is greater than it is in the Soviet Union, where the values of these two groups tend to cluster around a politically endorsed nucleus. The result, he suggests, is that adolescents in the United States (and in cultures with similar ecological structures) will be more likely to be influenced by peer group pressures. On the other hand, in a now classic comparison of human development in the United States and the Soviet Union, Bronfenbrenner (1970) expresses his concern that the Russians "have gone too far in subjecting the child and his peer group to conformity to a single set of values imposed by the adult society" (p. 165). With the breakup of the Soviet Union and the infusion of democratic ideals into Russian society, it would be interesting to revisit this issue and consider any changes that may have resulted from these events. Schlegel and Barry (1991), in a well-designed and pioneering interdisciplinary study, looked at a wide range of preindustrial societies located in such present-day countries as Argentina, Indonesia, Turkey, West Africa, Brazil, Cameroon, Canada, China, Peru, and the United States and the role played by the cultural context in adolescent development, particularly the influence of group similarities and differences. They take a cross-cultural approach, viewing adolescence as a universal social and cultural phenomenon. Although the samples in this study "represent a world that has vanished," it provides a model for future research on cross-cultural human development, especially in modernizing societies, where once traditional peoples are making a transition to industrialization and experiencing rapid, and often overwhelming, social change. Using data from 186 cultures and 340 variables representing a broad range of adolescent issues, Schlegel and Barry offer detailed comparisons and contrasts on parent–adolescent relationships, adolescent sexuality, social markers defining transitions from childhood to adolescence and to adulthood, rites of passage, changes in social roles, and a variety of other topics. Throughout their investigation, they attempt to assess adolescent behavior as it occurs across cultures, while carefully analyzing which behaviors appear to be culture-specific and which can be considered universal.

Among their many findings are the following: (1) passage into adolescence is easier for girls than boys because the break from childhood is not as severe, (2) girls are not innately less competitive than boys, and when gender differences are shown to exist, they are likely a result of factors within the social settings that promote or inhibit such behavior, (3) the length of the adolescent period is not arbitrarily defined but instead is the outcome of a number of factors in the "cultural manipulation of biological givens," and (4) adolescent antisocial behavior has its roots in childhood, perhaps even as early as infancy.

Schlegel and Barry conclude their study by stating, "The societies in our sample are very different today from what they were when the first ethnographic reports on them were made. Many important aspects of life have changed, and the experience of adolescence has altered in irrevocable ways. Are the patterns we have established for this preindustrial sample characteristic of the 'other' and not the West and the industrializing societies following its lead? We think not." (1991, p. 208).

To lend support to this, they comment on adolescence in modernizing societies and consider the implications of their findings for understanding adolescence in industrialized Western societies by presenting several hypotheses and suggestions for further research. These include speculations about adolescent-family-peer relationships, development of antisocial and delinquent behavior, and adolescent-motherhood issues at the forefront in many of today's modern societies.

One final comment from White (1993) effectively illustrates how parental belief systems affect the way parents perceive the role of peers in the United States and in Japan: "Peer pressure in America is popularly seen as a negative force, rather than, as in Japan, a source of support and socialization for adult roles" (p. 37). With this said, we move to adulthood and aging.

◇ ADULTHOOD AND AGING

Early in this book, we noted that we would be looking at development from a lifespan orientation. There is a good reason for this, as illustrated by parent–child relationships in the years of adulthood and old age. As Zarit and Eggebeen (1995) make clear, "Parent–child relationships are a life-span issue. Rather than ceasing when children are launched from the family, these relationships endure with often complex patterns of interaction, support, and exchange that wax and wane around key transitions in the adult years" (p. 119). If couples have been successful in meeting the challenges of parenthood and have been able to get their own children grown up and on the way to parenthood themselves, they may look forward to the day when they achieve a new status in the life cycle—that of grandparents.

Grandparenthood

While much has been written about parents, relatively little attention has been given to the role played by grandparents in the lives of their grandchildren. This is surprising, since nearly three-quarters of adults will become grandparents, most will be a grandparent for about a third of their lives (Smith, 2005), and evidence suggests that the role they play in a variety of diverse cultures is becoming increasingly important (Hagestad, 2000; Smith & Drew, 2004).

Smith (1991) has pointed out that when the first articles focusing on grandparents appeared during the 1930s and 1940s, they tended to portray grandparents in negative terms. During the next two decades, a more balanced view began to emerge (Staples, 1952). Adkins (1999) presents evidence showing that grandparents have a positive effect on children's affective and cognitive development, serve as a major support system during divorce and family breakdown, and when raising grandchildren on their own are as successful as are biological parents.

With a few notable exceptions, the majority of grandparent research has been conducted in the United States (Kornhaber, 1996; Smith & Drew, 2004). However, more recent studies from European industrialized societies and African nonindustrialized cultures have become available (Smith, 1991; Sangree, 1992). Several studies comparing grandparent behaviors across cultures, notably China and the United States, and across generations have begun to appear in recent years (Strom & Strom, 2000; Strom, Strom, Wang, Shen, Griswold, Chan, & Yang, 1999). Nevertheless, it is clear that more comparative cross-cultural studies, using the ecological systems model and other theories, are necessary if we are to describe, explain, and understand both the similarities and differences in grandparenting between and across cultures.

According to Smith (1995), the study of grandparenting is at the same time both easier and more difficult than the study of parenting. It is easier because objective analysis of grandparent–parent–grandchild relationships does not involve as intense emotions as those present in parent–child relationships. It is more difficult because "there are more varieties of grandparent than of parent, and one is studying three generations rather than two. . . . The study of grandparenthood is also challenging, in that the grandparent–parent–grandchild set of relationships confronts us squarely with the processes of socialization, intergenerational transmissions, and change over historical periods" (p. 89).

Due to the high divorce rate in the United States and the increase in single parents, who often have difficulty managing childrearing on their own, increasing numbers of grandparents are actively involved in raising their grandchildren. This adds a new layer of influence to the ecological system, as grandparents represent specific beliefs and values from a different historical period that may be contrary to the values of their children or even their own parents (Mills, 1999; Smith & Drew, 2002). Recalling the definition of culture (Chapter 1), just as individuals in Thailand or Mexico exhibit cultural differences, so do grandparents and parents represent two distinct cultures, each with their own shared set of values and beliefs.

In a pioneering longitudinal study of contemporary grandparenting, Kornhaber (1996) has noted that a body of research, based on a historical and cross-cultural perspective, is beginning to emerge and helping to clarify the meaning of grandparenthood and its function in various cultural settings. While pointing to the stable and important role grandparents play in modern societies, he also comments that "one of the dangers of 'modernization' most feared by leaders of emerging countries is the possible dismembering of the family and the inevitable loss of the grandparent's honored place in the family and society" (p. 22). Considering what we have said in earlier chapters about a culture's attitudes toward the aging process and the elderly, it should be apparent that these attitudes contribute to determining the status of grandparents. In cultures characterized by large extended families and a reverence for elders (e.g., China, Mexico, and many Asian and African societies), grandparents are likely to live with their families, be part of the social support system, and contribute to an intergenerational ecological setting.

In reviews of grandparenthood, Smith and Drew (2002, 2004) propose several theoretical perspectives for structuring and interpreting research on the topic of grandparenting, including lifespan development and gerontology, psychoanalysis and attachment theory, family systems theory, and evolutionary theory—a topic about which we have more to say in Chapter 11, when we consider future directions in cross-cultural human development. Among the many issues they discuss as fundamental to the study of grandparenthood are the characteristics of grandparents and grandchildren, the frequency and nature of contacts between them, perceptions and styles of grandparenting, grandparents affected by divorce or death of a grandchild, step-grandparenting, and the nature of grandparenting in different cultures. Also considered is the role grandparents sometimes play as surrogate parents, along with their contributions to the intergenerational transmission of behaviors, values, and attitudes. Let us now look at some of the interactions among these characteristics and the specific roles played by grandparents in several of the world's cultures.

Fingerman (2004), in a recent study of the role of offspring and children-in-law in grandparents' relationships with grandchildren, suggests that children-in-law may contribute to grandparents' relationships with their grandchildren in a variety of ways. In fact, she points out that such relationships "may play a greater role in the fabric of adults' lives than has been thought, particularly when grandchildren are in the picture" (p. 1046).

Japan

Japan, a country continuing to experience modernization, is an interesting example of a culture dealing with the changing role of contemporary grandparents. Traditionally, Japanese grandparents have been respected, honored, and provided with ritualized status through a rite of passage that allows grandmothers to "wear the color red as a badge of her status" (Kornhaber, 1996, p. 22). This once-privileged role is undergoing dramatic change, causing increased concern among some social scientists (Strom et al., 1995; Strom & Strom, 1993). Before World War II, most Japanese lived in an extended family made up of three or more generations and governed by a rigid hierarchical system characterized by filial piety (respect) and strong parental authority. Following the democratization of the country at the end of the war, family life underwent significant changes (e.g., abolishment of the patriarchal family structure and granting of equal legal status to women).

In an extensive three-generation study, Strom and colleagues (1995) found that Japanese grandparents believe their status in the family is eroding. While they want to continue to have an influence, social policy has yet to include education for their changing role in society. The authors analyzed responses to a questionnaire identifying strengths and needs of Japanese grandparents as perceived by 239 grandparents, 266 parents, and 274 school-age grandchildren from cities and small towns across Japan. Their findings reveal that grandparents report more satisfaction, greater success, and more extensive involvement in teaching than was observed by parents and grandchildren. In addition, grandparents said they felt greater difficulty, more frustration, and less informed to carry out their grandparenting role than was reported by parents and grandchildren. According to the authors, the factors most influencing responses related to grandparent performance were generation, grandchild's gender and age, generations living together, frequency of

A Japanese grandfather enjoys time with his granddaughter. (© AM Corporation/Alamy)

grandchild care by grandparent, and the amount of time they spent together. The authors have proposed the development of education programs to assist grandparents in adapting to their changing roles in Japan (Strom et al., 1995), as well as other cultures including China and the United States (Strom, 1999).

In a study of adolescents coming of age in Japan and the United States, White (1993) noted that grandparents often play a crucial role, particularly when they live near, although not with, the family and are able to provide support for the young person without creating dissension within the family. White quotes one working adolescent who delays going home by stopping at her grandmother's: "My mother asks too many questions. . . . So I go to my grandmother's house whenever I can, and I sometimes even call home to say I'm staying overnight there. She empties her refrigerator to cook wonderful meals for me. I am her favorite. And when I leave, she loads me down with fruit and food and sweets" (p. 68). Another adolescent, who takes care of a disabled grandmother, said, "I give her a massage every afternoon after school. I like to do it because she tells me stories about living in Nagano in the old days, and she really listens to me, and helps me with my problems" (p. 68).

Urbanization and technological advancements have contributed to a steady decrease in the number of Japanese extended families, from about 44 percent in 1955 to approximately 15 percent in 1985. The result is that the number of elderly (*rojin*) living on their own has risen sharply and will continue to rise in the future, presenting serious problems for a nation once known for its extended family structure. Still, Japan is finding creative ways to make use of its elderly and their skills. One such innovative concept is "silver banks." *Rojin* with superior abilities or knowledge in various fields are matched, through applications, with those needing their expertise and are paid for their services.

China

In the People's Republic of China (mainland China), grandparents have historically played a critical function in family life. According to Tien and Lee (1988), in the 1980s, about 40 percent of rural families and 24 percent of urban families were made up of three generations. Wolf (1978) notes that it was common for grandmothers to frequently intervene when they felt parents were punishing children too harshly. In commenting on the role of Chinese grandfathers, Wolf states that they are "a source of pennies for sweets, an occasional place for solace when the rest of the childhood world turns against them, and a good place for stories when nothing else is doing" (p. 142).

In an extensive investigation, similar to the one conducted among Japanese grandparents, Falbo (1991) surveyed almost 1,500 Chinese schoolchildren between the ages of six and ten to determine the impact of quality contact on children's behavior. Among her findings, she reports that contrary to the popular image of grandparents overindulging their grandchildren, there appears to have been no negative effect on personality or academic performance. In fact, "contact with educated grandparents was correlated with positive academic achievement. Contact with better educated grandfathers was correlated with . . . a more desirable personality as judged by both mothers and teachers" (p. 372). Her conclusion is that Chinese grandparents have a very positive influence on their grandchildren.

Stevenson, Chen, and Lee (1992) suggest that this influence, and the role grandparents play in families, largely depends on the sex of their own child as well as the sex of their grandchildren. For example, they state that "their son's children are considered to be their 'true' grandchildren . . . the ones for whose socialization they bear an important responsibility and for whom they assume a role as disciplinarian. . . . Grandparents feel no great need to be responsible for the children of their daughter, for their daughter's children are considered the children of their son-in-law. In fact, they are called 'outside' grandchildren, with whom it is permissible to establish a more playful relationship than with the 'true' grandchildren" (p. 23).

United States

According to Smith and Drew (2002), about three-fourths of adults in the United States will one day be grandparents. Women will typically become grandmothers around the age of fifty, and men will be grandfathers about two years later. They will be grandparents for approximately twenty-five years or one-third of their lifetime. Thus, grandparenthood becomes an important aspect of the life cycle for grandparents themselves, as well as those upon whom they have an impact.

As mentioned earlier, most of the relatively limited research on grandparenting has been conducted in modern, urban, industrialized societies, such as the United States, and, to a lesser degree, some of the countries in Western Europe and, more recently, Asia. In one study of American grandparents and their satisfaction with their role, Brubaker (1985) reported that 80 percent were happy in their relationships and a majority found it easier and more enjoyable than parenting.

The role grandparents play and their interactions within families will change significantly as family structures change and life expectancy increases. For example, four-generation families are becoming more common, with some grandparents becoming great-grandparents. In one study (Doka & Mertz, 1988), a sample of elderly great-grandparents reported that they found their role significant and emotionally fulfilling, providing them with a sense of personal and familial renewal, as well as a sign of longevity. With higher rates of divorce and remarriage, the issue of visitation rights for grandparents is also becoming an increasing concern for many (Stanton, 1998).

Another aspect of grandparenting in the United States that is different than that in other countries results from ethnic diversity. According to Lockery (1991), grandparents of Asian American, African American, Hispanic American, and Italian American backgrounds are more likely to play an active role in the lives of their grandchildren than are those of other ethnicities. In fact, as Barresi

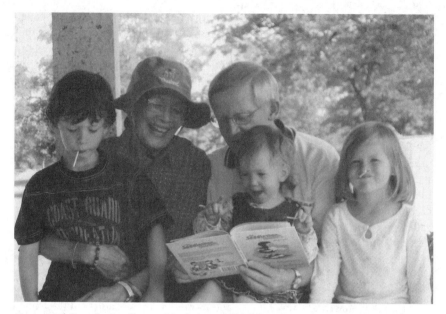

Harry and Ormsin Gardiner with their grandchildren—Macinnes Charoen Lamont, 6, Malinee Kathryn Lamont, 4, and Sirina Francis Lamont, 2. (Courtesy of authors)

and Menon (1990) report, increasing numbers of older African Americans are becoming actively involved in caregiving among their grandchildren and great-grandchildren. According to Minkler and Roe (1991), approximately 13 percent of African American children, 3 percent of Hispanic American children, and 2 percent of European American children live with their grandparents.

Having active and vital grandparents can provide grandchildren with positive role models for old age, as illustrated by the following quote from a young girl named Patty, who said with great admiration about her grandmother, "She is a dynamo. A speedball. When my mom was in the hospital, she came over and cleaned the house and did the cooking. I helped her; we did it together. We dance, and I get tired before she does. She even chops wood. I hope I am like that. She says I am" (Kornhaber, 1996). (For more about grandparenting in the United States, we recommend the book by Kornhaber in the "Further Readings" section of this chapter.)

Caring for the Elderly

For generations, respect for those who have reached their later years has been higher in Japan, China, and many other countries than it has in the United States. While this may still be true, in the case of the Japanese, the image may be overly idealized. As we pointed out earlier in this chapter, fewer elderly

Japanese today are living with their children, and more are returning to low-paying jobs to support themselves.

Just as Japan is changing, so too is China, another of the world's oldest cultures. In China, the elderly were once revered, and the extended family was the primary unit of care for the elderly. While the family is still a central focus, it is facing problems and its role is changing. For example, with increased industrialization, many rural farmers are moving to the cities, leaving their aging relatives behind. Those families that remain in rural areas often develop a reciprocal arrangement in which a married son provides for his elderly parents and, in return, receives help from them with childcare, housework, and even gardening. Those who are elderly and have no children may be eligible to move into one of the country's new homes for the elderly. To do so, one must meet four criteria: (1) have no living children nearby to provide care, (2) not be bedridden or require constant medical care, (3) be willing to enter the home, and (4) qualify for local welfare assistance (Olson, 1994). In addition to the difficulties already mentioned, elder abuse, inadequate housing, and insufficient retirement programs are becoming serious problems.

In Germany, community-based services are also increasing but are unable to meet the growing numbers of elderly, 75 percent of whom need help with daily activities and 10 percent of whom are bedridden.

In the United States, and many other countries, as individuals live longer, it is becoming increasingly common that adult children in middle adulthood are required to provide care for aging relatives, particularly parents, as well as for their own children. Finding themselves caught between the needs of two generations, these individuals are often referred to as the *sandwich generation*. As Olson (1994) has shown, up to 70 percent of this caregiving is currently provided by women, most often adult daughters, wives, and daughters-in-law. In the United States, families provide about 80 percent of all long-term care for the elderly.

In many countries—notably France, Sweden, Finland, and Israel—health care and social services are considered "rights," not privileges for those who can afford them. This is becoming a particularly difficult problem in France, where in the last couple of decades there has been a drop in the fertility rate accompanied by a corresponding increase in life expectancy. Currently, France has one of the longest life expectancies in the world, with approximately 3.8 million people over the age of seventy-five. This figure is expected to increase to 5.6 million by the year 2020 (Olson, 1994). The French microsystem is not working very well, as less than 10 percent of those sixty-five years or older live with family members and barely 5 percent live in institutions. This means the majority of elderly are living on their own. It is obvious that new ways of providing care are needed, and soon. For a view of how Koreans, Latinos, Africans, and Arabs treat their elderly, see Box 9.2.

While the elderly in most nonindustrialized traditional societies continue to receive respect from younger people and to play a role in their culture, this is not as true in faster-changing, modern, industrialized societies.

BOX 9.2

CULTURAL VIEWS AND TREATMENT OF THE ELDERLY

As individuals grow older, they experience changes in physical, cognitive, and social abilities. The following sections highlight some of the ways in which elderly are viewed and treated across cultures.

Korean Elderly

Historically, Korean society has been strongly influenced by Chinese culture and, in particular, Confucianism, which provides guidelines governing relationships between father and son, minister and ruler, husband and wife, elder and younger brothers, and friends. Broadly speaking, Korea is a collectivist or "relationship culture," in which the group is placed above the individual, resulting in pressure to conform to cultural norms and group demands.

The *Book of Rites* states that Koreans must respect parents, take good care of them, and bring no dishonor to them or family. Filial responsibility is the obligation of an adult child, and elderly parents typically live with their first married son who, with help from siblings, provides financial support and health care. The family remains of utmost importance in Korea today, although the proportion of elderly living apart from their children has been on the rise. Growing concern over rapid industrialization, urbanization, and changes in filial care by the younger generation has resulted in recent welfare laws and an increase in the provision of social and health services for the elderly (Sung, 1992).

Latino Elderly

While Latinos or Hispanics come from many different countries, they are united by a common language; and although differences exist across cultures, some generalizations are possible. For example, certain attitudes and values are common in Latino cultures. One of these is *familialism*, emphasizing sharing and cooperation, rather than competition. A sense of family pride and loyalty and extended family support is the norm. Families remain the traditional support system despite urbanization and modernization. Other cultural values include *simpatia*, with its stress on loyalty, dignity, friendliness, politeness, affection, and respect for others; *personalismo*, emphasizing the importance of personal goodness and getting along with others over individual ability and individual success; *respecto*, valuing and acknowledging hierarchies that define an individual's proper place in society on the basis of age, gender, race, and class (Levitt, Guacci-Franco, & Levitt, 1993). These values play a major role in beliefs about care of the elderly, as does the Catholic religion with its emphasis on charity as a virtue. The result is that Latinos often do not behave assertively and believe that problems or events are meant to be and cannot be altered (Sue & Sue, 1990).

BOX 9.2 CONTINUED

In Latino cultures, the elderly are believed to have an inner strength that can be a resource for the younger generation. They see themselves as important members of the family because they are links to the past, and do not feel useless or like a burden and are not ashamed to ask for help (Holmes & Holmes, 1995; Paz, 1993). They occupy a central role in the family and are treated with respect (*respecto*), status (*su lugar*), and authority (*su experiencia y sabiduria*; Paz, 1993).

Children, particularly daughters, play a major role in caring for the elderly and providing assistance, although not all elderly may necessarily live with their children. Interestingly, if daughters do not care for their mothers, complaints are more hostile than if they are neglected by their sons. Daughters are also expected to visit and phone more frequently than sons (Holmes & Holmes, 1995; Paz, 1993). When a parent's condition severely deteriorates, formal services may be used by the family, although institutionalization is rare (Holmes & Holmes, 1995).

African Elderly

Black African societies vary in their views and treatment of the elderly. At times, older individuals are held in esteem as vast storehouses of knowledge and power. At other times, their legitimacy to knowledge and power is questioned (Diop, 1989).

In a majority of African societies, old age is viewed as a sign of divine blessing. In fact, in several African languages the elder is the "big person" (Diop, 1989). Many African women who reach middle age experience the removal of restrictions in an often gender-typed society, and their status and power is approximately the same as men. However, not all views and treatment of the elderly are positive. In many societies, young people no longer fear the influence or ancestral powers of elders and, as poverty increases, there is less support for the elderly.

In Nigeria, many older persons have little personal income and usually live with their children. Typically, first sons and all daughters care for their aged parents, although homes for the elderly have existed since the early 1900s for elders without family support (Ekpenyong, 1995). Most elderly would prefer to die where they were born, and those physically able to make the journey often do so.

Among the Hausa, a Muslim society concentrated primarily in Northern Nigeria, elderly women have control over the respect and tolerance from male children and have a voice in the selection of a wife for their sons, frequently for their grandsons, and in some cases a brother's child. Old Muslim Hausa women, but not young or middle-aged women, may pray in the mosque along with men (Holmes & Holmes, 1995).

(continued)

BOX 9.2 CONTINUED

Arab Elderly

Arabs have many traits in common, but generalizing about Arab culture is difficult because of major regional differences. Nevertheless, some generalizations help in understanding how elderly are treated in Arab cultures.

Muslim ideology, as presented in the *Qur'an*, provides a sociological and legal framework of life containing the doctrines that guide Muslims to "correct" behaviors. The word "Islam" means "submission to the will of God," and a Muslim is "one who submits" (Nydell, 1987). Thus, religion guides and affects an Arab's entire way of life and thinking.

The extended family has always been highly valued in Arab cultures. Typically, fathers provide for the family, discipline the children, and maintain the cohesiveness, order, honor, and social standing of the family, while mothers are responsible for the care and nurturance of the children. An elderly person's status commands authority in an Arab Muslim household and increases with age. Honor and respect for the elderly is contained in the Qur'an and it is assumed that families will look after the elderly. Traditionally, elderly parents live with the oldest son.

Although a small number of nursing home facilities exist, they are still rare in the Middle East. The thought of "putting one's parents in a nursing home" is not acceptable to Arab Muslims. Arab families do not abandon their elderly or their sick, no matter how impractical the demands and responsibilities for their care.

Interestingly, senility among older Arab Muslims is rare and might be related to the fact that in the Middle East, elderly gain status and do not experience the loss of self-esteem or self-worth that often occurs in Western culture (Elkholy, 1981).

Source: Adapted from *Culture and Aging* by Vicki Ritts, 2000, unpublished manuscript, St. Louis Community College. Reprinted by permission.

Considering what has been covered in this section, the ecological systems approach seems to be alive and well and functioning effectively in more traditional cultures. Perhaps it is time to return to this model, consider its many positive characteristics, and possibly adapt and finetune it to the evolving cultures of today's contemporary world.

◇ THE CHANGING CONTEXT OF FAMILIES

Before bringing this chapter to a close, it should be recognized that the ecological settings of families throughout the world have been changing over the last several decades. This is especially true in the United States. The stereotype of the "all-American family," consisting of two children (a girl and a boy) living in a single-family home in a middle-class neighborhood with the father working and the mother staying at home to provide childcare, is no longer the norm—if it ever were.

According to Fuller (1992), only 7 percent of mothers in two-parent homes stay with children while their spouses go to work. Today's families are more likely to consist of single parents, parents who are not married but living together, or gay parents; blended families made up of stepparents and stepchildren; or families in which grandparents are responsible for raising minor-age children. As Fay (1993) has reported, families headed by a married couple declined from 40.3 percent in 1970 to 25.9 percent in 1991, while only 30 percent of adults in 1991 were married with children, down 9 percent from 1977.

In addition to these changing demographics, efforts to understand the ecology of families and the developmental niche of children within them are complicated by the fact that some children are born into an intact family, spend time in a single-parent family following a divorce, move into one of thirty-two different types of blended family environments when the custodial parent remarries, and may even be cared for by grandparents at some point (Fuller, 1992). While the challenges may be great, the need to understand how families throughout the world raise their children and the influence culture has on this process is even greater.

◇ SUMMARY

This chapter opened with a description of the family life cycle and was followed by a discussion of mate selection and marriage rites in a variety of cultures throughout the world, stressing the influence of one's ecological setting in determining the important influences on each of these events. In an exploration of the birth process, the focus was on the ecology of birth and similarities and differences in cultural practices, most notably in Yucatan, Holland, Sweden, and the United States. With the transition to parenthood, cultural belief systems begin to play a major role in family decision making, as illustrated in mothering and fathering behavior during the years of infancy and childhood. Next, adolescence was viewed from the standpoint of the ecological model, and the importance of peer relationships was discussed from a cross-cultural perspective. For many, the years of adulthood frequently consist of the raising of adolescent children (and even adult children), as well as caring for elderly parents. Finally, the transition to becoming a grandparent in Japan, China, and the United States received considerable attention, as did the recognition that family ecology is undergoing dramatic change.

◇ STUDY QUESTIONS

Discuss cultural variations in mate selection and marriage.

Define and give examples of parental belief systems from different cultures.

Consider adolescence from the ecological model point of view.

Discuss the changing context of families, and comment on cultural approaches to grandparenting and care for the elderly.

◇ FURTHER READINGS

Leonore Loeb Adler. (Ed.). (1991). *Women in Cross-Cultural Perspective*. Westport, CT: Praeger.

> A vivid presentation of traditional and evolving socialization of women and cultural perceptions of their contemporary roles. Seventeen chapters range across the globe from the Arctic to Latin America, Poland to Egypt and the Sudan, Thailand to Australia, India to Samoa. Each chapter contains short historical background sketches followed by chronologically organized information from infancy through school years, marriage, pregnancy and childbirth, adult activities, and aging.

Robbie E. Davis-Floyd & Carolyn F. Sargent (Eds.). (1997*). Childbirth and Authoritative Knowledge: Cross-Cultural Perspectives*. Berkeley, CA: University of California Press.

> This interdisciplinary book extends the work of Brigitte Jordan on the ecology of birth. In a series of essays, authors present first-hand ethnographic research findings on reproduction and childbirth in sixteen different societies and cultures.

Raeann R. Hamon & Bron B. Ingoldsby (Eds.). (2003). *Mate Selection Across Cultures*. Thousand Oaks, CA: Sage.

> An exploration of mate selection in Ecuador, Trinidad, Ghana, Egypt, Turkey, Spain, and more, with chapters authored by experts in each country. Chapters include case studies, vignettes, photographs of courtship and wedding traditions, and original research and methodologies used by contributing authors. Lively and interesting for student readers and others.

Arthur Kornhaber. (1996). *Contemporary Grandparenting*. Thousand Oaks, CA: Sage.

> The first text of its kind, written by one of the key figures in the grandparenting activist movement. This book brings to life the diversity of today's grandparents in a lively and readable way.

Robert Levine, Suguru Sato, Tsukasa Hashimoto, & Jyoti Verma. (1995). Love and marriage in eleven cultures. *Journal of Cross-Cultural Psychology*, 26, 554–571.

> What kinds of views do college students have on the topics of love and marriage? This study reports on students from India, Pakistan, Thailand, Mexico, Brazil, Japan, Hong Kong, the Philippines. Australia, England, and the United States.

Journal of Grandparenting Research.

This is an online journal of grandparenting for anyone interested in the various aspects of this topic. It contains abstracts of relevant articles in current publications, with information on how to obtain complete articles. It also includes a research questionnaire that can be used by anyone interested in researching grandparents' attitudes. It can be accessed at the following web site: http://www.grandparenting .org/Research.htm.

◇ DEVELOPMENTAL ANALYSIS

THE FAMILY IN CULTURAL CONTEXT

While I was growing up, the most common family structure included two married parents, with the father providing financial security and the mother acting as the family nurturer and caregiver. My own family seemed to fit this model quite well. While my father was frequently working outside on the farm, my mother was at home, raising three children, and keeping the house in order. My father felt that it was his responsibility to provide a roof over our heads, food on the table, and be a loving caregiver for his children. My mother and father seemed to effectively balance their roles and were both equally involved in teaching us the values they lived by. With clean clothes in the drawers, hearty food to eat, and periodic visits to grandparents, our home life felt very comfortable.

Outside of the home, I spent time with a rather large group of friends that included boys and girls. Most of us remained platonic friends throughout high school, with occasional thoughts of romance or finding a future mate. As I entered college, I began to think about the possibilities in the next phases of my life, including college, marriage, and children. My parents met while still in high school and married shortly thereafter. I went against this model by first going to college, continuing on to graduate school, and not marrying until I was almost thirty years old. I am also two years older than my husband, something quite rare in each of our cultures.

I will always remember when I first met Giorgio Carlo Conte, a fellow student from Italy. I was studying Economics in England as a PhD candidate; he was completing his studies in International Relations. Giorgio sat across from me at the table in the library and struck up a conversation about football (a game that I knew in the United States as "soccer"). He shared his passion for the game and grew very animated as he described the techniques of various players. Over the next several weeks, Giorgio continued to come to the library, settle into the seat across from me, and strike up conversation. We enjoyed casual talk and learning more about one another, until one day he asked me out. I initially refused, explaining the need to focus on my studies

(continued)

and thanked him for his kindness. I figured that was the end of that. Seven requests later (he was persistent!), I eventually accepted his invitation to tea. We soon discovered that we had many of the same goals and ambitions in life. For example, it was very important for me to find a mate that would provide a healthy environment for children and who would respect my devotion to education and a career. I quickly found that these things were also very important to Giorgio. We were married four years later.

The births of each of our children were significant moments in our life together. Both of our children were born in a sanitized, brightly lit hospital room. I was not sedated, nor did I receive any type of anesthesia or pain reliever during delivery. My husband was unable to be present in the hospital room while I delivered our children because it was not permitted at the time. These days, fathers are often in the birthing room serving as coaches to the mother. When our daughter gave birth to her first child, she opted for a midwife and labored at home for several hours. In fact, when she arrived at the hospital she was just 15 minutes away from giving birth! She tells me that while she would have liked to experience the entire birth at home, she appreciated having access to modern medicine in the hospital.

Because both Giorgio and I had full-time careers, we shared in the parenting of our two children. We came to rely on our parents more as the children grew, and Giorgio's parents eventually came to live with us in the United States. I think the transition was difficult for them, but the benefit of time with their grandchildren was worth it. Giorgio's parents have both passed away, and our children feel blessed to have such wonderful memories of their grandparents.

We are grandparents ourselves now and thoroughly enjoy our roles. It is wonderful to see our own children as parents and quite flattering when they ask us for parenting advice! I frequently feel the need to balance my roles as mother, wife, grandmother and daughter. I try to spend as much time with my grandchildren as possible while also caring for my aging mother, who is living in an assisted living home. I'm a living example of the "sandwich generation."

CHAPTER TEN

CULTURE AND HEALTH

Hiroki Hashimoto is fourteen and lives with his family in the northern city of Akita on the island of Honshu. He attends a private school, where one of his British teachers, Alison Perrin, is concerned about Hiroki's obsessive neatness, extreme shyness, and apparent lack of many close friends. Based on her previous experiences with adolescents in her own country and during a teaching appointment in Canada, she feels he may have an obsessive-compulsive neurosis as well as very poorly developed interpersonal skills. She mentions to a Japanese colleague that she is about to recommend that his parents take him to see a child psychologist. Her colleague explains that Hiroki is more likely showing signs of a rather common disorder in Japan known as taijin-kyofu-sho syndrome (TKS), in which an individual is afraid of offending others while engaged in social situations. Loosely translated as "interpersonal anxiety," or simply "fear of people," TKS appears related to two salient behavior patterns in Japanese culture: an almost universal appearance of shyness or modesty and a great concern with cleanliness.

The sun has just appeared over the small village near Huascaran, an extinct volcano and the highest peak in the Andes Mountains, in the Peruvian highlands, where Eric Summerville, an Australian physician, works among the runakuna (native Quechua people). He has just been summoned to the thatched-roof home of a family whose young daughter appears to be suffering from susto, a disorder he has observed many times before among Indian tribes in Peru, Colombia, and Bolivia. Susto (Spanish for fright) is frequently the result of a frightening experience, and its symptoms may include excitability, severe anxiety, depression, rapid heartbeat, and often loss of weight. According to cultural beliefs, it can be caused by a variety of circumstances, including contact with strangers, supernatural spirits, or even "bad air" from cemeteries. The village healer has already made the traditional diagnosis by examining a guinea pig's intestines. Dr. Summerville now assists with the usual treatment of rubbing a variety

265

of plants over the girl's skin, while the healer performs an animal sacrifice to pacify the Earth, where it is believed the girl's soul is trapped.

Each of the above vignettes illustrates a unique cultural orientation to the diagnosis and practice of medicine. In both cases, making an accurate diagnosis and planning effective treatment are of chief importance. However, the explanations for the behavior and the etiology (causes) of the symptoms differ, as well as the response to the illness and its treatment. In the case of Hiroki, cultural beliefs about social behavior and expectations within his ecological setting play a major role in his symptoms. In Peru, native beliefs about a variety of frightening circumstances lead to a culturally unique diagnosis and treatment, using indigenous methods that are an extension of the developmental niche and shaped by the ecological system.

◇ CULTURAL CONCEPTS OF HEALTH AND HEALING

Cultural traditions determine, in large part, how individuals look at their physical and mental health. What is considered healthy behavior in one society may be viewed as unhealthy in another. For example, there are many ways in which people deal with stress and tension (e.g., withdrawal, overt expressions of anger, overeating, or not eating at all). Which approach to dealing with problems would one consider healthy and which unhealthy? The answer varies depending on the culture, developmental niche, and interaction among unique ecocultural systems: the individual (microsystem), who lives and interacts with others in a particular village or neighborhood (mesosystem), and the specific cultural health beliefs and practices that help to shape what goes on within the wider exosystem and macrosystem.

Culture influences attitudes toward health in a variety of ways. A reciprocal process exists in which cultural beliefs, traditions, and progression of knowledge about health shape the views of a particular society; and the views of society, in turn, determine methods and treatments. Frequently, the signs and treatment of an illness are manifested in the beliefs themselves. For example, in remote parts of Sabah and Sarawak in East Malaysia, an individual who exhibits the symptoms of depression would seek the treatment of a village *bomoh* (medicine man) to remove the charms presumably evoked by jealous clans. In contrast, many North Americans view depression as a biological disorder, explainable as a chemical imbalance in the brain and usually treated with antidepressants. You can imagine how the nature and treatment of depression in either culture might be perceived by the other.

This gives rise to an important concept in cross-cultural psychology discussed earlier—the distinction between emic and etic factors. As you may recall, **emic** refers to *culture-specific concepts,* whereas **etic** refers to *culture-general concepts.* In this regard, the symptoms characteristic of certain illness in one culture cannot be generalized across cultures. For example, Beardsley and Pedersen (1997) point out that while eating disorders are particularly unique to young women in Western countries, such disorders may not be as common in developing countries, where the food supply is scarce. Each culture's delicate balance of ecological systems and developmental niches make up the emic values to be considered when diagnosing and treating illness.

Culture-Bound Syndromes

Medical anthropologists and ethnopsychiatrists have known about seemingly unique forms of psychological illnesses for a long time. These researchers observed (1) symptoms of known illnesses that expressed themselves in unique ways in different cultures and (2) certain illnesses that occurred only among members of a specific cultural group. Because the unique patterns of symptoms did not fit any conventional classification system of disorders, these disorders were largely ignored by the medical community. Finally, in 1994, the fourth edition of the *Diagnostic and Statistical Manual of the American Psychiatric Society* (DSM-IV) acknowledged the existence of these culture-bound syndromes. The DSM-IV defines culture-bound syndrome as: "recurrent, locality-specific patterns of aberrant and troubling experience that may or may not be linked to a particular DSM-IV diagnostic category. Many of these patterns are indigenously considered to be 'illnesses,' or at least afflictions, and most have local names" (p. 844). Box 10.1 on pages 268–270 presents examples of some of the better known syndromes. While the inclusion of culture-bound syndromes represents an improvement in the validity of Western diagnostic systems, current researchers suggest that this is just the foundation for the practice of culturally sensitive medicine. For instance, Azhar and Varma (2000) suggest that a new form of psychotherapy could be used to treat culture-bound syndromes (*koro, amok*) in Malaysia. This treatment is based on Western techniques of cognitive therapy, but includes culture-specific religious beliefs and practices to reduce symptoms and achieve overall well-being.

Medical Diagnosis Across Cultures

The emic–etic distinction is germane to another important issue in culture and health—namely, the reliability and validity of diagnostic tests and measurement. Before making a diagnosis, physicians and other health professionals need to consider the medical criteria on which they base their treatment decisions. Often, doctors trained in Western societies use their familiar inventories and diagnostic criteria to evaluate medical conditions in patients from nonWestern societies, with a resulting misdiagnosis. The emic- or culture-specific values and beliefs that are part of a particular doctor's ecocultural

BOX 10.1

 CULTURE-BOUND SYNDROMES AND
PSYCHOLOGICAL DISORDERS

How individuals view their mental and physical health is determined, in part, by cultural traditions; for example, what is considered healthy in one society may be seen as unhealthy in another. While psychological disorders can be found in all cultures, the ways in which they are formed and expressed appear to be highly influenced by cultural belief systems, and, according to Draguns (1997), shaped by cultural factors.

China

Koro, found primarily in China (as far back as 3000 B.C.) and some other South and East Asian countries, is associated with acute anxiety involving the fear that one's genitals (the penis in a man and the vulva and nipples in women) are shrinking and retracting into the body and may result in death. Chinese folk culture provides some insight into the syndrome's origins, which can be found in fears about nocturnal emissions and impotence. These fears originated in the traditional Chinese beliefs about the balance of *yin* (female) and *yang* (male) humors, which held that during masturbation or nocturnal emissions, an unhealthy loss of *yang* was thought to occur and to place an individual in an unbalanced condition (Pfeiffer, 1982).

Koro has been identified primarily in younger men, twenty-one to forty years of age. It is believed that guilt and anxiety arise out of real or imagined sexual excesses. People with *koro* demonstrate typical anxiety symptoms, such as sweating, breathlessness, and heart palpitations. Men with the disorder have been known to use mechanical devices, such as chopsticks, to try to prevent the penis from retracting into the body. Reassurance by medical professionals that the genitals are not retracting often puts an end to *koro* episodes, and the disorder passes with time (Pfeiffer, 1982). Most cases, however, are handled by traditional medical or folk healers outside of the established health care system.

Japan

Taijin-kyofu-sho (TKS) is characterized by an excessive fear and anxiety that a person will behave in ways that will embarrass or offend other people (for example, blushing, emitting odors, staring inappropriately, or presenting improper facial expressions), and results in social withdrawal and avoidance. Affecting primarily young Japanese men, the syndrome is believed to be related to an emphasis in Japanese culture on not embarrassing others as well as deep concerns about issues of shame (Kirmayer, 1991). TKS is also found in Korea (Kim, 1995).

Upon examining the symptoms of TKS and using a Western diagnostic system, patients with TKS would typically be diagnosed as having anxiety

BOX 10.1 CONTINUED

reactions, obsessive-compulsive reactions, or social phobias. Traditional therapy for TKS occurs in the context of a ritual setting and includes physiological applications (sweating and massage), behavioral restrictions (diet), and social support (Kirmayer, 1991; Pfeiffer, 1982).

Korea

Shin-byung (a divine illness) is a possession syndrome often occurring in the course of a prolonged psychosomatic illness. People believe they are possessed by a dead ancestor and, through a dream or a hallucination, are persuaded to become a shaman, after which the patient becomes "cured" of the ailment. The occurrence of *shin-byung* is reported to be decreasing (Kim, 1995).

India

Dhat is a disorder affecting Indian males and involves intense fear or anxiety over the loss of semen through ejaculations or through nocturnal emissions. Some men also believe, incorrectly, that semen mixes with urine and is excreted by urinating. In Indian culture, semen is considered to be the elixir of life, on both the physical and mystical sense. There is a popular belief that loss of semen drains a man of his vital natural energy, while its preservation guarantees health and longevity. Loss of semen through masturbation, excessive sexual intercourse, or nocturnal emission is believed to lead to weakness. The most common symptoms of *dhat* are fatigue, weakness, body aches, severe headaches, depression, anxiety, loss of appetite, and suicidal feelings. Indian males believe that this is caused by heated foods, a fiery constitution, sexual excesses, and the use of intoxicants. A "cooling diet," "cooling medications," and baths are recommended. A tonic may also be given to increase sperm production (Chadda & Ahuja, 1990; Pfeiffer, 1982).

Nigeria

"Missing genitals" is a syndrome that has been reported in Nigeria. The victim of this syndrome, typically a man, might exchange greetings by shaking hands with another man and is suddenly overcome by fear that the genitals have disappeared. It is usually claimed that supernatural forces have been invoked to make the genitals disappear. While objective examination of the genitals reveals that they are intact, pointing this out to the victim does not convince him (Sijuwola, 1995).

Latino Culture

Susto ("magical fright") is found in some Latino cultures, primarily among the Kechua-speaking Indians of the Andes. It is triggered by a frightening experience, in which the soul is thought to separate from the body and become

(continued)

BOX 10.1 CONTINUED ▬▬▬▬▬▬▬▬▬▬▬▬▬▬▬▬▬

trapped on earth, and the person falls to the ground. Symptoms include loss of appetite and weight, physical weakness, restless sleep, depression, introversion, and apathy. By looking at the intestines of a guinea pig, a healing expert makes the diagnosis and then attempts to appease the earth through sacrifices so that the soul will return to the body (Pfeiffer, 1982).

Native American Culture

Amok, a type of dissociative episode or a sudden change in consciousness or self-identity, is found in traditional Puerto Rican and Navajo cultures in the West. It is marked by a violent or aggressive outburst followed by a period of brooding, often precipitated by a perceived slight or insult. The person, who sometimes experiences amnesia, returns to his or her usual state of functioning following the episode. In the West, the expression "running amuck" refers to an episode of losing oneself and running around in a violent frenzy (Pfeiffer, 1982).

  Windigo, also known as witiko, is a rare, culture-bound disorder reported among some North American Indian tribes, including the Cree and Ojibwa. It is characterized by symptoms of melancholia and a delusion of transformation into a *witiko* or man-eating monster, who either has a heart of ice or vomits ice, and who will turn the victim into a homicidal cannibal. Cannibalism seldom, if ever, occurs. Suicidal ideation to avoid acting on the cannibalistic urges may take place (Trimble, Manson, Dinges, & Medicine, 1984).

Source: Adapted from *Infusing Culture into Parenting Issues: A Supplement for Psychology Instructors* by Vicki Ritts, 2000, unpublished manuscript, St. Louis Community College. Reprinted by permission.

perspective cannot be readily applied in diagnosing and treating people raised in a culturally different developmental niche. Lonner and Ibrahim (2002) suggest that accurate assessment should take into consideration the beliefs, values, and perceptions of the patient and that doctors should employ culture-specific criteria when diagnosing illnesses.

  In an interesting study focusing on illness beliefs, Cook (1994) asked 182 adult Chinese, Indian, and Anglo Celtic Canadians about their beliefs concerning chronic illness and how they should be treated. He found that each ethnic group viewed the causes and treatment differently, depending on geographical orientation, generation, and age. For example, older first- or second-generation Chinese emphasized a more traditional, spiritual dimension to help explain and treat physical illness, whereas younger Chinese tended to look to biomedical intervention. Once again, an individual's unique developmental niche and place in a specific ecological system help shape attitudes toward health. Failure to recognize this important link may result in misdiagnosis of medical conditions.

When individuals are misdiagnosed, their health generally deteriorates even more. There is little or no relief because treatment is completely ineffective. The chances of this occurring are greatest when physicians and health care professionals from one cultural orientation treat individuals from another. For example, in 1985, more than one hundred Cuban refugees were initially rejected from applying for U.S. citizenship, because a medical review board composed entirely of American psychiatrists diagnosed them as having antisocial personality disorder. However, this diagnosis was overturned after an official appeal was made to a second medical board composed of physicians and psychiatrists from several different countries. Many of the psychiatrists serving on the initial screening board subsequently admitted not being aware of crucial ethnic and cultural differences when they made their original diagnosis.

Lisa Beardsley (1994) has outlined several reasons for misdiagnoses. A first reason is the use of clinical manuals (e.g., the *Diagnostic and Statistical Manual,* Fourth Edition, DSM-IV) in societies significantly different from the ones for which they were originally intended. For example, while Chinese and American psychiatrists largely agree on some clinical evaluations, such as schizophrenia, they disagree on others, including depression and anxiety disorders.

A second reason for misidentifying a health problem frequently centers on the difference in definition between disease and illness behavior. According to Beardsley, **disease** is *a biological process,* whereas **illness behavior** is *a psychological experience and the social expression of disease* (p. 281). She goes on to point out that "cultural variables interact with biological processes, and as a result, there is overlap between culture-specific (emic) and culture-general (etic) features of a disease" (p. 281).

Finally, the use of culturally biased instruments and tests may contribute to misdiagnosis. For example, standardized intelligence tests, such as the Stanford-Binet and the Wechsler Intelligence Scale for Children (WISC), and personality inventories, such as the Minnesota Multiphasic Personality Inventory (MMPI), were developed for use with specific American populations and even when carefully translated are not always appropriate for use in other cultures. Consequently, use of these instruments may result in a patient or client receiving ineffective treatment. For example, one of the authors (Gardiner) once had a Chinese student come to his office in tears because she had been given the results of her MMPI, and the computerized analysis indicated she "demonstrates bizarre behavior and should be institutionalized and treated immediately." Knowing the cultural specificity of certain items on this test used to assess "psychopathological tendencies," he was able to calm her down by showing her how the answers she gave, while reasonable and healthy for her particular culture, were considered inappropriate and unhealthy when given by someone born and raised in the American culture. He strongly recommended that the personnel in the college counseling office, none of whom had had cross-cultural training, not use this instrument as a measure of anything with international students. As Brislin (1990) aptly states, "It is decidedly a creation of the 'Western' view of etiology and psychiatric classification (and is, therefore, culture-bound); its original normative samples came from small, rural parts of Minnesota (in the United States); and there is little or no 'theory' guiding its cross-cultural use" (p. 69). Nevertheless, the MMPI is available in more than one hundred languages and, since the incident mentioned above, has undergone revision and is seen by some as worthy of cross-cultural attention (Butcher, 2006). However, we still agree with Brislin, who argues for caution if employing this instrument, because "its misuse can lead to terrible errors and tragic consequences" (1990, p. 70).

The World Health Organization (WHO) has as its goal the promotion of health and prevention of misdiagnoses, as well as the provision of medical services to countries throughout the world. One of WHO's major efforts is the Mental Health Program, which is aimed at protecting and promoting mental health. According to Sartorius (1994), this program consists of four parts:"(1) Mental Health programme formulation and evaluation, (2) psychosocial and behavioural factors affecting health and development, (3) organization of services for the prevention and treatment of mental and neurological illnesses, and (4) biomedical research on mental functioning in health and disease" (p. 262). Developing guidelines for improving mental health care and training mental health professionals are also integral parts of this program. As a result of these and other efforts, health care professionals are becoming more culturally sensitive (see Box 10.2).

Success in these efforts requires an understanding of human development from a cross-cultural perspective. The focus of this chapter, therefore, is to investigate how health is mediated by cultural factors across the lifespan.

Illness, Stress, and Coping

Illness, at any age and in any ecological system, creates considerable stress. We know today that stressful life events affect physical health in complex ways. Behavior, cognition, and emotion interact with the central nervous system and the endocrine system in ways that might suppress or boost the immune system (Tosevski and Milovancevic, 2006), thus setting the stage for optimal health or risk of illness.

The ability to cope with the stress of illness is not only important for survival, but it is also the foundation for growth and change. You may know people in your life who experienced a seemingly devastating illness at some point in their lives. Yet, they were able to adapt to their limitations and develop abilities and strategies that allowed them to achieve goals. One could argue that coping with and adapting to their illness allows them to grow—they grow not despite the illness but because of it. Hampel and colleagues

BOX 10.2

 TRAINING HEALTH CARE PROFESSIONALS
TO BE CULTURALLY SENSITIVE

Although the world's 6 billion inhabitants live in 191 countries and speak more than 6000 languages, relatively little is known about the effects of culture on health care. In the United States, emergency rooms are treating increasing numbers of individuals from ethnically and culturally diverse backgrounds. For example, in 2006 it was estimated that there were more than 35,000,000 legal immigrants living in the United States, along with approximately 12,000,000 to 20,000,000 illegal immigrants, many speaking little or no English. In an article in Pediatrics (2000), Flores emphasizes the importance of physicians becoming more sensitive to cultural diversity, and provides a framework for understanding the clinical consequences of culture. The specific impact of five cultural components (normative cultural values, language, folk illnesses, parent/patient beliefs, and provider practices) is examined, along with practical solutions to ensure that culturally sensitive care is provided to patients. Most importantly, Flores proposes a model for cultural competency in health care, which can be used to guide clinicians in interactions with any cultural group. Today, hospital staff are taking steps to ensure greater awareness and better understanding of cultural differences. Failure to do this will only increase the possibility of misdiagnosis, as in the case of a Mexican peasant woman who invented her symptoms because she was too embarrassed to describe her real problem (rectal fistula). Needless to say, such misunderstanding not only jeopardizes patients' health but also opens up the possibility of a lawsuit. Thus, many physicians are taking courses in multiculturalism and are enlisting the help of relatives or friends of patients when making daily rounds. In New York, a Chinatown outreach team from St. Vincent's Hospital is learning about the use of herbal remedies to treat ailments of the elderly. Also, folk healers are recruited at University Hospital in Minneapolis to help serve the large community of Laotian Hmong refugees.

(2006) showed that children and adolescents with chronic health conditions coped with everyday stressors (e.g., tension with family or friends, school-related issues) better than their healthy counterparts. Perhaps adjusting to the stresses related to a chronic illness has helped these children to develop coping strategies for stressors in other areas of their lives. The Chinese view of stress emphasizes that stress presents a crisis and an opportunity (for growth) at the same time. In other words, stress is part of life, and adaptation is growth. Yet, individuals and cultural groups differ in how susceptible they are to stress and illness and how they cope with these situations (Hashim & Zhiliang, 2003). Ecological factors that shape responses to illness include differences in access to health care (Snowden and Yamada, 2005), social stigma, and parental modeling of illness behavior (Kirmayer and Looper, 2006). The focus of this chapter, therefore, will be to investigate how health, illness, and response to illness are mediated by cultural factors across the lifespan.

◇ INFANCY AND CHILDHOOD

Professionals in today's health care delivery systems see infant care as one of their major challenges. Technological advances allow premature and extremely low-birth-weight babies that would not have survived a decade ago to live and grow into healthy children and adults. But the process is not always easy, and success or failure frequently depends on cultural factors.

Sudden Infant Death Syndrome (SIDS)

In addition to the problem of premature and low-birth-weight babies, **sudden infant death syndrome (SIDS)** is another public health concern. In the United States, SIDS is the second leading cause of infant mortality, after complications from birth defects (USDHHS, 1992). In SIDS, for reasons still not clearly understood, *newborns who test normal on post-delivery neurological and respiratory tests and appear healthy for much of the first year of life, suddenly stop breathing and die.* While several medical explanations have been offered, little is known for certain about the precise causes, and no proven method for absolute prevention is available. However, some physicians now recommend that infants sleep on their backs in order to prevent suffocation.

The fear of suffocating infants is not new and has existed for centuries. In the Middle Ages, infants were sometimes asphyxiated when their mothers, sleeping in the same bed, rolled over on them in the middle of the night. This happened so frequently that local church authorities wrote a decree forbidding parents to sleep next to their newborns (Nakajima & Mayor, 1996). Since then, health officials in many Western countries have attempted to discourage the practice of mothers and infants sleeping in the same bed, because it is believed to increase the chances of the infant dying from SIDS. However, cross-cultural research conducted in Japan, where cosleeping is common, has shown this not to be the case. In fact, fewer babies die from SIDS in Japan and Sweden each year than almost anywhere in the world. Nakajima and Mayor (1996) report research carried out in sleep laboratories in California that shows that infants who slept with their mothers, rather than in separate bedrooms, doubled their chance of being breastfed, which provides nutrition and promotes healthy attachment (see Chapter 3). In addition, infants who slept with their mothers showed less distress and cried less often during the day.

Breastfeeding young infants is commonly practiced throughout the world. (© Jim Whitmer/Stock Boston)

Childhood Mental Health

Concerns about mental health are not commonly associated with "childhood." Nonetheless, in recent years it has become clear that several psychological and developmental disorders may first occur during this early life phase, among them multiple personality disorder, depression, autism, and attention deficit hyperactivity disorder (ADHD).

Viewed from an ecological systems perspective, culture plays a role in how childhood disorders are diagnosed and interpreted within the social context. Studies of autism, depression, and ADHD seem to suggest that, overall, mental health professionals in various countries agree on and correctly recognize the symptoms of these disorders. While reliable diagnostics can help identify these illnesses, ecological factors influence how family, peers, teachers, and health professionals interpret and deal with these disorders. Teachers, for example, are central in the diagnosis of ADHD, because one criterion in diagnosing this illness requires that the symptoms present themselves in at least two different contexts. One context is home;

the other is usually school. A study by Jacobson (2002) showed that teachers in the United States and the United Kingdom correctly identified ADHD-typical behaviors, but the two groups differed significantly in what they considered "appropriate" classroom behaviors. The cultural differences in these children's ecological systems brings into question the interpretation of some ADHD behaviors as "disordered." Another example of the interaction between ecological systems and a child's mental health status is Pribilsky's (2001) discussion of the culture-specific disorder "nervios." This illness occurs among children living in the southern Equadorian Andes mountains. Children suffer from a variety of depression-like symptoms, including melancholy and anger. A common trigger of the illness is children's separation (mainly) from their fathers, who usually migrate to the United States for economic reasons. The author argues that this childhood disorder is clearly defined by changes in lifestyles, family structure, and migration, all representing disturbing changes in the child's ecological system.

◇ ECOLOGICAL INFLUENCES ON EARLY COPING BEHAVIOR

The ecological conditions in which a child grows up set the stage for many potential health risks and stressors. These conditions include physical settings, such as climate, hygienic conditions, and access to vaccinations and medication. The health of children is one of the world's most important concerns, since the survival of any society rests, to some extent, on the health of its children. How healthy are the world's children? In a United Nations report on the state of children's health only a decade ago, Grant (1994) estimated that the largest proportion of child deaths are caused by pneumonia, diarrhea, tetanus, and tuberculosis. Most of these illnesses occur in countries with the fewest resources to deal with them and could be prevented if a variety of antibiotics and vaccines were available. On a more positive note, over the past one hundred years, we have witnessed a significant reduction in such often fatal communicable childhood illnesses as measles, smallpox, and scarlet fever. Many international health organizations are dedicated to developing and maintaining programs that address the ecological aspects of health. UNESCO and WHO have been successful in making preventative and acute health care more accessible and educating parents and communities.

In 2006, Microsoft founder Bill Gates and his wife, Melinda, through their foundation, pledged billions of dollars to vaccinate children in the world's poorest countries, primarily in Africa. Among the couple's long-term goals are the eradication of poverty and childhood diseases by helping governments improve basic services, such as clean water, and by providing financial incentives to developing nations to improve the health and lives of their people.

In addition to physical settings and resources, parental characteristics and family dynamics are a very salient aspect of the early ecological system, which influences the ways in which children perceive stress and illness and how they adapt to it. Findings from a landmark longitudinal study conducted by Werner (1989), provide important information on this topic. Beginning in the 1950s, more than 650 infants born on the Hawaiian island of Kauai were monitored for cognitive and emotional development throughout childhood and adulthood. While most were born without complications and were raised in supportive homes, a substantial number experienced a variety of difficulties, including some perinatal stress and prematurity. The researchers reported that infants raised in supportive and nurturing homes showed more competence than those who were not reared in such environments. Not surprisingly, they also found that premature and low-birth-weight infants developed significantly more slowly when their prenatal problems were combined with impoverished living conditions, dysfunctional family situations, and inadequate parenting. The premature infants who made the greatest progress tended to grow up in families with a great deal of physical stimulation, interaction with other family members, and supportive caregiving.

Beckwith, Rodning, and Cohen (1992) lent additional support to the importance of providing premature infants with warm and caring home environments. They reported that children born premature but raised in responsive environments had several advantages over those not raised in some homes, including improved self-esteem, higher measures of intelligence, and fewer behavioral problems. More recently, developmental researchers acknowledge that parenting influences children's coping in multiple phases of the coping process: how and when children may be exposed to a stressor, the appraisal of an event as stressful, modeling stress behavior, and modeling coping behavior (Power, 2004; Eisenberg and Valiente, 2004). This argument seems to gain some support from Chen and Kennedy (2005), who studied children's coping in different cultural environments. They learned that children of different ethnicities (the sample consisted of European-American, Chinese-American, and Mexican-American children within the Untied States, and Taiwanese children in their native country) reported different types of stressors, and they also preferred and used different coping strategies. The authors relate these differences to parental characteristics, family dynamics, and early socialization.

◇ ADOLESCENCE

Writing about the hurried child, Elkind (1988) characterizes American youth as growing up too fast too soon and states that "like Superman, Superkid has spectacular powers and precocious competence even as an infant. This allows us to think that we can hurry the little powerhouse with impunity" (p. xii).

The pressure to grow up affects most children at some point, but each culture has its own beliefs about when this is supposed to occur. In some

Latin American street children help each other survive the challenges of everyday life. (© Timothy Ross/The Image Works)

societies, the process is gradual, whereas in others it is abrupt. No matter how smooth the transition might be, it brings with it challenges, possibilities, and health concerns.

Adolescence, *the time between childhood and adulthood,* was initially called a period of "storm and stress" by the "father" of modern adolescent psychology, G. Stanley Hall (1904), who described the frequent mood swings and conflict thought to characterize the period. Many of these early ideas have been refuted by more recent researchers. Today, most lifespan psychologists view adolescence as a continuous process rather than a fixed stage in the life cycle.

Adolescence is nevertheless a complex concept and is shaped by sociocultural beliefs and historical events. For example, just before the start of the twentieth century in the United States, the concept of adolescence did not exist. Young persons were simply expected to take on adult responsibilities and contribute to the welfare of the family as soon as they were physically able to do so. Over time, however, this idea changed, and societies (especially those in the West) became more accepting of adolescence as a distinct stage in adult preparation. In recent years, the period of adolescence has shown signs of expanding so that children enter it earlier and stay in it longer, in some cases well into their early to mid-twenties. For many, biological changes during the adolescent years can be enormously stressful. (For a review of adolescent physical development, see Chapter 4.) For example, hormonal changes associated with puberty are frequently accompanied by fluctuations in social and emotional development. For many adolescents, these changes produce only minimal health risks, although, for others, they can contribute to serious health problems, including eating disorders or alcohol and drug addiction. Adolescence is also the time when many severe adult mental disorders manifest themselves.

Eating Disorders

Over the years, the topic of adolescent health has taken on new dimensions in cross-cultural human development. Because of the impact childhood illnesses can have on adult development (e.g., obesity and diabetes), international health organizations and relief agencies have devoted increasing attention to the identification of physical and mental illnesses among the world's adolescents. Today, a growing health concern among many professionals is the dramatic rise in the incidence of eating disorders, especially in highly industrialized societies.

While in some societies stoutness is associated with good health and prosperity, in others it is not. For example, in parts of Southeast Asia, a plump waistline suggests abundance, wealth, and good fortune. It has been reported that young women of the nomadic Moors of Mauritania or the Annang of Nigeria are force fed because large women are considered the most desirable (Brink, 1989; Cassidy, 1991). On the other hand, in North America, being slim and fit is important, whereas being overweight can be embarrassing. An obsession with being thin appears to be especially common among young women.

Crystal, Watanabe, and Chen (2000) studied the attitudes of 12-year-old and 16-year-old American and Japanese children towards obese peers. Overall, more Japanese than American children expressed positive and inclusive attitudes toward the obese peer. However, the study also showed older Japanese teenagers to be similar to Americans in showing even less willingness to include and more negative attitudes towards their overweight peers.

A particularly interesting example of the desire for thinness in American society was the celebration of the one-hundredth birthday of the Statue of Liberty. A new coin was issued with a likeness designed to resemble the original, with one exception: Lady Liberty's figure on the new coin had been "slimmed down" to more closely represent the culturally popular Western ideal of feminine thinness (Nichter & Nichter, 1991).

Research, as well as everyday experience, has demonstrated that adolescent girls are more likely to be dissatisfied with their physical appearance, particularly their weight, than are adolescent boys and are, therefore, more likely to go on diets. While dieting alone does not produce a health risk, excessive dieting can lead to a number of serious disorders, including anorexia nervosa and bulimia.

Cultural Variations in Anorexia and Bulimia

Anorexia nervosa is *an eating disorder,* found primarily among young adolescent girls, *characterized by loss of appetite and extreme loss of weight.* In severe cases, hospitalization becomes necessary, menstruation may stop, and an individual may lose 15 to 25 percent or more total body weight. It is estimated that between 5 and 15 percent of anorexic girls die of this disorder each year. By contrast, adolescents suffering from **bulimia,** again typically young women, *eat extremely large amounts of food, then purge it all by means of self-induced vomiting.* The aim is not to lose or gain weight but to maintain a specific weight. This practice dates back to the Roman Empire, when guests of the emperor were invited to the coliseum to celebrate an auspicious occasion by stuffing themselves with food and wine, followed by a trip to the "vomitorium" where they would ceremonially throw it all up. This was thought to relieve gas and stuffiness as well as cleanse the body from the inside out.

Both of these eating disorders can have serious adverse effects on one's personal health. But just how common are these disorders in countries throughout the world? Among the small number of cross-cultural studies looking at this problem, findings reveal fewer eating disorders and less dissatisfaction with body image among samples in Japan (Iwawaki & Kerner, 1974), Australia (Tiggemann & Rothblum, 1988), and Spain (Raich et al., 1992). There also is evidence showing a relationship between acculturation into some Western societies (e.g., the United States and Great Britain) and increases in negative body image, as well as a preference for a thin figure (Mumford, Whitehouse, & Choudry, 1992; Nasser, 1986). Unfortunately, the number of studies focusing on these disorders in developing countries remains small. Future research might well look at this and its possible relationship to ecological settings and the concept of the developmental niche.

In one cross-cultural study, Mukai and McCloskey (1996) investigated attitudes toward eating among 108 Japanese and American schoolgirls between eight and eleven years of age. Administering a children's version of an eating disorder test (ChEAT-26) and a revised form of the Demographic and Dieting Questionnaire, the authors report that nearly half of the girls in both Japan and the United States wished they were thinner, and about a third indicated they had attempted to lose weight. In both countries, the dieting practices of friends had a significant influence on eating attitudes.

In another study (Furnham & Alibhai, 1983), comparisons were made among three groups of subjects: Caucasian women residing in Great Britain, Asian women living in Kenya, and Asian women living in Great Britain who had once resided in Kenya. In all cases, subjects rated drawings of women depicting body types ranging from anorexic to obese. Findings showed that the drawings of thin women were rated more positively and drawings of heavier women more negatively by the Asian immigrants and Caucasian women than they were by those Asian women who lived in Kenya. Our interpretation of these results suggests that these women were responding to these drawings on the basis of their developmental niche and the cultural beliefs that helped to define it.

Indran (1995) administered the EAT questionnaire to 140 Form Five women students (equivalent to approximately grade eleven or twelve in the United States) at a secondary school in the suburbs surrounding Kuala

Lumpur, Malaysia. The findings, once again, support the interaction of our recurring themes, ecological systems theory and developmental niche, revealing that culture and family attitudes play a pivotal role in the Malaysian girls' eating habits. Interestingly, Malaysian girls paid less attention to being thin (than did Western girls) and paid greater attention to working hard to please their parents through academic success.

Finally, Cogan, Bhalla, Sefa-Dedeh, and Rothblum (1996) conducted a study of perceptions of obesity and thinness using 349 Ghanaian undergraduate students at the University of Ghana and 219 American undergraduates at the University of Vermont. All subjects completed a questionnaire containing demographic information and six measures of perceptions of obesity and thinness, including an eating disorders inventory. As hypothesized, compared to U.S. students, Ghanaian men and women rated a larger body size as the ideal. In addition, more Ghanaian than American students tended to select from a wider range of body sizes as "acceptable figures." For example, American subjects tended to have a narrower definition of the ideal figure and also tended

Anorexia nervosa affects many young women
throughout the world. (© Ed Quinn/CORBIS)

to identify with figures smaller than they were and, in some cases, two sizes smaller than Ghanaian students, reflecting a thinner ideal. This was more true for females than for males. When weight preference was considered, both Ghanaian men and women agreed that heavier was best and idealized heavier-set body builds. For the U.S. sample, men tended to prefer somewhat heavier models than did women. Furthermore, Americans associated thinness with such positive attributes as extroversion, attractiveness, self-discipline, and self-confidence. Many American women also associated thinness with happiness. This was not the case for any of the Ghanaian students. Finally, American women reported more incidents of eating disorders than did American men or Ghanaian men or women.

These findings, along with others already mentioned, reflect a cultural orientation in which young American women place a higher value on being thin and have a higher occurrence of eating disorders than young women in developing countries. Tiggemann and Rothblum (1988) provide further evidence in a comparison of Australian and American students' perceptions of thinness and obesity. They found that while students in both countries were concerned about weight, the U.S. sample reported significantly more concern. For example, dieting was more common among American students, who also reported being more self-conscious about their bodies than were Australian students.

A final example is a study by Banks (1992) that looks at anorexia nervosa and its possible relationship to religious and cultural contexts. Banks cites the cases of two anorectic women as evidence that for some, self-starvation may be interwoven with religious idioms and symbols about the body, food, and self. In an exhaustive review of the literature, she notes an interesting link between anorexia nervosa and **asceticism,** or the *practice of self-denial,* and hypothesizes that asceticism may be subjectively expressed through religious concepts about the body and food. She encourages further cross-cultural research examining the relationship between religion and other rituals of fasting and vomiting. An interesting recent study of this type was conducted by Ali & Maharajh (2004), in which an 18-year-old Islamic student, enrolled in a Roman Catholic Convent, was exposed to ambivalent religious values, which appeared to act as an etiological factor in her development of this disorder.

Taken as a group, these studies are important, because they indicate that negative perceptions of body image and incidences of eating disorders tend to occur more often in Western societies in which thinness is viewed as a cultural ideal that young women feel they need to achieve.

Culture and Sexually Transmitted Diseases (STDs)

As adolescents become sexually active, they are more likely to acquire sexually transmitted diseases (STDs) than any other age group. One sexually transmitted disease in particular, acquired immunodeficiency syndrome (AIDS), which is caused by the human immunodeficiency virus (HIV), has become a critically important international health issue. Since 1981, when AIDS was first diagnosed in Los Angeles, people with HIV have been found in more than 169 countries. **AIDS** is *a disease that attacks the body's immune system,* leaving an individual weak and susceptible to infections that generally prove fatal. With an increasing number of adolescents becoming sexually active at younger ages and large numbers engaging in unsafe practices, there is serious concern that many have become infected with the HIV virus and will die of AIDS when they reach the third decade of their lives (Harvard Mental Health Letter, 1999).

Discussion of HIV and the AIDS epidemic should be made within the context of culture and how it influences the interpretation, diagnosis, and treatment of the disease. In an unusually persuasive article on the relationship between culture and the media's influence on HIV and AIDS in Asia, Wolffers (1997) stresses that culture is not a passive entity but rather a dynamic process within which members of a society are continuously acting on their needs and interpreting what they see and experience. One of the major sources of cultural influence throughout the world is the media. In Southeast Asia, the media has devoted considerable time and energy to informing and educating the public about the causes and transmission of HIV. However, as Wolffers points out, many local newspapers have a policy of not printing information about HIV and its relationship to sexual behavior, because this sometimes conflicts with religious and cultural beliefs. Instead, in an effort to combat the illegal use and trafficking of drugs, emphasis is often placed on the occurrence of HIV and AIDS among drug users and their use of dirty needles. The concern, as Wolffers points out, is that under these circumstances many people, particularly those who are young, uneducated, and living at the poverty level, will not be adequately informed about the potential sources of contracting the virus, and that this ignorance will substantially contribute to the increasingly large number of AIDS cases throughout the world.

Culture and Adolescent Drug Use

Misuse of drugs and alcohol has also become a global health concern. In North America, young people are experimenting with alcohol and drugs at increasingly younger ages. It is estimated that nine out of ten high school seniors have consumed alcohol on occasion and many have experimented with illegal drugs at least once. Drugs most often abused are alcohol, tobacco, and marijuana. Health problems associated with such abuse include chemical dependency, diabetes, cirrhosis of the liver, kidney failure, cardiac and lung complications, fetal anomalies, injuries from accidents, and homicide. In addition, adolescents who use drugs and alcohol regularly are likely to engage in unprotected sex, thereby increasing the chance of contracting HIV.

In a longitudinal study involving male adolescents who consumed alcohol regularly in France, Weill and Le Bourhis (1994) identified several psychological correlates predictive of future drinking. They found the heaviest

Adolescents experiment with smoking and drinking at increasingly younger ages.
(© Photofusion Picture Library/Alamy)

drinkers were those who possessed negative, self-defeating attitudes, whereas those who were positive and enthusiastic and exhibited more religiosity consumed less alcohol and were more aware of the health dangers associated with drinking.

In the United States, drug use is highest among minority populations living in the inner city or on Indian reservations. However, the strongest factor in predicting drug use among adolescents is the type of friends with whom they associate.

Swaim and colleagues (1993) investigated the nature and extent of drug use among eleven- and twelve-year-olds on American Indian reservations, using the peer cluster theory—dyads of best friends who support and encourage each other in the use of alcohol and drugs. Over four hundred northern Plains and Southwest American Indians from two reservations were given a survey consisting of several different scales, including a Religious Identification and Peer Drug Association Scale. Data were compared to findings reported in an earlier study by Oetting and Beauvais (1987) among Anglo adolescents. With rare exception, most variables correlated higher among Anglos than among American Indians. For example, there were more peer clusters formed among Anglo adolescents than among American Indian adolescents. Swaim and colleagues (1993) conclude, "Association with drug-using peers does not appear to play as central a role in the substance use of Indian youths as it does among Anglos" (p. 640). These and other health concerns not only directly affect the lives of adolescents, but also have relevance for the health of adults.

⋄ EARLY AND MIDDLE ADULTHOOD

The transition from adolescence to adulthood is more gradual than that from childhood to adolescence. Exactly when an individual becomes an adult is not always clear, and there is likely to be just as much variation within cultures as there is among cultures.

Mental Health Issues

In addition to the effects of stress, other mental health issues concern adults. Among these are depression and schizophrenia. While it is not our intention to provide a comprehensive analysis of psychopathology in adulthood, we examine some of the different approaches to viewing these illnesses from a cross-cultural perspective.

Depression

As already noted, every culture has its own beliefs regarding the causes and treatment of illness and stress. This is true for depression as well, and once again, there is often more variation in interpretation within cultures than among cultures. For example, in the United States, individuals react in many different ways when hearing that someone is experiencing depression. Responses may range from "There's nothing to worry about, he's just a little moody these days. He'll soon be fine" to "She's had a long history of serious depression, just like her mother and father. It seems to run in the family." Because the term tends to be used so freely in everyday conversation and in the media, it is sometimes difficult to recognize the symptoms of depression.

Depression is *a serious psychological disorder involving periods of sadness and other negative feelings, such as hopelessness, despair, sleep disturbance, and loss of energy.* Cultural variations in beliefs about depression and other illnesses have important implications for the health status of individuals worldwide. Health authorities have become increasingly alarmed by the growing number of reported cases of depression among adults. It is estimated that at least one hundred million people around the world experience the symptoms of depression each year (Douki & Tabbane, 1996). This figure is expected to rise as people live longer and more people are exposed to chronic stress. It is also feared that the sudden exodus of families migrating to new countries and abandoning native customs and traditions, as well as the breakup of the extended family, will result in increased incidences of depression in younger people. Some experts worry that this will lead to greater consumption of alcohol and the abuse of drugs, which will only intensify the depression. Obviously, the magnitude of this problem presents enormous public health concerns.

Since depression has varying emotional, physical, and behavioral symptoms, it is common for many cases to go undetected. For this and other reasons, diagnosing and treating depression among young adults continue to be major problems for health care professionals in many cultures. In Western countries, depression is described in terms of being sad, disconnected, and withdrawn. Sometimes, these are accompanied by somatic complaints, such as headaches, stomach cramps, or nausea. However, in parts of India and South Africa, depression is described in quasi-spiritual or metaphysical terms—"suffering of the spirit" (Douki & Tabbane, 1996). Recent findings suggest that depression in some developing countries is gradually beginning to mimic depressive symptoms seen in the West. For example, an epidemiological study done among adults in Tunisia revealed that out of the five thousand patients sampled, most registered the same complaints concerning depression as their Western counterparts. Rapid socioeconomic development and mass urbanization were two of the reasons given to explain the depressive symptoms of young Tunisians (Douki & Tabbane, 1996). Thus, it appears that while there are certain culture-specific characteristics associated with depression, there also are several universal features.

In 1983, the World Health Organization (WHO) conducted a cross-national study of patients in Canada, Japan, Switzerland, and the Islamic Republic of Iran. Findings revealed a cluster of core depressive symptoms, including long periods of sadness, lack of energy and affect, inability to concentrate, feelings of inadequacy, and loss of self-esteem. As Douki and Tabbane (1996) indicate, while the frequency and extent of reported depressive cases may vary among cultures, depression is a major universal problem that usually requires treatment.

In China, depressive episodes and stress-related disorders among adults are often accompanied by somatization. This has also been reported in parts of Latin America, Asia, and Africa. **Somatization** refers to *physical ailments resulting from stress or emotional distress.* One explanation may be that in many collectivistic societies, individuals are discouraged from voicing their psychological complaints in the company of friends or extended family members. Furthermore, depression is viewed as a minor, transient illness not requiring immediate family intervention. Consequently, an individual who experiences a depressive episode is often forced to use somatization to signal distress and thereby gain attention. As Draguns (1990a) states, in the case of depression, "somatization serves as a culturally sanctioned cry for help" (p. 311). Thus, the nature and treatment of depression, like many other illnesses, reflects the interaction among ecocultural systems, historical and sociocultural factors, and developmental niche.

Today, depression is often referred to as the "common cold" of psychological disorders, and Prozac (used to treat depression) is one of the most widely prescribed drugs in the world. It is customary to think of depression as occurring primarily in developed countries, often as a result of living and working in a highly industrialized and hurried society. However, as Draguns (1994) points out, "Depression is not the exclusive property of Judeo-Christian cultures" (p. 168). In fact, depression is probably experienced to some degree in most, if not all, of the world's cultures. Even so, health care professionals

Many young people seek counseling for their depression. (©Will Hart)

have yet to agree on a set of depression symptoms that can be universally applied, and it is unlikely that they ever will because of the role played by cultural variables. Draguns (1994) affirms this: "The cross-cultural study of depression has not yet progressed to the point of being able to pinpoint the worldwide invariant manifestations of depression" (p. 168).

Schizophrenia

During the last two hundred years, schizophrenia has been one of the most frequently studied psychopathic disorders. **Schizophrenia** refers to *a group of severe psychological disorders characterized by disturbances in thought, perception, and affect or emotion.* In recent years, increasing attention has been given to the study of cultural variations in schizophrenia. For example, in 1973, the World Health Organization began conducting a series of studies in China, Taiwan, Colombia, Czechoslovakia, Denmark, India, Nigeria, the former Soviet Union, the United Kingdom, and the United States. The goal of these investigations has been to determine the extent of schizophrenia and the sociocultural and historical factors surrounding it. Findings have pointed to the identification of several core symptoms, including restricted affect, thinking aloud, lack of insight, poor rapport, incoherent speech, and widespread bizarre delusions (Draguns, 1994). In addition, three symptoms were identified that, although exotic or unusual, would not be considered symptoms of schizophrenia: waking early, depressed facial features, and expressions of extreme elation (Draguns, 1990b). Subsequent research conducted by WHO (1979) and Sartorius and colleagues (1986) reports a greater likelihood of these symptoms occurring in Colombia, India, and Nigeria than in the other industrialized countries mentioned earlier. One explanation may lie in the finding that schizophrenia is inversely proportionate to educational and occupational level. In fact, according to Draguns (1994), poorer and less educated patients in developing countries (e.g., India and Nigeria) recovered most quickly from this illness.

In the last ten years, WHO has continued to conduct cross-cultural research on more than three thousand schizophrenic patients in over twenty countries. Results indicate that schizophrenia occurs in nearly all cultures and that the prognosis is better in developing countries than it is in highly industrialized developed countries. Apparently, the support and encouragement provided by extended family members help reduce some of the symptoms associated with schizophrenia.

Day and his colleagues (1987) investigated the nature and prevalence of schizophrenia in nine countries in Asia, Europe, and South and North America. Contrary to the medical model often used to explain schizophrenia in the West, most of these schizophrenias were associated with stressful events not initiated by the patients themselves but caused by external forces (e.g., charms or evil spirits).

Schizophrenia has been studied in India and Nigeria, where Katz and his colleagues (1988) found the symptoms to be similar to those reported by schizophrenics in Western countries and to include hallucinations, delusions, and withdrawal. The separation of the schizophrenic from others and the disruption of the cohesive family system is the most mysterious aspect of this illness to the normal population. It is not the disease itself that is puzzling but rather the inclination toward withdrawal and obsessive self-focus. The nature of the disease threatens collectivist values and clashes with ecological orientation and developmental niche.

Acculturation and Adaptation

The challenge of living, working, or studying in another culture is a common experience for an increasing number of today's young adults. It brings with it stresses that have both physical and psychological consequences for health. Perhaps more so than other life transitions, moving to a different culture changes a person's ecological systems at all levels. Changes in food and climate, language, financial issues, work/study problems, and loss of social network are among the concerns when one moves to a different culture. Therefore, it should not be a surprise that most "sojourners" experience their acculturation as stressful (Ryan and Twibell, 2000).

Although all acculturation is stressful, we differ in how we perceive stress and how we cope with it. The difference in response to acculturative stress is a result of the dynamics of a person's ecological system earlier in life (e.g., such as parents' characteristics), as well as the dynamics of the ecological system into which the person enters. Kim and Won (1997) learned that Chinese students reported experiencing more daily stress in their adaptation to a new environment than did Korean and Japanese students in comparable situations. Similarly, among African and Western students studying at Chinese universities, African students reported more stress in their daily lives than Western students, particularly in areas like climate, finances, reading and writing in Chinese, social activities, and academic performance (Hashim and Zhiliang, 2003).

Cross (1995) focused her research not so much on the perception of acculturative stress but on adaptation strategies employed by East Asian and American graduate students at the University of Michigan (U.S.A.). Students in the study came from South Korea, the People's Republic of China, Japan, and North America. East Asian students placed more emphasis on community and interdependence than did American students. On the other hand, American students exercised strong self-reliance and independence. When adapting to new surroundings, Americans considered expressing oneself and being an autonomic thinker as important cognitive skills. Those East Asian students who showed more preference for independence also used more direct coping strategies when addressing problems related to daily stress. More direct strategies were correlated with reduced level of stress, i.e., students of both cultures who were willing to take direct action when confronted with problems of adaptation were less distressed and healthier.

Adult Taiwanese, adjusting to life in the United States, experienced similar adaptation patterns. Ying and Liese (1990) recruited individuals at a seminar designed to prepare them for their overseas study and followed them through their "abroad experience." The researchers inquired about such areas as homesickness, physical complaints, levels of control, loneliness, social support, relationship problems, and perception of host country. The results indicated that those adults who took greater risks and became more actively involved during their studies were healthier and better adjusted. They experienced fewer physical difficulties than those who practiced traditional Chinese customs and declined involvement in day-to-day activities on campus. Good adjustment was also related to a sense of control; individuals felt more secure when they made decisions on their own, apart from family interference. Conversely, a decline in perceived control was associated with feelings of pressure to comply with family directives to strictly adhere to Chinese traditions. These and other findings lend support for the use of training programs as preparation for study or work-abroad experiences. If people can learn about the ecological system they are about to experience ahead of time, they may be able to adjust their coping strategies accordingly, making the transition from one culture to another a less stressful experience.

◇ LATER ADULTHOOD

When we think of aging, we frequently have mixed reactions. On the one hand, we think of a group of elderly people enjoying their "golden years" by visiting grandchildren, traveling, and perhaps volunteering. On the other hand, we sometimes perceive the elderly as frail, weak, dependent, and in need of extensive medical care. Certainly, among many North Americans and increasing numbers of older people in other cultures, this can be a disturbing and confusing time.

Disease and Premature Aging

Senescence, or *the process of biological aging,* and the health issues surrounding it have been the topic of much research and debate. Elderly persons experiencing the normal signs of aging often complain of reduced energy, vision and hearing loss, dried and wrinkled skin, brittle bones, slower reaction time, diminished motor skills, and sometimes a loss of memory. These complaints, some subtle and others less so, are common in most cultures and are often legitimate. But what about those who age before their time?

Following research conducted on a rare and cruel disease known as Werner's syndrome, scientists at the University of Washington put forth some ideas regarding the aging process. People suffering from this disorder experience all the signs of normal aging, but they do so beginning in their midtwenties and usually die before they reach their fiftieth birthday. They gray prematurely and develop wrinkled skin, first on the face, then on their hands, legs, and feet. They catch frequent colds, which often lead to pneumonia, and develop cancer, kidney and heart trouble, and osteoporosis. In addition, they show some of the same symptoms seen in Alzheimer's patients (e.g., problems in concentration, remembering, and decision making). In April 1996, scientists released findings that could be a major breakthrough in explaining why we age. They identified the Werner's gene, the first gene known to cause human aging. Although optimistically cautious, scientists at the National Institute on Aging called this discovery remarkable.

With more accurate identification and treatment of illnesses, as well as rapid advancements in technology, many cultures are experiencing lower mortality rates and longer life expectancies. However, the longer people live, the greater the chance of encountering a major physical or psychological problem. Throughout the world, many elderly die each year from heart disease, cancer, or stroke, and arthritis, osteoporosis, and injuries resulting from falls and other accidents require extended hospitalization or nursing home and hospice care for elderly sufferers.

Cultural Views on Dementia and Alzheimer's Disease

What is the relationship between age and psychological decline? How do a culture's ecocultural system and an individual's developmental niche contribute to the aging process? As just noted, in many industrialized nations people are living longer but at a cost to society. As the average lifespan has expanded, we have seen dramatic increases in cases of **dementia,** especially Alzheimer's disease (Ritchie & Lovestone, 2002). In the United States persons diagnosed with Alzheimer's represent about 10 percent of the population over the age of sixty-five and as much as 50 percent of those eighty-five and older

In the early stages, Alzheimer's disease resembles normal aging, with periodic memory loss, frequent agitation, problems speaking, and difficulty concentrating for long periods of time. However, as the disease worsens, the signs become more apparent. In the later stages, individuals forget how to perform the most basic tasks, such as changing clothes, eating, and going to the bathroom. They become completely dependent, require twenty-four-hour supervision, and are unable to recognize family members and medical personnel.

While older age and genetic predisposition may be two of the greatest risk factors in developing the illness, cultural influences may play a role that needs yet to be fully understood. An interesting study by Yamada and colleagues (2002) suggests that diet and eating habits may be an additional risk factor. These researchers found a notably higher frequency and severity of symptoms in their Japanese-Brazilian Alzheimer patients than in comparable samples of Japanese patients. An analysis of patients' dietary patterns revealed that the Japanese-Brazilian diet includes little fish and large amounts of meat—the opposite of the typical Japanese diet. While one study does not establish dietary patterns as a single risk factor, it certainly points to the desirability of considering ecocultural factors along with biological ones.

One factor that compounds the tragedy of Alzheimer's disease is our lack of understanding regarding its causes and diagnosis. Currently, the only reliable way of determining whether a person has Alzheimer's is after death, when an autopsy is performed. Analyses from some autopsies have shown a cluster of plaques and neuron tangles located near the hippocampus; these have been associated with rapid destruction of healthy brain tissue. This is a crippling disease that touches many people, including the late Ronald Reagan, former president of the United States.

How do caregivers in different cultures respond to an elderly person suffering from Alzheimer's or similar diseases of aging? How do cultural beliefs about family values and relationships influence the course of these diseases?

Regardless of where it strikes, the devastating effects of Alzheimer's disease affect many people. For example, caring for a loved one with Alzheimer's can be very stressful. This is evident in Strong's (1984) study of caregiver support for Alzheimer's disease patients, in which she compared American Indian and Caucasian caregivers and found that both groups felt equally frustrated, angry, guilty, anxious, and helpless. The gradual deterioration of the patient left caregivers in both groups searching for answers. American Indian caregivers were much more communal and interdependent and employed more supportive, although passive, strategies in coping with the stress. For instance, common comments were "We just have to get used to this. There's nothing you can do about it but try and make them comfortable." Caucasian caregivers, on the other hand, initially tried to handle the situation by themselves, rarely turning to others for help and support.

The difference in the way the two groups responded to the stress of caregiving reflects their culture's ecocultural system and their own developmental niche. Strong (1984) reports the perspective of an American Indian caregiver: "The white man . . . is torn between two ideals; on the one hand he believes in freedom, in minding his own business, and in the right of people to make up their own minds; but on the other hand, he believes that he should be his brother's keeper" (p. 29). In Indian society, taking care of family members is the chief responsibility of each person, and nobody is exempt.

In another study, Cox (1993) conducted personal interviews with eighty-six Hispanic caregivers in New York to examine the ways in which cultural values and norms influence behavior. Her findings concur with those of Strong's (1984), suggesting that family cohesiveness plays a significant role in caregivers' behavior. As with American Indian caregivers, Hispanics appeared to accept passively the stresses of caregiving and believe it is part of their heritage to take care of the afflicted member. At no point did caregivers in either study consider admitting their relative to a nursing home or hospice.

In 1991, Meng conducted a survey in China and reported that 96 percent of elderly persons reside with family members and are cared for until they die. Strong family interdependence and cohesiveness were shown to have a positive impact on the physical and mental health of weak and frail elderly parents living at home. At no point in caring for their aging parents did caregivers consider the possibility of sending them to a medical facility or nursing home. To do so would have brought immediate disapproval and shame from the community. These findings are consistent with those obtained by Frazier and Glascock (1994) in their work with the frail elderly living in a kibbutz community in Israel. Kalu and Kalu (1993) found that frail elderly parents in Nigeria responded somewhat differently. Those who were plagued by physical and mental infirmities retrieved their umbilical cords, buried at birth in their native village. This act is believed to help slow down the aging process. The event is a festive, colorful celebration attended by family members and friends, who surround their loved one with love and support.

As we learn more about the genetic and environmental foundations of Alzheimer's and other diseases common among the elderly, along with methods of treatment from different parts of the world, we can anticipate that cures will be found in the future. These were among the goals discussed at the first Alzheimer's Association International Conference on the Prevention of Dementia held in Washington, D.C., in June 2005. In the meantime, efforts to discover why a person's brain at some point in the lifespan begins to self-destruct continue.

Coping with Chronic Illness in Older Age

Faced with the prospect of failing health and developing chronic illness in older age, coping becomes more critical for survival and maintenance of one's quality of life in later years. Geriatric researchers Becker and Newsom (2005) provide a good example of how the specific historical, cultural, and social context of African Americans in the United States has shaped their responses to, and coping with, chronic illness later in life. In particular, this segment of the population has developed coping strategies that emphasize reliance on self, community, and spirituality rather than reliance on health services. Johnson, Elbert-Avila, and Tulsky (2005) add that these coping strategies develop in response to ecological systems in which older African Americans often experience economic disadvantages and a lack of access to health services. As a result, they seek out the resources available to them such as the support of family, community, and spiritual leaders. Similarly, Polyakova and Pacquaio (2006) describe how older immigrants from the former Soviet Union bring their cultural values and beliefs about illness and coping to their new cultural environment, building a unique developmental niche. Older immigrants cope with chronic illness by using distractions and by keeping active with hobbies. They also describe family support as important, especially the assurance by family members that the person's illness is just part of life and he or she can deal with the problem successfully.

◇ SUMMARY

When we think about health and related issues, we usually don't consider the many ways these might be affected by culture. How do cultural beliefs influence one's well-being and ill health? This chapter explores cultural differences in health care and beliefs that influence development across the lifespan. We began with an overview of how standardized tests and diagnostic techniques often are incapable of detecting medical problems in cultures other than those for which they were originally designed. We discussed the expression of illness symptoms and how they may be interpreted differently across cultures. Furthermore, the way individuals respond to illness and cope with it is also largely influenced by the cultural and ecological system.

Health problems, at birth and shortly afterward (e.g., preterm and low-birth-weight infants), can cause considerable concern for parents in many cultures. Variations in parental cultural beliefs, discussed extensively in previous chapters, play a major role in the way cultures care for problem birth infants.

Health issues during adolescence focus on the adolescent's search for the perfect body and physical appearance. Cultural variations in the occurrence and treatment of eating disorders such as anorexia and bulimia were examined in depth. Sexually transmitted diseases (STDs), including AIDS, also were discussed.

In early adulthood, pressures to achieve and to form interpersonal relationships with one's peers are frequently accompanied by the stress of adaptation and acculturation; these stressors produce a variety of medical problems.

The ability to maintain a healthy lifestyle grows increasingly difficult for families that migrate to different countries. Similar difficulties exist for students who pursue formal education in other countries. Several cross-cultural studies involving the resettlement of young adults were examined.

Middle adulthood is sometimes referred to as the "sandwich generation," during which parents attempt to balance their own needs with the physical and emotional needs of their aging parents and growing children. This period can present unique challenges and produce medical problems, including depression and schizophrenia. Cross-cultural research indicates that each culture approaches and treats these illnesses differently, depending on the ecocultural system and developmental niche.

The last stage in the lifespan, later adulthood, is often viewed as the "golden years," with opportunities for retirement and travel. However, this stage is also characterized by health problems. In the closing section, a cross-cultural comparison of the status of the elderly was addressed, along with cultural practices for nurturing those afflicted with dementia and Alzheimer's disease. In the end, older adults often create an ecological system for themselves that supports them in their adjustment to the health challenges of older age.

◇ STUDY QUESTIONS

Provide examples of how cultural beliefs and traditions affect the delivery of health care in Western and nonwestern cultures.

Define culture-bound syndrome, and explain the reciprocal process that exists between cultural beliefs and the methods used to diagnose and treat physical and psychological disorders.

Distinguish between emic and etic aspects of health and culture, and discuss how each culture's delicate balance of ecological systems and developmental niche need to be considered when diagnosing and treating illness.

Discuss research devoted to the relationship between culture and sudden infant death syndrome, childhood mental health, eating disorders, STDs and adolescent drug use, depression, schizophrenia, and dementia.

◇ FURTHER READINGS

Boston Women's Health Book Collective. (1992). *The New Our Bodies, Ourselves.* New York: Simon & Schuster.

> This highly enjoyable and easy-to-read paperback addresses a wide range of women's health concerns. Topics covered include STDs and AIDS, chronic fatigue syndrome, sexual myths, menopause, breast reconstruction after mastectomy, and depression. A great book for either casual reading or for sparking open classroom discussion.

S. Kazarian and D. Evans (Eds). (2001). *Handbook of Cultural Health Psychology.* San Diego, CA: Academic Press.

> This collection provides a state of the art understanding of what is known and not known about the rapidly emerging field of cultural health psychology. The editors take a multicultural approach providing a diversity of perspectives by acknowledged experts in a wide range of crucial topics. Case studies are well designed and helpful in highlighting the major concepts within a chapter.

David B. Morris. (1998). *Illness and Culture in the Postmodern Age.* Berkeley: University of California Press.

> In a narrative account, the author follows the concept of health and illness through modern history into the late twentieth century, providing a context for talk about health and illness, medicine and suffering. Anyone who wants to understand why people get sick differently in different cultures and what's making us sick here and now will enjoy this book.

Renee Rose Shield and Stanley M. Aronson (2003). *Aging in Today's World: Conversations Between an Anthropologist and a Physician.* New York: Berghahn Books.

> In a unique approach, each author explores a different aspect of aging in alternating chapters, in turn followed by a commentary by the other. The authors interrupt each other within chapters to raise questions, contradict, ask for clarification, and explore related ideas—emphasizing the dynamic nature of their ideas about age. Finally, a third "voice," that of a random old man, periodically "speaks" to remind the authors of their limited understanding of the subject.

Ronald C. Simons and Charles C. Hughes. (Eds.). (1985). *The Culture-Bound Syndrome: Folk Illnesses of Psychiatric and Anthropological Interest.* Dodrecht, Netherlands: D. Reidel Publishing Company.

> One of the best available compilations on culture-bound syndromes from many areas of the globe.

E. M. Suh and S. Oishi. (2002). Subjective well-being across cultures. In W. J. Lonner, D. L. Dinnel, S. A. Hayes, & D. N. Sattler (Eds.), *Online Readings in Psychology and Culture* (Unit 7, Chapter 1), (http://www.wwu.edu/~culture), Center for Cross-Cultural Research, Western Washington University, Bellingham, Washington.

> This on-line chapter suggests that all individuals strive to be happy. How they pursue this ultimate human goal, however, seems to vary in interesting ways across cultures. Three key findings have emerged from recent scientific research: 1) individualist cultures are happier than collectivists, 2) psychological attributes characterizing the self (e.g., self-esteem, self-consistency) are more relevant to the happiness of Western individualists than to the happiness of collectivists, and 3) the self-judgment of happiness is anchored on different types of cues and experiences across cultures.

◇ DEVELOPMENTAL ANALYSIS

CULTURE AND HEALTH

My parents and older relatives have often told me that I was a very healthy baby. As I looked at pictures of my younger days, I came to wonder whether "healthy" was another way of saying "plump." I weighed nearly nine pounds at birth, which was quite rare for that era. From the time I was just two months old, I slept in a crib alone in my own bedroom. My parents often teased that they thought I would become an opera singer one day so I could put the strong set of lungs I developed (through countless hours of crying) to good use! Some of the more difficult cries to comfort a baby though are those related to teething. While my siblings and I were teething, my mother's favorite remedy was to put a little brandy on her finger and let us suck on it. The brandy tasted good and helped to numb the feeling of pain in our gums. Not exactly modern medicine, but it seemed to work!

As a child, I remained active by playing outdoors and doing chores on the farm. I was a little larger than the other children my age but always felt accepted by my peers and family. Through regular exercise, and an eventual growth spurt at age 14, I grew into a well-proportioned adolescent. During adolescence, I learned about intoxicants. My parents received a letter from my health teacher, explaining that we were learning about the dangers of drugs at school. The teacher suggested that these messages be reinforced at home. Although the legal drinking age was only 18 years at the time, underage drinking was a problem parents and teenagers had to address. When my parents discussed the dangers of alcohol, tobacco, and other drugs, they spoke about the legal ramifications as well as the physical consequences. I learned that my ability to think, breathe, exercise, and even have children could be compromised by the effects of intoxicants. Fortunately, my peer group was strong, and we encouraged one another to stay clear of drugs. (My mother assured me that the brandy I consumed at age one was not detrimental to my health!). As a parent, I was impressed with the public movement to educate children on the dangers of drugs. When my son, Alexander, was 15 years old, he participated in a school program focused on keeping children's bodies free of drugs. The group hosted alcohol-free parties and dances. He and his friends remained very involved in the program through graduation. These types of programs provide adolescents with useful information, education, and a solid sense of peer support.

Both of our children are grown now and have young children of their own. It has been delightful to watch our children grow as adults and into the roles of parents. Giorgio and I have also watched our own parents age and pass on. Both of Giorgio's parents passed away about ten years ago of heart disease and cancer, and my father passed away peacefully of old age two years later. My mother is still living and has begun to show early signs of Alzheimer's disease. As a result, we decided to move her to an assisted living facility last year so that she could receive more attentive care. The facility is a wonderful way for my mom to maintain her sense of independence, while also receiving excellent care by health professionals. She is active enough to participate in group activities and receives frequent visits from friends and family.

Giorgio and I have retired and fill our time with travel, visits with family, excursions with friends, and caring for those we love. We feel fortunate to be in good health and spirits. We try to keep our minds and bodies sharp by remaining active in the community and continually gaining new experiences. Last year, we began learning Tae Kwon Do and have earned our yellow belts! Our grandson is catching up to us by attempting to get *his* orange belt!

It has been fun documenting my life in this way and to observe the various cultural influences on my development. I also enjoyed exploring the changing cultural influences my husband Giorgio and I have had on the lives of our own children. Perhaps they, like you, will document their lives and cultural journey as well. I wish you all the best—*buona fortuna!*

CHAPTER ELEVEN

LOOKING TO
THE FUTURE

*Phyllidia Ramirez is eleven and lives with her mother, Nina, in a village high in the
mountains in the middle of Nicaragua's Central Highlands. Like many Nicaraguan
women, Nina has lived a large part of her life as a single mother. Her husband, Luis,
was a migrant laborer who left home each year for several months to harvest cotton in
the lowlands of the Pacific region. The long absences caused serious disruptions, and he
abandoned the family when Phyllidia was five years old. Nina and Phyllidia both
work part time harvesting coffee. Although schools in the area are underfunded and
inadequate, family and kinship are important, and through compadrazgo—a system
of "coparenthood" that links parents, children, and godparents—Phyllidia is learning
Spanish and weaving skills from her godmother, Maria.*

*Montreal, the largest city in the province of Quebec, differs greatly from the rest of
Canada due to the prominence of its French culture and language, as well as the fact
that most of its inhabitants belong to the Roman Catholic Church. Michel Lamoureux,
thirteen years old, lives here with his mother Sylvie, father Jacques, brother Pierre,
and sister Lise. His parents are well-to-do and are able to send their children to private
Catholic schools and provide private lessons in foreign language, golf, and tennis. They
set high standards for their children and, because their careers frequently keep them
away from home, give Michel, the oldest child, a great deal of responsibility for the care
of his younger brother and sister.*

Our exploration of lives across cultures is nearly over. Before our journey
comes to an end, we would like to briefly revisit our major themes, reconsider
some of the theories we have discussed, and offer suggestions for modifying
these to meet the needs of a rapidly changing world. A few simple revisions

in specific theoretical positions might help make these theories more useful and appropriate for the study of lives across cultures. Finally, as we come to the end of our journey, we would like to gaze into our crystal ball and speculate as to where the young field of cross-cultural human development might be heading and make some recommendations for future research as we move towards the end of the first decade of the twenty-first century.

◇ LOOKING BACK: A REVIEW OF MAJOR THEMES AND THEORIES

We begin with a review of the major theories introduced in Chapter 2 and addressed throughout subsequent chapters. Our purpose in doing this is to take one last look at the ideas we have scattered throughout chapters and pull them together into a final statement stressing the importance of viewing human development from a cross-cultural perspective and within a cultural context.

The chapter closes with a look at the future—the theories, topics, issues, and research that will determine the directions that the study of cross-cultural human development will take in the future and how this new knowledge will lead to a better understanding of the effects of culture on behavior and how these might help improve lives across cultures.

Ecological Model

As you will recall, the ecological model of Bronfenbrenner (1989, 1993, 2000, 2005) focuses on the reciprocal relationships between and among children, their parents, and other family members, and their connection with larger social and cultural traditions as well as the interaction among biological, sociocultural, and psychological factors in human development. Throughout the pages of this book, we have seen, through the use of opening vignettes, how the lives of individuals are deeply embedded in distinctly different ecocultural systems reflecting long-held and well-established patterns of thought and behavior governed by the interaction of micro-, meso-, exo-, and macrosystems (see Figure 2.1 in Chapter 2).

In terms of the microsystem (the cultural setting in which adult–child interactions take place at home or at school), we can see that the young lives of Phyllidia in Nicaragua and Michel in Canada, at the opening of this chapter, have been influenced in a variety of ways by their cultural surroundings.

At the same time, parts of each of their microsystems have been in contact with a second, larger circle of influence, the mesosystem, consisting of a number of overlapping social settings that have also helped to shape the individual development of Phyllidia and Michel. For example, Michel's private tutorial sessions are a routine activity among the upper-middle-class families in the educational community in Montreal.

The work of harvesting coffee is regularly performed
by Nicaraguan women and girls. (© Larry Luxner/
D. Donne Bryant Stock)

Beyond this is the exosystem, consisting of community institutions that individuals experience indirectly. In Michel's case, his private school curriculum reflects the content and skill areas believed to be important in attaining competency, even though he was not directly involved in setting curricula.

Then, there is the macrosystem made up of the prominent cultural values and attitudes that influence a person's maturation. In Michel's case, religious beliefs provide the foundation for worship and daily living. In Phyllidia's single-parent household, her part-time job and close contact with extended family reflect the values of the macrosystem found in most Nicaraguan villages.

As we saw in earlier chapters, sometimes several macrosystems operate within a single culture. In Malaysia and Singapore, for example, one macrosystem consists of a rapidly emerging group of young middle-class wage earners who are moving out of their parents' homes in an effort to achieve personal success and financial independence. Another represents the more traditional extended family system, in which parents and grandparents serve as principal caregivers for children, even those well into their adult years.

Since one of the major goals of cross-cultural research is to be aware of the varying influences of culture on behavior, by looking at how children interact within their culture's unique ecological system and gradually carve out a developmental niche, we hopefully have laid the foundation for a better understanding of how these forces shape and change development across the cultures we have considered, as well as those the reader may encounter in the future.

Developmental Niche

The concept of a developmental niche has contributed greatly to our understanding of the ways in which different components of a culture work together as a system and how parents and children behave within normal everyday settings.

Applying the developmental niche concept to the vignettes at the opening of this chapter, we can see how Nina's experience as a single mother affects her daughter Phyllidia's views of work and family relationships. Similarly, Michel's parents' expectations regarding his responsibilities toward caring for his younger brother and sister help shape Michel's values and attitudes. Each of these vignettes presents the child's unique developmental niche and how it operates within the larger ecological system (see Figure 2.2 in Chapter 2). Over the lifespan, Phyllidia and Michel will each continue to react and respond to thousands of cultural messages that will eventually become internalized and help them understand their world and themselves.

Taken together, the ecological model and the developmental niche provide a method for examining the social context of any group of people and explaining the similarities and differences in behavior from a cross-cultural and developmental perspective.

While relatively few cross-cultural studies have been specifically designed to compare cultures based on the developmental niche framework, a recent example is worth noting. Schwarz, Schafermeier, & Trommsdorff (2005) report results of two studies on the relationship among cultural values, parental beliefs, and parenting practices, with a focus on similarities and differences between German and South Korean mothers. Among the findings were those that showed Korean mothers to be less individualistic than German mothers, with a preference for group-oriented and achievement-oriented child-rearing goals. They were also more strict and controlling with their children. The authors emphasize that the results " . . . have shown that child-rearing goals are related to parenting behavior . . . [and] . . . this is in line with some of the assumptions of the developmental niche" (p. 224).

Vygotsky's Sociocultural Theory

As we discussed in Chapter 2, Vygotsky offers a contextualist's approach to the study of cognitive development. While most mainstream Western developmental theories have traditionally viewed individuals as separate from their physical and social environments, Vygotsky believed that human development occurs over time *within* the context of culture. His influential mentor and friend, Alexandria Luria (1981), captured the essence of Vygotsky's theory best when he stated, "In order to explain the highly complex forms of human consciousness one must go beyond the human organism. One must seek the origins of conscious activity . . . in the external processes of social life, in the social and historical forms of human existence" (p. 25). Notice the contrast between the strong individualistic assumptions found in much of the psychological research conducted in Western societies and the historical and sociocultural contextualist approach employed by Vygotsky.

As Kagitcibasi (1996) has cogently observed, "This important body of thinking and research has brought in a corrective to traditional work in mainstream developmental psychology that was oblivious of culture. It has also helped to create a recognition of the 'indigenous' cognitive competence of people (children and adults alike) who were too readily labeled as lacking in competence because they did not perform well on standard psychometric tests . . . or school-related activities. Finally, it has contributed to a better understanding of the interactive nature of the learning process" (pp. 39–40).

If we apply Vygotsky's zone of proximal development (the amount of assistance an individual needs from others in contrast to how much he can do without help) to this chapter's opening vignettes, we see that the guided instructions provided by Phyllidia's godmother in the teaching and learning of weaving reflects both the family's ecological surroundings, as well as her developmental niche. As Maria, the godmother, mentors Phyllidia's apprenticeship, she will move through the zone and increase her weaving skills. Her contributions to the family's collection of woven blankets and other objects strengthen her creativity, while promoting family cohesiveness, cultural identification, and interdependency.

In the case of Michel, he is being carefully trained by his golf coach to develop good putting skills. In the early stages, Michel needed lots of advice and practice drills to master the basics of good form. As Michel has improved and moved through the zone, demonstrating increased competency, his coach gradually removes the amount of assistance offered until Michel can proceed without further help. In both of these situations, it is likely that elements of the ecological context—such as climate, types of terrain, urban or rural setting, population density, health care, and other factors—will be intertwined within a variety of social contexts. In short, culture is, to a large extent, a group's response to its physical ecology, ancestral heritage, and developmental niche.

While Vgotskly's theory does have its problems, we believe it is certain to receive increased attention from cross-cultural developmental researchers in the decades ahead. This has surely been the case with the theorist we look at next—Jean Piaget.

Piaget's Cognitive Developmental Theory

Applying Piaget's theory to our opening vignettes, it is clear that eleven-year-old Phyllidia's ability to recreate her godmother's weaving skills requires that she has the ability to distinguish between types and amounts of materials used, to be able to use symbols creatively, and to infer cause-and-effect relationships—all characteristics of concrete operational thinking described in Chapter 2. On the other hand, Michel's ability to hold the golf club properly and to speculate what will happen if the ball is driven three hundred yards or more requires that he be able to make use of hypotheses and form abstractions regarding golf skills. When he is able to do this, he displays some of the characteristics associated with formal operational thinking.

While each of these vignettes describes life in different cultures, the unique ecological settings, specific developmental niche, and distinctive social interactions experienced by Michel and Phyllidia strongly influence the nature and timing of the development of their cognitive abilities.

Kohlberg's Theory of Moral Development

According to Kohlberg, morality is based on a belief in general principles of justice and consists of six levels, ranging from an immature obedience and punishment orientation to an advanced application of universal ethical principles (see Chapter 2 for a detailed description).

Gilligan (1982) severely criticized Kohlberg's approach and suggested that moral reasoning among women is more likely defined by a caring attitude and the maintenance of a network of relationships rather than by rules and abstract principles of justice. However, Gilligan did not take the next logical step and formulate an alternative developmental model that would integrate both orientations (caring and justice) into an understanding of moral development.

From a cross-cultural perspective, Kohlberg's model is clearly limited in its research application. Based on Gilligan's critique that the justice orientation is not the only way of viewing morality, we wonder how many other moral orientations may be present in other cultures. For example, in Japan, an individual frequently makes moral decisions based on a strict code of honor in which behavior is seen as right because it is the honorable thing to do. A common example involves the resignation of a company's president when someone in the organization behaves badly or commits an immoral act (e.g., overbilling), even though the president had no direct knowledge of, or connection to, the misbehavior. Moral reasoning such as this fits neither the justice nor the caring orientation and suggests that there are significant opportunities for more research in the area of moral development.

In this regard, a rarely cited model of moral development has been put forth by Haan, Aerts, and Cooper (1985). She and her colleagues propose that development of moral reasoning is not determined by general orientations, such as caring or justice, but is the result of understanding the interdependence of self and others that occurs in social interactions. In her model, morality is viewed as a form of social agreement that equalizes individuals' relations with each other, taking into account that when disagreements or disputes arise, all parties make their issues clearly known (Haan, 1991). Thus, moral solutions generally focus on a specific situation, involving a specifc group of people, at a given time, and devote careful consideration to what each person needs and deserves, recognizing that these may vary at different times. In other words, the most mature moral reasoner attempts to make a moral decision that balances her needs, desires, strengths, and weaknesses with those of others affected by a particular moral issue. Situations involving conflicting needs frequently become severely emotional, because the fundamental form of moral action is dialogue or talk, which often provokes high levels of stress, which, in turn, also play a major role in moral decision making. In her research focusing on stressful moral situations, Haan found that individuals who were able to control their emotions, objectively consider a variety of possible solutions, be empathetic, and demonstrate the ability to "cope rather than defend" showed higher levels of moral action. In this view, moral reasoning would take on different forms in different cultures, simply because of wide variations in what is considered a need, desire, strength, or weakness and, unlike many other models of moral development, emphasizes the interactional nature of morality.

The potential usefulness of Haan's model (1991) for the study of moral development across cultures, as well as its relevance to the major themes expressed throughout this book, permit us to study moral reasoning within the context of culture-specific interactions and culture-specific moral issues, resulting in an emic approach to moral development. For example, in a highly individualistic culture such as the United States, most individuals accept as fair the notion that those of greater ability receive higher pay. However, in a collective setting, like the one found in a kibbutz, it may be equally fair that individuals get paid according to their needs, not what they actually earn by their own work. While both concepts of what is fair or right are valid in each culture, they can only be reasonably evaluated within the appropriate context.

Applying these concepts of moral development to our opening vignettes suggests that Michel's view of what is right or wrong is strongly influenced by the religious values taught as part of his Roman Catholic faith, a centerpiece of the Quebec culture in which he lives. Although the majority of Nicaraguans during the early 1990s were nominally Roman Catholic, according to Merrill (1994), the church "touches the lives of most Nicaraguans only sporadically at best" (p. 84). Like most living in rural villages far from an organized church, Phyllidia has likely been taught the basics of moral behavior as defined by her parents and community—for example, being nice to others, saying only good things, not stealing, and "having a strong belief in divine power over human affairs . . . reflected in the use of phrases such as 'God willing' or 'if it is God's desire' in discussions of future events" (Merrill, 1994, p. 85).

Erikson's Theory of Psychosocial Development

We can think of Erikson's theory (1963) as analogous to a book with eight chapters. Like chapters in a "Book of Life," his developmental stages follow one another. Sometimes an issue introduced in one chapter is carried over into the next and may not be fully resolved until much later in the book. In order to understand the story completely and make sense of the plot, the reader must read the eight chapters in chronological order. As infants and children pass through the first four stages of Erikson's theory, they are confronted by a series of psychosocial crises (turning points with two possible resolutions, one positive and one negative) requiring successful resolution if healthy development is to take place at a later stage. These crises center on trust versus mistrust, autonomy versus shame and doubt, initiative versus guilt, and industry versus inferiority. The adolescent and young adult encounter the issue of identity versus role confusion, or identity diffusion. The mature adult first faces the challenge of intimacy versus isolation, followed by generativity versus stagnation or self-absorption. Finally, the older adult needs to resolve issues related to integrity versus despair. Erikson views these crises as a natural development common to everyone, regardless of their culture, through which we come to understand ourselves and our relationships with others. However, as with other stage theories, Erikson's approach is subject to the criticism that stages may vary from one culture to another in the time of occurrence, duration, and content.

Considering what we know about the subjects in our opening vignettes, we might hypothesize that Phyllidia and Michel have both been raised in warm and caring family environments, in which they developed the trust that allowed them to explore their surroundings and establish positive social relationships with family members. With supportive parents, they gradually developed control over their behavior, realizing that their intentions could be acted out through imitation of those around them. Michel, guided by his teachers in school, influenced by his golfing instructor in private lessons, and encouraged by his parents to take responsibility for his younger siblings, has developed a strong sense of industry and is on the verge of establishing a strong personal identity. Phyllidia, working part time alongside her mother, harvesting coffee as well as learning her culture's weaving skills from her godmother, feels an equally strong sense of industry and, in the life of her village, is on the verge of womanhood and preparing to assume an adult identity.

While Erikson's theory works well as a general framework within which some specific lifespan changes can be described and interpreted, it is less useful as a model for cross-cultural experimentation. This is not to say, that with some modification and attention to cultural considerations, his ideas could not be usefully applied to human development within the cultural context. In fact, efforts directed at such endeavors might prove quite interesting as we have shown at various places throughout this book. On the other hand, an approach that may be more useful in accounting for the cultural context of lifespan development has been offered by Cantor and her associates (Cantor, Norem, Niedenthal, Langston, & Brower, 1987; Cantor et al, 1991).

Using the concept of "life-tasks" (the underlying goals that guide an individual's life or everyday behavior at a given time), Cantor and others (1987) studied a group of undergraduate students in the United States by having them keep records detailing their daily activities. While recording their activities, they also answered questions about the people they were with and their feelings about the activities. Findings revealed that students shared several "life-tasks," the two most important being "making friends" and "getting good grades." One advantage of using an approach like Cantor's in cross-cultural research is that it relies on self-generated "themes" based on people's culture-specific experience. This makes for a more emic approach than imposing a set of preformulated "themes" on individuals, as is the case with universalist theories such as Erikson's.

We are encouraged by the development of new approaches like this and encourage others to consider using them in formulating their cross-cultural human development research efforts.

◇ WHERE DO WE GO FROM HERE? THOUGHTS AND CHALLENGES FOR THE FUTURE

Traditionally, the literature in mainstream developmental psychology has emphasized a Western European and North American orientation. For too long there has been what we might call a "psychological research ethnocentrism," that is, the assumption that research findings reported from studies conducted in one culture applied equally well to other cultures. Yet, Harkness and Keefer (2000) caution that "in our search for cross-cultural validity in comparative research, we must make sure to avoid a new kind of ethnocentrism based on non-Western constructs or measures. Such an approach would be as unrealistic as the former mistake of imposing Western measures on other contexts . . . [and we must avoid the] . . . problem of oversimplification of cultural variability—complete relativism, in which cross-cultural comparisons become impossible" (p. 105).

Although Harkness & Keefer's point is well-taken, we do believe it is important to continue to conduct additional indigenous developmental studies. Recent research has demonstrated that concepts first identified indigenously (in one culture, often nonWestern) frequently have a significant degree of validity when operationally defined and incorporated into multicultural studies. For example, Yamuguchi's (2004) study of *amae* has shown that this concept is related to constructs (e.g., attachment) in the United States (and other cultures). Japanese researchers, as well as others, admit that the term **amae,** a Japanese word, is difficult to define. It is generally used to describe *behavior aimed at inducing another person, such as a parent, spouse, teacher, boss or other individual, to take care of oneself.* Takeo Doi (1973), the first to discuss the concept, defined it as *indulgent dependency.* In other words, the person who is carrying out *amae* may selfishly beg, plead, or act childishly, knowing that the caregiver will forgive and indulge the person. While once thought to be unique to Japan, similar behavior has been observed throughout Asia and may have its equivalent in some Western or African countries as well (Smith & Nomi, 2000). Here is an emic or culture-specific concept that, with further research, may be shown to be an etic or universal or culture-general concept. For these reasons, we would like to see more research conducted on this interesting cultural concept.

Other research worthy of recognition and further investigation includes the work of Cheung & Leung (1998) on indigenous measures of Chinese personality dimensions, and Kwan, Bond, & Singelis (1997) on measurement of relationship harmony. In addition, measures of **budi values** (*generosity, respect, sincerity and righteousness*) in Malaysia have been shown to account for variances explained by Schwartz's value survey items (an approach receiving increasing attention among cross-cultural developmentalists). Finally, Boski (2005) has identified **humanism** (defined as *a concern for personal relationships combined with endorsement of personal responsibility and a rejection of materialism*) and **sarmatism** (*a mix of impulsive self-assertion and social hedonism,* deriving from values once espoused by the Polish nobility) as key Polish values.

In the future we also hope to see additional studies that enhance our understanding of the nature of cultural differences and their importance. This would include studies that challenge the validity of derogatory ethnic and national stereotypes by publicizing empirically-based findings on the values, beliefs, and life experiences of different groups, as well as studies that challenge those people who assert that cultural differences either do not exist or can be ignored.

Although we have seen a steady increase in developmental studies in recent years, much of this research still focuses on childhood and adolescence within a Western context. By comparison, relatively few studies have addressed cultural variations in adulthood and old age, and even fewer have examined the end of the lifespan in nonWestern societies.

A welcome addition to the applied developmental literature is a recent volume that focuses on the contemporary culture of Japan, but demonstrates the universality of the research problems discussed (Shwalb, Nakazawa, & Shwalb, 2005). Included among the topics are the effects of video games, *manga,* comics, and television on children's development, literacy acquisition (Japan's rate is nearly 100%), innovative techniques for dealing with children's disabilities, and concern with bullying (a topic on which Japanese researchers have been at the forefront). One of the strengths of this book is the easy access for international researchers and readers to important findings by contemporary Japanese developmentalists. Another strength is the authors' choice of key issues and an emphasis on how culture guides research and theory and ways in which findings have been shown to have universal applications beyond the culture in which they were found. If only we had more books like this one. We are hopeful that the authors' strong emphasis on originality of topics and research approaches, along with attempts at universal applications, will serve as a model for activities in other cultural contexts.

By placing culture at the center of human development, we gain a better appreciation for the enormous influence culture has on our physical, cognitive, social, and emotional development. In the process, we may also find solutions for some of our most pressing global concerns. More than twenty-five years ago, Heron and Kroeger (1981) stated that "any serious and systematic attempt to study human behavior and experience must, in the very nature of things, be both developmental in depth and cross-cultural in breadth" (p. 1). Not many years ago, a similar concern was expressed by Valsiner and Lawrence (1997), who make the point that "to understand how development occurs throughout life it is necessary to locate developing individuals within their specific cultures" (p. 71).

In the next several years, we predict an increasing interest in viewing human development within an ecological and cross-cultural developmental perspective. Several recent efforts are at the forefront of this movement. One is the previously mentioned work of Kagitcibasi (1996), whose perspective is similar to ours, in that she takes a contextual-developmental-functional approach to human development, with the added goal of applying her findings to social policy issues in her native Turkey, most notably in the "Turkish Early Enrichment Project." In doing this, she moves from a position of theory to one of application, focusing on the fields of early childhood care and education. These are areas of induced change in which cross-cultural findings on human development can be used to develop intervention strategies and policy positions relevant to children and families within varying cultural contexts (Bronfenbrenner, 2005; Harkness et al., 2006).

An extensive study by Mishra, Sinha, and Berry (1996), examining the psychological adaptation of tribal groups in India, is yet another example of the type of research we hope to see more of in the future. Three groups (the Asur, Oraon, and Birhar), differing in settlement and occupation patterns, were compared in terms of cultural lifestyles, patterns of child socialization, cognitive behavior, and acculturation attitudes and experiences. These authors also focus on the application of their findings, this time to problems of acculturative stress. In the decades ahead, we predict there will be more studies that focus on the practical application of findings to real-world problems. We only wish there were more such examples at the present time.

In a review of cultural influences on child development, Super and Harkness (1997) have presented theoretical principles and research evidence in support of three specific approaches that, while varying in focus, emphasize "the structured, dynamic and integrative nature of the environment."

These approaches include their developmental niche concept, which we have referred to extensively throughout this book, Worthman's proposed theory of developmental microniche (1994, 1995), and Weisner's work on the ecocultural niche (Weisner, 2002).

Following a comprehensive review of contemporary evidence, they point to three recurring themes they believe "will continue to occupy a central place in the work that lies ahead: how best to conceptualize variability within and across cultural settings, to characterize activities of the child's mind, and to improve methodological rigor in research in culture and development" (p. 30).

In a review of cross-cultural human development research, Gardiner (2004) raised several critical and challenging questions that need to be answered in the near future: What types of cross-cultural developmental studies will be conducted in the future? How similar or different should these be to current research? In what ways will these studies contribute to our understanding of human development and the ever-changing and increasingly complex world in which people live? What implications will future research findings have for the construction of new developmental theories, and how will these new theories affect the design of even newer studies?

We are, in fact, beginning to see some possible answers to a few of these questions (Smith, 2004). Before we bring our discussions to a close, let us look at some of the topics to which we have given a great deal of attention, consider the implications of recent research and some of the proposals for future research, and comment on the benefits of understanding cross-cultural development and how this might help readers apply the ideas and findings to their own everyday lives. We shall do this, more or less, in the order in which topics were originally introduced, beginning with theories and methodology.

In Chapter 2, we pointed out that a single macrotheory (one designed to describe, explain, understand, and predict all aspects of an individual's development) is unlikely ever to appear, although some theories will explain more behavior than will others. Instead, recent trends toward the development of "minitheories" (efforts focused on limited and specific facets of development and behavior) are likely to continue in the future. In a summary of recent trends in human development theorizing, Thomas (2001) asserts that a conflict exists between traditional and more recent interpretations of development, and this is expected to continue "with traditional belief systems probably losing adherents as a result of the spread of literacy and the inevitable increase in international communication and intercultural exchange during the coming years" (p. 278).

Michael Cole introduced a "somewhat unorthodox" strategy for conducting cross-cultural developmental research that shows promise for those interested in designing specific environments for the study of children. He took this approach because of his . . . "long term dissatisfaction with the difficulties of conducting methodologically adequate cross-cultural research involving large demographic groups or entire nations, combined with my growing interest in specifying the role of culture in development in rather precise detail" (2005, p. 54). In order to conduct these kinds of studies, he borrowed Gary Alan Fine's (1989) concept of an **idioculture,** or " . . . *a cultural formation that emerges in a small group: system of knowledge, beliefs, behaviors, and customs shared by members of an interacting group to which members can refer and that serve as the basis of further interatction*" (p. 125). He illustrates his approach in which he uses cross-cultural psychology to design afterschool educational activities in a variety of cultural settings in what he calls the "**Fifth Dimension,**" or *"an educational activity system that offers school-aged children a specially designed environment in which to explore a variety of off-the-shelf computer games and game-like educational activities during the afterschool hours"* (2005, p. 56). For more about this approach, see Cole's chapter in the *Culture and Human Development* book listed in the "Further Readings" section at the close of this chapter. Additional information on the "Fifth Dimension" and after-school programs can be found at *www.uclinks.org*.

Also in Chapter 2, we identified some of the problems in conducting cross-cultural research. A researcher who has dealt extensively with these issues, Fons van de Vijver, looks at the future in this way: "The major methodological task ahead of us is the change from an 'adjustment perspective,' by which we adopted and adjusted prevailing methodologies, to a truly cultural perspective that transcends the borders of a specific cultural context" (2001, p. 91). He proposes that future efforts will be directed at developing methodologies "tailor-made" for cross-cultural research and, in order to accomplish this, he suggests that the field draw on experiences from the various branches of psychology (e.g., developmental, experimental, social, abnormal, etc.). We would also encourage, as we have many times before, closer interdisciplinary cooperation and sharing of ideas, where appropriate, with our colleagues in sociology and anthropology who, in many cases, are confronting similar problems and concerns.

Before these long-term goals of cross-cultural research can be accomplished, van de Vijver cites the need for two antecedent developments: (1) innovations in statistical approaches; e.g., development of multilevel models allowing for the simultaneous study of individual and cultural differences to determine if a concept such as individualism is the same at the individual and cultural levels, and (2) wider distribution and acceptance of guidelines for the appropriate design and carrying out of cross-cultural research; e.g., awareness of bias in selection of subjects and populations, equivalence in meaning of concepts, instruments, methodology, interpretation of scores, etc. See our earlier discussion in Chapter 2 regarding some of these guidelines.

In Chapter 3 we focused on what we believe to be one of the most important concepts in human development, namely socialization. In a review of parental socialization and children's values, Grusec (2002) points out that researchers have significantly altered their theoretical approaches to the study of socialization and introduced more refined and sophisticated methods for measuring its dimensions and outcomes. She states that, "At the moment, developmentalists are only beginning to understand how biology, context, and environment interact, and the amount of variance explained in studies is generally not large" (p. 162). However, she asserts that future studies that employ longitudinal designs, larger sample sizes, variables in interaction, "will help to untangle the specific contributions of parent and child to the socialization process . . . [and will] . . . allow the use of causal modeling techniques . . . to suggest the relative contributions of parent and child at given points in time to various outcomes having to do with socialization" (p. 162). Many of these ideas and suggestions for future research are discussed in *Handbook of Socialization* (Grusec & Hastings, 2006). Also contributing to a better understanding of parenting and socialization, will be findings emerging from the field of molecular genetics and the associations beginning to be made between genes and behavioral traits and characteristics (Plomin & Rutter, 1998).

In terms of physical growth and development (Chapter 4), efforts are being made worldwide to better understand cultural differences in these processes and to identity, understand, and treat children with a variety of disorders. With the completion of the human genome project and the advent of recombinant (synthetic) growth hormone for human beings, we expect a number of significant breakthroughs in this area. Adding to this are new discoveries and research emerging from the field of developmental neuroscience, showing the close relationships among genes, physical development, and environmental contexts. We anticipate exciting results in the years ahead from the various projects being conducted under the sponsorship of the National Institute of Child Health and Human Development (2001), aimed at ensuring that "every individual is born healthy, is born wanted, and has the opportunity to fulfill his or her potential for a productive life unhampered by disease or disability" (p. i).

A number of thought-provoking ideas receive attention in a volume by Richerson and Boyd (2004). Their interdisciplinary approach demonstrates how culture and biology are linked, and how we might speculate about their interaction in a way that provides a better understanding of the ways in which human behavior develops.

In Chapter 5 we learned that individuals throughout the world tend to use the same or similar cognitive processes, but that cultural differences distinguish the way they are employed in specific cultural contexts. Our understanding of the relationship between culture and cognition requires a careful synthesis of what is currently known about these topics. Norbert Ross (2003), who knows both cognitive anthropology and cognitive psychology well, has provided such a synthesis in his book—*Culture and Cognition: Implications for Theory and Method*—and suggests a number of useful directions for future investigation that are not only interesting but could be quite productive.

Mishra (2001), looking to the future, points out that while cross-cultural research studies "still fail to capture the day-to-day psychological life of individuals . . . Interest in the study of everyday cognition reflects an attempt to capture this reality" (p. 131). As evidence he cites developments in cultural psychology, indigenous psychologies, and indigenization of psychology in numerous countries around the world.

Along similar lines, Williams and Sternberg (2001), building on the ideas of Vygotsky and Rogoff, have set forth ten lessons parents can use to maximize children's cognitive abilities (e.g., recognizing what can and can not be changed, aiming to *meaningfully challenge* them, and teaching them to take responsibility both for their successes and their failures).

Regarding the topic of children's temperament discussed in Chapter 6, individual differences can be observed in the earliest hours following birth, become more apparent during infancy, and remain an important, although often modifiable influence (depending on age, gender, social and cultural factors, and parental characteristics) on later developments in behavioral, social, and cognitive areas.

As to future research, Rothbart and Bates (1998) point out that even the best contemporary measures of temperament are inadequate, and future research should be directed at the development of measures with better construct validity—the extent to which a test measures the construct it is designed to measure (e.g., temperamental characteristics of Indonesian infants). See also the work of Rothbart & Hwang (2005). Efforts should also be made to examine parental expectations before the birth of a child to determine how these may influence socialization strategies employed with a child's actual behavior after birth. For example, imagine you are expecting a child. You or your mate may be "hoping for" a boy or a girl. When the baby arrives, whether it is or isn't the gender you expected, you may already have preconceived ideas about how the child will behave and how you will react to those behaviors, which may or may not be appropriate. Knowing more about temperament, the characteristic styles of children and typical parental patterns of responding, will help you to be a more effective parent as you provide socialization experiences appropriate to the culture and world in which your newborn child will live.

Carefully designed longitudinal studies, beginning at infancy, may help to explain observed gender and cultural differences in temperament. In addition, a number of researchers have drawn attention to the importance of replicating previous parent-temperament interaction findings to be certain they are accurate—an argument we have made several times with regard to other types of research findings.

Putnam, Sanson, and Rothbart (2002) recommend that future research on temperament can be greatly improved by moving away from global measures (e.g., "difficult," "easy," and "slow-to-warm-up"), which can vary significantly from one study to another, to more specific measures (e.g., irritability, fear, self-regulation, and shyness). This suggests another promising area—the testing of hypotheses that focus on specific combinations of parenting characteristics and temperament traits (e.g., how fear might lead to a lessening of aggressive responses). These authors also note that almost all temperament research has focused on mothers and, with changes in parental roles, more attention should be given to the caregiving role of fathers and others (e.g., grandparents, extended family members, etc.).

Finally, and perhaps of greatest importance to those interested in human development within cultural contexts, is the issue of the generalizability of findings. Almost all of the research on temperament, with the exception of a few anthropological studies (e.g., Margaret Mead's work in New Guinea), has been conducted in individualistic Western cultures. As Kitayama and Markus (1994) have suggested, individuals raised in collectivist cultures (e.g., those in Asia, Africa, and among Indian tribes in the United States and Canada) are more frequently identified by their relationship to various groups, and, as a result, variations in temperament may, therefore, be less noticeable and relevant. We suggest that indigenous researchers should carefully examine the relationship between temperament and parenting within their cultures to expand our understanding of this crucial topic and provide parents with relevant information as they attempt to deal with their children's developing personalities. Putnam, Sanson, and Rothbart have expressed it well: "The task then for the parent and the practitioner is to foster 'respect for the individuality and integrity of each child, and flexibility in creating environments that may lead to positive outcomes for them and for us'" (2002, p. 272).

As we saw in Chapter 7, issues of gender and sexuality have been of increasing interest in cross-cultural psychology and anthropology. Best and Williams (2001) have provided one of the most comprehensive reviews of research on culture and gender, including findings on sociobiological factors, socialization practices, cultural influences, gender stereotypes, self-concept, mate selection, and male–female relationships. They conclude that there are relatively minor biological differences between men and women, that these differences can be expanded or reduced by cultural or socialization practices, and that male–female relationships are organized in strikingly similar ways across social groups. At the same time, they suggest that individuals can expect to live lives that are qualitatively different, dependent upon whether they are male or female.

Based on their knowledge of the issues related to culture and gender, Best and Williams pose a number of questions and challenges for the future of cross-cultural gender research. First, they express surprise that more of the cross-cultural research on gender is not "theory driven," that is, based on hypotheses derived from current theories (e.g., social learning, cognitive developmental, and gender schema). They suggest conducting longitudinal studies in societies experiencing rapid changes in socioeconomic development to determine if gender concepts change in theoretically predicted directions. Second, Best and Williams note that the relationship between cultural practices (e.g., initiation rites or rites of passage), frequently studied by anthropologists, and individual development (more often the focus of psychologists), needs greater research attention. The authors argue, as we have before, that psychologists and anthropologists, with shared interests in understanding how culture affects human behavior, should work more closely together and, thereby, learn from each other. They express this well when they suggest that, "Perhaps the growing field of cultural psychology, together with cross-cultural psychology, will provide a bridge between disciplines, recognizing that culture serves as both an independent and an organizing variable" (p. 212).

In Chapter 8, we discussed some aspects of culture and social behavior. What kinds of developments might we expect in the future, particularly from a cross-cultural perspective? Smith, Bond, & Kagitcibasi (2006) have suggested several possible areas of interest, including (1) expansion of our cultural theory base (e.g., consideration of cultural factors contributing to aggression and conflict resolution, as well as movement from Western, individualized theories of development to non-Western, collectivized theories of relatedness and interdependence), (2) universalization of social science measures (e.g., movement away from predominantly American instruments written in English to development of what Wierzbicka (1993) calls "cultural scripts" consisting of simple sentences that capture cultural norms from the point of view of "natives" and expresses these norms in terms of universal human concepts), and (3) diversification of input (e.g., greater interdisciplinary and cultural cooperation among social scientists in both the development of research projects and authorship of published writings). The authors speculate that attention to a number of dimensions of cultural variation are beginning to emerge. These include increasing contributions by Asian researchers from collectivist cultures interested in comparative studies, examination of relationships between cultural masculinity/femininity and measures of sexual norms and behaviors, as well as gender-related beliefs represented by the work of Hofstede (1996, 2001, 2004), and studies of values at the individual and cultural level (Knafo & Schwartz, 2003; Schwartz, 1995). In an expansion of his pioneering research on cultural values, Hofstede (2004) maintains that individuals carry around "mental programs," developed within the family during the years of early childhood, containing elements of national culture, reinforced in organizations and schools. The clearest expression of these "programs" can be found in the cluster of values that characterize and distinguish one cultural group from another. According to Smith and Bond (1999), these changes had to "await the diffusion of 'Western' psychology to different cultural milieux and the nurturing of local psychologists who are capable of challenging the biases of the discipline in its own terminology, using its established procedures" (p. 322). Now that cross-cultural social psychology has reached this stage, the authors believe there will be "an intellectual synergy that will enable us to transcend the limitations imposed by our different cultural origins. We may then be able to claim that we have a more truly universal understanding of humanity's social behaviour" (p. 323).

Another topic receiving attention in Chapter 8 was attachment. In the view of Waters & Cummings (2000), "Cross-cultural research on key issues in attachment theory is one of the most exciting prospects for the next generation of attachment research" (p. 169). Rothbaum and Morelli (2005) express a similar view by pointing out the necessity of understanding how "biological dispositions to develop attachments and real environments in which these attachments occur are co-mingled" (p. 119). They suggest a multimethod approach to look at cultural variations that will lead to better understanding of child security and caregiver behavior. For more information on recent attachment measures and a discussion of issues and difficulties in assessing the topic of attachment, visit this website: *http://www.psychology. sunysb.edu/attachment/measures/measures_index.html.*

In Chapter 9 we looked at families in cultural context and learned that it is a complex topic including mate selection, marriage and other long-term relationships, birth, transition to parenthood, parental belief systems, grandparenthood, and the need to care for elderly parents. While a great deal of progress has been made in describing diverse family systems (Roopnarine & Gielen, 2004) and the variety of cultural contexts in which they develop and thrive (Gielen & Roopnarine, 2004), much remains to be done. For example, we need to broaden our examination of different forms of families (e.g., extended or multigenerational, single-parent, stepfamilies, and families headed by gay and lesbian parents). Cross-culturally, we need to encourage indigenous researchers to take an emic (culture-specific) approach to the study of families, parenting, and development to refine and extend our understanding of family dynamics and processes in diverse ecological settings, setting the stage for more etic (universal or cultural general) studies and comparisons.

In their book, *Handbook of Parenting*, Hoghughi and Long (2004) assess the current status of parenting around the world and discuss possible trends affecting parents and children in the twenty-first century. These include onset of earlier sexual activity in children and parents' role in sex education, increasing influence of entertainment media and new technologies on children, the increasing exposure of children to dysfunctional parenting models in the media, the trend for children in their early twenties to continue living, (or returning to live), with parents and the effects on all involved, advances in genetic engineering and ability to create "designer babies," increased family mobility and erosion of neighborhood ties, and increase in frequency and severity of children's emotional behavioral problems throughout the world. Each of these topics is worthy of further cross-cultural investigation.

Advances in reproductive technology (e.g., *in vitro* fertilization—IVF—or "test-tube" babies, donor insemination or egg donation, surrogate parenting) have dramatically changed the way in which some families are formed and the manner in which some individuals become parents. Much of this technology is still new enough that we are uncertain how it affects parents and the psychological, social, and emotional development of their children. Golombok (2002) sums it up this way: "Although existing knowledge about the impact of the contemporary reproductive technologies does not give undue cause for concern, there remain many unanswered questions about the consequences for parenting of creating families in this way" (p.355).

As we pointed out earlier, the transition to parenthood represents a major change in most people's lives. To understand how this transition takes place, the manner in which parent–child relationships are formed, and the effects on children's development, Cowan, Powell, and Cowan (1998) have proposed that future research employ a family systems model of parenting that collects information on six critical aspects of family functioning, including the quality of relationships: (1) among parents, grandparents, and grandchildren, (2) between siblings, (3) between each parent and child, (4) between nuclear family members and individuals or institutions outside the family (e.g., friends, peers, school, childcare, government, etc.), (5) between parents and their roles and communication patterns within the family, and (6) the biological and psychological characteristics of each family member.

What parents know and believe about parenting is, in large part, a result of the way their parents raised them. While the scientific study of parental beliefs is about fifty years old and has been characterized by a variety of perspectives, Sigel and McGillicuddy-De Lisi (2002) suggest a new approach to the topic that views cognition as the core component, especially the effects on children's cognitive and social development and academic achievement. At the same time, they admit that their approach is controversial, with the most extensive argument against it being made by Wachs (2000a). However, they believe their dynamic belief systems model deserves further attention and provides evidence from cross-cultural studies of parental beliefs within specific cultures, across cultures, and between groups from different cultural backgrounds within a society to bolster their view of cultural perspectives.

In the latter part of Chapter 9, we devoted attention to grandparenthood and the roles played by grandparents in several cultures including those of Japan, China, and the United States. In reviews of this topic, Smith and Drew (2002, 2004) discuss some of the historical issues related to grandparenting, many classic research studies, and several of the theoretical approaches frequently used in its study (e.g., psychoanlysis and attachment theory, evolutionary theory, lifespan development and gerontology, and family systems theory). While information on this topic has grown rapidly over the past twenty years, Smith and Drew (2004) acknowledge there are limitations, including limited methodology (interviews or structured questionnaires), narrow range of cultures (primarily in the United States), and a lack of theoretical structuring. To improve and extend our knowledge of grandparenting, they suggest utilizing a wider range of methods (e.g., naturalistic home observations of grandparent–grandchild interactions, children's drawings of grandparents, and essays written about them), employing more cultures (e.g., those in Asian, African, and Latin American and industrial, nonindustrial, urban, rural), which would allow for testing biocultural theories to account for differences between cultures as well as similarities across cultures, and greater use of theoretical frameworks, like those mentioned previously, to interpret new and previously collected data.

In addition to these topics, even less is known about step-grandparenthood, the role of grandparents in lesbian and gay families, and the extended intergenerational role of great-grandparenthood. There are numerous opportunities to explore these topics in a wide variety of cultural and cross-cultural contexts.

In Chapter 10, we noted that when it comes to health and related issues, we often do not consider the many ways these might be affected by culture. Fortunately, a number of recent efforts have begun to give greater attention to the role played by cultural factors in health, illness, and well-being. In their handbook of cultural health psychology, two Canadian researchers, Kazarian and Evans (2001), have set forth a conceptual framework that considers the interface between health behavior and cultural psychology, a necessary step for the advancement of a more culturally competent and ethnically sound approach to health. Among the topics discussed by contributors to this handbook are (1) approaches to multiculturalism, the relationship between culture and health, and the need to understand variations in health concepts and practices in multicultural societies including the physical, popular, and folk sectors, (2) provider–patient relationships and the success or failure of treatments that are frequently embedded in cultural differences in individualism and collectivism and the illness models and cultural expectations for health care that result from these differences, (3) the need to more fully integrate the role of culture into the critical topics of health promotion and disease prevention, areas from which it has been conspicuously absent, and (4) efforts to identify issues and strategies relevant to cultural and ethnic groups at highest risk for HIV/AIDS to provide guidance for the development of health programs and research tailored to these groups.

The final part of this handbook focuses on health issues related to specific cultural groups and includes material on (1) health concerns of Latinos (e.g., heart disease, HIV/AIDS, cancer, and diabetes), (2) health issues among African Canadians and African Americans with detailed discussions of each group's demographics, health status, and health determinants, (3) clinical issues encountered by professionals working with native peoples, specific health-related issues they face, and a proposal for a "culturally congruent model" that integrates the values and beliefs of the target groups (e.g., present-time orientation, harmony with nature, sharing, respect for elders, and non-materialism), (4) discussion of the principles of Confucianism and Taoism as they apply to beliefs about health and illness and some of the ways in which the cultural context shapes both collective and individual health behaviors in traditional and contemporary Chinese societies, (5) information on a wide variety of South Asian cultural groups from India, Bangladesh, Nepal, Bhutan, and Maldives and their perspectives on health and illness as reflected in their religious customs, languages, traditions, unique political contexts, paths of immigration, and culture-specific physical and mental health issues (e.g., acculturation stress, depression, and culture-bound syndromes), and (6) methodological limitations in much of the available research on women's health. They present a case for future research aimed at defining specific determinants of health status in minority women, as well as development of a better classification system of "race/ethnicity" to collect more relevant and accurate data and permit better application of findings to specific cultural groups.

Taken as a whole, this collection provides a state-of-the-art understanding of what is known and not known about the rapidly emerging field of cultural health psychology, along with valuable detailed suggestions for designing needed multicultural studies to expand the field and lead to important findings related to each of the health issues discussed.

In another timely effort, Tinsley et al. (2002) reviewed and attempted to integrate research findings concerned with specific ways parents try to promote children's health in a variety of cultural settings. They examine traditional approaches to child health care (e.g., the biomedical disease model, which has largely ignored psychological, social, and behavioral factors) and more contemporary developmental models (e.g., the transactional, which includes these factors along with consideration of the intellectual, social, and physical environment and systems theory approaches, which take into account the reciprocal influence of experiential and biological factors). They also discuss parent's socialization of children's sick role behavior as well as their wellness behavior. The authors conclude that health research is limited (e.g., focusing on mother's role in health promotion). They would like to see more attention given to the role of fathers, and the influence of entire families as they function in a cultural and ecological context.

In an effort to understand and explain the relationship between culture and health, Maclachlan (2006) introduces new techniques for assessment and treatment of disorders found in a variety of cultures. Making use of psychological, anthropological, sociological, and medical research, the authors provide case studies and guidelines for good practice that show promise for future research.

An area of the world that has not received as much cross-cultural attention as it deserves, particularly in light of recent global events, is the Middle East/North Africa, sometimes referred to as MENA. In fact, until recently we have known relatively little about the people living in this important region of the world. A major contribution to our understanding of the societies and cultures that exist here, along with insights into their struggles with traditions and modernity, self and identity, stereotypes and misunderstandings and the universality as well as unique behaviors that characterize their citizens, are discussed in a book by Gary Gregg, *The Middle East: A Cultural Psychology* (2005). Most importantly, he provides a "social ecology" of psychological development and explores development across the same life stages as we have from infancy to adulthood. His contributions are theoretical, empirical, pragmatic, and add significantly to our cross-cultural understanding of societies we do not know very well but certainly should. in addition, the majority of the reported research has been conducted by Arab-Muslim scholars and has previously been unavailable to Westerners and others.

As stated in the Foreword to this book, "The theoretical perspectives on culture, personality, self, identity, and development; empirical contributions of the study of lives approach; and the carefully crafted writing make this volume one that is sure to make a strong and lasting contribution to the scholarly literature on culture, psychology, and the Middle East/North Africa" (p. vii).

Gregg closes with thoughtful suggestions for further research based on the writings of indigenous scholars with a focus on emic–etic influences on development. Among the priorities that researchers might consider are care practices among the growing urban poor, mastering of the "honor-modesty" system, the nature and consequences of patriarchal or authoritarian parenting styles, adolescent dealings with the contradictory world views associated with tradition and modern institutions, as well as their effect on identity formation. The book contains a wealth of ideas that can be applied not only to the study of MENA cultures but to other cultures as well.

In bringing the third edition of *Lives Across Cultures* (2005) to a close, we said that "Cross-cultural study of development frequently resembles a confused mosaic of often contradictory findings. Yet therein lies the promise and excitement of future endeavors. . . . Much more needs to be done, and as the cross-cultural perspective reveals, discovery of similarities and dissimilarities in human behavior will make our understanding both easier and more difficult" (p. 310). This was true then, and it is even more true now.

Ahead of us lie tremendous challenges and opportunities. Speculating about where our cross-cultural journey will take us next is difficult. Wherever we go, it is certain to be an interesting and exciting adventure. Perhaps some of you will be the pioneer theorists and researchers who take us to the next point on this journey. We eagerly look forward to that day.

◇ SUMMARY

In this final chapter, we looked back at the major theories introduced at the beginning of our journey into human development and commented on their usefulness for explaining cultural similarities and differences in behavior across the lifespan. These included the ecological systems approach and developmental niche as well as the work of Piaget, Vygotsky, Erikson, and Kohlberg. We concluded with our view of some of the current challenges we face and promising directions the field of cross-cultural human development will (or should) take as it attempts to expand our knowledge and understanding of a most fascinating topic—ourselves.

◇ STUDY QUESTIONS

Comment critically on the theories of Kohlberg and Erikson, and explain how these theories might be made more useful to cross-cultural researchers.

Explain why there is a need for conducting more comparative cross-cultural studies of human development.

Describe some of the examples of the type of research the authors outlined in "Thoughts and Challenges for the Future."

◇ FURTHER READINGS

Roy D'Andrade. (2000). The sad story of anthropology 1950–1999. *Cross-Cultural Research, 34,* 219–232.

> The author discusses how changing political attitudes over the past fifty years have affected the field of anthropology and its effectiveness as a discipline and what directions it might take in the future.

Wolfgang Friedlmeier, Pardeep Chakkarath, and Beate Schwarz (2005). *Culture and Human Development.* NY: Psychology Press.

> This book provides an interdisciplinary approach to key developmental processes, with particular focus on theoretical and methodological issues in cross-cultural research. An invaluable source of information and very readable.

Gary S. Gregg (2005). *The Middle East: A Cultural Psychology.* New York: Oxford University Press.

> A book that provides a long overdue synthesis of psychological research on Middle Eastern and North African societies. Readers will become familiar with the lives of individuals in this critical region of the world who are attempting to resolve differences between adherence of traditional values and the attraction of Westernized lifestyles.

Cigdem Kagitcibasi and Ype H. Poortinga. (2000). Cross-cultural psychology: Issues and overarching themes. *Journal of Cross-Cultural Psychology, 31,* 129–144.

> The authors consider the difficulties of defining behavior–culture relationships, how the notion of culture is used in empirical studies, possible future trends in cross-cultural psychology, and how findings might be applied to problems of economic and social inequality to contribute globally to human well-being.

Heidi Keller and Patricia M. Greenfield. (2000). History and future of development in cross-cultural psychology. *Journal of Cross-Cultural Psychology, 31,* 52–62.

> A view of the future of cross-cultural human development and how developmental issues and methods can be used to advance theory and research.

David Shwalb, Jun Nakazawa, & Barbara J. Shwalb (Eds.) (2005). *Applied Developmental Psychology: Theory, Practice, and Research from Japan*. Greenwich, CT: Information Age Publishing.

This book consists of sixteen chapters in which the editors and authors provide valuable insights into theories, approaches, and applications of findings in a nonWestern culture, which have important implications for other cultures. Not only are the presentations original, but easy to read and understand.

REFERENCES

Abbott, S. (1997). *"You give 'em lots of love and use the flat of your hand": Patterns of child rearing in the mountains.* Paper presented at the twenty-sixth annual meeting of the Society for Cross-Cultural Research, San Antonio, TX.

Abel, E., & Sokol, R. (1987). Incidence of fetal alcohol syndrome and economic impact of FAS-related anomalies. *Drug and Alcohol Dependency, 19,* 51–70.

Abdel-Khalek, A. M. & Soliman, H. H. (1999). A cross-cultural evaluation of depression in children in Egypt, Kuwait, and the United States. *Psychological Reports, 85,* 973–980.

Adelson, J. (1985). Observations on research in adolescence. *Genetic, Social, and General Psychology Monographs, 111,* 249–254.

Adkins, V. K. (1999). Grandparents as a national asset: A brief note. *Activities, Adaptations, & Aging, 24,* 13–18.

Adler, L. (2001). Women and gender roles. In L. L. Adler and U. P. Gielen (Eds.), (2001). *Cross-cultural topics in Psychology* (2nd ed.) (pp. 103–114). Westport, CT: Praeger Publishers/Greenwood Publishing Group.

Ahadi, S. A., & Rothbart, M. K. (1994). Temperament, development, and the big five. In C. F. Halverson, Jr., G. A. Kohnstamm, & R. P. Martin (Eds.), *The developing structure of temperament and personality from infancy to adulthood* (pp. 189–207). Hillsdale, NJ: Erlbaum.

Ahmed, R. A. (1991). Women in Egypt and the Sudan. In L. L. Adler (Ed.), *Women in cross-cultural perspective* (pp. 107–133). Westport, CT: Praeger.

Ahnert, L., Meischner, T., & Schmidt, A. (2000). Maternal sensitivity and attachment in East German and Russian family networks. In P. M. Crittenden & A. H. Claussen (Eds.), *The organization of attachment relationships: Maturation, culture, and context.* New York: Cambridge University Press.

Ainsworth, M. D. S. (1982). Attachment: Retrospect and prospect. In C. M. Parks & J. Stevenson-Hinde (Eds.), *The place of attachment in human behavior* (pp. 3–30). New York: Basic Books.

Ainsworth, M. D. S., & Wittig, B. A. (1969). Attachment and exploratory behavior of one-year-olds in a strange situation. In B. M. Foss (Ed.), *Determinants of infant behavior IV* (pp. 111–136). London: Methuen.

Aldous, J., Mulligan, G. M., & Bjarnason, T. (1998). Fathering over time: What makes the difference? *Journal of Marriage & the Family, 60,* 809–820.

Ali, A., & Maharajh, H. D. (2004). Anorexia nervosa and religious ambivalence in a developing country. *The Internet Journal of Mental Health, 2* (1). *http://www.ispub.com/ostia/index.php?xmlFilePath=journals/ijmh/vol2n1/anorexia.xml*

Anderson, J. A. (1999). Hot flashes or power surges? A contextual analysis of menopause and its meaning. *Dissertation Abstracts International: Section B: The Sciences and Engineering, 60* (6-B), 2979.

Annett, M. (1985). *Left, right, hand, and brain: The right shift theory.* Hillsdale, NJ: Erlbaum.

Antonucci, T. C. (1990). Social Supports and Social Relationships. In R. H. Binstock and K. George (Eds.), *Handbook of Aging and the Social Sciences* (3rd ed., pp. 205–226). New York: Academic Press.

Aptekar, L. (1988). Colombian street children: Their mental health and how they can be served. *International Journal of Mental Health, 17,* 81–104.

Aptekar, L. (1989). Colombian street children: *Gamines* and *chupagruesos. Adolescence, 24,* 783–794.

Aptekar, L. (1994). Street children in the developing world: A review of their condition. *Cross-Cultural Research, 28*(3), 195–224.

Aptekar, L., & Ciano-Federoff, L. M. (1999). Street children in Nairobi: Gender differences in mental health. In M. Raffaelli (Ed.), *Homeless and working youth around the world: Exploring developmental issues.* San Francisco, CA: Jossey-Bass.

Archetti, E. P. (1999). *Masculinities: Football, polo, and the tango in Argentina.* Oxford, UK: Berg Publishers.

Ardelt, M. (2004). Wisdom as expert knowledge system. *Human Development, 47* (5), 257–285.

Arnett, J. (1992). Reckless behavior in adolescence: A developmental perspective. *Developmental Review, 12,* 339–373.

Ashmore, R. D. (1990). Sex, gender, and the individual. In L. Pervin (Ed.), *Handbook of personality: Theory and research* (pp. 486–526). New York: Guilford Press.

Atkinson, P, & Delamont, S., (Eds.). (2006). *Narrative methods.* London, UK: Sage Publications, Ltd.

Azhar, M. Z., & Varma, S. L. (2000). Mental illness and its treatment in Malaysia. In I. Al-Issa (Ed.), *Al-Junun: Mental illness in the Islamic world.* Madison, WI: International Universities Press.

Azuma, H. (2005). Foreword. In D. W. Shwalb, J. Nakazawa, & B. J. Shwalb (Eds.), *Applied developmental psychology: Theory, practice, and research from Japan.* Greenwich, CT: Information Age Publishing.

Baca Zinn, M., & Eitzen, D. S. (1993). *Diversity in families* (3rd ed.). New York: HarperCollins.

Baltes, P. B. (1987). Theoretical propositions of life-span developmental psychology: On the dynamics between growth and decline. *Developmental Psychology, 23,* 611–626.

Baltes, P. B., Reese, H. W., & Lipsett, L. P. (1980). Life-span developmental psychology. *Annual Review of Psychology, 31,* 65–110.

Baltes, P. B., & Staudinger, U. M. (2000). Wisdom. *American Psychologist, 55,* 122–136.

Bandura, A. (1990). *Multidimensional scales of perceived academic efficacy.* Stanford, CA: Stanford University.

Bandura, A. (1997). *Self-efficacy: The exercise of control.* New York: Freeman.

Banks, C. G. (1992). "Culture" in culture-bound syndromes: The case of anorexia nervosa. *Social Science & Medicine, 34*(8), 867–884.

Barnard, K. E., & Martell, L. K. (1995). Mothering. In M. H. Bornstein (Ed.), *Handbook of parenting* (Vol. 3, pp. 3–26). Mahwah, NJ: Erlbaum.

Barnard, K. & Solchany, J. (2002). Mothering. In M. Bornstein (Ed.), *Handbook of parenting, Vol. 3: Becoming and being a parent* (pp. 3–26). Mahwah, NJ: Earlbaum.

Barnlund, D. C., & Araki, S. (1985). Intercultural encounters: The management of compliments by Japanese and Americans. *Journal of Cross-Cultural Psychology, 16,* 9–26.

Barresi, C. M., & Menon, G. (1990). Diversity in black family caregiving. In Z. Harel, E. A. McKinney, & M. Williams (Eds.), *Black aged: Understanding diversity and service needs.* Newbury Park, CA: Sage.

Barrett, D. E., Radke-Yarrow, M., & Klein, R. E. (1982). Chronic malnutrition and child behavior: Effects of early caloric supplementation on social and emotional functioning at school age. *Developmental Psychology, 18,* 541–556.

Beardsley, L. M. (1994). Medical diagnosis and treatment across cultures. In W. J. Lonner & R. Malpass (Eds.), *Psychology and culture.* Boston: Allyn & Bacon.

Beardsley, L. M., & Pedersen, P. (1997). Public health and culture-centered intervention. In J. Berry, M. Segall, & C. Kagitcibasi (Eds.), *Handbook of cross-cultural psychology: Vol 3: Social psychology, personality, and psychotherapy.* Boston: Allyn & Bacon.

Beatty, S. E., Jeon, J. O., Albaum, G., & Murphy, B. (1994) A cross-national study of leisure activities. *Journal of Cross-Cultural Psychology, 25*(3), 409–422.

Becker. G., & Newsom, E. (2005). Resilience in the face of serious illness among chronically ill African Americans in later life. *Journal of Gerontology: Series B: Psychological Sciences and Social Sciences, 60,* 214–223.

Beckwith, L., Rodning, C., & Cohen, S. (1992). Preterm children at early adolescence, and continuity in discontinuity in maternal responsiveness from infancy. *Child Development, 63,* 1198–1208.

Beidelman, T. O. (1997). *The cool knife: Metaphors of gender, sexuality and moral education in Kaguru initiation ritual.* Washington, DC: Smithsonian Institute Press.

Belsky, J. (1985). Exploring individual differences in marital change across the transition to parenthood: The role of violated expectations. *Journal of Marriage and the Family, 47,* 1037–1044.

Bereczkei, T., Voeroes, S., Gal, A., & Bernath, L. (1999). Adaptive algorithms and reproductive decisions in human mating. *Magyar Pszichologiai Szemle, 54,* 523–549.

Berndt, A. L., & Zook, J. M. (1993). Effects of friendship on adolescent development. *Bulletin of the Hong Kong psychological Society, 30/31,* 15–34.

Berry, J. W. (1983). The sociogenesis of social sciences: An analysis of the cultural relativity of social psychology. In B. Bain (Ed.), *The sociogenesis of language and human conduct.* New York: Plenum.

Berry, J. W., & Dasen, P. (Eds.). (1974). *Culture and cognition.* London: Methuen.

Berry, J. W., Dasen, P. R., & Saraswathi, T. S. (Eds.). (1997). *Handbook of cross-cultural psychology: Vol. 2. Basic processes and human development* (2nd ed.). Boston: Allyn & Bacon.

Berry, J. W., Poortinga, Y. H., & Pandey, J. (Eds.). (1997). *Handbook of cross-cultural psychology: Vol. 1. Theory and method* (2nd ed.). Boston: Allyn & Bacon.

Berry, J. W., Poortinga, Y. H., Segall, M. H., & Dasen, P. R. (2002). *Cross-cultural psychology* (2nd ed.). Cambridge, England: Cambridge University Press.

Bersoff, D. M., & Miller, J. (1993). Culture, context, and the development of moral accountability judgments. *Developmental Psychology, 29*, 669–676.

Bertrand, J. T., Ward, V., & Pauc, F. (1992). Sexual practices among the Quiche-speaking Mayan population of Guatemala. *International Quarterly of Community Health Education, 12*, 265–282.

Best, D. (2001). Gender concepts: Convergence in cross-cultural research and methodologies. *Cross-Cultural Research, 35*, 23–43.

Best, D. L., & Williams, J. E. (2001). Gender and culture. In D. Matsumoto (Ed.), *The handbook of culture and psychology* (pp. 195–219). New York: Oxford University Press.

Bhogle, S. (1999). Gender roles: The construct in the Indian context. In T. S. Saraswathi (Ed.), *Culture, socialization and human development: Theories, research, and applications in India.* Thousand Oaks, CA: Sage.

Biller, H. B. (1993). *Fathers and families.* Westport, CT: Auburn House.

Birdsong, D., & Molis, M. (2001). On the evidence for maturational constraints in second-language acquisition. *Journal of Memory & Language, 44*, 235–249.

Birren, J. E., & Schaie, K. W. (Eds.). (1995). *Handbook of psychology and aging.* San Diego, CA: Academic Press.

Bochner, S. (1994). Cross-cultural differences in the self-concept. A test of Hofstede's individualism/collectivism distinction. *Journal of Cross-Cultural Psychology, 25*, 273–283.

Boesch, E. E. (1991). *Symbolic action theory for cultural psychology.* Berlin: Springer.

Bolton, R. (1994). Sex, science, and social responsibility: Cross-cultural research on same-sex eroticism and sexual intolerance. *Cross-Cultural Research, 28*, 134–190.

Bond, T. G. (1998). Fifty years of formal operational research: The empirical evidence. *Archives de Psychologie, 66*, 221–238.

Book, A. S., Starzyk, K. B., & Quinsey, V. L. (2001). The relationship between testosterone and aggression: A meta-analysis. *Aggression & Violent Behavior, 6*, 579–599.

Borgatti, S. P. (1992). ANTHROPAC 4.0: *Methods guide.* Columbia, SC: Analytic Technologies.

Bornstein, M. H. (1995). Parenting infants. In M. H. Bornstein (Ed.), *Handbook of parenting* (Vol. 1, pp. 3–39). Mahwah, NJ: Erlbaum.

Bornstein, M. H. (2000). Infant to conversant: Language and non-language processes in developing early communication. In N. Budwig, I. C. Uzgiris, and J. V. Wertsch (Eds.), *Communication: An arena of development.* Stamford, CT: Ablex Publishing.

Bornstein, M. H. (2002). Parenting infants. In M. H. Bornstein (Ed.), *Handbook of parenting* (Vol. 1, 2nd ed., pp. 3–43). Mahwah, NJ: Erlbaum.

Bornstein, M. H., Tal, J., Rahn, C., Galperin, C. Z., Pecheux, M.-G, Lamour, M., Azuma, H., Toda, S., Ogino, M., & Tamis-LeMonda, C. S. (1992). Functional analysis of the contents of maternal speech to infants of five and thirteen months in four cultures: Argentina, France, Japan, and the United States. *Developmental Psychology, 28*, 593–603.

Bornstein, M. H., Tal, J., & Tamis-LeMonda, C. S. (1991). Parenting in cross-cultural perspective: The United States, France, and Japan. In M. H. Bornstein (Ed.), *Cultural approaches to parenting* (pp. 69–90). Hillsdale, NJ: Erlbaum.

Boski, P. (2005). Humanism–materialism: Century-long Polish cultural origins and twenty years of research in cultural psychology. In U. Kim, Yang, K-S., & Hwang, K-K. *Indigenous and cultural psychology:* New York: Springer.

Bouchard, T. J., Lykken, D. T., McGue, M., Segal, N. L., & Tellegen, A. (1990). Sources of human psychological differences: The Minnesota study of twins reared apart. *Science, 250*, 223–228.

Bourguignon, E. (1979). *Psychological anthropology: An introduction to human nature and cultural differences.* New York: Holt, Rinehart & Winston.

Bowlby, J. (1988). *Secure and insecure attachment.* New York: Basic Books.

Brannigan, M. C. (Ed.). (2004). *Cross-cultural biotechnology.* Rowman & Littlefield.

Brink, P. J. (1989). The fattening room among the Annang of Nigeria. *Medical Anthropology, 12*, 131–143.

Brislin, R. (Ed.). (1990). *Applied cross-cultural psychology.* Newbury Park, CA: Sage.

Brislin, R. (1993). *Understanding culture's influence on behavior.* New York: Harcourt Brace Jovanovich.

Bronfenbrenner, U. (1967). Response to pressure from peers versus adults among Soviet and American school children. *International Journal of Psychology, 2*, 199–207.

Bronfenbrenner, U. (1970). *Two Worlds of Childhood: U.S. and U.S.S.R.* New York: Russell Sage Foundation.

Bronfenbrenner, U. (1975). Reality and research in the ecology of human development. *Proceedings of the American Philosophical Society, 119*, 439–469.

Bronfenbrenner, U. (1977). Toward an experimental ecology of human development. *American Psychologist, 32*, 513–531.

Bronfenbrenner, U. (1979). *The ecology of human development: Experiments by nature and design.* Cambridge, MA: Harvard University Press.

Bronfenbrenner, U. (1986). Ecological systems theory. In R. Vasta (Ed.), *Annals of Child Development* (Vol. 6, pp. 187–251). Greenwich, CT: JAI Press.

Bronfenbrenner, U. (1989). Ecological systems theory. In R. Vasta (Ed.), *Six theories of child development* (Vol. 6, pp. 187–250). Greenwich, CT: JAI Press.

Bronfenbrenner, U. (1993). The ecology of cognitive development: Research models and fugitive findings. In R. H. Wozniak & K. W. Fischer (Eds.), *Development in context: Acting and thinking in specific environments* (pp. 3–44). Hillsdale, NJ: Erlbaum.

Bronfenbrenner, U. (1994). Ecological models of human development. In T. Husen & T. N. Postlethwaite (Eds.), *International encyclopedia of education*, 2nd ed., Vol. 3 (pp. 1643–1647). Oxford, UK: Pergamon/Elsevier Science.

Bronfenbrenner, U. (1999). Environments in developmental perspective: Theoretical and operational models. In S. L. Friedman & T. D. Wachs (Eds.), *Measuring environment across the life span*. Washington, DC: American Psychological Association.

Bronfenbrenner, U. (Ed.). (2005). *Making human beings human*. Thousand Oaks, CA: Sage.

Bronfenbrenner, U., & Evans, G. W. (2000). Developmental science in the 21st century: Emerging questions, theoretical models, research designs and empirical findings. *Social Development, 9*, 115–125.

Bronfenbrenner, U., & Morris, P. (1998). The ecology of developmental processes. In R. M. Lerner (Ed.), *Handbook of child psychology, Vol. 1: Theoretical models of human development* (5th ed.). New York: Wiley.

Brooks, P. J., Jia, X., Braine, M. D. S., & DaGraca Dias, M. (1998). A cross-linguistic study of children's comprehension of universal quantifiers: A comparison of Mandarin Chinese, Portuguese, and English. *First Language, 18*, 33–79.

Brown, B. B., Lohr, M. J., & Trujillo, C. (1990). Multiple crowds and multiple life-styles: Adolescents' perceptions of peer-group stereotypes. In R. E. Muuss (Ed.), *Adolescent behavior and society* (4th ed.). New York: McGraw-Hill.

Brubaker, T. H. (1985). *Later life families*. Newbury Park, CA: Sage.

Budwig, N., Wertsch, J. V., & Uzgiris, I. C. (2000). Introduction: Communication, meaning, and development: Interdisciplinary perspectives. In N. Budwig, I. C. Uzgiris, and J. V. Wertsch (Eds.), *Communication: An arena of development*. Stamford CT: Ablex Publishing.

Bulbeck, C. (2005). "The mighty pillar of the family": Young people's vocabularies on household gender arrangements in the Asia-Pacific region. *Gender Work and Organization, 12*, 14–31.

Burbank, V. K. (1988). *Aboriginal adolescence: Maidenhood in an Australian community*. New Brunswick, NJ: Rutgers University Press.

Buss, D. M. (1994a). *The evolution of desire: Strategies of human mating*. New York: Basic Books.

Buss, D. M. (1994b). Mate preferences in 37 cultures. In W. J. Lonner & R. Malpass (Eds.), *Psychology and culture* (pp. 197–201). Boston: Allyn & Bacon.

Buss, D. M. (2003). *The evolution of desire: Strategies of human mating* (Revised edition). New York: Basic Books.

Buss, D. M., & Schmitt, D. P. (1993). Sexual strategies theory: An evolutionary perspective on human mating. *Psychological Review, 100*, 204–232.

Butcher, J. N. (2006). *MMPI-2: A practitioner's handbook*. Washington, DC: American Psychological Association.

Cabaj, R. P., & Purcell, D. W. (Eds.) (1998). *On the road to same-sex marriage: A supportive guide to psychological, political, and legal issues*. San Francisco, CA: Jossey-Bass.

Calabrese, R. L., & Noboa, J. (1995). The choice for gang membership by Mexican-American adolescents. *High School Journal, 78*, 226–235.

Calhoun, D. W. (1987). *Sport, culture, and personality* (2nd ed). Champaign, IL: Human Kinetics Publishers.

Cantor, N., Norem, J. K., Langston, C. A., Zirkel, S., Fleeson, W., & Cook-Flannagan, C. (1991). Life tasks and daily life experience. *Journal of Personality, 59*, 425–451.

Cantor, N., Norem, J. K., Niedenthal, P. M., Langston, C. A., & Brower, A. M. (1987). Life tasks, self-concept ideals, and cognitive strategies in a life transition. *Journal of Personality and Social Psychology, 53*, 1178–1191.

Carey, G. (2003). *Human genetics for the social sciences*. Thousand Oaks, CA: Sage.

Carpo, R. H. (1995). Factors in the cross-cultural patterning of male homosexuality: A reappraisal of the literature. *Cross-Cultural Research, 29*, 178–202.

Caselli, C., Casadio, P., & Bates, E. (1999). A comparison from first words to grammar in English and Italian. *Journal of Child Language, 26*, 69–111.

Cassidy, C. M. (1991). The good body: When big is better. *Medical Anthropology, 13*, 181–213.

Chadda, R. K., & Ahuja, N. (1990). Dhat Syndrome. *British Journal of Psychiatry, 156*, 577–579.

Chagnon, N. A. (1997). *Yanomamo* (5th ed.) Fort Worth, TX: Holt, Rinehart & Winston.

Chamberlain, P., & Patterson, G. R. (1995). Discipline and child compliance in parenting. In M. Bornstein (Ed.), *Handbook of parenting* (Vol. 4, pp. 205–225). Hillsdale, NJ: Erlbaum.

Charles, M., & Hopflinger, F. (1992). Gender, culture and the division of household labor: A replication of U.S. studies for the case of Switzerland. *Journal of Comparative Family Studies, 23,* 375–387.

Chen, J-L., & Kennedy, C. (2005). Cultural variations in children's coping behavior, tv viewing time, and family functioning. *International Nursing Review, 52,* 186–195.

Cheung, K., & Leung, K. (1998). Indigenous personality measures: Chinese examples. *Journal of Cross-Cultural Psychology, 29,* 233–248.

Chisholm, J. S. (1983). *Navajo Infancy.* New York: Aldine.

Chiu, M. L., Feldman, S. S., & Rosenthal, D. A. (1992). The influence of immigration on parental behavior and adolescent distress in Chinese families residing in two western nations. *Journal of Research on Adolescence, 2*(3), 205–239.

Chuang, Y. C. (2002), Sex differences in mate selection preferences and sexual strategy: Tests for Evolutionary hypotheses. *Chinese Journal of Psychology, 44,* 75–93.

Clark, K. B., & Clark, M. P. (1947). *Racial identification and preference in Negro children.* New York: Holt.

Cogan, J. C., Bhalla, S. K., Sefa-Dedeh, A., & Rothblum, E. D. (1996). A comparison study of United States and African students on perceptions of obesity and thinness. *Journal of Cross-Cultural Psychology, 27*(1), 98–113.

Cole, M. (1995). Culture and cognitive development: From cross-cultural research to creating systems of cultural mediation. *Culture and Psychology, 1,* 25–52.

Cole, M. (1998). *Cultural psychology: A once and future discipline.* Cambridge: Belknap.

Cole, M. (2005). Using cross-cultural psychology to design afterschool educational activities in different cultural settings. In W. Friedlmeier, P. Chakkarath, & B. Schwarz (Eds.), *Culture and human development* (pp. 53–71). New York: Psychology Press.

Cole, M., & Cole, S. R. (1993). *The development of children* (2nd ed.). New York: Freeman.

Cole, M., & Cole, S. R. (1996). *The development of children* (3rd ed.). New York: Freeman.

Cole, M., & Cole, S. R. (2001). *The development of children* (4th ed.). New York: Worth Publishers.

Colin, V. L. (1996). *Human attachment.* New York: McGraw-Hill.

Condon, J. C. (1984). *With respect to the Japanese.* Yarmouth, ME: Intercultural Press.

Connolly, M. (1990). Adrift in the city: A comparative study of street children in Bogota, Colombia and Guatemala City. In N. Boxhill (Ed.), *Homeless children: The watchers and the waiters* (pp. 129–149). New York: Haworth Press.

Cook, P. (1994). Chronic illness beliefs and the role of social networks among Chinese, Indian, and Anglo-celtic Canadians. *Journal of Cross-Cultural Psychology, 25,* 452–465.

Cooley, C. H. (1902). *Human nature and the social order.* New York: Scribner's.

Corman, H. H., & Escalona, S. K. (1969). Stages in sensori-motor development: A replication study. *Merrill-Palmer Quarterly, 15*(4), 351–361.

Corsaro, W. A. (1988). Routines in the peer culture of American and Italian nursery school children. *Social Education, 61,* 1–14.

Corsaro, W. A., & Eder, D. (1990). Children's peer cultures. *Annual Review in Sociology, 16,* 197–220.

Cosgrove, J. (1990). Towards a working definition of street children. *International Social Work, 33,* 185–192.

Cousins, S. D. (1989). Culture and self-perception in Japan and the United States. *Journal of Personality and Social Psychology, 56,* 124–131.

Cowan, P. A., Powell, D., & Cowen, C. P. (1998). Parenting interventions: A family systems perspective. In I. E. Sigel and K. A. Renninger (Eds.), *Handbook of child psychology* (5th ed.). New York: Wiley

Cox, C. (1993). Hispanic culture and family care of Alzheimer's patients. *Health and Social Work, 18*(2), 92–101.

Crittenden, K. S. (1991). Asian self-effacement or feminine modesty? Attributional patterns of women university students in Taiwan. *Gender and Society, 5,* 98–117.

Cross, S. E. (1995). Self-construals, coping, and stress in cross-cultural adaptation. *Journal of Cross-Cultural Psychology, 26,* 673–697.

Crystal, D. S., Watanabe, H., & Chen, R. (2000). Reactions to morphological deviance: A comparison of Japanese and American children and adolescents. *Social Development, 9,* 40–61.

Cummings, L. L. (1994). Fighting by the rules: Women street-fighting in Chihuahua, Mexico. *Sex Roles, 30,* 189–198.

Cushner, K. (1990). Cross-cultural psychology and the formal classroom. In R. W. Brislin (Ed.), *Applied cross-cultural psychology* (pp. 98–120). Newbury Park, CA: Sage.

D'Abreu, R. C., Mullis, A. K., & Cook, L. A. (1999). The resiliency of street children in Brazil. *Adolescence, 34*(136), 745–751.

Damon, W. (1973). Early conceptions of positive justice as related to the development of logical operations. *Child Development, 46,* 301–312.

Dasen, P. R. (1972). Cross-cultural Piagetian research: A summary. *Journal of Cross-Cultural Psychology, 7,* 75–85.

Dasen, P. R. (2003). Theoretical frameworks in cross-cultural developmental psychology: An attempt at integration. In T. S. Saraswathi (Ed.), *Cross-cultural perspectives in human development: Theory, research, & applications.* New Delhi: Sage India.

Dasen, P. R., & Heron, A. (1981). Cross-cultural tests of Piaget's theory. In H. C. Triandis & A. Heron (Eds.), *Handbook of cross-cultural psychology* (Vol. 4). Boston: Allyn & Bacon.

Dasen, P. R., Inhelder, B., Lavellee, M., & Retschitzki, J. (1978). *Naissance de l'intelligence chez l'enfant Baoule de Côte d'Ivoire.* Berne: Hans Huber.

Datan, N., Antonovsky, A., & Moaz, B. (1984). Love, war, and the life cycle of the family. In K. A. McCluskey & H. W. Reese (Eds.), *Life-span developmental psychology: Historical and generational effects* (pp. 143–159). New York: Academic Press.

Day, R. D., & Lamb, M. B. (2004). (Eds.). *Conceptualizing and measuring father involvement.* Mahwah, NJ: Lawrence Earlbaum.

Day, R., Nielsen, J., Korten, A., Ernberg, M., et al. (1987). Stressful life events preceding the onset of schizophrenia: A cross-cultural study from the World Health Organization. *Culture, Medicine, and Psychiatry, 11,* 123–205.

Delaney, C. H. (1995). Rites of passage in adolescence. *Adolescence, 30,* 891–897.

Dennis, W. (1973). *Children of the crèche.* New York: Appleton-Century-Crofts.

Dennis, W., & Dennis, M. G. (1940). The effect of cradling practices upon the onset of walking in Hopi children. *Journal of Genetic Psychology, 56,* 77–86.

Dentan, R. K. (1968). *The Semai: A nonviolent people of Malaya.* New York: Holt, Rinehart & Winston.

DeRosier, M. E., & Kupersmidt, J. B. (1991). Costa Rican children's perceptions of their social networks. *Developmental Psychology, 27,* 656–662.

de St. Aubin, E., McAdams, D. P., & Kim, T.C. (Eds.). (2003). *The generative society: Caring for future generations.* Washington, D.C.: American Psychological Association Press.

DeVries, M. W. (1994). Kids in context: Temperament in cross-cultural perspective. In W. B. Carey & S. C. Devitt (Eds.), *Prevention and early intervention: Individual differences as risk factors for the mental health of children.* New York: Brunner/Mazel.

DeVries, M. W., & Sameroff, A. J. (1984). Culture and temperament: Influences on temperament in three East African societies. *American Journal of Orthopsychiatry, 54,* 83–96.

Dhawan, N., & Roseman, I. J. (1988). *Self-concept across two cultures: India and the United States.* Paper presented at the ninth conference of the International Association for Cross-Cultural Psychology, Newcastle, Australia.

Diamond, L. M., & Savin-Williams, R. C. (2002). Gender and sexual identity. In R. M. Lerner, F. Jacobs, & D. Wertlieb, (Eds.), *Handbook of applied developmental science,* Volume 1. (pp. 101–121). Thousand Oaks, CA: Sage.

DiLalla, L. F., & Jones, S. (2000). Genetic and environmental influences on temperament in preschoolers. In V. J. Molfese & D. Molfese (Eds.), *Temperament and personality development across the life span.* Mahwah, NJ: Erlbaum.

Dion, K. L., & Dion, K. K. (1993). Gender and ethnocultural comparisons in styles of love. *Psychology of Women Quarterly, 17,* 463–473.

Diop, A. M. (1989). The place of the elderly in African society. *Impact of Science on Society, 153,* 93–98.

Doi, T. (1973). *The anatomy of dependence.* Tokyo: Kodansha International.

Doka, K. J., & Mertz, M. E. (1998). The meaning and significance of great-grandparenthood. *Gerontologist, 28,* 192–197.

Domino, G. (1992). Cooperation and competition in Chinese and American children. *Journal of Cross-Cultural Psychology, 23*(4), 456–467.

Douki, S., & Tabbane, K. (1996). Culture and depression. *World Health Magazine, 49*(2), 22–26.

Draguns, J. (1990a). Applications of cross-cultural psychology in the field of mental health. In R. Brislin (Ed.), *Applied cross-cultural psychology* (pp. 302–324). Newbury Park, CA: Sage.

Draguns, J. G. (1990b). Normal and abnormal behavior in cross-cultural perspective: Toward specifying the nature of their relationship. In J. J. Berman (Ed.), *Nebraska symposium on motivation 1989* (pp. 236–277). Lincoln: University of Nebraska Press.

Draguns, J. G. (1994). Pathological and clinical aspects. In L. L. Adler & U. P. Gielen (Eds.), *Cross-cultural topics in psychology.* Westport, CT: Praeger.

Draguns, J. R. (1997). Abnormal behavior patterns across cultures: Implications for counseling and psychotherapy. *International Journal of Intercultural Relations, 2,* 213–248.

Draper, P., & Cashdan, E. (1988). Technological change and child behavior among the !Kung. *Ethnology, 27,* 348.

Durbin, D. L., Darling, N., Steinberg, L., & Brown, B. B. (1993). Parenting style and peer group membership among European-American adolescents. *Journal of Research on Adolescence, 3,* 87–100.

Dybdahl, R. (1996, August). *The child in context: Exploring childhood in Somalia*. Paper presented at the Twenty-sixth International Congress of Psychology, Montreal.

Dybdahl, R. (2001). Children and mothers in war: An outcome study of a psychological intervention program. *Child Development, 72,* 1213–1230.

Dybdahl, R. (2002). Children in war in sociocultural context. In R. Dybdahl, *Bosnian women and children in war: Experiences, psychological consequences and psychosocial intervention*. Doctoral thesis. Department of Psychology, Faculty of Social Science: University of Tromsø, Norway.

Dybdahl, R. (2005). Psychosocial assistance to civilians in war—the Bosnian experience. In L. Barbanel & R. Sternberg (Eds.), *Psychosocial intervention in times of crisis*. New York: Springer.

Dybdahl, R., & Hundeide, K. (1998). Childhood in the Somali context: Mothers' and children's ideas about childhood and parenthood. *Psychology and Developing Societies, 10,* 131–145.

Eckensberger, L. H. (1994). Moral development and its measurement across cultures. In W. J. Lonner and R. S. Malpass (Eds.), *Psychology and culture* (pp. 71–78). Boston: Allyn & Bacon.

Edwards, C. P. (1989). The transition from infancy to early childhood: A difficult transition, and a difficult theory. In V. R. Bricker & G. H. Gossen (Eds.), *Ethnographic encounters in Southern Mesoamerica: Essays in honor of Evon Z. Vogt, Jr.* (pp. 167–175). Austin: University of Texas.

Edwards, C. P. (1996). Parenting toddlers. In M. H. Bornstein (Ed.), *Handbook of parenting* (Vol. 1, pp. 41–63). Hillsdale, NJ: Erlbaum.

Edwards, M. (1994). Pollution in the former U.S.S.R.: Lethal legacy. *National Geographic Magazine, 186*(2), 70–99.

Eisenberg, N., Boehnke, K., Schuhler, P., & Silbereisen, R. K. (1985). The development of prosocial behavior and cognition in German children. *Journal of Cross-Cultural Psychology, 16,* 69–82.

Eisenberg, N., & Valiente, C. (2004). Elaborations on a theme: Beyond main effects in relations of parenting to children's coping and regulation. *Parenting: Science and Practice, 4,* 319–323.

Ekpenyong, S. (1995). The structural adjustment programme and the elderly in Nigeria. *International Journal of Aging and Human Development, 41,* 266–280.

Elder, G. H., Jr. (1998a). Life course and development. In R. M. Lerner (Ed.), *Handbook of child psychology Vol. 1: Theoretical models of human development* (5th ed.). New York: Wiley.

Elder, G. H., Jr. (1998b). *Children of the great depression (25th anniversary edition)*. Boulder, CO: Westview Press.

Elder, G. H., Modell, J., & Parke, R. D. (Eds.). (1993). *Children in time and place*. New York: Cambridge University Press.

Eldering, L. (1995). Child rearing in bicultural settings: A culture-ecological approach. *Psychology and Developing Societies, 7,* 133–153.

Elgin, S. H. (2000). *The language imperative*. Cambridge, MA: Perseus Books.

Elkholy, A. (1981). The Arab American family. In C. Mindel & P. Habenstein (Eds.), *Ethnic families in America: Patterns and variations* (pp. 145–162). New York: Elsevier.

Elkin, F., & Handel, G. (1989). *The child and society: The process of socialization* (5th ed.). New York: Random House.

Elkind, D. (1988). *The hurried child: Growing up too fast too soon*. Reading, MA: Addison-Wesley.

Ellis, R. (1994). *The study of second-language acquisition*. Oxford, UK: Oxford University Press.

Ellison, P. T. (Ed.). (2001). *Reproductive ecology and human evolution*. New York: Aldine de Gruyter.

Ember, C. R., & Ember, M. (2000). *Cross-cultural research methods*. Walnut Creek: AltaMira Press.

Ember, C. R., & Ember, M. (2003). *Cultural anthropology*. (11th ed). Englewood Cliffs, NJ: Prentice Hall.

Engels, J. (1993). *Pocket guide to pediatric assessment* (2nd ed.). St. Louis: Mosby.

England, P., Hermsen, J. L., & Cotter, D. (2000). The devaluation of women's work: A comment on Tam. *American Journal of Sociology, 105,* 1741–1751.

Engle, P. L., Zeitlin, M., Medrano, Y., & Garcia, L. M. (1996). Growth consequences of low-income Nicaraguan mothers' theories about feeding 1–year-olds. In S. Harkness & C. M. Super (Eds.), *Parents' cultural belief systems* (pp. 428–446). New York: Guilford Press.

Enright, R. D., Bjerstedt, A., Enright, W. F., Levy, V. M., Buss, R. R., Harwell, M., & Zindler, M. (1984). Distributive justice development: Cross-cultural, contextual, and longitudinal evaluations. *Child Development, 55,* 1737–1751.

Enright, R. D., Franklin, C. C., & Manheim, L. A. (1980). Children's distributive justice reasoning: A standardized and objective scale. *Developmental Psychology, 16,* 193–202.

Epstein, J. L. (1983). Longitudinal effects of family–school–person interactions on student outcomes. *Research in Sociology of Education and Socialization, 4,* 101–107.

Erikson, E. H. (1963). *Childhood and society* (2nd ed.). New York: Norton.

Erikson, E. H. (1982). *The life cycle completed*. New York: Norton.

Erikson, E. H., Erikson, J. M., & Kivnick, H. G. (1986). *Vital involvement in old age*. New York: Norton.

Fagot, B. I., & Leinbach, M. D. (1989). The young child's gender schema: Environmental input, internal organization. *Child Development, 60,* 663–672.

Falbo, T. (1991). The impact of grandparents on children's outcomes in China. *Marriage & Family Review, 16*(3–4), 369–376.

Farver, J. A. M., & Wimbarti, S. (1995). Indonesian children's play with their mothers and older siblings. *Child Development, 66,* 1493–1503.

Fasold, R. (1999). Ebonic need not be English. *ERIC Issue Paper.* Washington, D.C.: ERIC Clearinghouse On Languages and Linguistics.

Fay, W. B. (1993). Families in the 1990s. *Marketing Research, 5*(1), 47.

Ferrante, J. (1992). *Sociology: A global perspective.* Belmont, CA: Wadsworth.

Fine, G. A. (1989). *With the boys: Little baseball and preadolescent culture.* (3rd ed.). Chicago, IL: University of Illinois Press.

Fingerman, K. L. (2004). The role of offspring and children-in-law in grandparents' relationships with grandchildren. *Journal of Family Issues, 25,* 1026–1049.

Fishbein, H. D. (1984). *The psychology of infancy and childhood: Evolutionary and cross-cultural perspectives.* Hillsdale, NJ: Erlbaum.

Fitzgerald, M. H. (1990). The interplay of culture and symptoms: Menstrual symptoms among Samoans. *Medical Anthropology, 12,* 145–167.

Flanagan, C. A., & Eccles, J. S. (1993). Changes in parents' work status and adolescents' adjustment to school. *Child Development, 64,* 246–258.

Fleming, J., Watson, C., McDonald, D., & Alexander, K. (1991). Drug use patterns in Northern Territory Aboriginal communities, 1986–1987. *Drug and Alcohol Review, 10,* 367–380.

Floderus-Myrhed, B., Pedersen, N., & Rasmuson, I. (1980). Assessment of heritability for personality, based on a short form of the Eysenck Personality Inventory: A study of 12,898 twin pairs. *Behavior Genetics, 10,* 153–162.

Flores, G. (2000). Culture and the patient–physician relationship: Achieving cultural competency in health care. *Journal of Pediatrics, 136,* 14–23.

Flouri, E. (2005). *Fathering and child outcomes.* New York: John Wiley & Sons.

Forman, G. E., & Sigel, I. E. (1979). *Cognitive development: A life-span view.* Monterey, CA: Brooks/Cole.

Francis-Connally, E. (2000). Toward an understanding of mothering: A comparison of two motherhood stages. *American Journal of Occupational Therapy, 54,* 281–289.

Frazier, C. L., & Glascock, A. P. (1994). Aging and old age in cross-cultural perspective. In L. L. Adler & U. P. Gielen (Eds.), *Cross–cultural topics in psychology* (pp. 103–111). Westport, CT: Praeger.

Freeman, D. (1983). *Margaret Mead and Samoa.* Cambridge, MA: Harvard University Press.

Friedlmeier, W., Chakkarath, P., & Schwarz, B. (Eds.). (2005). *Culture and human development.* New York: Psychology Press.

Friedman, A., Todd, J., & Kariuki, P. W. (1995). Cooperative and competitive behavior of urban and rural children in Kenya. *Journal of Cross-Cultural Psychology, 26*(4), 374–383.

Friedman, S. L., & Wachs, T. D. (Eds.) (1999). *Conceptualization and assessment of environment across the lifespan.* Washington DC: American Psychological Association.

Fuller, M. L. (1992). Today's demographics don't leave it to Beaver. *Education Digest, 58*(6), 54–57.

Furnham, A., & Alibhai, N. (1983). Cross-cultural differences in the perception of female body shapes. *Psychological Medicine, 13,* 829–837.

Furnham, A., Kirkcaldy, B. D., & Lynn, R. (1994). National attitudes to competitiveness, money, and work among young people: First, second, and third world differences. *Human Relations, 47*(1), 119–132.

Gallimore, R., Weisner, T. S., Kaufman, S. Z., & Bernheimer, L. P. (1989). The social construction of ecocultural niches: Family accommodation of developmentally delayed children. *American Journal on Mental Retardation, 94,* 216–230.

Gander, M. J., & Gardiner, H. W. (1981). *Child and adolescent development.* Boston: Little, Brown.

Gangestad, S. W. (1993.) Sexual selection and physical attractiveness: Implications for mating dynamics. *Human Nature, 4,* 205–235.

Garbarino, J. (1985). *Adolescent development: An ecological perspective.* Columbus, OH: Merrill.

Garbarino, J. (2000). The soul of fatherhood. *Marriage and Family Review, 29,* 11–21.

Gardiner, H. W. (1966). *Newspapers as personalities: A study of the British national daily press.* Unpublished doctoral dissertation. Manchester, UK: University of Manchester.

Gardiner, H. W. (1994). Child development. In L. L. Adler & U. P. Gielen (Eds.), *Cross-cultural topics in psychology* (pp. 61–72). New York: Praeger.

Gardiner, H. W. (1995, March/April). The life of a Buddhist monk. *Calliope: World history for young people.* Peterborough, NH: Cobblestone Publishing.

Gardiner, H. W. (1996). *Cross-cultural content in contemporary developmental textbooks.* Paper presented at the thirteenth congress of the International Association for Cross-Cultural Psychology, Montreal, Canada.

Gardiner, H. W. (2001a). Child and adolescent development. In L. L. Adler and U. P. Gielen (Eds.), *Cross-cultural topics in psychology* (2nd ed.). Westport, CT: Greenwood.

Gardiner, H. W. (2001b). Culture, context, and development. In D. Matsumoto (Ed.), *The handbook of culture and psychology.* New York: Oxford University Press.

Gardiner, H. W. (2004). Follow the yellow brick road: New approaches to the study of cross-cultural human development. In U. P. Gielen & J. L. Roopnarine (Eds.), *Childhood and adolescence. Vol. 2: Cross-cultural applications.* Westport, CT: Greenwood Press.

Gardiner, H. W., & Gardiner, O. S. (1991). Women in Thailand. In L. L. Adler (Ed.), *Women in cross-cultural perspective* (pp. 174–187). New York: Praeger.

Gardiner, H. W., & Mutter, J. D. (1994). *Measuring multicultural awareness and identity: A model.* Paper presented at the twenty-third annual meeting of the Society for Cross-Cultural Research, Santa Fe, NM.

Gauvian, M., & Cole, M. (Eds.) (2005). *Readings on the development of children* (4th ed.) New York: Worth.

Geertz, C. (1973). *The interpretation of cultures.* New York: Basic Books.

Gibbons, J. L., Stiles, D. A., Perez-Prada, E., Shkodriani, G. M., & Medina, M. (1996, February). *Adolescents' beliefs about women's and men's roles in Iceland, Mexico, Spain, and the United States.* Paper presented at the 25th annual meeting of the Society for Cross-Cultural Research, Pittsburgh, PA.

Gibson, J. T., Westwood, M. J., Ishiyama, F. I., Borgen, W. A., et al. (1991). Youth and culture: A seventeen nation study of perceived problems and coping strategies. *International Journal for the Advancement of Counselling, 14,* 203–216.

Gielen, U., & Jeshmaridian, S. S. (1999). Lev S. Vygotsky: The man and the era. In H. Adler (Ed.), *Piaget and Vygotsky.* New York: New York Academy of Sciences.

Gielen, U., & Roopnarine, J. L. (Eds.). (2004). *Childhood and adolescence across cultures.* Westport, CT: Praeger.

Gilligan, C. (1982). *In a different voice: Psychological theory and women's development.* Cambridge, MA: Harvard University Press.

Ginsberg, H. P., Choi, Y. E., Lopez, L. S., Netley, R., & Chao-Yuan, C. (2000). Happy birthday to you: Early mathematical thinking of Asian, South American, and U.S. children. In T. Nunes & P. Bryant (Eds.), *Learning and teaching mathematics: An international perspective.* New York: Psychology Press.

Gladwin, T., & Sarason, S. B. (1953). *Truk: Man in paradise.* (Viking Fund Publications in Anthropology No. 20). New York: Wenner-Gren Foundation for Anthropological Research.

Goh, D., & Gardiner, H. W. (2004). Culture and achievement. In C. Spielberger (Ed.), *Encyclopedia of Applied Psychology.* New York: Academic Press.

Goldberg, S. (1972). Infant care and growth in urban Zambia. *Human Development, 15,* 77–89.

Golombok, S. (2002). Parenting and contemporary reproductive technologies. In M. H. Bornstein (Ed.), *Handbook of parenting* (Vol. 3, 2nd ed., pp. 339–360). Mahwah, NJ: Erlbaum.

Gonzales, G. F., & Villena, A. (1996). Body mass index and age at menarche in Peruvian children living at high altitudes and at sea level. *Human Biology, 68*(2), 265–276.

Goodnow, J. J. (1990). The socialization of cognition. In J. W. Stigler, R. A. Shweder, & G. Herdt (Eds.), *Cultural psychology: Essays on comparative human development.* Cambridge, England: Cambridge University Press.

Goodnow, J. J., & Bethon, G. (1966). Piaget's tasks: The effects of schooling on intelligence. *Child Development, 37,* 573–582.

Gopal-McNicol, S. (1995). A cross-cultural examination of racial identity and racial preference of preschool children in the West Indies. *Journal of Cross-Cultural Psychology, 26,* 141–152.

Gotowiec, A., & Beiser, M. (1993). Aboriginal children's mental health: Unique challenges. *Canada's Mental Health, 41,* 7–11.

Graf, P., & Ohta, N. (Eds.) (2000). *Lifespan Development of Human Memory.* Boston, MA: MIT Press.

Grant, J. P. (1994). *The state of the world's children.* New York: UNICEF and Oxford University Press.

Green, J. A., Irwin, J. R., & Gustafson, G. E. (2000). Acoustic cry analysis, neonatal status and long-term developmental outcomes. In R. G. Barr, B. Hopkins, & J. A. Green (Eds.), *Crying as a sign, a symptom, & a signal.* New York: Cambridge University Press.

Greenfield, P. M. (1997). Culture as process: Empirical methods for cultural psychology. In J. W. Berry, Y. H. Poortinga, & J. Pandey, (Eds.), *Handbook of cross-cultural psychology: Vol. 1: Theory and method* (2nd ed.). Boston: Allyn & Bacon.

Greenfield, P. M., Brazelton, T. B., & Childs, C. P. (1989). From birth to maturity in Zinacantan: Ontogenesis in cultural context. In V. R. Bricker & G. H. Gossen (Eds.), *Ethnographic encounters in Southern Mesoamerica: Essays in honor of Evon Z. Vogt, Jr.* (pp. 177–216). Austin: University of Texas.

Greenfield, P. M., & Cocking, R. R. (1994). *Cross-cultural roots of minority child development.* Hillsdale, NJ: Erlbaum.

Gregg, Gary S. (2005). *The Middle East: A cultural psychology*. New York: Oxford University Press.

Grossman, B., Wirt, R., & Davids, A. (1985). Self-esteem, ethnic identity, and behavioral adjustment among Anglo and Chicano adolescents in West Texas. *Journal of Adolescence, 8*, 57–68.

Grossmann, K. E., Grossman, K. G., & Waters, E. (2005). *Attachment from infancy to adulthood: The major longitudinal studies*. New York: Guilford Press.

Grusec, J. E. (2002), Parental socialization and children's acquisition of values. In M. H. Bornstein (Ed.), *Handbook of parenting* (Vol. 5, 2nd ed., pp. 143–167). Mahwah, NJ: Erlbaum.

Grusec, J. E., & Hastings, P. D. (Eds.). (2006). *Handbook of socialization*. New York: Guilford Press.

Haan, N. (1991). Moral development and action from a social constructivist perspective. In W. M. Kurtines, & J. L. Gewirtz (Eds.), *Handbook of moral behavior and development, Vol. 1: Theory* (pp. 251–273). Hillsdale, NJ: Erlbaum.

Haan, N., Aerts, E., & Cooper, B. B. (1985). *On moral grounds: The search for a practical morality*. New York: New York University Press.

Hagestad, G. O. (2000). Adult intergenerational relationships. Ch. 4, *Generations and Gender Programme. Exploring future research and data collection options*. United Nations/New York and Geneva.

Hakuta, K., Bialystok, E., & Wiley, E. (2003). Critical evidence: A test of the critical-period hypothesis for second-language acquisition. *Psychological Science, 14*, 31–38.

Hall, G. S. (1904). *Adolescence*. New York: Appleton-Century-Crofts.

Hall, G. S. (1922). *Senescence: The last half of life*. New York: Appleton-Century-Crofts.

Hall, M. (1997). *The big book of sumo: History, practice, ritual, fight*. Berkeley, CA: Stone Bridge Press.

Hamilton, C. E. (2000). Continuity and discontinuity of attachment from infancy through adolescence. *Child Development, 71*, 690–694.

Hamon, R. R., & Ingoldsby, B. B. (Eds.). (2003). *Mate selection across cultures*. Thousand Oaks, CA: Sage.

Hampel, P., & Petermann, F. (2006). Perceived stress, coping, and adjustment in adolescents. *Journal of Adolescent Health, 38*, 409–415.

Harkness, S. (2005). Themes and variations: Parental ethnotheories in seven Western cultures. In K. Rubin (Ed.), *Parental beliefs, parenting, and child development in cross-cultural perspectives*. New York: Psychology Press.

Harkness, S., Hughes, M., Muller, B., & Super, C. M. (2005). Entering the developmental niche: Mixed methods in an intervention program for inner city children. In T. Weisner (Ed.), *Discovering successful pathways in children in development: Mixed methods in the study of childhood and family life*. Chicago: University of Chicago Press.

Harkness, S., & Keefer, C. H. (2000). Contributions of cross-cultural psychology to research and interventions in education and health. *Journal of cross-cultural psychology, 31*, 92–109.

Harkness, S., Moscardino, U., Bermudez, M. R., Zylicz, P. O., Welles-Nystrom, B., Blom, M., Parmar, P., Axia, G., Palacios, J., & Super, C. M. (2006). Mixed methods in international collaborative research: The experiences of the international study of parents, children, and schools. *Cross-cultural research, 40*, 1–18.

Harkness, S., & Super, C. M. (1985). The cultural context of gender segregation in children's peer groups. *Child Development, 56*, 219–224.

Harkness, S., & Super, C. M. (1995). Culture and parenting. In M. Bornstein (Ed.), *Handbook of parenting* (Vol. 2, pp. 211–234). Hillsdale, NJ: Erlbaum.

Harkness, S., & Super, C. M. (Eds.). (1996). *Parents' cultural belief systems: Their origins, expressions, and consequences*. New York: Guilford Press.

Harkness, S., & Super, C. M. (2003) Culture and parenting. In M. Bornstein (Ed.), *Handbook of parenting* (2nd ed.). (Vol. 2, pp. 253–280). Mahwah, NJ: Erlbaum.

Harlow, H. F., & Harlow, M. K. (1962). Social deprivation in monkeys. *Scientific American, 207*, 136–146.

Harlow, H. F., & Zimmermann, R. R. (1959). Affectional responses in the infant monkey. *Science, 130*, 421–432.

Harris, J. A. (1999). Review and methodological considerations in research on testosterone and aggression. *Aggression & Violent Behavior, 4*, 273–291.

Harrison, A. O., Stewart, R. B., Myambo, K., & Teveraishe, C. (1995). Perceptions of social networks among adolescents from Zimbabwe and the United States. *Journal of Black Psychology, 21*, 382–407.

Harter, S. (1982). The perceived competence scale for children. *Child Development, 53*, 87–97.

Hartup, W. W. (1983). Peer groups. In P. H. Mussen (Gen. Ed.), *Handbook of child psychology* (Vol. 4, pp. 103–196). New York: Wiley.

Harvard Mental Health Letter (March, 1999). AIDS and mental health, Part 1. *The Harvard Mental Health Letter, 15*, 1–4.

Hashim, I. H., & Zhiliang, Y. (2003). Cultural and gender differences in perceiving stressors: A cross-cultural investigation of African and Western college students in Chinese colleges. *Stress and Health, 19*, 217–225.

Hatfield, E., & Rapson, R. L. (2005). *Love & sex: Cross-cultural perspectives*. Lanham, MD: University Press of America.

Hatta, T. (1994). Cohort effects in the lateral preference of Japanese people. *Journal of General Psychology, 21,* 377–380

Heinicke, C. M. (1995). Determinants of the transition to parenting. In M. H. Bornstein (Ed.), *Handbook of parenting* (Vol. 3, pp. 277–303). Mahwah, NJ: Erlbaum.

Helson, R., Kwan, V. S. Y., John, O. P. and Jones, C. (2002). The growing evidence for personality change in adulthood: Findings from research with personality inventories. *Journal of Research in Personality, 36,* 287–306.

Helson, R., Mitchell, V., & Moane, G. (1984). Personality patterns of adherence and nonadherence to the social clock. *Journal of Personality and Social Psychology, 46,* 1079–1096.

Hendrick, J. B. (1990). Early childhood. In R. Thomas (Ed.), *The encyclopedia of human development and education: Theory, research, and studies.* Oxford: Pergamon.

Hendry, J. (1986). *Becoming Japanese.* Honolulu: University of Hawaii Press.

Hendry, J. (1993). Becoming Japanese: The arenas and agents of socialization. In R. H. Wozniak (Ed.), *Worlds of childhood reader.* New York: HarperCollins.

Herdt, G., McClintock, M. (2000). The magical age of 10. *Archives of Sexual Behavior, 29,* 587–606.

Heron, A., & Kroeger, E. (1981). Introduction to developmental psychology. In H. C. Triandis, & A. Heron (Eds.), *Handbook of cross-cultural psychology,* (1st ed., Vol. 4). Boston: Allyn & Bacon.

Herskovits, M. J. (1948). *Man and his works: The science of cultural anthropology.* New York: Knopf.

Ho, D. Y. F. (2000). Dialetical thinking: Neither Eastern nor Western. *American Psychologist, 55,* 1064–1065.

Hobbs, D, & Wright, R. (Eds.). (2006). *The Sage Handbook of Fieldwork.* London, UK: Sage Publications, Ltd.

Hofstede, G. (1996). *Masculinity, religion, gender and sex.* Paper presented at 13th Congress of the International Association for Cross-Cultural Psychology, Montreal, Canada.

Hofstede, G. (2001). *Culture's consequences: Comparing values, behaviors, institutions, and organizations across cultures,* 2nd ed. Thousand Oaks, CA: Sage.

Hofstede, G., & Hofstede, G. J. (2004). *Cultures and organizations: Software of the mind* (2nd ed.). New York: McGraw-Hill.

Hoghughi, M., & Long, N. (2004). (Eds.). *Handbook of parenting.* Thousand Oaks, CA: Sage.

Hollos, M., & Leis, P. E. (1989). *Becoming Nigerian in Ibo society.* New Brunswick, NJ: Rutgers University Press.

Hollos, M., & Richards, F. A. (1993). Gender-associated development of formal operations in Nigerian adolescents. *Ethos, 21,* 24–52.

Holmbeck, G. N., Paikoff, R. L., & Brooks-Gunn, J. (1995). Parenting adolescents. In M. H. Bornstein (Ed.), *Handbook of parenting* (Vol. 1, pp. 91–118). Mahwah, NJ: Erlbaum.

Holmes, E. R., & Holmes, L. D. (1995). *Other cultures, elder years.* Thousand Oaks, CA: Sage.

Hopkins, B., & Westra, T. (1988). Maternal handling and motor development: An intracultural study. *Genetic, Social and General Psychology Monographs, 14,* 377–420.

Horn, J. L., & Cattell, R. B. (1967). Age differences in fluid and crystalized intelligence. *Acta Psychologica, 26,* 107–129.

Horn, J. L., & Hofer, S. M. (1992). Major abilities and development in the adult period. In R. J. Sternberg and C. A. Berg (Eds.), *Intellectual development.* Cambridge, England: Cambridge University Press.

Hrdy, S. (1999). *Mother nature: Material instincts and how they shape the human species.* Ballantine Group.

Hsu, F. L. K. (1985). The self in cross-cultural perspective. In A. J. Marsella, G. DeVos, & F. L. K. Hsu (Eds.), *Culture and self: Asian and Western perspectives* (pp. 24–55). New York: Tavistock.

Hsu, F. L. K., Watrous, B. G., & Lord, E. M. (1961). Culture pattern and adolescent behaviour. *International Journal of Social Psychiatry, 7,* 33–53.

Hu, Y.-H. (1995). Elderly suicide risk in family context: A critique of the Asian family care model. *Journal of Cross Cultural Psychology, 10,* 199–217.

Huebner, A. M., & Garrod, A. C. (1993). Moral reasoning among Tibetan monks. A study of Buddhist adolescents and young adults in Nepal. *Journal of Cross-Cultural Psychology, 24,* 167–185.

Hymes, D. (1996). *Ethnography, linguistics, narrative inequality: Toward an understanding of voice.* London: Taylor & Francis.

Hymes, D. (Ed.). (1999). *Reinventing anthropology.* Ann Arbor: University of Michigan Press.

Indran, S. K. (1995). Brief report: Eating attitudes among adolescent girls in Malaysian secondary school using the EAT questionnaire. *International Journal of Social Psychiatry, 41*(4), 299–303.

Inhelder, B., & Piaget, J. (1959). *The early growth of logic in the child: Classification and seriation.* New York: Harper & Row.

Isralowitz, R. E., & Hong, O. T. (1990). Singapore youth: The impact of social status on perceptions of adolescent problems. *Adolescence, 98,* 357–362.

Iwawaiki, S., & Kerner, R. M. (1974). Cross-cultural analysis of body build stereotypes of Japanese and American males and females. *Psychologia, 17,* 75–81.

Jablensky, A., Sartorius, N., Ernberg, G., Anker, M., Korten, A., Cooper, J. E., Day, R., & Bertelsen, A. (1992). Schizophrenia: Manifestations, incidence and course in different cultures: A World Health Organization ten-country study. *Psychological Medicine (Monograph Suppl.* No. 20).

Jacobson, K. (2002). ADHD in cross-cultural perspective: Some empirical results. *American Anthropologist, 104,* 283–286.

Jahoda, G. (1982). *Psychology and anthropology: A psychological perspective.* London: Academic Press.

Jahoda, G. (1986). A cross-cultural perspective on developmental psychology. *International Journal of Behavioral Development, 9,* 417–437.

Jahoda, G., & Krewer, B. (1997). History of cross-cultural and cultural psychology. In J. W. Berry, Y. H. Poortinga, & J. Pandey (Eds.), *Handbook of cross-cultural psychology: Theory and method* (Vol. 1, pp. 1–42). Boston: Allyn & Bacon.

Janssen, J. P. (2000). Foundations of a functional theory of human handedness. *Theory & Psychology, 10,* 375–398.

Jenni, O. G., & O'Connor, B. B. (2005). Children's Sleep: An Interplay Between Culture and Biology. *Pediatrics,* Vol. 115, pp. 204–216.

Jensen, L. A. (2003). Coming of age in a multicultural world: Globalization and adolescent cultural identity formation. *Applied Developmental Science, 7,* 188–195.

Johnson, J. S., & Newport, E. L. (1989). Critical period effects in second-language learning: the influence of maturational state on the acquisition of English as a second language. *Cognitive Psychology, 21,* 60–99.

Johnson, K. S., Elbert-Avila, K. I., & Tulsky, J. A. (2005). The influence of spiritual beliefs and practices on the treatment preferences of Africans Americans: A review of the literature. *Journal of the American Geriatrics Society, 53,* 711–719.

Jordan, B. (1978). *Birth in four cultures: A crosscultural investigation of childbirth in Yucatan, Holland, Sweden and the United States.* St. Albans, VT: Eden Women's Publications.

Jordan, B., & Davis-Floyd, R. (1993). *Birth in four cultures: A crosscultural investigation of childbirth in Yucatan, Holland, Sweden and the United States* (4th ed.). Prospect Heights, IL: Waveland Press.

Judge, T.A., Erez, A., Bono, J. E., and Thoresen, C. J. (2002). Are measures of self-esteem, neuroticism, locus of control, and generalized self-efficacy indicators of a common core construct? *Journal of Personality and Social Psychology, 83,* 693–710.

Kaffman, M. (1993). Kibbutz youth: Recent past and present. *Journal of Youth and Adolescence, 22,* 573–604.

Kagan, J., Kearsley, R. B., & Zealazo, P. (1978). *Infancy: Its place in human development.* Cambridge, MA: Harvard University Press.

Kagitcibasi, C. (1996). *Family and human development across cultures.* Mahwah, NJ: Erlbaum.

Kalu, W., & Kalu, O. (1993). Nigeria. In L. L. Adler (Ed.), *International handbook on gender roles* (Chap. 17). Westport, CT: Greenwood Press.

Kamara, A. I., & Easley, J. A., Jr. (1977). Is the rate of cognitive development uniform across cultures? A methodological critique with new evidence from Themne children. In P. R. Dasen (Ed.), *Piagetian psychology: Cross-cultural contributions* (pp. 26–63). New York: Gardner/Wiley.

Kasuya, H. (2002). Bilingual context for language development. In S. Blum-Kulka & C. E. Snow (Eds.), *Talking to Adults: The contribution of multi-party discourse to language acquisition* (pp. 299–325). Mahwah, NJ: Erlbaum.

Katz, M. M., Maesella, A., Dube, K. C., Olatawura, M., Takahashi, R., Nakane, Y., Wynne, L. C., Gift, T., Brennan, J., Sartorius, N., & Jablensky, A. (1998). On the expression of psychosis in different cultures: Schizophrenia in an Indian and in a Nigerian community. *Culture, Medicine, and Psychiatry, 12:* 331–355.

Kazarian, S. S., & Evans, D. R. (2001). *Handbook of cultural health psychology.* San Diego, CA: Academic Press.

Kazdin, A. E. (Ed.). (2000). *Encyclopedia of Psychology.* Washington, DC: American Psychological Association.

Keller, H., & Greenfield, P. M. (2000). History and future of development in cross-cultural psychology. *Journal of Cross-Cultural Psychology, 31,* 52–62.

Kelly, M. (1977). Papua New Guinea and Piaget—An eight-year study. In P. R. Dasen (Ed.), *Piagetian psychology: Cross-cultural contributions* (pp. 169–202). New York: Gardner Press.

Kelso, B. J. (1994, September/October). Movement to combat female mutilation. *African Report,* 60–61.

Kemper, S. (1992). Language and aging. In F. I. M. Craik & T. A. Salthouse (Eds.), *The handbook of aging and cognition.* Hillsdale, NJ: Erlbaum.

Kerig, P. K., Alyoshina, Y. Y., & Volovich, A. (1993). Gender-role socialization in contemporary Russia: Implications for cross-cultural research. *Psychology of Women Quarterly, 17,* 389–408.

Kenkel, W. F. (1985). *The family in perspective* (5th ed.). Houston, TX: Cap and Gown Press.

Kim, K. (1995). Culture and mental illness in South Korea. In I. Al-Issa (Ed.), *Handbook of culture and mental illness.* Madison, WI: International Universities Press.

Kim, K., & Won, H. (1997). Students' stress in China, Japan and Korea: Transcultural study. *International Journal of Social Psychiatry, 43,* 87–94.

Kim, U., Park, Y-S., & Park, D. (2000). The challenge of cross-cultural psychology: The role of the indigenous psychologies. *Journal of Cross-Cultural Psychology, 31,* 63–75.

Kim, U., & Yang, K. S. (Eds.). (2005). *Indigenous and cultural psychology: Understanding people in context.* New York: Kluwer/Academic Plenum.

Kimm, S. Y. S., Glynn, N. W., Obarzanek, E., Kriska, A. M., Daniels, S. R., Barton, B. A., & Liu, K. (2005). Relation between the changes in physical activity and body-mass index during adolescence: a multicentre longitudinal study. *www.thelancet.com, Vol 366, July 23, 2005.*

Kirkby, R. J., Kolt, G. S., & Habel, K. (1998). Cultural factors in exercise participation of older adults. *Perceptual and Motor Skills, 87,* 890.

Kirmayer, L. J. (1991). The place of culture in psychiatric nosology: Taijinkyofusho and the DSM-III-R. *Journal of Nervous and Mental Disease, 179,* 19–28.

Kirmayer, L. J., & Looper, K. J. (2006). Abnormal illness behavior. Physiological, psychological, and social dimensions of coping with illness. *Current Opinion in Psychiatry, 19,* 54–60.

Kirmayer, L. J., & Minas, H. (2000). The future of cultural psychiatry: an international perspective. *Canadian Journal of Psychiatry, 45,* 438–46.

Kitayama, S., & Markus, H. (Eds.) (1994), *Culture and emotion.* Washington, DC: American Psychological Association.

Klineberg, O. (1980). Historical perspectives: cross-cultural psychology before 1960. In H. C. Triandis & W. W. Lambert (Eds.), *Handbook of cross-cultural psychology: Vol. 1,* (pp. 1–14). Boston: Allyn & Bacon.

Knafo, A., & Schwartz, S. H. (2003). Parenting and adolescents' accuracy in perceiving parental values. *Child Development, 74,* 595–612.

Koffka, K. (1935). *Principles of gestalt psychology.* New York: Harcourt Brace.

Kohlberg, L. (1981). *Essays on moral development* (Vol. 1). New York: Harper & Row.

Kohlberg, L., & Gilligan, C. (1971). The adolescent as philosopher: The discovery of self in a post-conventional world. *Daedalus, 100,* 1051–1086.

Kohler, K. (1938). *The place of value in a world of facts.* New York: Liveright.

Konner, M. J. (1976). Maternal care, infant behavior and development among the !Kung. In R. B. Lee & I. DeVore (Eds.), *Kalahari hunter-gatherers: Studies of the !Kung San and their neighbors.* Cambridge, MA: Harvard University Press.

Korn, S., & Gannon, S. (1983). Temperament, culture variation, and behavior disorders in preschool children. *Child Psychiatry and Human Development, 13,* 203–212.

Kornhaber, A. (1996). *Contemporary grandparenting.* Thousand Oaks, CA: Sage.

Kostelny, K., & Garbarino, J. (1994). Coping with the consequences of living in danger: The case of Palestinian children and youth. *International Journal of Behavioral Development, 17,* 595–611.

Kozulin, A. (1990). *Vygotsky's psychology: A biography of ideas.* New York: Harvester Wheatsheaf.

Krishnan, L. (1999). Socialization and cognitive–moral influences on justice rule preferences: The case of Indian culture. In T. S. Saraswathi (Ed.), *Culture, socialization and human development: Theory, research, and applications in India.* Thousand Oaks, CA: Sage Publications.

Kroeber, A. L., and Kluckhohn, C. (1952). *Culture, Part III.* Papers of the Peabody Museum of Harvard University.

Kumari, R. (1988). *Female sexuality in Hinduism.* Delhi: Joint Women's Programme by ISPCK.

Kunzmann, U., & Baltes, P. B. (2005). The psychology of wisdom. *Personality and Social Psychology Bulletin, 29,* 1104–1119.

Kwan, V. S. Y., Bond, M. H., & Singelis, T. M. (1997). Pancultural explanations for life-satisfaction: Adding relationship harmony to self-esteem. *Journal of Personality and Social Psychology, 73,* 1038–1051.

Labouvie-Vief, G. (1986). *Mind and self in life-span development.* Symposium on developmental dimensions of adult adaptation: Perspectives in mind, self, and emotion. Presented at the 1986 meeting of the Gerontological Association of America, Chicago, IL.

Laland, K. N., Kumm, J., van Horn, J. D., & Feldman, M. W. (1995). A gene-culture model of human handedness. *Behavior Genetics, 25,* 433–445.

Lalor, K. J. (1999). Street children: A comparative perspective. *Child Abuse & Neglect, 23,* 759–770.

Lamb, M. E. (Ed.). (1987). *The role of the father: Cross-cultural perspectives.* Hillsdale, NJ: Erlbaum.

Lamb, M. E. (Ed.). (2003). *The role of the father in child development* (4th ed.). New York: Wiley & Sons

Lamb, M. E., Pleck, J., Charnov, E. L., & Levine, J. A. (1987). A biosocial perspective on paternal behavior and involvement. In J. B. Lancaster, J. Altmann, A. Rossi, & L. R. Sherrod (Eds.), *Parenting across the life span: Biosocial perspectives* (pp. 111–142). Chicago, IL: Aldine.

Lambert, W. W. (1971). Cross-cultural backgrounds to personality development and the socialization of aggression: Findings from the six cultures study. In W. Lambert and R. Weisbrod (Eds.), *Comparative perspectives on social psychology* (pp. 49–61). Boston: Little, Brown.

Lancy, D. (1980). Work and play: The Kpelle children during rapid cultural change. In D. F. Lancy & B. A. Tindall (Eds.), *The anthropological study of play: Problems and prospects.* West Point, NY: Leisure Press.

Landale, N. S., Oropesa, R. S., & Gorman, B. K. (2000). Migration and infant death: Assimilation and selective migration among Puerto Ricans. *American Sociological Review, 65,* 888–909.

Launer, L. J. (1993). The work patterns of lactating women in Madura. *Social Science & Medicine, 37*(4), 555–563.

Laurendeau-Bendavid, M. (1977). Culture, schooling, and cognitive development: A comparative study of children in French Canada and Rwanda. In P. R. Dasen (Ed.), *Piagetian psychology: Cross-cultural contributions* (pp. 123–168). New York: Gardner Press.

Lebra, T. (1999). *Feminism from a Japanese perspective: The experience of Japanese professional women.* Paper presented at the Feminists Doing Psychological Anthropology Year 2000 Conference, Stockholm, Sweden.

Lefrancois, G. R. (1996). *The lifespan* (5th ed.). Belmont, CA: Wadsworth.

Lennartsson, C. (1999). Social ties and health among the very old in Sweden. *Research in Aging, 21,* 657–681.

Lerner, R., Brennan, A. L., & Noh, E. R. (1998). *The parenting of adolescents and adolesce nts as parents: A developmental contextual perspective. http://parenthood.library.wisc.edu/Lerner/ Lerner.html.*

le Roux, J., & Smith, C. S. (1998). Psychological characteristics of South African street children. *Adolescence, 33,* 891–899.

Levitt, M. J., Guacci-Franco, N., & Levitt, J. L. (1993). Convoys of social support in childhood and early adolescence: Structure and function. *Developmental Psychology, 29,* 811–818.

Levy, B. S., Wilkinson, F. S., & Marine, W. M. (1971). Reducing neonatal mortality rate with nurse midwives. *American Journal of Obstetrics and Gynecology, 109,* 50–58.

Levy, R. (1996). Essential contrasts: Differences in parental ideas about learners and teaching in Tahiti and Nepal. In S. Harkness & C. M. Super (Eds.), *Parents' cultural belief systems: Their origins, expressions, and consequences.* New York: Guilford.

Lewin, K. (1935). *A dynamic theory of personality.* New York: McGraw-Hill.

Lewis, M., Feiring, C., & Rosenthal, S. (2000) Attachment over time. *Child Development, 71,* 707–720.

Li, J., & Yue, X. (2004). Self in learning among Chinese children. *New directions in child and adolescent development, 104,* 27–43.

Liu, X. C, Liu L. Q., & Wang, R. Z. (2003). Bedsharing, sleep habits, and sleep problems among Chinese school-aged children. *Sleep, 26,* 89–94.

Liu, Z., Liu, L., Owens, J. A., & Kaplan, D. L. (2005). Sleep patterns and sleep problems among schoolchildren in the United States and China, *Pediatrics, 115,* 241–249.

Lock, M. (1991). Contested meanings of the menopause. *Lancet, 337,* 1270–1272.

Lockery, S. (1991). Caregiving among racial and ethnic minority elders. *Generations, 15*(4), 58–62.

Lonner, W. J. (2005). The psychological study of culture: Issues and questions of enduring importance. In W. Friedlmeier, P. Chakkarath, & B. Schwarz (Eds.), *Culture and human development* (pp. 9–25). New York: Psychology Press.

Lonner, W. J., & Ibrahim, F. A. (2002). Appraisal and assessment in cross-cultural counseling. In P. Pedersen, J. Draguns, W. Lonner, & J. Trimble (Eds.), *Counseling across cultures* (5th ed.). Honolulu: University of Hawaii Press.

Lonner, W. J., & Malpass, R. (Eds.). (1994). *Psychology and culture.* Boston: Allyn & Bacon.

Loscocco, K., & Kalleberg, A. (1988). Age and the meaning of work in the United States and Japan. *Social Forces, 67,* 337–357.

Low, B. S. (1989). Cross-cultural patterns in the training of children: An evolutionary perspective. *Journal of Comparative Psychology, 103,* 311–319.

Luria, A. R. (1981). *Language and cognition* (J. V. Wertsch, Ed.). New York: Wiley Intersciences.

Lusk, M. (1992). Street children of Rio de Janeiro. *International Social Work, 35,* 293–305.

Lykken, D. T. (2000). Reconstructing fathers. *American Psychologist, 55,* 681–682.

Ma, H. K. (1989). Moral orientation and moral judgment in adolescents in Hong Kong, Mainland China, and England. *Journal of Cross-Cultural Psychology, 20,* 152–177.

Maccoby, E. E. (1990). Gender and relationships. A developmental account. *American Psychologist, 45,* 513–520.

Maccoby, E. E. (1998). *The two sexes: Growing up apart, coming together.* Cambridge, MA: Harvard University Press.

Maccoby, E. E. (2002). Gender and group processes: A developmental perspective. *Current Directions in Psychological Science, 11,* 55–58.

MacDorman, M., & Singh, G. (1998). Midwifery care, social and medical risk factors, and birth outcomes in the USA. *Journal of Epidemiology Community Health, 52,* 310–317.

Maclachlan, M. (2006). *Culture and health.* New York: John Wiley & Sons.

MacLeod, R. B. (1947). The phenomenological approach to social psychology. *Psychological Review, 54,* 193–210.

MacNeilage, P. F., & Davis, B. L. (2000). On the origin of internal structure of word forms. *Science, 288,* 527–531.

Main, M., & Solomon, J. (1990). Procedures for identifying infants as disorganized/disoriented during the Ainsworth strange situation. In M. Greenberg, D. Cicchetti, & E. M. Cummings (Eds), *Attachment in the preschool years: Theories, research, and intervention.* Chicago, IL.: University of Chicago Press.

Mallinckrodt B. (2000). Attachment and social competencies, social support, and interpersonal process in psychotherapy. *Psychotherapy Research 10,* 239–266.

Markus, H., & Kitayama, S. (1991). Culture and the self: Implications for cognition, emotion, and motivation. *Psychological Review, 98,* 224–253.

Marshall, L. (1976). *The !Kung of Nyae Nyae.* Cambridge, MA: Harvard University Press.

Marsiglio, W., & Cohan, M. (2000). Contextualizing father involvement and paternal influence: Sociological and qualitative themes. *Marriage & Family Review, 29,* 75–95.

Martin, C. L. (1990). Attudes and expectations about children with nontraditional and traditional gender roles. *Sex Roles, 22,* 151–165.

Mascolo, M. F., Misra, G., Rapisardi, C. (2004). Individual and relational conceptions of self in India and the United States. *New Directions in Child and Adolescent Development, 104,* 9–26.

Matchinda, B. (1999). The impact of home background on the decision of children to run away: The case of Yaounde city street children in Cameroon. *Child Abuse & Neglect, 23,* 245–255.

Matsumoto, D. (2000). *Culture and psychology: People and the world* (2nd ed.). Belmont, CA: Wadsworth.

Matsumoto, D. (Ed.). (2001) *The handbook of culture and psychology.* New York: Oxford University Press.

Matsumoto, D., & Juang, L. (2004). *Culture and psychology* (3rd ed.). Belmont, CA: Wadsworth.

McCrae, R. R. (2004). Human nature and culture: A trait perspective. *Journal of Research in Personality, 38,* 3–14.

McCrae, R. R., & Allik, J. (Eds.), (2002). *The Five-factor Model of personality across cultures.* New York: Kluwer Academic/Plenum Publishers.

McCrae, R. R., & Costa, P. T., Jr. (1990). *Personality in adulthood.* New York: Guilford.

McCrae, R. R., & Costa, P. T. (2003). *Personality in adulthood: A five-factor theory perspective* (2nd ed.). Guilford, New York.

McCrae, R. R., Costa, P. T., Jr., de Lima, M. P., Simoes, A., Ostendorf, F., Angleitner, A., Marusic, L., Bratko, D., Chae, J.-H., & Piedmont, R. L. (1999). Age differences in personality across the adult life span: Parallels in five cultures. *Developmental Psychology, 35,* 466–477.

McCrae, R. R., & John, O. P. (1992). An introduction to the five-factor model and its applications. *Journal of Personality, 60,* 175–216.

McGann, P. J. (1999). Skirting the gender normal divide: A tomboy life story. In: M. Romero and A. J. Stewart (Eds.), *Women's untold stories: Breaking silence, talking back, voicing complexity.* (pp. 105–124). New York: Routledge.

McKenna, J. (1999). Cultural influences on infant and childhood sleep biology and the science that studies it: Toward a more inclusive paradigm. In J. Loughlin, et al. (Eds.), *Sleep in development and pediatrics.* New York: Marcel Dekker.

McKenna, J. (2002). Breastfeeding and bedsharing: Still useful (and important) after all these years (Special Issue). *Mothering,* 28–37.

Mead, G. H. (1934). *Mind, self, and society.* Chicago: University of Chicago Press.

Mead, M. (1973). *Coming of age in Samoa: A psychological study of primitive youth.* New York: American Museum of Natural History. (Original work published 1928.)

Meijer, L., Super, C. M., & Harkness, S. (1997). *Culture, temperament, and parents' perceptions of children's "difficult" behavior in the Netherlands and the U.S.* Paper presented at the twenty-sixth annual meeting of the Society for Cross-Cultural Research, San Antonio, TX.

Meng, J. M. (1991). The pattern of family and quality of life. *Journal of Gerontology, 3,* 135–140.

Meredith, H. V. (1978). Research between 1960 and 1970 on the standing height of young children in different parts of the world. In H. W. Reece & L. P. Lipsitt (Eds.), *Advances in Child Development and Behavior* (Vol. 12). New York: Academic Press.

Merrill, T. (Ed.). (1994). *Nicaragua: A country study.* Library of Congress (3rd ed.). Washington, DC: U.S. Government Printing Office.

Meyers, S. A. (1993). Adapting parent education programs to meet the needs of fathers: An ecological perspective. *Family Relations, 42*(4), 447–453.

Miller, B. D., Van Esterik, P., & Van Esterik, J. (2004). *Cultural anthropology,* 2nd Canadian ed. Toronto: Pearson Education.

Miller, J., & Bersoff, D. M. (1994). Cultural influences on the moral status of reciprocity and the discounting of endogenous motivation. *Personality and Social Psychology Bulletin, 20,* 592–602.

Miller, J. G. (1984). Culture and the development of everyday social explanation. *Journal of Personality and Social Psychology, 46,* 961–978.

Mills, T. L. (1999). When grandparents grow up: Role transition and family solidarity among baby boomer grandchildren and their grandparents. *Journal of Aging Studies, 13,* 219–239.

Minkler, M., & Roe, K. (1991). *Preliminary findings from the grandmother caregiver study of Oakland, California.* Berkeley: University of California Press.

Mishra, R. C. (2001). Cognition across cultures. In D. Matsumoto (Ed.), *The handbook of culture and psychology* (pp. 119–135). New York: Oxford University Press.

Mishra, R. C., Sinha, D., & Berry, J. W. (1996). *Ecology, acculturation and psychological adaptation.* Thousand Oaks, CA: Sage.

Miyake, K., Chen, S. J., & Campos, J. J. (1985). Infant temperament, mother's mode of interaction, and attachment in Japan: An interim report. In I. Bretherton & E. Waters (Eds.), Growing points of attachment theory and research. *Monographs of the Society for Research in Child Development, 50,* 276–297.

Moeller, S., & Schoenweiler, R. (1999). Analysis of infant cries for the early detection of hearing impairment. *Speech Communication, 28,* 175–193.

Moghaddam, F. M., Taylor, D., & Wright, S. C. (1993). *Social psychology in cross-cultural perspective.* New York: Freeman.

Molitor, A., & Eckerman, C. O. (1992). *Behavioral cues of distress/avoidance in preterm infants.* Paper presented at the International Conference on Infant Studies, Miami, FL.

Morelli, G. A., Rogoff, B., Oppenheim, D., & Goldsmith, D. (1992). Cultural variation in infants' sleeping arrangements: Questions of independence. *Developmental Psychology, 28,* 604–613.

Morinaga, Y., Frieze, I. H., & Ferligoj, A. (1993). Career plans and gender-role attitudes of college students in the United States, Japan, and Slovenia. *Sex Roles, 29,* 317–334.

Mukai, T., & McCloskey, A. A. (1996). Eating attitudes among Japanese and American elementary schoolgirls. *Journal of Cross-Cultural Psychology, 27*(4), 424–435.

Mumford, D. B., Whitehouse, A. M., & Choudry, I. Y. (1992). Survey of eating disorders in English-medium schools in Lahore, Pakistan. *International Journal of Eating Disorders, 11,* 173–184.

Mundy-Castle, A. C. (1974). Social and technological intelligence in Western and non-Western cultures. *Universita* (University of Ghana), *4,* 46–52.

Mundy-Castle, A. C., & Okonji, M. D. (1976). *Mother–infant interaction in Nigeria.* Unpublished manuscript, University of Lagos.

Munroe, R. L., & Romney, A. K. (2006). Gender and age differences in same-sex aggregation and social behavior. *Journal of Cross-Cultural Psychology, 37,* 3–19.

Murdock, G. P. (1967). *Ethnographic atlas.* Pittsburgh, PA: Pittsburgh University Press.

Murphy-Berman, V., & Berman, J. J. (2002), Cross-cultural differences in perception of distribution of justice: A comparison of Hong Kong and Indonesia. *Journal of Cross-Cultural Psychology, 33,* 1157–1170.

Muuss, R. E. (1988). *Theories of adolescence* (5th ed.). New York: Random House.

Muuss, R. E. (1996). *Theories of adolescence* (6th ed.). New York: McGraw-Hill.

Muuss, R. E., & Porton, H. D. (1998). *Adolescent behavior and society: A book of readings* (5th ed.). New York: McGraw-Hill.

Mwamwenda, T. S. (1992). Cognitive development in African children. *Genetic, Social, and General Psychology Monographs, 118*(1), 7–72.

Naito, T. (1994). A survey of research on moral development in Japan. *Cross-Cultural Research, 28,* 40–57.

Nakajima, H., & Mayor, F. (1996). Culture and health. *World Health, 49*(2), 13–15.

Nasser, M. (1986). Comparative study of the prevalence of abnormal eating attitudes among Arab female students of both London and Cairo Universities. *Psychological Medicine, 16,* 621–625.

National Institute of Child Health and Human Development (2001). *From cells to selves: Biobehavioral development.* Bethesda, MD: U.S. Department of Health and Human Services.

Nelson, L. W. (1992). Cultural context and cultural code in the oral life narratives of African-American women: An ethnography of speaking. *Dissertation Abstracts International, 53* (2A), 544.

Nelson, M. B. (1994). *The stronger women get, the more men love football: Sexism and the American culture of sport.* New York: Harcourt Brace.

Nesdale, D., & Naito, M. (2005). Individualism–collectivism and the attitudes to school bullying of Japanese and Australian students. *Journal of Cross-Cultural Psychology, 36,* 537–556.

Neyer, F. J. & Asendorpf, J. B. (2001). Personality–relationship transaction in young adulthood. *Journal of Personality and Social Psychology, 81,* 1190–1204.

Nichter, M., & Nichter, M. (1991). Hype and weight. *Medical Anthropology, 13,* 249–284.

Niethammer, C. (1977). *Daughters of the earth: The lives and legends of American Indian women.* New York: Macmillan.

Numes, T., Schliemann, A. D., & Carraher, D. W. (1993). *Street mathematics and school mathematics.* Cambridge, England: Cambridge University Press.

Nurmi, J. E. (1991). How do adolescents see their future? A review of development of future orientation and planning. *Developmental Review, 11,* 1–59.

Nydell, M. K. (1987). *Understanding Arabs.* Yarmouth, ME: Intercultural Press.

Nyiti, R. M. (1982). The validity of "cultural differences explanations" for cross-cultural variation in the rate of Piagetian cognitive development. In D. A. Wagner & H. W. Stevenson (Eds.), *Cultural perspectives on child development.* San Francisco: Freeman.

Obermeyer, C. M. (1999). Female genital surgeries: The known, the unknown, and the unknowable. *Medical Anthropology Quarterly, 13,* 79–106.

O'Connor, T. G., Marvin, R. S., Rutter, M., Olrick, J. T., Pritner, P. A., and the English and Romanian Adoptees Study Team (2003). Child-parent attachment following early institutional deprivation. *Development and Psychopathology, 15,* 19–38.

Ochs, E. (1988). *Culture and language development.* Cambridge, UK: Cambridge University Press.

Ochse, R., & Plug, C. (1986). Cross-cultural investigation of the validity of Erikson's theory of personality development. *Journal of Personality and Social Psychology, 50*(6), 1240–1252.

Oetting, E. R., & Beauvais, F. (1987). Common elements in youth drug abuse: Peer clusters and other psychosocial factors. *Journal of Drug Issues, 17*(1–2), 133–151.

Offer, D., Ostrov, E., Howard, K. I., & Atkinson, R. (1988). *The teenage world: adolescents' self-image in ten countries.* New York: Plenum.

Okafor, N. A. O. (1991). Some traditional aspects of Nigerian women. In L. L. Adler (Ed.), *Women in cross-cultural perspective* (pp. 134–141). Westport, CT: Praeger.

Olowu, A. A. (1990). The self-concept in cross-cultural perspective. In A. A. Olowu (Ed.), *Contemporary issues in self-concept studies.* Ibadan, Kenya: Shaneson C. I., Ltd.

Olson, L. K. (Ed.). (1994). *The graying of the world: Who will care for the frail elderly?* Binghamton, NY: Haworth Press.

Page, R. C., & Berkow, D. N. (1991). Concepts of the self: Western and Eastern perspectives. *Journal of Multicultural Counseling and Development, 19,* 83–93.

Parke, R. D. (2000). Father involvement: A developmental psychological perspective. *Marriage and Family Review, 29,* 43–58.

Parke, R. D. (2002). Fathers and families. In M. H. Bornstein (Ed.), *Handbook of parenting* (Vol 3., 2nd ed., pp. 27–74). Mahwah, NJ: Erlbaum.

Parke, R. D., Ornstein, P. A., Rieser, J. J., & Zahn-Waxler, C. (Eds.). (1994). *A Century of Developmental Psychology.* Washington, DC: American Psychological Association.

Parker, R. (1989). Youth, identity, and homosexuality: The changing shape of sexual life in contemporary Brazil. *Journal of Homosexuality, 17,* 269–289.

Parmar, P., Harkness, S., & Super, C. M. (2004). Asian and Euro-American parents' ethnotheories of play and learning: Effects on pre-school children's home routines and school behavior. *International Journal of Behavioral Development, 28*(2), 97–104,

Pastorelli, C., Caprara, G. V., Barbaranelli C., Rola, J., Rosza, S., & Bandura, A. (2001). The structure of children's perceived self-efficacy: A cross-national study. *European Journal of Psychological Assessment, 17,* 87–97.

Paz, J. J. (1993). Support of Hispanic elderly. In H. McAdoo (Ed.), *Family ethnicity* (pp. 177–190). Newbury Park, CA: Sage.

Penfield, W., & Roberts, L. (1959). *Speech and brain mechanisms.* New York: Atheneum Press.

Peng, K., & Nisbett, R. E. (1999). Culture, dialecticism, and reasoning about contradiction. *American Psychologist, 54,* 741–754.

Pfeiffer, W. M. (1982). Culture-bound syndromes. In I. Al-Issa (Ed.), *Culture and psychopathology.* Baltimore: University Park Press.

Phillips, A. S. (1973). *Adolescence in Jamaica.* Kingston: Jamaica Publishing House.

Phinney, J. S., Lochner, B., & Murphy, R. (1990). Ethnic identity development and psychological adjustment in adolescents. In A. Stiffman & L. Davis (Eds.), *Ethnic issues in adolescent mental health.* Newbury Park, CA: Sage.

Piaget, J. (1954). *The construction of reality in the child.* New York: Basic Books.

Piaget, J. (1972). Intellectual evolution from adolescence to adulthood. *Human Development, 15,* 1–12.

Pillemer, D. B., & White, S. H. (Eds.). (2005). *Developmental psychology and social change.* New York: Cambridge University Press.

Plomin, R., & Rutter, M. (1998). Child development, molecular genetics, and what to do with genes once they are found. *Child Development, 69,* 1223–1242.

Pollitt, E., Gorman, K. S., Engle, P., Martorell, R., & Rivera, J. (1993). Early supplemental feeding and cognition: Effects over two decades. *Monographs of the Society for Research in Child Development, 235*(58), No. 7.

Polyakova, S. A., & Pacquaio, D. F. (2006). Psychological and mental illness among elder immigrants for the former Soviet Union. *Journal of Transcultural Nursing, 17,* 40–49.

Posada, G., Gao, Y., Wu, F., Posada, R., Tascon, M., Schöelmerich, A., Sagi, A., Kondo-Ikemura, K., Haaland, W., & Synnevaag, B. (1995). The secure-base phenomenon across cultures: children's behavior, mothers' references, and experts' concepts. *Monographs of the Society for research in Child Development, 60* (2–3, Serial No. 244), 27–48.

Power, T. (2004). Stress and coping in childhood: The parents' role. *Parenting: Science and Practice, 4,* 271–317.

Pretorius, E., & Naude, H. (2002). A culture in transition: Poor reading and writing ability among Children in South African townships. *Early Childhood Development & Care, 172,* 439–449.

Pribilsky, J. (2001) Nervios and "modern childhood": Migration and shifting contexts of child life in the Ecuadorian Andes. *Childhood: A Global Journal of Child Research, 8,* 251–273.

Price-Williams, D. R., Gordon, W., & Ramirez, M., III. (1969). Skills and conservation: A study of pottery-making children. *Developmental Psychology, 1,* 769.

Proos, L. A., Hofvander, Y., & Tuvemo, T. (1991). Menarchael age and growth pattern of Indian girls adopted in Sweden I. Menarcheal Age. *Acta Pediatrica Scandinavia, 80,* 852–858.

Putnam, S. P., Sanson, A. V., and Rothbart, M. K. (2002). Child temperament and parenting. In M. H. Bornstein (Ed.), *Handbook of parenting* (Vol. 1, 2nd ed., pp. 255–277). Mahwah, NJ: Erlbaum

Radin, N. (1993). Primary caregiving fathers in intact families. In A. Gottfried & A. Gottfried (Eds.), *Redefining families* (pp. 11–54). New York: Plenum.

Raeff, C. (2004). Within-culture complexities: Multifaceted and interrelated autonomy and connectedness characteristics in late adolescent selves. *New Directions in Child and Adolescent Development, 104,* 61–78.

Rahula, W. (1959). *What the Buddha taught.* New York: Grove Press.

Raich, R. M., Rosen, J. C., Deus, J., Perez, O., Requene, A., & Gross, J. (1992). Eating disorders symptoms among adolescents in the United States and Spain: A comparative study. *International Journal of Eating Disorders, 11,* 63–72.

Randhawa, B. S., & Gupta, A. (2000). Cross-national differences in mathematics achievement, attitude, and self-efficacy within a common intrinsic structure. *Canadian Journal of School Psychology, 15,* 51–66.

Recio Adrados, J. L. (1995). The influence of family, school, and peers on adolescent drug misuse. *International Journal of the Addictions, 30,* 1407–1423.

Retschitzki, J. (1989). Evidence of formal thinking in Baule airele players. In D. M. Keats, D. Munro, & L. Mann (Eds.), *Heterogeneity in cross-cultural psychology.* Amsterdam: Swets & Zeitlinger.

Rhode, D. L. (Ed.). (1990). *Theoretical perspectives on sex differences.* New Haven, CT: Yale University Press.

Richerson, P. J., & Boyd, R. (2004). *Not by genes alone: How culture transformed human evolution.* Chicago: University of Chicago Press.

Richman, A. L., LeVine, R. A., New, R. S., Howrigan, G. A., Welles-Nystrom, B., & LeVine, S. (1988). Maternal behavior to infants in five cultures. In R. A. LeVine, P. M. Miller, & M. M. West (Eds.), *Parental behavior in diverse societies: New directions for child development* (No. 40). San Francisco: Jossey-Bass.

Richman, A. L., Miller, P. M., & LeVine, R. A. (1992). Cultural and educational variations in maternal responsiveness. *Developmental Psychology, 28,* 614–621.

Ritchie, K., & Lovestone, S. (2002). The dementias. *Lancet, 360,* 1767–1769.

Ritts, V. (2000). *Culture and aging.* St. Louis Community College: Unpublished manuscript.

Ritts, V. (2000). *Infusing culture into parenting issues: A supplement for psychology instructors.* St. Louis Community College: Unpublished manuscript.

Ritts, V. (2001). *Culture and gender.* St. Louis Community College. Unpublished manuscript.

Ritts, V. (2001). *Personality, the self, and culture.* St. Louis Community College: Unpublished manuscript.

Robarchek, C. A., & Robarchek, D. (1998). Reciprocities and realities: World views, peacefulness, and violence among Semai and Waorani. *Aggressive Behavior, 24,* 123–133.

Roberts, B. W., & Bogg, T. (2004). A longitudinal study of the relationships between conscientiousness and the social—environmental factors and substance-use behaviors that influence health. *Journal of Personality, 72,* 325–353.

Roberts, B. W., Wood, D., & Smith J. L. (2005). Evaluating Five Factor Theory and Social investment perspective on personality trait development. *Journal of Research in Personality, 39,* 166–184.

Roberts, G. W. (1994). Brother to brother. African-American modes of relating among men. *Journal of Black Studies, 24,* 379–390.

Robinson, G. (2002). Cross-cultural perspectives on menopause. In A. E. Hunter and C. Forden (Eds.). *Readings in the psychology of gender: Exploring our differences and commonalities* (pp. 140–149). Needham Heights, MA: Allyn & Bacon.

Rogoff, B. (1990). *Apprenticeship in thinking: Cognitive development in social context.* New York: Oxford University Press.

Rogoff, B., & Chavajay, P. (1995). What's become of research on the cultural basis of cognitive development? *American Psychologist, 50,* 859–873.

Roopnarine, J. L., & Carter, D. B. (1992). *Parent-child socialization in diverse cultures.* Norwood, NJ: Ablex.

Roopnarine, J. L., & Gielen, U. P. (Eds.). (2004). *Families in global perspective.* Boston: Allyn & Bacon.

Rosenblith, J. F. (1995). *In the beginning: Development from conception to age 2,* 2nd ed. Newbury Park, CA: Sage.

Ross, N. O. (2003). *Culture and cognition: Implications for theory and method.* Thousand Oaks, CA: Sage.

Rothbart, M. K., & Bates, J. E. (1998). Temperament. In N. Eisenberg (Ed.), *Handbook of child psychology,* (Vol. 3, 5th ed., pp. 105–176). New York: Wiley.

Rothbart, M. K., & Hwang, J. (2005). Temperament. In A. J. Elliot & C. S. Dweck (Eds.), *Handbook of Competence and Motivation* (pp. 167–184). New York: Guilford Press.

Rothbaum, F., & Morelli, G. (2005). Attachment and culture: Bridging relativism and universalism. In W. Friedlmeier, P. Chakkarath, & B. Schwarz (Eds.), *Culture and human development* (pp. 100–123). New York: Psychology Press.

Rothbaum, F., Weisz, J., Pott, M., Miyake, K., & Morelli, G. (2000). Attachment and culture. Security in the United States and Japan. *American Psychologist, 55,* 1093–1104.

Ruan, F. F. (1991). *Sex in China: Studies in sexology in Chinese culture.* New York: Plenum Press.

Rushton, J. P. (1998). Ethnic differences in temperament. In Y. Lee, C. McCauley and J. Draguns (Eds.), *Personality and person perception across cultures* (pp. 45–63). Mahwah, NJ: Erlbaum.

Rutter, M., & the ERA Study team (1998). Developmental catch-up and deficit, following adoption and after severe global early privation. *Journal of Child Psychology and Psychiatry and Allied Disciplines, 39,* 465–476.

Ryan, A. S., Rush, D., Krieger, F. W., & Lewandowski, G. E. (1991). Recent declines in breast-feeding in the United States, 1984 through 1989. *Pediatrics, 88,* 719–727.

Ryan, E. B., Giles, H., Bartolucci, G., & Henwood, K. (1986). Psycholinguisitc and social psychological components of communication by and with the elderly. *Language and Communication, 6,* 1–24.

Ryan, M. E., & Twibell, R. S. (2000). Concerns, values, stress, copying health and educational outcomes of college students who studied abroad. *International Journal of Intercultural Relations, 24,* 409–435.

Sagi, A. (1990). Attachment theory and research in cross-cultural perspective. *Human Development, 33,* 10–22.

Sagi-Schwartz, A., & Aviezer, O. (2005). Correlates of attachment to multiple caregivers in kibbutz children from birth to emerging adulthood: The Haifa Longitudinal Study. In K. E. Grossmann, K. Grossmann, and E. Waters (Eds.), *Attachment from infancy to adulthood: The major longitudinal studies* (pp. 165–197). New York: Guilford Publications.

Sahin, N., & Sahin, N. H. (1995). Dimensions of concerns: The case of Turkish adolescents. *Journal of Adolescence, 18,* 49–69.

Salamone, F. A. (1983). Children's games as mechanisms for easing ethnic interaction in ethnically heterogeneous communities: A Nigerian case. In J. C. Harris and R. J. Park (Eds.), *Play, games, and sports in cultural contexts* (pp. 461–472). Champaign, IL: Human Kinetics.

Salthouse, T. A. (1987). The role of experience in cognitive aging. In K. W. Schaie & K. Eisdorfer (Eds.), *Annual Review of Gerontology and Geriatrics* (Vol. 7). New York: Springer.

Sanchez, L. (1993). Women's power and the gendered division of labor in the third world. *Gender and Society, 7,* 434–459.

Sangree, W. H. (1992). Grandparenthood and modernization: The changing status of male and female elders in Tiriki, Kenya, and Irigwe, Nigeria. *Journal of Cross-Cultural Gerontology, 7,* 331–361.

Sartorius, N. R. (1994). Description of WHO's Mental Health Programme. In W. J. Lonner & R. Malpass (Eds.), *Psychology and culture.* Boston: Allyn & Bacon.

Sartorius, N. R., Jablensky, A., Korten, A., Ernberg, G., Anker, M., Cooper, J. E., & Day, R. (1986). Early manifestations and first contact incidence of schizophrenia in different cultures: A preliminary report on the initial evaluation phase of the WHO Collaborative Study on Determinants of Outcome of Severe Mental Disorders. *Psychological Medicine, 16,* 909–928.

Scabini, E., Marta, E., & Lanz, M. (2006). *The transition to adulthood and family relations.* New York: Psychology Press.

Schaie, K. W. (1984). The Seattle Longitudinal Study: A 21–year exploration of psychometric intelligence in adulthood. In K. W. Schaie (Ed.), *Longitudinal studies of adult psychological development.* New York: Guilford.

Schlegel, A., & Barry, H. (1991). *Adolescence: An anthropological inquiry.* New York: Free Press.

Schwartz, S. H. (1995). Are there universal aspects in the structure and contents of human values? *Journal of Social Issues, 50,* 19–46.

Schwartz, T. (1981). The acquisition of culture. *Ethos, 9,* 4–17.

Schwarz, B., Schafermeier, E., & Trommsdorff, G. (2005). Relations between value orientation, childrearing goals, and parenting: A comparison of German and South Korean mothers. In W. Friedlmeier, P. Chakkarath, & B. Schwarz (Eds.), *Culture and human development* (pp. 203–230). New York: Psychology Press.

Schwartzman, H. B. (1983). Socializing play: Functional analysis. In J. C. Harris & R. J. Park (Eds.), *Play, games, and sports in cultural contexts.* Champaign IL: Human Kinetics.

Scully, E. (2000). Acculturation and language learning: Filipina wives in a rural Japanese village. *Dissertation Abstracts International Section A: Humanities & Social Sciences, 60,* 2340.

Searle-White, J. (1996). Personal boundaries among Russians and Americans: A Vygotskian approach. *Cross-Cultural Research, 30*(2), 184–208.

Segall, M. H. (1979). *Cross-Cultural Psychology.* Belmont, CA: Wadsworth.

Segall, M. H., Dasen, P. R., Berry, J. W., & Poortinga, Y. H. (1999). *Human behavior in global perspective* (2nd ed.). Boston: Allyn & Bacon.

Segall, M. H., Lonner, W. J., & Berry, J. W. (1998). Cross-cultural psychology as a scholarly discipline: On the flowering of culture in behavioral research. *American Psychologist, 53,* 1101–1110.

Segalowitz, S. J., & Schmidt, L. A. (2003). Developmental psychology and the neurosciences. In J. Valsiner & K. Connolly (Eds.), *Handbook of developmental psychology* (pp. 48–71). London: Sage Publications.

Serpell, R. (1993). *The significance of schooling: Life-journeys in an African society.* New York: Cambridge University Press.

Sharma, N., & Sharma, B. (1999). Children in difficult circumstances: Familial correlates of advantage while at risk. In T. S. Saraswathi (Ed.), *Culture, socialization and human development: Theory, research and applications in India* (pp. 398–418). Thousand Oaks, CA: Sage Publications.

Shea, J. D. (1985). Studies of cognitive development in Papua New Guinea. *International Journal of Psychology, 20,* 33–61.

Shields, D. L. L., & Bredemeier, B. J. L. (1995). *Character development and physical activity.* Champaign, IL: Human Kinetics.

Shostak, M. (1981). *Nissa: The life and words of a !Kung woman.* Cambridge, MA: Harvard University Press.

Shwalb, D. W., Nakazawa, J., & Shwalb, B. J. (Eds.). (2005). *Applied developmental psychology: Theory, practice, and research from Japan.* Greenwich, CT: Information Age Publishing.

Shwalb, D. W., Nakazawa, J., Yamamoto, T., & Hyun, J-H. (2003). Fathering in Japanese, Chinese, and Korean cultures: A review of the research literature. In M. E. Lamb (Ed.), *The role of the father in child development,* 4th ed. New York: Wiley.

Shweder, R., Mahapatra, M., & Miller, J. G. (1987). Culture and moral development. In J. Kagan & S. Lamb (Eds.), *The emergence of morality in young children* (pp. 1–82). Chicago: University of Chicago Press.

Sigel, I. E. (Ed.). (1985). *Parental belief systems: The psychological consequences for children.* Hillsdale, NJ: Erlbaum.

Sigel, I. E., & McGillicuddy-DeLisi, A. V. (2002). Parental beliefs are cognitions: The dynamic belief system model. In M. H. Bornstein (Ed.), *Handbook of parenting: Being and becoming a parent* (pp. 485–508). Mahwah, NJ: Lawrence Erlbaum.

Sigel, I. E., McGillicuddy-DeLisi, A. V., & Goodnow, J. J. (Eds.). (1992). *Parental belief systems: The psychological consequences for children* (2nd ed.). Hillsdale, NJ: Erlbaum.

Sijuwola, O. A. (1995). Culture, religion, and mental illness in Nigeria. In I. Al-Issa (Ed.), *Handbook of culture and mental illness* (pp. 65–72). Madison, WI: International Universities Press.

Silverstein, M., & Parker, M. G. (2002). Leisure activities and quality of life among the oldest old in Sweden. *Research on Aging, 24,* 528–547.

Singh, D. (1993). Body shape and women's attractiveness: The critical role of waist-to-hip ratio. *Human Nature, 4,* 297–331.

Smith, D. E., & Blinn Pike, L. (1994). Relationship between Jamaican adolescents' drinking patterns and self-image: A cross-cultural perspective. *Adolescence, 29,* 429–437.

Smith, D. E., & Reynolds, T. E. (1992). Adolescents' self-image: A cross-cultural perspective. *Child Study Journal, 22,* 303–315.

Smith, H. W., & Nomi, T. (2000), Is Amae the key to understanding Japanese culture? *Electronic Journal of Sociology.* ISSN: 1198–3655. *http://www.sociology.org/content/vol 005.001/Smith-nomi. html.*

Smith, J., & Baltes, P. B. (1990). Wisdom-related knowledge: Age/cohort differences in response to life-planning problems. *Developmental Psychology, 26*(3), 494–505.

Smith, J. S. (1992). Women in charge: Politeness and directiveness in the speech of Japanese women. *Language in Society, 21*, 59–82.

Smith, M. G. (1965). The Hausa of northern Nigeria. In J. L. Gibbs, Jr. (Ed.), *Peoples of Africa* (pp. 119–155). New York: Holt, Rinehart & Winston.

Smith, P. B. (2004). Nations, cultures, and individuals: New perspectives and old dilemmas. *Journal of Cross-Cultural Psychology, 35*, 6–12.

Smith, P. B., & Bond, M. H. (1999). *Social psychology across cultures*, 2nd ed. Boston: Allyn & Bacon.

Smith, P. B., Bond, M. H., & Kagitcibasi, C. (2006). *Understanding social psychology across cultures: Living and working in a changing world*. Thousand Oaks, CA: Sage.

Smith, P. K. (1991). Introduction: The study of grandparenthood. In P. K. Smith (Ed.), *The psychology of grandparenthood: An international perspective* (pp. 1–16). London: Routledge & Keagan Paul.

Smith, P. K. (1995). Grandparenthood. In M. H. Bornstein (Ed.), *Handbook of parenting* (Vol. 3, pp. 89–112). Mahwah, NJ: Erlbaum.

Smith, P. K. (2005). Grandparents and grandchildren. *The Psychologist, 18*, 684–687.

Smith, P. K., & Drew. L. M. (2002). Grandparenthood. In M. H. Bornstein (Ed.), *Handbook of parenting* (Vol. 3, 2nd ed., pp. 141–172). Mahwah, NJ: Erlbaum.

Smith, P. K., & Drew, L. M. (2004). Grandparenting and support networks. In M. S. Hoghughi & N. Long (Eds.), *The handbook of parenting: Theory, research and practice* (pp. 146–159). London: Sage Publications, Ltd.

Snarey, J. R. (1985). Cross-cultural universality of socio-moral development. A critical review of Kohlbergian research. *Psychological Bulletin, 97*, 202–232.

Snowden, L. R., & Yamada, A. (2005). Cultural differences in access to care. *Annual Review of Clinical Psychology, 1*, 143–166.

Solomon, G. B. (1997). Fair play in the gymnasium: Improving social skills among elementary school children. *Journal of Physical Education, Recreation, and Dance, 68*, 22–25.

Sommers, I., Fagan, J., & Baskin, D. (1993). Sociocultural influences on the explanation of delinquency for Puerto Rican youths. *Hispanic Journal of Behavioral Sciences, 15*, 36–62.

Sparkes, K. K. (1991). Cooperative and competitive behavior in dyadic game-playing: A comparison of Anglo-American and Chinese children. *Early Child Development and Care, 68*, 37–47.

Spencer, M. B., Harpalani, V., Fegley , S., Dell'Angelo, T., & Seaton, G. (2003). Identity, self, and peers in context: A culturally sensitive developmental framework for analysis. In R. Lerner, F. Jacobs, & D. Wertlieg, (Eds.), *Handbook of Applied Developmental Science*, Volume 1, pp. 123–142.

Spiro, M. E. (1993). Is the Western conception of the self "peculiar" within the contexts of world cultures? *Ethos, 21*, 107–153.

Spock, B., & Rothenberg, M. B. (1992). *Dr. Spock's baby and child care*. New York: Pocket Books.

Stack, C. B. (1974). *All our kin: Strategies for survival in a black community*. New York: Harper & Row.

Stanton, A. M. (1998). Grandparents' visitation rights and custody. *Child & Adolescent Psychiatric Clinics of North America, 7*, 409–422.

Staples, R. (1952). Appreciations and dislikes regarding grandmothers as expressed by granddaughters. *Journal of Home Economics, 44*, 340–343.

Steinberg, L., & Brown, B. B. (1989). *Beyond the classroom: Parent and peer influences on high school achievement*. Invited paper presented to the Family as Educators Special Interest Group at the annual meetings of the American Educational Research Association, San Francisco.

Steinberg, L. (1987). Impact of puberty on family relations: Effects of pubertal status and pubertal timing. *Developmental Psychology, 23*, 451–460.

Steinberg, L. (1988). Reciprocal relation between parent–child distance and pubertal maturation. *Developmental Psychology, 24*, 122–128.

Steinberg, L., Darling, N. E., & Fletcher, A. C. (1995). Authoritative parenting and adolescent adjustment: An ecological journey. In P. Moen, G. H. Elder, Jr., & K. Luscher (Eds.), *Examining lives in context: Perspectives on the ecology of human development* (pp. 423–466). Washington, DC: American Psychological Association.

Steinberg, L., & Silk, J. S. (2002). Parenting adolescents. In M. H. Bornstein (Ed.), *Handbook of parenting* (Vol. 1, 2nd ed., pp. 103–133). Mahwah, NJ: Erlbaum.

Sternberg, R. J., & Grigorenko, E. (Eds.) (2004). *Culture and competence: Contexts of life success*. Washington, DC: American Psychological Association.

Steube, A. M., Rich-Edwards, J. W., Willett, W. C., Manson, J. E., & Michels, K. B. (2005). Duration of lactation and incidence to type 2 diabetes. *Journal of the American Medical Association, 294*, 2601–2610.

Stevenson, H. W., Chen, C., & Lee, S. (1991). Chinese families. In J. L. Roopnarine & D. B. Carter (Eds.), *Parent–child socialization in diverse cultures* (pp. 17–33). Norwood, NJ: Ablex.

Stevenson, H. W., & Stigler, J. W. (1992). *The learning gap: Why our schools are failing and what we can learn from Japanese and Chinese education.* New York: Simon & Schuster.

Stigler, J., & Fernandez, C. (1995). Learning mathematics from classroom instructions: Cross-cultural and experimental perspectives. In C. Nelson (Ed.), *Contemporary perspectives on learning and development: Twenty-seventh Minnesota symposium on child psychology.* Hillsdale, NJ: Erlbaum.

Stiles, D. A., & Gibbons, J. L. (1995). *Gender role expectations of Norwegian adolescents.* Paper presented at the twenty-fourth annual meeting of the Society for Cross-Cultural Research, Savannah, GA.

Strom, R. D., & Strom, S. K. (1993). Grandparents raising grandchildren: Goals and support groups. *Educational Gerontology, 19,* 705–715.

Strom, R. D., & Strom, S. K. (2000). Intergenerational learning and family harmony. *Educational Gerontology, 26,* 261–283.

Strom, R. D., Strom, S., Collinsworth, P., Sato, S., Makino, K., Sasaki, Y., Sasaki, H., & Nishio, N. (1995). Grandparents in Japan: A three-generational study. *International Journal of Aging and Human Development, 40*(3), 209–227.

Strom, R. D., Strom, S. K., Wang, C., Shen, Y., Griswold, D., Chan, H., & Yang, C. (1999). Grandparents in the United States and the Republic of China: A comparison of generations and cultures. *International Journal of Aging and Human Development, 49,* 279–317.

Strong, C. (1984). Stress and caring for elderly relatives: Interpretations and coping strategies in an American Indian and White sample. *Gerontologist, 24*(3), 251–256.

Sue, D. W., & Sue, D. (1990). Counseling American Indians. In D. W. Sue & D. Sue (Eds.), *Counseling the culturally different: Theory and practice* (pp. 175–188). New York: Wiley.

Sullivan, R. (2004). (Ed.) *Focus on fathering.* Melbourne, Australia: AECR Press.

Sung, K. T. (1992). Motivations for parent care: The case of filial children in Korea. *International Journal of Aging and Human Development, 34,* 109–124.

Super, C. M. (1981). Cross-cultural research on infancy. In H. C. Triandis and A. Heron (Eds.), *Handbook of cross-cultural psychology: Vol. 4. Developmental Psychology.* Boston: Allyn & Bacon.

Super, C. M. (2005). The globalization of developmental psychology. In D. B. Pillemer & S. H. White (Eds.), *Developmental psychology and social change* (pp. 11–33). New York: Cambridge University Press.

Super, C. M., & Harkness, S. (1982). The infants' niche in rural Kenya and metropolitan America. In L. L. Adler (Ed.), *Cross-cultural research at issue* (pp. 47–55). New York: Academic Press.

Super, C. M., & Harkness, S. (1986). The developmental niche: A conceptualization of the interface of child and culture. *International Journal of Behavioral Development, 9,* 545–570.

Super, C. M., & Harkness, S. (1994a). The developmental niche. In W. J. Lonner & R. Malpass (Eds.), *Psychology and culture* (pp. 95–99). Boston: Allyn & Bacon.

Super, C. M., & Harkness, S. (1994b). Temperament and the developmental niche. In W. B. Carey & S. C. Devitt (Eds.), *Prevention and early intervention: Individual differences as risk factors for the mental health of children.* New York: Brunner/Mazel.

Super, C. M., & Harkness, S. (1997). The cultural structuring of child development. In J. W. Berry, P. R. Dasen, & T. S. Saraswathi (Eds.), *Handbook of cross-cultural psychology* (Vol. 2, 2nd ed., pp. 1–39). Boston: Allyn & Bacon.

Super, C. M., & Harkness, S. (1999). The environment as culture in developmental research. In S. L. Friedman & T. D. Wachs (Eds.), *Measuring environment across the life span.* Washington, DC: American Psychological Association.

Super, C. M., & Harkness, S. (2002). Culture structures the environment for development. *Human Development, 45,* 270–274.

Super, C. M., & Harkness, S. (2003). The metaphors of development. *Human Development, 46,* 3–23.

Suzuki, T. (1998). Children's comprehension of Japanese passives: A different perspective. In Eve Clark (Ed.), *The proceedings of the twenty-ninth annual child language research forum (pp. 91–100).* Stanford, CA: Center for Study of Language and Information.

Swaim, R. C., Oetting, E. R., Thurman, P. J., Beauvais, F., & Edwards, R. W. (1993). American Indian adolescent drug use and socialization characteristics: A cross-cultural comparison. *Journal of Cross-Cultural Psychology, 24*(1), 53–70.

Swanson, D. P., Spencer, M. B., Harpalani, V., Dupree, D., Noll, E., Ginzburg, S., & Seaton, G. (2003). Psychosocial development in racially and ethnically diverse youth: Conceptual and methodological challenges in the 21st century. *Developmental Psychopathology, 15,* 743–771.

Tajfel, H. (1981). *Human groups and social categories.* Cambridge, England: Cambridge University Press.

Talukder, M. (2000). The importance of breastfeeding and strategies to sustain high breastfeeding rates. In A. Costello & D. Manandhar (Eds.), *Improving newborn infant health in developing countries*. London: Imperial College Press.

Tang, T. L. (1996). Pay differential as a function of rater's sex, money ethic, and job incumbent's sex: A Test of the Matthew effect. *Journal of Economic Psychology, 17,* 127–144.

Tang, T. L-P., Furnham, A., & Davis, G. M-T. (2000). A cross-cultural comparison of pay differentials as a function of rater's sex and money ethic endorsement: The Matthew effect revisted. *Personality & Individual Differences, 29,* 685–697.

Thomas, A., & Chess, S. (1977). *Temperament and development*. New York: Brunner/Mazel.

Thomas, R. M. (1999). *Human development theories: Windows on culture*. Thousand Oaks, CA: Sage.

Thomas, R. M. (2001). *Recent theories of human development*. Thousand Oaks, CA: Sage.

Thomas, W. I., & Znaniecki, F. (1927). *The Polish peasant in Europe and America*. New York: Knopf.

Tien, H. Y., & Lee, C. F. (1988). New demographics and old designs: The Chinese family and induced population transition. *Social Science Quarterly, 69,* 605–628.

Tiggemann, M., & Rothblum, E. D. (1988). Gender differences in social consequences of perceived overweight in the United States and Australia. *Sex Roles, 18,* 75–86.

Ting-Toomey, S. (1991). Intimacy expressions in three cultures: France, Japan, and the United States. *International Journal of Intercultural Relations, 15,* 29–46.

Tinsley, B. J., Markey, C. N., Ericksen, A. J., Oritz, R. V., & Kwasman, A. (2002). Health promotion for parents. In M. H. Bornstein (Ed.), *Handbook of parenting* (Vol. 5, 2nd ed., pp. 311–328). Mahwah, NJ: Erlbaum

Tisak, M. S., Tisak, J., & Goldstein, S. E. (2006). Aggression, delinquency, and morality: A social–cognitive perspective. In M. Killen and J. G. Smetana (Eds.), *Handbook of Moral Development* (pp. 611–629). Mahwah, NJ: Lawrence Erlbaum Associates

Tosevski, D. L., & Milovancevic, M. P. (2006). Stressful life events and physical health. *Current Opinion in Psychiatry, 19,* 184–189.

Triandis, H. C. (1989). The self and social behavior in differing cultural contexts. *Psychological Bulletin, 96,* 506–520.

Trimble, J. E., Manson, S. M., Dinges, N. G., & Medicine, B. (1984). American Indian concepts of mental health: Reflections and directions. In P. B. Pedersen, N. Sartorius, & A. J. Marsella (Eds.), *Mental health services: The cross-cultural context*. Beverly Hills: Sage.

Tronick, E. Z., Morelli, G. A., & Ivey, P. K. (1992). The Efe forager infant and toddler's pattern of social relationships: Multiple and simultaneous. *Developmental Psychology, 28,* 568–577.

Tronick, E. Z., Thomas, R. B., & Daltabuit, G. (1994). The manta pouch: A regulatory system for Peruvian infants at high altitude. *Children's Environments, 11*(2), 142–146.

Tse, S., & Bailey, D. M. (1992). Tai chi and postural control in the well elderly. *American Journal of Occupational Therapy, 46*(4), 295–300.

Tsuneyoshi, R. K. (2001). *The Japanese model of schooling: Comparisons with the United States*. NY: Routledge Falmer.

Turiel, E. (2004). Commentary: Beyond individualism and collectivism: A problem or progress? *New Directions in Child and Adolescent Development, 104,* 91–100.

Tylor, E. B. (1871). *Primitive culture* (2 vols.). London: Murray.

Tzuriel, D. (1992). The development of ego identity at adolescence among Israeli Jews and Arabs. *Journal of Youth and Adolescence, 21,* 551–571.

United Nations Children's Fund/UNICEF (2001), *Progress since the World Summit for Children—A statistical Review*. New York: United Nations Publications.

United Nations Children's Fund/UNICEF (2003), *The state of the world's children, 2003*. New York: United Nations Publications.

United Nations Children's Fund/UNICEF (2006). *The state of the world's children, 2006*. New York: United Nations Publications.

UNESCO, *UNESCO Universal Declaration on Cultural Diversity*, issued on International Mother Language Day, February 21, 2002.

Uzgiris, I. C., & Raeff, C. (1995). Play in parent-child interactions. In M. H. Bornstein, *Handbook of parenting* (Vol. 4). Mahwah, NJ: Erlbaum.

Valsiner, J., & Lawrence, J. (1997). Human development in culture across the life span. In J. W. Berry, P. R. Dasen, & T. S. Saraswathi (Eds.), *Handbook of cross-cultural psychology* (Vol. 2, 2nd ed., pp. 69–106). Boston: Allyn & Bacon.

Van Acker, J., Oostrom, B., Rath, B., & de Kemp, R. (1999). Street children in Nairobi: Hakuna Matata? *Journal of Community Psychology, 27,* 393–404.

Van den Heuvel, H., Tellegen, G., & Koomen, W. (1992). Cultural differences in the use of psychological and social characteristics in children's self-understanding. *European Journal of Social Psychology, 22,* 353–362.

van de Vijver, F. (2001). The evolution of cross-cultural research methods. In D. Matsumoto (Ed.), *The handbook of culture and psychology* (pp. 77–97). New York: Oxford University Press.

van de Vijver, F. J. R., & Leung, K. (2000). Methodological issues in psychological research on culture. *Journal of Cross-Cultural Psychology, 31,* 33–51.

Van Esterik, P. (1989). *Beyond the breast-bottle controversy.* New Brunswick, NJ: Rutgers University Press.

Van Ijzendoorn, M. H., & Sagi, A. (1999) Cross-cultural patterns of attachment: Universal and contextual dimensions. In J. Cassidy & P. R. Shaver (Eds.), *Handbook of attachment; theory, research, and clinical applications.* (pp. 713–734). New York: Guilford Press.

Veale, A. (1992). Towards a conceptualization of street children: The case from Sudan and Ireland. *Troaire Developmental Review* (Dublin), 107–128.

Visano, L. (1990). The socialization of street children: The development and transformation of identities. *Sociological Studies of Child Development, 3,* 139–161.

Vondra, J., & Belsky, J. (1993). Developmental origins of parenting: Personality and relationship factors. In T. Luster & L. Okagaki (Eds.), *Parenting: An ecological perspective* (pp. 1–33). Hillsdale, NJ: Erlbaum.

Vygotsky, L. S. (1978). *Mind in society: The development of higher psychological processes.* Cambridge, MA: Harvard University Press.

Wachs, T. D. (2000a). *Necessary but not sufficient: The respective roles of single and multiple influences of individual development.* Washington, D.C.: American Psychological Association.

Wachs, T. (2000b). Linking nutrition and temperament. In V. J. Molfese & D. Molfese (Eds.), *Temperament and personality development across the life span.* Mahwah, NJ: Erlbaum.

Wainryb, C. (2006). Moral development in culture: Diversity, tolerance, and justice. In M. Killen and J. G. Smetana (Eds.), *Handbook of Moral Development* (pp. 211–240). Mahwah, NJ: Lawrence Erlbaum Associates.

Watanabe, Y. (1986). Distributive justice development. *Japanese Journal of Educational Psychology, 34,* 84–90.

Waters, E., & Cummings, E. M. (2000). A secure base from which to explore the environment. *Child Development, 71,* 164–172.

Waters, E., Hamilton, C. E., & Weinfield, N. S. (2000). The stability of attachment security from infancy to adolescence and early childhood: General introduction. *Child Development, 71,* 678–683.

Waters, E., Merrick, S., Treboux, D., Crowell, J., & Albersheim, L. (2000). Attachment security in infancy and early adulthood: A twenty-year longitudinal study. *Child Development, 71,* 684–689.

Watkins, D., & Dhawan, N. (1989). Do we need to distinguish the constructs of self-concept and self-esteem? *Journal of Social Behavior and Personality, 4,* 555–562.

Wei, M., Russell, D. W., Mallinckrod, B., & Zakalik, R. A. (2004). Cultural equivalence of adult attachment across four ethnic groups: Factor structure, structured means, and associations with negative mood. *Journal of Counseling Psychology, 51,* 408–417.

Weill, J., & Le Bourhis, B. (1994). Factors predictive of alcohol consumption in a representative sample of French male teenagers: A five-year prospective study. *Drug & Alcohol Dependence, 35,* 45–50.

Weinfield, N., Sroufe, L. A., & Egeland, B. (2000). Attachment from infancy to early adulthood in a high-risk sample: Continuity, discontinuity, and their correlates. *Child Development, 71,* 695–702.

Weisner, T. S. (2002). Ecocultural understanding of children's developmental pathways. *Human Development, 45,* 272–281.

Wellman, H. M., & Gelman, S. A. (1992). Cognitive development: Foundational theories of core domains. *Annual Review of Psychology, 43,* 337–375.

Werner, E. E. (1979). *Cross-cultural child development.* Belmont, CA: Wadsworth.

Werner, E. E. (1989). Children of the garden island. *Scientific American, 260,* 101–111.

West, A. (1999). Children's own research: Street children and care in Britain and Bangladesh. *Childhood: A Global Journal of Child Research, 6,* 145–155.

West, C., & Zimmerman, D. H. (1987). Doing gender. *Gender and Society, 1,* 125–151.

White, M. (1993). *The material child: Coming of age in Japan and America.* New York: Free Press.

Whiting, B. B. (1963). *Six cultures: Studies of child rearing.* Cambridge, MA: Harvard University Press.

Whiting, B. B., & Edwards, C. P. (1988). *Children of different worlds: The formation of social behavior.* Cambridge, MA: Harvard University Press.

Whiting, B. B., & Whiting, J. W. M. (1975). *Children of six cultures: A psycho-cultural analysis.* Cambridge, MA: Harvard University Press.

Whorf, B. L. (1956). *Language, thought and reality.* Cambridge, MA: MIT Press.

Wierzbicka, A. (1993). A conceptual basis for cultural psychology. *Ethos, 21,* 205–231.

Williams, J., & Best, D. (1990). *Sex and psyche: Gender and self viewed cross-culturally.* Newbury Park, CA: Sage.

Williams, W. M., & Sternberg, R. J. (2001). How parents can maximize children's cognitive abilities. In M. H. Bornstein (Ed.), *Handbook of parenting* (Vol. 5, 2nd ed., pp. 169–194). Mahwah, NJ: Erlbaum.

Wolf, A. P. (1964). *Marriage and adoption in a Hokkien village.* Unpublished doctoral dissertation, Department of Anthropology, Cornell University.

Wolf, A. P. (1978). *Studies in Chinese society.* Stanford, CA: Stanford University Press.

Wolf, M. (1972). *Women and the family in rural Taiwan.* Stanford, CA: Stanford University Press.

Wolfe, W. S., Campbell, C. C., Frongillo, E. A., Haas, J. D., & Melnik, T. A. (1994). Overweight schoolchildren in New York state: Prevalence and characteristics. *American Journal of Public Health, 84,* 807–813.

Wolffers, I. (1997). Culture, media, HIV/AIDS in Asia. *Lancet, 349* (9044), 52–59.

Woolf, L. M., Hulsizer, M. R., & McCarthy, T. (2002). *International psychology: Annotated bibliography, relevant organizations, and course suggestions.* Retrieved March 31, 2003 from APA Division 2, Society for the Teaching of Psychology, Office of Teaching Resources in Psychology Web Site: http//www.lemoyne.edu/OTRP/otrpresources/inter-comp.html.

Worchel, F. F., & Allen, M. (1997). Mother's ability to discriminate cry types in low-birthweight premature and full-term infants. *Children's Health Care, 26,* 183–195.

World Factbook. (2005). Washington, D.C.: Central Intelligence Agency.

World Health Organization. (1979). *Schizophrenia: An international follow-up study.* New York: Wiley.

World Health Organization. (1983). *Depressive disorders in different cultures: Report of the WHO collaborative study of standardized assessment of depressive disorders.* Geneva: WHO.

Worthman, C. M. (1994). Developmental microniche: A concept for modeling relationships of biology, behavior, and culture in development. *American Journal of Physical Anthropology Supplement, 18,* 210.

Worthman, C. M. (1995). Biocultural bases of human variation. *ISSBD Newsletter, 27*(1), 10–13.

Wylie, L. (1974). *Village in the Vaucluse* (3rd ed.). Cambridge, MA: Harvard University Press.

Yamada, T., Kadekaru, H., Matsumoto, S., Inada, H., Tanabe, M., Moriguchi, E. H., Moriguchi, Y., Ishikawa, P., Ishikawa, A. G., Taira, K., & Yamori, Y. (2002). Prevalence of dementia in the older Japanese-Brazilian population. *Psychiatry & Clinical Neuroscience, 56,* 71–75.

Yamaguchi, S. (2004). Further clarifications of the concept of *amae* in relation to dependence and attachment. *Human Development, 47* (January–February): 28–33.

Yang, C. K., & Hahn, H. M. (2002). Cosleeping in young Korean children. *Journal of Developmental Behavioral Pediatrics, 23,* 151–157.

Yang, J-A. (1999). An exploratory study of Korean fathering of adolescent children. *Journal of Genetic Psychology, 160,* 55–68.

Yi, S. H. (1993). Transformation of child socialization in Korean culture. *Early Childhood Development, 85,* 17–24.

Yi, Z., Yuzhi, L., & George, L. K. (2003). Gender differentials of the oldest old in China. *Research on Aging, 25,* 65–80.

Ying, Y., & Liese, L. (1990). Initial adaptation of Taiwan foreign students to the U.S: The impact of prearrival variables. *American Journal of Community Psychology, 18,* 825–845.

Yodanis, C. (2005). Divorce culture and marital gender equality. A cross-national study. *Gender and Society, 19,* 644–659.

Zarit, S. H., & Eggebeen, D. J. (1995). Parent–child relationships in adulthood and old age. In M. H. Bornstein (Ed.), *Handbook of parenting* (Vol. 1, pp. 119–140). Hillsdale, NJ: Erlbaum.

Zarit, S. H., & Eggebeen, D. J. (2002). Parent-child relationships in adulthood and later years. In M. H. Bornstein (Ed.), *Handbook of parenting* (Vol. 1, 2nd ed., pp. 135–161). Mahwah, NJ: Erlbaum.

Zeskind, P. S., Klein, L., & Marshall, T. (1992). Adults' perceptions of experiential modifications of durations of pauses and expiratory sounds in infant crying. *Developmental Psychology, 28,* 1153–1162.

Zeskind, P. S., Platzman, K., Coles, C. D., & Schuetze, P. A. (1996). Cry analysis detects subclinical effects of prenatal alcohol exposure in newborn infants. *Infant Behavior & Development, 19,* 497–500.

Zevalkink, J., Riksen-Walraven, J. M., & Van Lieshout, C. F. M. (1999). Attachment in the Indonesian Caregiving Context. *Social Development, 8,* 21–40.

Zhang, Y., Proenca, R., Maffel, M., Barone, M., et al. (1994). Positional cloning of the mouse obese gene and its human homologue. *Nature, 372,* 425–442.

NAME INDEX

SUBJECT INDEX